EARLY GREEK PHILOSOPHY AND THE ORIENT

EARLY GREEK PHILOSOPHY AND THE ORIENT

M. L. WEST

OXFORD
AT THE CLARENDON PRESS

This book has been printed digitally and produced in a standard specification in order to ensure its continuing availability

OXFORD
UNIVERSITY PRESS

Great Clarendon Street, Oxford OX2 6DP

Oxford University Press is a department of the University of Oxford.
It furthers the University's objective of excellence in research, scholarship,
and education by publishing worldwide in

Oxford New York

Auckland Bangkok Buenos Aires Cape Town Chennai
Dar es Salaam Delhi Hong Kong Istanbul Karachi Kolkata
Kuala Lumpur Madrid Melbourne Mexico City Mumbai Nairobi
São Paulo Shanghai Singapore Taipei Tokyo Toronto

Oxford is a registered trade mark of Oxford University Press
in the UK and in certain other countries

Published in the United States
by Oxford University Press Inc., New York

Reprinted 2002

ISBN 0-19-814289-7

TO

WALTER BURKERT

PREFACE

THIS is a work of construction. It aims on the one hand to advance the understanding of several early Greek writers, by new interpretations and combinations; on the other, to raise the subject suggested by the title out of the disrepute into which it has fallen, by bringing fuller documentation, avoiding vagueness, and employing a properly philological and historical approach to what are eminently philological and historical problems.

The discussion of Pherecydes of Syros is a development from the one published in *CQ* 57, 1963, 157–72: I have thought everything out afresh, added new evidence, and, I hope, achieved a much improved account of this intriguing figure. In leaving the comparative material out of account until I have finished with the Greek sources, I have followed a principle that obtains throughout the book, and one which is necessary to avoid the suspicion of circularity. The outcome is that three of the seven chapters are concerned wholly with Greek evidence.

It is no doubt an impertinence to publish the other four without having made myself a master of Egyptian, Akkadian, Hebrew, Avestan, Pahlavi, and Sanskrit, not to mention other languages of incidental relevance. But I have enjoyed the criticism of such expert orientalists as Professor J. W. B. Barns, Professor Sir Godfrey Driver, Dr. Ilya Gershevitch, Mr. W. G. Lambert, and Mrs. Wendy O'Flaherty, all of whom generously gave time to reading and discussing the parts that touched their fields. Thanks to them I may hope to have got my facts straight, whatever may be thought of my inferences.

Walter Burkert had the goodness to read a draft of the whole, and it owes much besides to the example of his published works. It is dedicated to him in gratitude and friendship.

M. L. W.

University College, Oxford
September 1970

CONTENTS

LIST OF ILLUSTRATIONS

(*Between pages 128 and 129*)

EXPLANATION OF ABBREVIATIONS

A. Works cited by author's name only, or author and abbreviated title

Budge, E. A. Wallis, *The Book of the Dead*, 1913. Cited from the University Books edition, New York, 1960.

Burkert, W., *Weisheit und Wissenschaft*, Nuremberg, 1962.

—— 'Iranisches bei Anaximandros', *Rheinisches Museum* 106, 1963, 97–134.

Burnet, J., *Early Greek Philosophy*, 4th ed., London, 1930.

Bywater, I., *Heracliti Ephesii Reliquiae*, Oxford, 1877.

Cumont, F., *Recherches sur le symbolisme funéraire des Romains*, Paris, 1942.

—— *Textes et monuments figurés relatifs aux mystères de Mithra*, 2 vols., Brussels 1899.

Diels, H., *Doxographi Graeci*, Berlin, 1879.

Eisler, R., *Orphisch-dionysische Mysteriengedanken in der christlichen Antike* (Vortr. d. Bibl. Warburg 1922/3, 2), Leipzig and Berlin, 1925.

—— *Weltenmantel und Himmelszelt*, 2 vols., Munich, 1910.

Fränkel, H., *Dichtung und Philosophie des frühen Griechentums*, 2nd ed., Munich, 1962.

—— *Wege und Formen frühgriechischen Denkens*, 2nd ed., Munich, 1960.

Frazer, J. G., *The Golden Bough*, 3rd ed., London, 1911–36. Cited by physical volume and page, thus *GB* ii = *The Magic Art* ii; *GB* xiii = *Aftermath* (supplementary volume).

Gigon, O., *Untersuchungen zu Heraklit*, Diss. Basel, Leipzig, 1935.

Guthrie, W. K. C., *A History of Greek Philosophy*, 3 vols. (to date), Cambridge, 1962– .

Jaeger, W., *The Theology of the Early Greek Philosophers*, Oxford, 1947.

Kahn, C. H., *Anaximander and the Origins of Greek Cosmology*, New York and London, 1960.

Kirk, G. S., *Heraclitus, The Cosmic Fragments*, Cambridge, 1954 (repr. with corrections 1962).

—— and Raven, J. E., *The Presocratic Philosophers*, Cambridge, 1957.

Kühner, R., and Gerth, B., *Ausführliche Grammatik der griechischen Sprache*, 2. Teil (Syntax), 2 vols., Hanover, 1898–1904.

Lobeck, C. A., *Aglaophamus*, 2 vols., Königsberg, 1829.

Marcovich, M., *Estudios de filosofía griega*, i, Mérida (Venezuela), 1965.

—— *Heraclitus*, ed. maior, Mérida, 1967. Fragments of Heraclitus are cited from this edition.

NILSSON, M. P., *Geschichte der griechischen Religion*, 2 vols., 3rd/2nd ed., Munich, 1967, 1961.

——*Griechische Feste von religiöser Bedeutung*, Leipzig, 1906.

—— *The Minoan-Mycenaean Religion*, 2nd ed., Lund, 1950.

REINHARDT, K., *Parmenides und die Geschichte der griechischen Philosophie*, Bonn, 1916.

—— *Vermächtnis der Antike*, Göttingen, 1960.

ROSCHER, W. H. (ed.), *Ausführliches Lexikon der griechischen und römischen Mythologie*, Leipzig and Berlin, 1884–1937.

SCHWABL, H., 'Weltschöpfung', *RE* Supp. ix. 1434–1582 (1958).

SELIGMAN, P., *The* Apeiron *of Anaximander*, London, 1962.

SOMIGLIANA, A., *Monismo indiano e monismo greco nei frammenti di Eraclito*, Padua, 1961.

THESLEFF, H., *The Pythagorean Texts of the Hellenistic Period*, Åbo, 1965.

van der WAERDEN, B. L., *Die Anfänge der Astronomie*, Groningen, *c.* 1966.

WILAMOWITZ-MOELLENDORFF, U. von, *Der Glaube der Hellenen*, 2 vols., Berlin, 1931–2. Cited after the second printing (1955), which has slightly different pagination.

ZAEHNER, R. C., *The Dawn and Twilight of Zoroastrianism*, London, 1961.

——*Zurvan, A Zoroastrian Dilemma*, Oxford, 1955.

ZELLER, E., *Die Philosophie der Griechen in ihrer geschichtlichen Entwicklung*, 1. Teil, 6th ed. revised by W. Nestle, Leipzig, 1919–20.

B. Other abbreviations

ANET	*Ancient Near Eastern Texts*, ed. J. B. Pritchard, 2nd ed., Princeton, 1955.
Arch. f. Rel.	*Archiv für Religionswissenschaft.*
Begriffswelt	*Um die Begriffswelt der Vorsokratiker*, ed. H.-G. Gadamer (Wege der Forschung, 9), Darmstadt, 1968.
BSOAS	*Bulletin of the School of Oriental and African Studies.*
CPh	*Classical Philology.*
DK	H. Diels, *Die Fragmente der Vorsokratiker*, 5th ed. by W. Kranz, Berlin, 1934–5.
ERE	*Encyclopaedia of Religion and Ethics*, ed. J. Hastings, Edinburgh, 1908–26.
GGN	*Nachrichten der Göttingischen Gesellschaft.*
Hes. Th.	Hesiod, *Theogony*, ed. M. L. West, Oxford, 1966.
JNES	*Journal of Near Eastern Studies.*
LSJ	Liddell–Scott–Jones, *A Greek–English Lexicon*, Oxford, 1925–40.
RE	*Real-Encyclopädie der classischen Altertumswissenschaft*, ed. Pauly–Wissowa–Kroll, Stuttgart, 1894– .

SBE	*Sacred Books of the East*, ed. F. Max Müller, Oxford, 1879–1910.
SVF	*Stoicorum Veterum Fragmenta*, ed. H. von Arnim, Leipzig, 1903–5.
ZDMG	*Zeitschrift der deutschen morgenländischen Gesellschaft.*

In abbreviations for ancient authors, papyrus and inscription collections, or periodicals not mentioned above, the lists in LSJ should resolve any obscurities.

1

PHERECYDES AND HIS BOOK

THERE may be many students of antiquity to whom Pherecydes of Syros is no more than a name, and others to whom he is even less. He deserves better. According to some, his book was the first work of Greek literature to be written in prose. Whether that is correct or not, it was a book with enormously interesting contents, as we can see from the scanty remains of it that have come down to us.

Biographical data

Pherecydes lived in the sixth century B.C., perhaps in the same generation as Anaximander, if that was the time when the idea of writing in prose first established itself in Ionia. Apollodorus in fact put his *floruit* in 544/3, flying in the face of the tradition that made him a contemporary, or one of the number, of the Seven Sages (585/4 in Apollodorus' chronology).[1] He said that Anaximander was 64 years old in 547/6;[2] if he picked out that age because he had reason to think that it was when Anaximander wrote his book, he was dating that slightly before Pherecydes' *floruit*, in spite of the latter's reputation as the first prose author.[3] Although we are ignorant of the justification for

[1] See Jacoby, *Apollodors Chronik*, pp. 210 ff.; a brief summary in Kirk–Raven, p. 49. The earlier dating was well enough compatible with the fixed belief that Pherecydes was the teacher of Pythagoras, and one might have expected Apollodorus to set his *floruit* in 571/0, the fortieth year before Pythagoras'. Theopompus 115 F 70 even associates him with the capture of Messene, presumably the one in the mid seventh century; compare the early datings of Pythagoras by Eratosthenes and Antigonus, Jacoby, pp. 222 ff.; Burkert, *WW*, p. 176; Livy 1. 18. 2 with Ogilvie.

[2] Jacoby, p. 189. See below, p. 76 n. 1.

[3] Ps.-Thales *ap*. D.L. 1. 43, Plin. *NH* 7. 205, Apul. *Flor.* 15 p. 22. 8 Helm, Isid. *orig*. 1. 38. 2, Porph. *ap*. *Sud*. s.v. Φερεκύδης Ἀθηναῖος, cf. s.vv. Ἑκαταῖος, ἱστορῆσαι, συγγράφω, Φερεκύδης Βάβιος. These are all later writers, but must be following an older source. Theopompus 115 F 71 said Pherecydes was the first to

the Apollodorean dating, we are bound to consider it slightly more worthy of credence than the one that is linked with the Seven Sages. That derives from the unhistorical, anecdotal tradition which credited Pherecydes with various feats of supernatural knowledge. Such stories attached themselves to several *σοφοί* (clever men, experts, pundits) of the sixth and fifth centuries—Thales, Anaximander, Pythagoras, Anaxagoras—and testify to the awe with which such people were regarded in certain circles, an awe which turned into fear and hatred at Athens under the stresses of the Peloponnesian War. Sometimes the same story is connected with different men. It is particularly remarkable that three feats of prophecy and an oracular command, which Theopompus attributed to Pherecydes, were all given to Pythagoras by Andron of Ephesus.[1] Pherecydes was held to be the teacher of Pythagoras, and by the fourth century there existed more than one version of the story that Pythagoras journeyed to attend his master's death-bed.[2] Whether the two really ever met must remain doubtful. But it is certain that there were similarities of style and content between their teachings. Even if Pherecydes was not Pythagoras' 'teacher', his book was soon discovered by Pythagoreans and studied with interest.[3] In this milieu it would be natural for the same legends to be associated now with him, now with Pythagoras; though it must be granted that the

write *περὶ φύσεως καὶ θεῶν*, cf. Aponius in DK 7 A 5. Cadmus of Miletus, sometimes called the first prose writer, sometimes only the first historian, seems to be a fictitious figure, see Jacoby on *FGrHist* 489. Themist. *or.* 26 p. 317 c, presumably following Apollodorus, makes Anaximander the first writer *περὶ φύσεως* (Favorinus *ap.* D.L. 8. 83 was certainly wrong to give this honour to Alcmeon of Croton), and Diels and some other modern scholars have put Anaximander earlier than Pherecydes because of supposed influence; but of this I can find no trace. The question of priority is neither soluble nor important.

[1] Porph. *ap.* Eus. *PE* 10. 3. 6–9 = DK 7 A 6; Burkert, *WW*, pp. 120 f.

[2] Dicaearchus, fr. 34 Wehrli, Aristoxenus? Diod. 10. 4, etc.; Burkert, *WW*, p. 182 n. 51.

[3] His name is linked with Pythagoras' as early as Ion of Chios (epigram *ap.* D.L. 1. 120 = fr. 5 Diehl, 30 Blumenthal; Burkert, *WW*, p. 100). Burkert suggested to me in 1964 that Pherecydes' book was one of the *συγγραφαί* that Pythagoras made use of according to Heraclitus, fr. 17 M. = B 129. This might be so, though other fifth-century and later sources associate Pythagorean forgery rather with the name Orpheus. Cf. p. 214 n. 4.

systematic disagreement between Theopompus and Andron smacks of tendentiousness.

Pherecydes is said to have had no teacher, but to have used 'the revelation of Ham'[1] or the 'secret books of the Phoenicians'.[2] Such allegations have of course no evidential value, though we shall find abundant eastern influence in Pherecydes. It is interesting to note that while he himself had a good Greek name, and called an island near Delos his home, his father's name, Babys or Babis,[3] belongs to a group (masc. Babas, Babes, Babis, Babous, Babys, Baboas, fem. Baba, Babba, Babou, Babeis, Babo, Babyla) which are certainly of Asiatic origin, being most frequent in Phrygia, Pisidia, and Galatia.[4]

Byzantine writers say that Pherecydes visited Egypt,[5] but this was said of many 'philosophers' from Solon and Thales to Plato, and cannot be taken very seriously, even if Egypt was one of the most interesting objects of foreign travel for an inquisitive man in the sixth century. Other places in which Pherecydes turns up in the anecdotal tradition are Delos (plausible), Samos (the home of Pythagoras, suspect), Ephesus and Magnesia (surprising), Delphi, Olympia, Messene, and Sparta. His death is put in as many as five different localities.

The association with Sparta may turn out to be important, and deserves a little attention. The relevant material is as follows.

1. While *en route* for Messene from Olympia, Pherecydes advised one Perilaos to flee with his household, and it turned out that Messene had fallen.[6] This came in Theopompus

[1] Clem. *Strom.* 6. 53. 5 (cf. 1. 62), from Isidorus the Gnostic. On this see Kirk–Raven, p. 65.

[2] *Suda*; cf. Philo of Byblos 790 F 4 § 50 = DK 7 B 4.

[3] *Βάβιος Suda*, Strabo 487 v.l.; *Βάβυος* Strabo cod. D, *Βάδυος* codd. D.L. 1. 116, *Βάδυος* and *Βάβους* codd. ibid. 119. Both *Βάβυς* and *Βάβις* occur on inscriptions (*IG* 7. 3615; *MAMA* 1. 407, 4. 244).

[4] See L. Zgusta, *Kleinasiatische Personennamen*, pp. 113–16. They also occur, though comparatively rarely, in Caria, Lydia, Pamphylia, Lycaonia, Isauria, and Bithynia.

[5] Cedrenus i. 165. 19 Bekker, Theodorus Meliteniotes in *Patrol. gr.* 149. 1000 b. Cf. Jos. *c. Ap.* 1. 14 (Pherecydes and others learned from the Egyptians and Chaldaeans).

[6] D.L. 1. 116, Porph. *ap.* Eus. *PE* 10. 3. 8–9.

(115 F 70), and was one of the stories that Andron told about Pythagoras, with Sybaris in place of Messene.

2. Heracles appeared in a dream to Pherecydes and instructed him to tell the Spartan kings not to honour gold and silver. In the same night he appeared to one of the kings and told him to obey Pherecydes. The Spartans accordingly changed their constitution and avoided the danger of oligarchy.[1] This too came in Theopompus (F 71).

3. Terpander, Thaletas, and Pherecydes were greatly honoured at Sparta because their teachings agreed with those of Lycurgus.[2] Lycurgus' prohibition of coinage appears in the context, so the reference to Pherecydes seems to be based on story 2 above.

4. The Spartans killed Pherecydes and the kings preserved his skin because of an oracle.[3] In the better-known version of Sosibius (*ap.* D.L. 1. 115), the skin was that of Epimenides. Plutarch or a predecessor may have substituted Pherecydes by a slip of memory, remembering his mantic role at Sparta from the other tradition; or the substitution may go back to Theopompus.

Everything *may* have come from Theopompus, and it is patently unhistorical; Pherecydes cannot have had anything to do with the 'Lycurgan' reform or the Messenian War. But the fiction is easier to understand if there was some prior tradition about Pherecydes at Sparta. It would find its place in a series of stories about eminent visitors to Sparta in the seventh and sixth centuries. The list includes Epimenides and Anaximander.

The book

Why did Pherecydes write in prose and not in verse, which was the standard medium for any formal composition, anything intended to be preserved, down to his time or shortly before it? His subject-matter was not unsuited for hexameters.

[1] D.L. 1. 117, Olympiod. *in Alc.* p. 104 Westerink; cf. E. N. Tigerstedt, *Eranos* 51, 1953, 9.

[2] Plut. *Agis* 10. 3.

[3] Plut. *Pelop.* 21. 3.

To see the question in its proper light we must consider what a book was in his time. It was not the means by which the poet communicated with his public, or only to a very restricted degree. He recited, or sang, or taught a choir to sing; his public knew his work from hearing it, and read books little or not at all. The written book was a record of the spoken or sung word and subordinate to it. It was primarily valuable to the author himself, as an aide-mémoire, a way of fixing his liquid thoughts, or just as a pleasing visible token of his creativity. We hear of books being dedicated in temples, as if, once written, there was nothing further to be done with them.[1] Of course people would see them there, and those who could and were interested might read or even copy them, but systematic multiplication of copies was a thing of the future.

The first prose books must have been what poetry-books were at the time, records of the spoken word. That is why early writers refer to their work as a 'discourse', *λόγος*,[2] and to particular statements in it with phrases like 'as I have said', 'this is what I say on the matter', 'I shall speak of this later', habits which have remained with us through a continuous tradition ever since. The book was a 'write-up', *συγγραφή*, and the man who produced it was a 'discourse-writer', *λογογράφος*. It cannot be an accident that the three oldest prose books that survived—Pherecydes, Anaximander, Anaximenes—were all expositions of the origin and nature of the world. I infer that it was not unusual for a man who had views on these topics to deliver himself of some sort of lecture on them before an interested audience. Heraclitus does not say 'of all those whose books I have read' but 'of all those whose discourses I have heard' (fr. 83 M., DK 22 B 108). Later doxographers too will report that a philosopher

[1] *Hymn to Apollo*, *Cert.* 18 line 320 Allen; Heraclitus, D.L. 9. 6; Pindar's Seventh Olympian, Gorgon 515 F 18; even Crantor, D.L. 4. 25. This gives point to the (possibly genuine) apophthegm of Aeschylus in Ath. 347 e. Later, prize poems were often dedicated. See W. H. D. Rouse, *Greek Votive Offerings*, 1902, pp. 64 f.

[2] Heraclitus, fr. 1 *τοῦ λόγου τοῦδε*, etc. (see below, p. 115); Ion of Chios B 1; Hdt. 1. 5, 95, 2. 123, etc.; Hecataeus 1 F 1 *Ἑκαταῖος Μιλήσιος ὧδε μυθεῖται·* (but then) *τάδε γράφω ὥς μοι δοκεῖ ἀληθέα εἶναι*; Alcmeon B 1 *Ἀλκμέων Κροτωνιήτης τάδε ἔλεξε Πειρίθου υἱὸς Βροντίνῳ καὶ Λέοντι καὶ Βαθύλλῳ.*

'heard' such and such of his seniors. They distinguish between the θεολόγος and the φυσιολόγος, the preacher who declared that things were so, as if he had access to hidden knowledge, and the reasoner who tried to establish laws of nature.

Pherecydes was the former. His account was partly narrative in form, and partly a statement of how the world works now, the functions of the gods, and the fate of souls after death. To judge from the longest verbatim fragment (B 2; below, p. 16), he told his tale easily and artistically, in an unaffected style that was content with the simplest syntax and connectives, the informal present tense (strictly avoided in epic narrative), and such carefree repetition as in ἐπεὶ δὲ ταῦτα ἐξετέλεσαν πάντα καὶ χρήματα καὶ θεράποντας καὶ θεραπαίνας καὶ τἆλλα ὅσα δεῖ πάντα, ἐπεὶ δὴ πάντα ἕτοῖμα γίνεται, τὸν γάμον ποιεῦσιν, characteristic of speech but soon eliminated from literary prose. If later readers found Pherecydes enigmatic, it was only because of their conviction that he was to be interpreted allegorically.[1] His language seems to have been extremely clear, and the tempo of the story unhurried. He has room for inessential details like the servants, and for little formal speeches by bridegroom to bride and by bride to bridegroom. In telling of the battle in which the forces of Chronos drove those of Ophioneus into Ogenos, he prepared for the event in the Homeric manner, by referring to challenges and ἅμιλλαι (duels ?), and to an advance agreement between the two sides that those who fell into Ogenos should be held the losers.[2]

One of the lines in the papyrus fragment about the wedding is numbered 600. It may be reckoned that the text preceding this point in the roll amounted to the equivalent of eight or nine Teubner pages, and the chances are that the roll began with the beginning of Pherecydes' book. The whole work was probably

[1] Cf. the forged epistle to Thales, D.L. 1. 122 τὰ ἄλλα χρὴ νοέειν· ἅπαντα γὰρ αἰνίσσομαι, Clem. *Strom.* 5. 50, 6. 53. 5, Orig. *c. Cels.* 1. 18, Porph. *antr. nymph.* 31, Procl. *in Tim.* i. 129. 15.

[2] Compare for example the way in which at the games for Patroclus a prize is prearranged for the archer who misses the target-bird but severs the string that holds it (*Il.* 23. 857), the contingency that is actually realized in the contest.

of no great length. Diogenes Laertius (I. 119) refers to it as a βιβλίον, and Olympiodorus (*in Alc.* p. 104 Westerink) as a βίβλος. It is true that these expressions need not imply a work in one volume;[1] but Josephus states that Pherecydes, Pythagoras, and Thales are universally agreed to have learned from the Egyptians and Chaldaeans and to have written little.[2] The statement in the *Suda* that Pherecydes' work was in ten books is generally admitted to represent a confusion with the fifth-century Athenian historian of the same name, for identical information is given about him a few lines later.

Transmission, title

For an ancient book to survive it was necessary that it should arouse interest within fifty years or so of its composition. The people who were mainly interested in Pherecydes in the fifth century were, I have suggested, the Pythagoreans. It is only among them that we find significant echoes of his peculiar conceptions. Plato never mentions him,[3] though there is a general similarity between the Platonic myths and the kind of eschatology expounded by Pherecydes. It may be that Plato owes this style of teaching to a Pythagorean tradition. Aristotle and Eudemus certainly know Pherecydes and speak of him explicitly.

The papyrus fragment published in 1897, dated to the third century A.D., shows that he remained available well into the Roman period. Historians and others with an interest in the east, like Philo of Byblos, Josephus, and Isidorus the Gnostic, referred to him in order to derive the earliest Greek philosophy from abroad. Grammarians like Apollonius Dyscolus and his son Herodian used him as a source for the Ionic dialect. But he was mainly of interest to theologians and philosophers who found in him anticipations of their own ideas. We hear of allegorical

[1] See *CQ* 57, 1963, 157.

[2] 'And the Greeks consider these to be the most ancient of all writings, and can scarcely bring themselves to believe in their authenticity' (*c. Ap.* I. 14). 'Was von Pythagoras und Thales gilt, ist tendenziös auf Pherekydes übertragen' (Diels, *S.B. Berl. Ak.* 1897, 146 n. = *Kl. Schr.*, p. 25 n.).

[3] Unless, as some have thought, *Soph.* 242 c–d is an allusion (see Zeller–Nestle, i. I. 116 n. 4); but the parallel with Isoc. 15. 268 points to Ion of Chios.

interpretation by the late-second-century Platonist Celsus and perhaps by Numenius, and from this circle we can trace a continuing tradition through Porphyry to the later Neoplatonists, Proclus, Hermias, Damascius, Lydus. Pherecydes was not necessarily still extant then; Damascius at any rate uses Eudemus' account (fr. 150 Wehrli).

Apollonius Dyscolus quotes *Φερεκύδης ἐν τῇ θεολογίᾳ* (B 10), and this designation should have been sufficient for anyone. After all, people spoke simply of Hesiod's *θεογονία*, and Presocratics who wrote only one work were catalogued as so-and-so *περὶ φύσεως*. The *Suda*, however, offers a more elaborate title: *ἑπτάμυχος ἤτοι θεοκρασία ἢ θεογονία*.[1] I take *ἑπτάμυχος* to be (*a*) an error for *πεντέμυχος*,[2] and (*b*) an adjective qualifying whichever one chooses of the following nouns.[3] I should have thought that *ἤτοι* at this stage of Greek ought to mean either 'either (. . . or)' or 'i.e.', and the latter is inappropriate. And *Πεντέμυχος* would be an odd book-title by itself: in cases like Ptolemy's *Τετράβιβλος*, Ostanes' *'Οκτάτευχος*, or the Orphic *'Ογδοηκοντάλιθος*, we can more easily understand a noun like *βίβλος* or *πραγματεία*.

On the other hand, *πεντέμυχος θεοκρασία* or *πεντέμυχος θεογονία* is also odd. *θεοκρασία* is a rare word; the only other occurrences of it known to me come from Neoplatonist writers. In Iambl. *VP* 240 and Dam. *Isid.* p. 8 Zintzen it means 'uniting oneself with God', while in Dam. *Isid.* pp. 146–7 Z. it appears to be used of two gods merging with each other in a single identity. The phrase *πεντέμυχος θεοκρασία* in relation to Pherecydes would refer to the formation of gods from fire, wind, and water distributed in five nooks (A 8; below, pp. 12–15). The same event could be called a *θεογονία*, especially as the fire, wind, and water came from Chronos' seed. But it is difficult to believe that phrases describing this one stage in Pherecydes'

[1] The following words *ἔστι δὲ θεολογία {ἐν βιβλίοις ῑ} <περι>έχουσα θεῶν γένεσιν καὶ διαδόχους* (*διαδοχάς* Preller) do not add another title, but are descriptive. Similar sentences begin with *ἔστι δέ* s.vv. *Ἀριγνώτη*, *'Ερμαγόρας Ἀμφιπολίτης*, *Φερεκύδης Ἀθηναῖος*, and I daresay elsewhere.

[2] See below, p. 13.

[3] So apparently Wilamowitz, *Kl. Schr.* v (2). 129.

cosmogony were commonly used to designate his book as a whole, and the word θεοκρασία seems not to have been invented until a late period. I suspect that some Neoplatonist writer spoke of 'Pherecydes' five-nook god-mixing, or should one say god-generating', intending a reference to the particular doctrine, and that the *Suda* title comes from an unintelligent misinterpretation of this.

Pherecydes himself, of course, used no title. He probably began with a '*sphragis*' such as Φερεκύδης Σύριος τάδε ἔλεξε Βάβυος υἱός. This is customary in early prose books, at any rate from the time of Hecataeus. After the fifth century the practice was discontinued, presumably because the author and title were now written as a heading. The use of a heading meant that a copyist might omit a *sphragis* in the older style, provided that it was not too closely integrated with more important prefatory sentences (as was the case in Hecataeus, Alcmeon, Herodotus, Thucydides, Antiochus of Syracuse). Consequently a text of Heraclitus, instead of beginning (e.g.) Ἡράκλειτος Βλόσωνος Ἐφέσιος τάδε λέγει· τοῦ δὲ λόγου τοῦδε ἐόντος αἰεί κτλ., now began *ΗΡΑΚΛΕΙΤΟΥ ΠΕΡΙ ΦΥΣΕΩΣ*. τοῦ δὲ λόγου τοῦδε κτλ. (Aristotle and Sextus say that this was the beginning of the book. The δέ is absent in some quotations, and was no doubt expelled from some texts.) Ion's *Triagmoi* now began ἀρχὴ δέ μοι τοῦ λόγου πάντα τρία, again with an unneeded connective. Philolaus began ἁ φύσις δ' ἐν τῷ κόσμῳ ἁρμόχθη ἐξ ἀπείρων τε καὶ περαινόντων.[1]

The three pre-existing deities

It is therefore no argument against the assumption of a Pherecydean *sphragis* that the opening sentence of the book is quoted as Ζὰς μὲν καὶ Χρόνος ἦσαν αἰεὶ καὶ Χθονίη· Χθονίῃ δὲ ὄνομα ἐγένετο Γῆ, ἐπειδὴ αὐτῇ Ζὰς γῆν γέρας διδοῖ. Pherecydes signed his name, and then without further ado[2] embarked upon his narrative.

[1] Cf. Burkert, *WW*, p. 234 n. 73.

[2] Without, for example, a disclaimer such as is attributed to him in the letter to Thales: ἔστι δὲ οὐκ ἀτρεκηίη πρηγμάτων, οὐδὲ ὑπίσχομαι τἀληθὲς εἰδέναι. Alcmeon puts such a disclaimer in his preface. If Pherecydes uttered one he must have put it somewhere else.

Ζάς, genitive *Ζαντός*, is Pherecydes' name for Zeus; we are informed that he also used *Ζής*.[1] Both these forms are peculiar to him. Lydus, *de mens.* 4. 3, cites Pherecydes as an authority for the identification of Zeus with the sun. This may be based on someone's allegorical interpretation of Pherecydes, for in 3. 10 (p. 47. 7 Wünsch, cf. p. 45. 20) the identification is ascribed to physical philosophers who similarly explained Hera as the moon. We know that someone else interpreted Zas as the aither (Probus, Hermias, DK 7 A 9), and this would be surprising if Pherecydes himself had said that Zas was the sun. There is no certain case of the identification of Zeus with the sun before the Hellenistic period.[2]

Chronos speaks for himself: he is the god Time. Hermias read 'Kronos', and so the tradition of Origen in B 4; Damascius, Probus, and Diogenes give Chronos. Confusion was easy, Kronos and Chronos being widely regarded as identical. Zeller preferred *Κρόνος* on the ground that it was 'scarcely credible that such an ancient thinker had placed the abstract idea of Time among the first principles'.[3] In the next chapter it will be shown how mistaken this is. For the moment it is sufficient to observe that the Kronos of Hesiodic tradition is a figure of mythology who plays no part in the world's affairs, but rules in the Isles of the Blessed Ones or else sits huddled in misty Tartarus. He could not assume any cosmic importance until he was identified with Chronos. We do not know whether in fact Pherecydes associated his Chronos with Kronos.[4]

He himself explains who Chthonie is. The Earth familiar to us first appeared when an embroidered robe was given to a goddess

[1] Herodian ii. 911. 8 Lentz *καὶ γὰρ Δὶς καὶ Ζὴν καὶ Δὴν καὶ Ζὰς καὶ Ζὴς παρὰ Φερεκύδει κατὰ κίνησιν ἰδίαν*. Confused? The grammarians' various notices are collected by A. B. Cook, *Zeus* ii. 351 n. 2.

[2] See Cook, *Zeus* i. 186 ff. In *IG* 12 (7). 87 (Amorgos, vi/v B.C.) *ΖΕΥΣ ΗΛ*[. .]*Σ*, the second word may be the dedicator's name in the genitive. Orph. fr. 21 a. 6 was composed by a Stoic, and fr. 47 mainly by Diels. On the other hand, Helios as chief of all the gods in Sophocles (cf. p. 109) may point in that direction.

[3] Zeller–Nestle, i. 1. 103 n. 4; cf. Wilamowitz, *Kl. Schr.* v (2). 165.

[4] The earliest evidence for the association is probably Pind. *Ol.* 10. 49/55. See also F. M. Cornford, *CR* 26, 1912, 181, and *From Religion to Philosophy*, p. 171 n. 4; J. van Leeuwen, *Pindarus' Tweede Olympische Ode*, pp. 73–5, 429–32 (nn. 197 ff.).

at her wedding: Chthonie is the name Pherecydes chooses to give her for the time before her marriage, and so that we shall not be puzzled, he immediately mentions the change into Ge which is to take place later in his story. *χθόνιος* was established by his time as an epithet of gods who are in the earth.[1] 'Earth', then, for Pherecydes, is 'Goddess-inside-the-earth' plus a robe, and the robe, as we shall see, has the visible outer surface of the earth depicted on it.

Chaos

Probus and Hermias ignore the distinction between Chthonie and Ge, and explain Chthonie as earth. This accounts for Sextus Empiricus' statements[2] that Pherecydes took earth as the *ἀρχὴ τῶν πάντων* (a view which Aristotle, who knew Pherecydes, says no philosopher had held: *Metaph.* 989^{a}5). By contrast, Achilles Tatius, *Isag. in Arat.* p. 31.28 Maass, writes: *Θαλῆς ὁ Μιλήσιος καὶ Φερεκύδης ὁ Σύριος ἀρχὴν τῶν ὅλων τὸ ὕδωρ ὑφιστῶσιν, ὃ δὴ καὶ Χάος καλεῖ ὁ Φερεκύδης, ὡς εἰκὸς τοῦτο ἐκδεξάμενος παρὰ τοῦ Ἡσιόδου οὕτω λέγοντος· "ἤ τοι μὲν πρώτιστα Χάος γένετο"* (*Th.* 116). *παρὰ γὰρ τὸ χεῖσθαι ὑπολαμβάνει τὸ ὕδωρ Χάος ὠνομάσθαι.*[3] It may be inferred that Pherecydes introduced 'Chaos' in some context where a later interpreter was able to represent it as the material *ἀρχή*. The Stoic interpretation of Hesiod's Chaos as water, supported by the etymology from *χεῖσθαι*, was not only applied to Pherecydes but even attributed to him. There is in

[1] If someone spoke of the *θεὸς χθόνιος* (Hes. *Th.* 767), he would be understood to mean Hades, and by the same token *Χθονίη* might suggest Persephone. 'Musaeus' (DK 2 B 11, uncertain date) used the name for a goddess who gave oracles at Delphi, so apparently as the equivalent of Ge. A late inscription from Myconos (compared by Diels, *S.B. Berl. Ak.* 1897, 149 f. = *Kl. Schr.*, pp. 28 f.; Wilamowitz, *Kl. Schr.* v (2). 128, 165 n. 4) records sacrifices *Δὶ Χθονίῳ Γῇ Χθονίῃ* (*SIG*[3] 1024. 20; but one might expect *Δὶ Χθονίῳ καὶ Χθονίῃ*, cf. *IG* 7. 1814 *Δὶ Μιλίχυ κὴ Μιλίχῃ*).

[2] *Pyrrh.* 3. 30, *adv. math.* 9. 360. Cf. Epiphanius, *adv. haer.* 3. 7 (Diels, *Doxogr.* p. 590); Galen, *hist. phil.* 18 (ibid. p. 610); sch. in Basilium p. 195. 4 Pasquali (*GGN* 1910).

[3] Similar information in a more abridged form appears in sch. Hes. loc. cit. and Tz. in Lyc. 145. The *Suda* says casually of Pherecydes *ἐζηλοτύπει δὲ τὴν Θάλητος δόξαν*, and among the pairs of rivals listed in D.L. 2. 46 (from Aristotle, fr. 75) Pherecydes is given as Thales' rival; but these notices need not be doxographically intended.

fact no reason to believe that when he said Chaos he meant water, and in view of the usage of the word before and after him it is in the highest degree improbable. The associations of Chaos in the archaic period are with darkness and depth. Like such figures as Erebos and Night, it always appears in the earliest stages of cosmogonies, before heaven and earth.[1] In Pherecydes too it must have appeared early, or it could not have been held to be the ἀρχή. Yet it was not one of the three first deities. One might imagine something on these lines: 'Zas and Chronos always were, and Chthonie; but Chthonie's name became Ge, because Zas gave her the earth as a gift of honour. For earth was not at first, nor heaven, but Chaos extended over all.' It may have been argued that if Chaos was not earth or heaven, it was water.

The five nooks

Of the three first deities, Zas and Chthonie married each other, while Chronos produced offspring from his own seed without a consort. Damascius (after Eudemus) speaks of this as if it came directly after the mention of the three, before the wedding.

Φερεκύδης δὲ ὁ Σύριος Ζάντα μὲν εἶναι ἀεὶ καὶ Χρόνον καὶ Χθονίαν, τὰς τρεῖς πρώτας ἀρχάς, τὴν μίαν φημὶ πρὸ τῶν δυοῖν καὶ τὰς δύο μετὰ τὴν μίαν. τὸν δὲ Χρόνον ποιῆσαι ἐκ τοῦ γόνου ἑαυτοῦ πῦρ καὶ πνεῦμα καὶ ὕδωρ—τὴν τριπλῆν οἶμαι φύσιν τοῦ νοητοῦ—ἐξ ὧν ἐν πέντε μυχοῖς διῃρημένων πολλὴν ἄλλην[2] *γενεὰν συστῆναι θεῶν, τὴν πεντέμυχον καλουμένην, ταὐτὸν δὲ ἴσως εἰπεῖν πεντέκοσμον.*

It is of Chronos, then, that we must understand Aristotle's statement (*Metaph.* 1091^{b}10) that Pherecydes and others τὸ γεννῆσαν πρῶτον ἄριστον τιθέασιν.[3] The implication of ἄριστον is that Chronos was somehow said to have power now, an idea for which there are plenty of fifth-century parallels. But Pherecydes

[1] Hes. loc. cit., Acusilaus 9 B 1–2, cf. Ar. *Av.* 693. Orph. fr. 54 is of later date.

[2] πολλὴν BEW: πάλιν FI. ἄλλην om. BFW.

[3] Everyone seems to take it of Zas. This led Kern to alter ἑαυτοῦ to αὑτοῦ. (Diels should not have said that τοῦ γόνου ἑαυτοῦ was bad Greek. See Kühner–Gerth, i. 620.)

thought of Zas as exercising power among the gods too (B 5: he throws unruly ones into Tartarus).

Out of his seed Chronos made fire, wind, and water. These were distributed among five nooks, and a number of gods arose from them, the 'so-called five-nook generation'. Was this a phrase that Pherecydes himself had used? At first sight it might appear so. But we must remember that Damascius was the heir to a long tradition of exegesis of Pherecydes' work, and it may well be that it is to this that he owes the expression. Pherecydes would have said *πεντάμυχος*, not *πεντέμυχος*, if he had used such an adjective at all.[1] Nor is there any ground for supposing that the word *γενεά* comes from Pherecydes, for it is fully accounted for by the usage of Damascius in the rest of the doxographical passage.[2]

What and where were the five *μυχοί*? The word is vague, and that is why I have used the non-committal 'nook' in rendering it. We can only guess at what Pherecydes had in mind; fortunately nothing much rests on the answer. The number presents another problem. As was mentioned above, the *Suda* gives, as if the title of Pherecydes' book, 'seven-nook theocrasy or theogony'. Theocrasy/theogony is what takes place in Damascius' five nooks (see below). It is difficult to believe that Pherecydes' cosmogony involved one such process in a set of five nooks and another somewhere else in a set of seven. No convincing attempt to explain the discrepancy has ever been made, and I think we must adopt Preller's proposal to abolish it by emending the *Suda*.[3]

[1] Cf. Hdt. 1. 136 *πενταέτης*, 144 *πεντάπολις*, 2. 10 and 4. 47 *πεντάστομος*, 6. 89 *πεντάδραχμος*, 9. 83 *πεντάπηχυς* (v.l. *πεντέ-*); A. Debrunner, *Griech. Wortbildungslehre*, p. 69.

[2] Cf. the account of Epimenides a few lines before, *ἐξ οὗ πάλιν ἄλλην γενεὰν προελθεῖν* (this may be held either to support or to condemn the variant *πάλιν* for *πολλήν* in the report on Pherecydes); or that of Acusilaus, *παράγει δὲ ἐπὶ τούτοις ἐκ τῶν αὐτῶν καὶ ἄλλων θεῶν πολὺν ἀριθμὸν κατὰ τὴν Εὐδήμου ἱστορίαν*; or that of the Babylonians, *ἐκ δὲ τῶν αὐτῶν ἄλλην γενεὰν προελθεῖν, Λαχὴν καὶ Λαχόν*. Similarly Irenaeus, *c. haeres.* 2. 14 (Antiphanes, i, p. 318 Meineke) *post quos rursus secundam deorum generationem inducit.*

[3] *Rh. Mus.* N.F. 4, 1845, 378. P. Walcot, *CQ* 59, 1965, 79, thinks that the seven nooks are guaranteed by the Ugaritic Baal epic, where El speaks 'from the seven chambers, from the eight openings of the closed room'. But the parallels that he tries to establish between El and Chronos are insubstantial, and I cannot see that El's chambers, whether seven or eight, have much relevance to Pherecydes'

The nooks serve as matrices, so to speak, in which the new generation of gods develops and is differentiated. It is generally the case in mythology that gods' semen produces new life, in whatever circumstances it is shed, but only after it has fallen on the earth or been received in some kind of womb.[1] One might suspect, with Kirk (Kirk–Raven, p. 58), that what was distributed in the nooks was simply Chronos' seed. Kirk dismissed the fire, wind, and water as intrusions from a physical exegesis of Pherecydes in the Stoic manner. I, in my earlier discussion, assumed that five gods were born in the nooks, representing physical elements, among which were the three named by Damascius, and that they were subsequently brought into creative mixture by Zas in the guise of Eros (B 3). But apart from the fact that Damascius says that the seed became fire, wind, and water before it was distributed in the nooks, it has to be admitted that the account he used (sc. Eudemus) only gave three elements, not five; for his interpretation as *ἡ τριπλῆ φύσις τοῦ νοητοῦ* cannot be based on a wanton falsification of his own. And I now think that B 3 may have to be understood very differently. If Damascius is to be trusted, we may perhaps suppose that Pherecydes combined a purely theological idea—the seed of Time in five wombs producing differentiated gods—with a physical rationale: semen contains *πῦρ*, *πνεῦμα*, and *ὕδωρ*, being hot, wet, and quickening,[2] and as the differing proportions of these constituents produce children with different temperaments, so the seed of Chronos, separated into its ingredients and then mixed in the nooks in different proportions, produced gods with contrasted characters. This interpretation does justice to the expression *θεοκρασία*, and to Aristotle's classification of Pherecydes as an 'intermediate' kind of philosopher who does not say everything in mythical terms (*Metaph.* 1091^{b}8).

cosmogony. Seven is of course common as a special number, particularly in the east. Walcot does not attempt to reconcile the *Suda* figure with the testimony of Damascius.

[1] I collected some examples in *CQ* 57, 1963, 159.

[2] Cf. Diog. Apoll. 64 A 24, B 6, Hippon 38 A 3, Philolaus 44 A 27, Democr. 68 A 140, and later philosophers cited by Kirk. I shall be told that Pherecydes lived too early to have thought in these terms; may I also be told a better explanation.

If there are five nooks, it must be because the gods whose birth Pherecydes wants to put at this stage are five in number,[1] or fall into five groups of differing temper, perhaps located in different regions of the universe. This is suggested by Damascius' tentative equation of πεντέμυχος with πεντέκοσμος,[2] and we shall see that Pherecydes did divide the universe into parts (perhaps five: heaven, earth, the regions outside Ogenos, Hades, Tartarus), at least some of which have particular gods permanently settled in them.

The wedding of Zas and Chthonie

These provinces, however, only became solid and actual after Zas married Chthonie. Since their existence is presupposed by the battle in which the Ophionidai were driven into Ogenos, I now put the wedding before the battle, though without much assurance. Maximus of Tyre 4. 4 writes: ἀλλὰ καὶ τοῦ Συρίου τὴν ποίησιν σκόπει, καὶ τὸν Ζῆνα καὶ τὴν Χθονίην καὶ τὸν ἐν τούτοις ἔρωτα, καὶ τὴν 'Οφιονέως γένεσιν καὶ τὴν θεῶν μάχην, καὶ τὸ δένδρον καὶ τὸν πέπλον; but there is no certainty that this list of contents is in correct order. We know that the robe was associated with Zas and Chthonie, though it may have been mentioned in more than one context. Analogies with the order of events in Hesiod and other theogonies are ambivalent and indecisive. Nor can we argue anything from the interval of eight or nine Teubner pages which we believe to have separated what we have of the wedding narrative from the beginning of the book.

[1] Cf. Ael. *HN* 12. 16 (DK 68 A 151) λέγει Δημόκριτος πολύγονα εἶναι ὗν καὶ κύνα, καὶ τὴν αἰτίαν προστίθησι, λέγων ὅτι πολλὰς ἔχει τὰς μήτρας καὶ τοὺς τόπους τοὺς δεκτικοὺς τοῦ σπέρματος, and similarly Hp. *nat. puer.* 31 (vii. 540 L.).

[2] F. G. Sturz, *Pherecydis Fragmenta*, [2]1824, p. 43, compared Plut. *def. or.* 422 f ἀλλὰ μὴν ὑμῶν, ἔφη, τῶν γραμματικῶν ἀκούομεν εἰς Ὅμηρον (*Il.* 15. 187 ff.) ἀγόντων τὴν δόξαν, ὡς ἐκείνου τὸ πᾶν εἰς πέντε κόσμους διανέμοντος, οὐρανόν, ὕδωρ, ἀέρα, γῆν, ὄλυμπον . . . οὕτω δὲ καὶ Πλάτων (*Tim.* 55 d) ἔοικε . . . πέντε κόσμους καλεῖν, τὸν γῆς, τὸν ὕδατος, τὸν ἀέρος, τὸν πυρός, ἔσχατον δὲ τὸν περιέχοντα τούτους τὸν τοῦ δωδεκαέδρου. Cf. *de E* 389 f. For κόσμος meaning 'cosmic region' in Aristotle and elsewhere see Jula Kerschensteiner, *Kosmos* (*Zetemata*, 30), 1962, pp. 45 ff. Cf. the Hermetic and Neoplatonic use of it in expressions like ὁ ὑπερουράνιος κόσμος, ὁ ἐπιχθόνιος κόσμος.

It may easily have been occupied by the account of the five nooks and the theocrasy, and the preliminaries of the wedding, or by other events of which we have no inkling.

What is known of the wedding is known primarily from the papyrus fragment, which reads as follows.[1]

Col. i]τῳ̣ ποιεῦσιν τὰ ο[ἰ]κία πολλά τε καὶ μεγάλα· ἐπεὶ δὲ ταῦτα ἐξετέλ̣εσαν πάντα καὶ χρήματα καὶ̣ θεράποντας καὶ θερα̣παίνας καὶ τἆλλα ὅσα δεῖ πάντα, ἐπεὶ δὴ πάντα ἑτοῖμα γίνεται, τὸν γάμον ποιεῦσιν. κἀπειδὴ τρί̣τη ἡμέρη γίνεται τῷ̣ γάμῳ̣, τότε Ζὰς ποιεῖ φᾶρος μέγα τε καὶ κ̣αλόν, καὶ ἐν αὐτῷ̣ π̣ο̣ι̣κ̣⌊ίλλει γῆν⌋ καὶ ὠγη̣̣⌊νὸν καὶ τὰ ὠ⌋γη̣νοῦ ⌊δώματα........]γι̣̣[

Col. ii]γάρ σεο τοὺς γάμου̣[ς] εἶναι, τούτῳ̣ σε τιμ̣[έω·] σ̣ὺ δέ μοι χαῖρε καὶ σ̣ύ[νι]σθι." ταῦτά φασ̣ιν ἀν̣[α]καλυπτήρια πρῶτον̣ γενέσθαι, ἐκ το̣ύτου δ̣[ὲ] ὁ νόμος ἐγένε[το] κ̣α̣ὶ θεοῖσι καὶ ἀνθρ̣[ώπ]-ο̣ι̣σιν. ἡ δέ μι[ν ἀμεί]β̣[ε]ται δ̣ε̣ξαμ̣[ένη εὖ τὸ] φᾶ̣[ρος - - - - -]επ̣ [- - - - -]ζ̣ι̣[- - - - -].[- - - - -]θ.[

The last lines of col. i are restored from the quotation by Clement, *Strom.* 6. 9. A detached fragment mounted in the same frame bears the letters]εθυετο.[. The papyrus and ink resemble those of the Pherecydes fragment, but the hand is cursive. If the scrap comes from the same roll, it may belong to a scholium, possibly on the word θυωρός 'sacrificial table', which Pherecydes said was the gods' word for τράπεζα (B 12). Of the material on the speech of the gods which I have collected on Hes. *Th.* 831, the passage most relevant to Pherecydes' dictum is Sannyrion fr. 1 (i. 793 Kock),

πελανὸν καλοῦμεν ἡμεῖς οἱ θεοί,
ἃ καλεῖτε σεμνῶς ἄλφιθ' ὑμεῖς οἱ βροτοί.

In other words, the name of a thing in religious cult is the gods' name.[2]

The match was one of love (Max. Tyr. l.c.), and it is of this that I now understand the passage of Proclus printed by Diels as

[1] For palaeographical details see *CQ* 57, 1963, 164 f.
[2] Cf. Lobeck, p. 868.

B 3. Proclus is talking about the function of Love as a unifying force in the physical cosmos, and he has quoted verses from the Chaldaean Oracles and the Orphic Rhapsodies to illustrate the importance accorded to it by various authorities. Then he says: *καὶ ἴσως πρὸς τοῦτο ἀποβλέπων καὶ ὁ Φερεκύδης ἔλεγεν εἰς ἔρωτα μεταβεβλῆσθαι τὸν Δία μέλλοντα δημιουργεῖν, ὅτι δὴ τὸν κόσμον ἐκ τῶν ἐναντίων συνιστὰς εἰς ὁμολογίαν καὶ φιλίαν ἤγαγε, καὶ ταυτότητα πᾶσιν ἐνέσπειρε καὶ ἕνωσιν τὴν δι' ὅλων διήκουσαν.* The *ὅτι*-clause is Proclus' own account of what Pherecydes might have meant, and need have no relation to anything he had said. The passage is usually taken to show that Zas at a certain stage underwent a metamorphosis into Eros, and in this identity set about a demiurgy of some kind. But *μεταβεβλῆσθαι*, on this interpretation, would mean that Zas became Eros *instead* of being Zas, and Pherecydes or any other theologian would surely have said that he was (or became called) Eros *as well as* Zas. Chthonie changes her name but not her identity; the Orphic Phanes is Zeus and Eros at once; Rhea becomes Demeter when she becomes the mother of Zeus, but does not cease to be Rhea (Orph. fr. 145). Surely what Pherecydes said was that Zas fell in love; e.g. *Χρόνος μὲν δὴ ταῦτα ἐποίει. ὁ δὲ Ζὰς τὰ μὲν πρῶτα οὐκ ἔπασχεν οὐδὲν περισσὸν μετὰ τῆς Χθονίης ἐών, τῷ δὲ πολλῷ χρόνῳ καὶ συνηθείῃ μετέβαλεν ἐς ἔρωτα.*[1] Looking for connections between love and cosmogony, Proclus or his source blindly or wilfully misconstrued the great god's experience. The 'demiurgy' that he was soon to accomplish was nothing but the weaving of the robe embroidered with earth, ocean, and the rest (so Kirk–Raven, p. 62). For it was this robe that turned Chthonie into the earth we know. When he gave it to her and said *τούτῳ σε τιμέω*, that was the same act that had been referred to in the opening sentence of the book, *Χθονίῃ δὲ ὄνομα ἐγένετο Γῆ, ἐπειδὴ αὐτῇ Ζὰς γῆν γέρας διδοῖ.*[2]

He made it and gave her it on the day of the *anakalypteria*,

[1] Cf. Hdt. 1. 65 *τὸ δὲ ἔτι πρότερον τούτων καὶ κακονομώτατοι ἦσαν . . . μετέβαλον δὲ ὧδε ἐς εὐνομίην.*

[2] *γέρας* and *τιμή* can be very close in meaning, e.g. Hes. *Th.* 393–6, 426–7, 449.

the third day of marriage,[1] a regular occasion for a gift from husband to bride.[2] Thus Pherecydes kills two birds with one stone. He explains how Goddess-within-the-earth came to have the earth put round her, and he incidentally provides an *αἴτιον* for a custom observed by men: *ἐκ τούτου δὲ ὁ νόμος ἐγένετο καὶ θεοῖσι καὶ ἀνθρώποισι.*

The decoration of the robe comprises the earth and its surroundings, namely Ogenos and the Mansions of Ogenos. (If there had been further items, such as heaven or sea, one might have expected Clement to include them in his quotation, since he is concerned to show that Pherecydes copied from Homer's description of Achilles' shield (quoted below).) Ogenos is, like Zas,[3] a peculiar Pherecydean substitute for a name that was familiar to all Greeks in a different form, in this case Okeanos. Clement, the papyrus, and Celsus in B 4, write *'Ωγην-*; Lycophron, however, uses the form *"Ωγενος* (231), and some other learned poet, probably Alexandrian, used *'Ωγενίδαι.*[4] Both *'Ωγηνός* and *"Ωγενος*[5] may have come from Pherecydes. The only sixth-century inscription from Syros shows inconsistent use of *E* and *H* for standard Greek *ε*, and the close relationship of its script with those of the nearby Delos and Ceos implies that the same two symbols might be used indiscriminately for standard Greek *η* too.[6] If Pherecydes wrote his book in his local script, he may well have written *ΟΛΕΝΟΣ* and *ΟΛΗΝΟΣ* in different passages. The great majority of such vagaries would be ironed out by early copyists who understood what he was saying. But Ogenos

[1] Hesych. *ἀνακαλυπτήριον· ὅτε τὴν νύμφην πρῶτον ἐξάγουσιν τῇ τρίτῃ ἡμέρᾳ.*

[2] Harpocr. s.v. *ἀνακαλυπτήρια*, Pollux 3. 36.

[3] *'Ρῆ* for Rhea (B 9) should not be added to the list. It represents a normal Ionic development, cf. *'Ερμῆς, Δημῆς* from *-είας, -έας, -έης.* (Wilamowitz, *Euripides Herakles*, [2]iii. 261 n. 2.) In what connection Pherecydes mentioned Rhea is unknown.

[4] St. Byz. s.v. *"Ωγενος*, *Suda* s.v. (explained as *ἀρχαῖοι*), Hesych. s.v. (explained as *'Ωκεανίδαι. '⟨Ω⟩γὴν γὰρ 'Ωκεανός*). Parthenius, fr. 5 Diehl, wrote *ὠγενίης Στυγὸς ὕδωρ*, whether meaning 'daughter of Ocean' or 'ancient' (Hesych. *ὠγένιον· παλαιόν*).

[5] The accents are immaterial; no one could have known Pherecydes' pronunciation, and the accent was assigned on the strength of supposed analogues. Pherecydes is likely to have followed the model of *'Ωκεανός*. If *'Ωγενίδαι* is formed on *'Ωγενος* (so St. Byz., *Suda*), *'Ωγήν* may be a grammarian's construction from it.

[6] L. H. Jeffery, *The Local Scripts of Archaic Greece*, pp. 296, 298.

was a wholly strange form, and they had no reason to make a uniform choice. The inconsistency may thus have been perpetuated at least into Hellenistic times.

The Mansions of Ogenos are something of a mystery. The Homeric Oceanus lives in a house,[1] or in Aeschylus' opinion a cave.[2] This is appropriate to a divine river,[3] and there is nothing objectionable in the idea that Pherecydes' Ogenos had a house, as do Zas and Chthonie. But in the present context a house of that kind would surely not deserve explicit mention. Pherecydes is telling us that the robe represented the terrestrial world, and like Homer in the account of Achilles' shield,[4] he is thinking in terms of the great divisions of the world: earth, ocean, and, I can only think, habitations beyond ocean, where Greek myth located many fabulous persons.[5] These are not usually thought of as taking up much space; at any rate, other authors make no provision for them when they carve up the cosmos into earth, sea, sky, etc. If Pherecydes mentions them specially, it is possibly because he has in view a map on which they were prominently marked. Maps of the world were believed to have first appeared in Greece in the mid sixth century. Anaximander was supposed to have made the first one, and we hear of them next in connection with two more Milesians, Aristagores and Hecataeus. We gather from Herodotus that they were commonly bordered by the circle of Oceanus.[6]

By the time col. ii of the papyrus begins, Zas has handed over the gift and begun a pretty little speech. Before *γάρ* a participle is evidently needed. Weil's *βουλόμενος* has been widely accepted,

1 *Il.* 14. 202 = 303, 311; cf. Orph. fr. 135.

2 *PV* 133, 300, cf. 396; *Ὠκεανοῖο ῥοὰς καὶ Τηθύος ἄντρα* Q.S. 3. 748, 12. 160. A cave can be described as *δώματα* (Hes. *Th.* 303, 777; or *δόμοι*, *H. Herm.* 27, 248; or *μέγαρα*, *Od.* 4. 557).

3 Cf. Hes. *Th.* 777 (Styx); Virg. *A.* 8. 65, Ov. *F.* 5. 661 (Tiber); id. *M.* 8. 560 (Achelous).

4 *Il.* 18. 483 f. *ἐν μὲν γαῖαν ἔτευξ', ἐν δ' οὐρανόν, ἐν δὲ θάλασσαν, ἐν δὲ τὰ τείρεα πάντα, τά τ' οὐρανὸς ἐστεφάνωται*, 606 *ἐν δ' ἐτίθει ποταμοῖο μέγα σθένος Ὠκεανοῖο.*

5 Cf. especially Hes. *Th.* 816 (Kottos and Gyges) *δώματα ναιετάουσιν ἐπ' Ὠκεανοῖο θεμέθλοις*. Note that Pherecydes uses the more poetic *δώματα* here (once in Herodotus, 2. 62), but *οἰκία* for the apartments of Zas and Chthonie.

6 Anaximander 12 A 6, cf. Burkert, 'Iranisches', pp. 103, 132; Hdt. 4. 36, 5. 49.

yielding the sense 'wishing marriages to be yours', i.e. under your patronage. But Ge is not the goddess of marriages, and even if she were, that would be no reason for giving her a cartographic robe. The sense of the missing participle was probably 'to make it known' or 'to mark the fact', and the sense of σέο τοὺς γάμους εἶναι 'that it is your wedding'.[1] Chthonie then seems to say something in reply (if the commonly accepted supplement is correct). What does she do with the robe? The natural and obvious answer is that she puts it on. That is what robes are for, and the act would be the perfect expression of her development into Ge. We expect her to put it on and to wear it ever after.

But Isidorus the Gnostic, reported by Clement (*Strom.* 6. 53 = DK 7 B 2), mentions as prime instances of Pherecydes' theological allegories ἡ ὑπόπτερος δρῦς καὶ τὸ ἐπ' αὐτῇ πεποικιλμένον φᾶρος, 'the winged oak (or tree) and the embroidered robe on it'.[2] Maximus of Tyre too (above, p. 15) associates 'the robe' with 'the tree' instead of with 'Zas and Chthonie and the love between them'. There cannot have been two embroidered robes. Yet if the robe made for Chthonie, with its ornamentation of earth, ocean, and so on, is located on a tree, where is Chthonie who is now Ge? Has the robe after all no cosmic significance, or is the physical earth sundered from the goddess Earth? Intolerable both. We are driven to the conclusion that the tree is in some way equivalent to Chthonie, or takes her place in a later part of the narrative. Some sense will be found in this in due course.

Ophioneus, the theomachy

Another episode in Maximus' list is the birth of Ophioneus, the leader of the force that fought against Chronos. His name suggests a serpent,[3] and there is evidence that he was one. Origen, answer-

[1] Plural γάμοι of a single wedding is frequently attested, from Aeschylus on. The singular was used in col. i.

[2] Not 'the robe embroidered on it' (H. Gomperz, *Wien. St.* 47, 1929, 22); that would be ποικιλλόμενον. In any case, a tree is not a loom, and if Zas had used it as such we might expect it to appear in the papyrus fragment.

[3] The Aetolian Ophioneis no doubt traced their origin from an earthborn serpent.

ing Celsus' contention that the Christian Satan was derived from allegorical accounts of cosmic strife in Heraclitus, Pherecydes, Homer, and elsewhere, claims that Pherecydes' Ophioneus was derived from the serpent of Genesis (*c. Cels.* 6. 43). Philo of Byblos (790 F 4 § 50), speaking of the divine nature of serpents which the Egyptians and Phoenicians recognize, says: 'And it was from the Phoenicians that Pherecydes took his point of departure when he theologized about the god that he calls Ophioneus, and the Ophionidai, of whom we shall speak in another place.'

These prose writers, speaking with explicit reference to Pherecydes, use the form *'Οφιονεύς*. Hellenistic and later poets know of a metrically more convenient *'Οφίων* [ῐ], who is evidently the same:[1] he too is pushed into ocean by Kronos (= Chronos),[2] he seems to be a serpent,[3] and Callimachus (fr. 177. 7) knows also of Ophionidai. In earlier literature there is no trace of Ophioneus or the Ophionidai except in Pherecydes, and it seems likely that he was the only source for the later writers. It does not follow that everything they say can be attributed to Pherecydes, for they may have added details of their own. But certain salient features deserve consideration, and I shall consider them in their place.

We do not know who Ophioneus' parents were. It would certainly be rash to conclude that they were Zas and Ge because Maximus mentions the birth after the love-affair. Ge would not, however, be an unsuitable mother for a serpent-god, whether or not her husband was involved.[4] It is less likely that he was a product of the five-nook theocrasy, seeing that his birth is mentioned as a separate episode preceding the theomachy, but this and other possibilities cannot be excluded. If the Ophionidai were his children, as the form of their name implies, he must have had a consort (unless he behaved like Chronos, or the Orphic Phanes);

[1] For the alternating forms cf. *Δηιών/Δηιονεύς, Γηρυών/Γηρυονεύς*.

[2] A.R. 1. 503 ff., quoted below, p. 22.

[3] Dion. Bass. fr. 18 recto 9 Heitsch *δυσ]αέϊ σίζεν 'Οφίων*. Cf. *'Εχίων*, the snake father of Pentheus.

[4] Eisler, *Weltenmantel*, p. 546; Kirk–Raven, p. 70.

and so he had, according to Apollonius Rhodius and Nonnus (*D.* 8. 161), namely Eurynome. She will have been known to Pherecydes as a goddess with aquatic associations and perhaps monstrous form. In Hesiod she was one of the most important of the daughters of Oceanus, wife of Zeus and mother of the Charites. In *Il.* 18. 398 ff. she lives in a cave in the middle of Oceanus, apparently with Thetis.[1] At Phigaleia she was worshipped in the form of a mermaid, anthropomorphic above the waist and fish below (Paus. 8. 41. 4). She was a good choice for the wife of a serpent-god who was himself to be relegated to ocean's stream. And if both parents were of monstrous nature, it must be judged likely that the Ophionidai were too.

War followed between forces led by Ophioneus—probably his family—and forces led by Chronos.[2] The matter at issue was the possession of heaven. Either the struggle represented a revolt by Ophioneus, or he actually enjoyed a period of overlordship, and Chronos then struck back. Apollonius makes Orpheus sing

> ὡς πρῶτον Ὀφίων Εὐρυνόμη τε
> Ὠκεανὶς νιφόεντος ἔχον κράτος Οὐλύμποιο,
> ὥς τε βίῃ καὶ χερσὶν ὁ μὲν Κρόνῳ εἴκαθε τιμῆς,
> ἡ δὲ Ῥέῃ, ἔπεσον δ' ἐνὶ κύμασιν Ὠκεανοῖο.

He is evidently combining Pherecydes with other material, which may include an actual Orphic theogony, the one known to Plato in which Kronos and Rhea were preceded by Oceanus and Tethys (*Tim.* 40 e = fr. 16 Kern; see below for the equation of Oceanus and Ophion). The picture that he presents of a succession of rulers may therefore be the result of combination. Aristotle (*Metaph.* 1091^b^6) contrasts people like Pherecydes with the poets who believe in changing rulers of the world. A series of scholiasts who say that Ophion (*sic*) and Eurynome ruled before Kronos (*sic*) and Rhea are dependent upon Apollonius.[3]

[1] A similar context in *Od.* 4. 366 led to her intrusion there.

[2] Celsus, p. 162 Bader *ap.* Orig. *c. Cels.* 6. 42 = B 4.

[3] This is particularly clear in Tz. in Lyc. 1191; the others are sch. Aesch. *PV* 957 = sch. Ar. *Nub.* 247, sch. Arat. 16. Similarly Lyc. 1192, 1196–7, Nonn. *D.* 2. 573, 12. 44. Cf. Luc. *Podagra* 101.

On the other hand, the *Suda* (if rightly emended) records that Pherecydes' book contained θεῶν διαδοχάς. Perhaps he gave Ophioneus a period of power without speaking of formal kingship.

It was arranged that whichever side fell into Ogenos should be held the losers, while the side that pushed them in should be the victors and rightful possessors of heaven. Ophioneus and the Ophionidai lost. They were cast into ocean, and that must be where they stayed. The defeat of the Titans in Hesiod explained why they dwell in Tartarus and play no part in the world's affairs; the overthrow of Typhon by Zeus explained how he came to be under Etna, to make the mountain burn and quake; the defeat of Ophioneus and his brood must explain how they came to be stationed on the stream that girdles the earth. It is tempting to guess that they are in fact the occupants of the Ὠγηνοῦ δώματα. In Nonnus (*D.* 8. 158 ff.) Ophion and Eurynome have a house at the ὑστατίη πέζα Ὠκεανοῖο. Dionysius Bassaricus (above, p. 21 n. 3), writing at a time when sea and Oceanus were no longer properly distinguished, seems to connect Ophion's hissing with the fury of the sea in a tempest. Allegorizing interpreters identified him with Oceanus: *Ophion et secundum philosophos Oceanus, qui et Nereus, de maiore Thetide* (= Tethys) *genuit caelum.*[1] It was probably this identification, or at any rate the close association of Ophioneus with ocean, that led Apollonius to combine the defeat of Ophion by Chronos (Pherecydes) with the succession of Oceanus by Kronos (Orphic theogony).[2]

Having defeated his opponent, Chronos wore a crown like a victorious athlete.[3] We recall the Aristotelian reference to his continued supremacy.

[1] *Myth. Vat.* 1. 204. For *philosophos*, cf. *Myth. Vat.* 3. 1. 5, Rufinus in Orph. fr. 55, Damascius, ibid., fr. 60.

[2] In Callimachus loc. cit. the Ophionidai appear as those for whom the sun shines after it has set here, and they are called]θεῶν τοῖσι παλαιοτέροις. They thus seem to be assimilated to the Titans in Tartarus (cf. Pfeiffer ad loc.). Lycophron too has Rhea throwing Eurynome into Tartarus.

[3] Tertull. *de corona militis* 7 (= B 4) *Saturnum Pherecydes ante omnes refert coronatum, Iouem Diodorus* (book 6, fr. 4) *post deuictos Titanas.* It is implied that the occasion in Pherecydes was similar to that in Diodorus.

Cosmography, eschatology

Besides telling of the past, Pherecydes gave an account of the world as it is now. We know that it did not come at the beginning of the book, and the probability is that it came at the end rather than in the middle. If it followed the battle and the casting-out of the Ophionidai, that would be like the Hesiodic *Theogony*, where the Titanomachy and the consigning of the Titans to Tartarus leads into a general description of the underworld and the gods who have their homes there. There is a similarity in the structure of the Hesiodic passage too. It is made up of a series of self-contained items, mostly introduced by ἔνθα or ἔνθα δέ, in one case by τῶν πρόσθε (746), which seems to mean 'as you go further'. In the same way, Pherecydes divided his cosmos into parts, which he described in turn. We have his description of one of the parts, or at least the beginning of it, and we can see how it was connected with what went before: 'And next below that division . . .' (B 5).

Whether Pherecydes proceeded in this downward direction throughout, and began in heaven, we cannot be certain, but it will be convenient to follow this order ourselves. A detail of the life of the celestial ones is preserved by Plutarch, *de facie lun.* 938 b (= B 13 a). How could men live on the moon where no plants grow? 'Unless we say that as Athena instilled a little nectar and ambrosia into Achilles when he refused food (*Il.* 19. 341 ff.), so the moon, which is rightly identified with Athena, nourishes the men by sending up ambrosia for them each day, as old Pherecydes thinks the gods themselves feed.'[1] This cannot mean merely that Pherecydes thought the gods lived on ambrosia; Plutarch would not have cited so recondite an authority for such a commonplace. It must mean that ambrosia grew, or issued forth from a spring, an idea which we find in Euripides (*Hipp.* 748 f., *pace* Barrett) and in the Hellenistic poetess Moiro (fr. 1. 4 f. Powell; cf. already *Od.* 12. 63). And it probably means that Pherecydes located this source on the moon.

[1] Reading αὐτοὺς ⟨τοὺς⟩ θεούς. Cf. p. 68 n. 4.

Below the world of the gods, where Chronos and his allies live, lies the world of men, surrounded by Ogenos and the Mansions of Ogenos, and the Ophionidai. Below this, presumably, is the world of the dead. Here Pherecydes will have had much to say to his hearers. He was remembered as the first author who declared that the human soul was immortal,[1] or more precisely, that it passed from body to body.[2] As in a Platonic myth, its adventures were placed in a complex topographical setting. Porphyry (*antr. nymph.* 31 = B 6) says that Pherecydes spoke of *μυχοὺς καὶ βόθρους καὶ ἄντρα καὶ θύρας καὶ πύλας*, and that by way of these, in his allegorical manner, he described the passage of souls to and from earthly life.[3] Like Plato again, he must have taught that the souls of the pure and the souls of the wicked go different ways. Bloodshed, in particular, he regarded as sinful.[4]

Somewhere in this region there was an 'outflow', *ἐκροή*, which was of importance to the souls. In another of his works,[5] Porphyry discusses the question when life enters an embryo. 'There will be much implausibility and artificiality,' he says, 'however the moment is defined. One answer is that it is when the semen is deposited—as if it were incapable of being caught in the womb so as to generate life, if a soul from outside did not effect the union by its own entry. And in this connection we hear a lot from Numenius and the people who expound the hidden meanings of Pythagoras, and who understand the river Ameles in Plato, the Styx in Hesiod and the Orphics, and the outflow in Pherecydes, to represent the semen.'

The nature of the 'outflow' must be deduced from the parallelism with the Ameles and the Styx. The Ameles appears in the

[1] Cic. *Tusc.* 1. 38 (= A 5), Lact. *divin. inst.* 7. 7. 12, Aug. *epist.* 137. 12, *c. Acad.* 3. 37.

[2] *Suda*, Tatian, *c. Graecos* 25 p. 27. 1–2 Schwartz (cf. 3 p. 4. 6); cf. Mart. Cap. 2. 142.

[3] *αἰνιττομένου* should not be taken to imply that Pherecydes did not actually speak of souls (Kirk–Raven, p. 60). Porphyry means that when Pherecydes speaks of souls going through gates etc. we should attach a symbolic value to the physical structures. For *μυχοί* in this connection cf. the *Ἑκάτης μυχός* on the moon, where souls atone for their sins, Plut. *de facie lun.* 944 c.

[4] Themist. *or.* 2 p. 38 a–b.

[5] *Ad Gaurum* 2. 2 p. 34 Kalbfleisch (*Abh. Berl. Ak.* 1895) = B 7. There is a translation of the work in Festugière's *La Révélation d'Hermès Trismégiste*, iii. 265 ff.

myth of Er, *Rep.* 621 a. It is a river which souls approach and drink from before being reincarnated. It is intelligible that it should later have been allegorically interpreted as the semen flowing into the womb. Of the Styx, Hesiod (*Th.* 793 ff.) and 'Orpheus' (Rhapsodies, fr. 295) said that a god who swore a false oath by it was banished from heaven for nine years. The interpreters who explained it as the semen must have taken their cue from Empedocles (B 115), who made the exiled perjurer god pass through a long series of lives in mortal bodies. As in Plato, then, the incarnation of souls could be linked up with their approach to a certain stream. If the outflow in Pherecydes was interpreted in the same way by the same people, it follows that it too was a stream or fountain associated with the souls of the dead. Since he, unlike Hesiod, did speak of reincarnation, it is hardly overbold to go a little further and say that it was associated with their return to life. Probably they drank from it; that is what is done with the Ameles, and the drinking of certain waters in the other world is also important in the gold plates.[1]

Finally, 'below that division is the division of Tartarus. Its guardians are daughters of Boreas, the Harpyiai and Thyella. There Zas casts out any god that commits violence.' Unlike some others in the sixth century, Pherecydes preserves the original distinction between Hades and Tartarus. Tartarus is for unruly gods, and it lies 'as far below Hades as heaven is from the earth' (*Il.* 8. 16). Zas is the chieftain who has the power to throw his subordinates into it—this too follows Hesiodic and Homeric tradition—though it is inconceivable that he could ever throw Chronos there. He exercises his power *ὅταν τις ἐξυβρίσῃ*, by which Pherecydes perhaps means bloodshed: we know that he treated bloodshed as sinful, and Empedocles links it with perjury as one of the two offences for which gods are cast out of heaven. The prison warders are the storm-winds; the idea that Tartarus is a very windy place occurs in one or two other authors.[2]

[1] Orph. fr. 32 Kern; others in Ἀρχ. Ἐφ. 89/90, 1950/1, 99, and 1953/4 *B'* (1958), 57, 58.

[2] Hes. *Th.* 742 (perhaps interpolated, but early); Pl. *Phd.* 112 b. The plural Ἅρπυιαι is oddly conjoined with the singular Θύελλα. Eisler, *Weltenmantel*, p. 456,

The tree

Somewhere in Pherecydes we have to fit in the winged tree which bore Earth's embroidered robe. I have said that it was in some way equivalent to Chthonie or took her place, and it was clearly in some sense a 'world tree', a central part of the physical framework of the cosmos. The robe that was upon it depicted earth and its surroundings: so at any rate we were told when Chthonie was due to develop into Ge, but we may perhaps suppose that the tree reached up into heaven, and its roots must certainly have reached down into the nether world. I say roots, but it was not rooted in any firm supporting matter, for then its wings would be altogether pointless. The whole structure was self-contained and self-supporting.

Did the tree appear in the narrative part of the book, or in the cosmography? The latter is easier to imagine. The description of Tartarus, admittedly, shows no sign of being the description of part of a tree. But we need not suppose that the conception of the tree dominated the entire account of the various regions of the universe. A single reference to the whole being like a winged tree, at the beginning or end, would be enough to arouse the interest of Isidorus and his sort.

So much can be gathered from the testimonia concerning the contents of Pherecydes' book.[1] It must have been a tale of peculiar charm that left these fascinating ruins; a novel tale, quite unlike the familiar poetic traditions about the origin of the world and the gods and the destiny of the soul. Its author must have drawn from strange and deep wells, which it is our next task to try and uncover.

conjectures Ἅρπυια. *Θύελλαι* is also possible; cf. Hes. loc. cit. *ἀλλά κεν ἔνθα καὶ ἔνθα φέροι πρὸ θύελλα θυέλλης*. The Aurai are daughters of Boreas in Q.S. 1. 684.

[1] Diels's B 8, like all other citations of 'Pherecydes' in the scholia to Apollonius Rhodius, belongs to the Athenian historian (3 F 109). Kern, *De Orphei Epimenidis Pherecydis theogoniis quaest. crit.*, 1888, p. 106, was the first to suppose otherwise.

2

PHERECYDES THE SYNCRETIST

The seed of Time

WE may start with Chronos, the god Time who always existed, who began everything by generating progeny from his own seed, and who remains powerful in the world of the present day. Here, right at the outset, is something entirely without precedents in earlier Greek accounts of the origins of things;[1] so much so that Zeller, as we saw, refused to believe in it. Zeller was a man with an enviably comprehensive and thorough knowledge of Greek philosophy, but he was sternly opposed to attempts to explain it in the light of barbarian material.[2] If he had taken non-Greek evidence into account here, he would have found, not only that his objection to a Pherecydean Chronos (above, p. 10) was based on a misjudgement of the capabilities of pre-philosophical speculation, but that the idea of the god Time as a cosmic progenitor was widely established in the east, at any rate by the fourth century B.C., and in India, at least, by a period which may be no later than Pherecydes. No one will pretend that Pherecydes was responsible for its currency there. The question is whether by some coincidence he arrived at it independently.

Eudemus reported of the cosmology of the Sidonians that they put Chronos, Pothos, and Omichle at the beginning of things.[3] Pothos appears in another Phoenician cosmogony as the first mutation of a primeval wind which existed in darkness in company with a liquid chaos.[4] According to a probable conjecture of

[1] The Orphic theogonies of Hieronymus and the Rhapsodies cannot come into question here. I shall show elsewhere that they were composed much later.

[2] See Zeller–Nestle^{6}, i. 21–44 (with continuation by Nestle).

[3] Fr. 150 Wehrli, *ap.* Dam. *princ.* 125 *ter* (i. 323. 1 R.).

[4] Sanchuniathon of Beirut as adapted by Philo of Byblos, 790 F 2 (Eus. *PE* 1. 10. 1). For a summary account of this source see *Hes. Th.* pp. 24 ff.

O. Eissfeldt's,[1] this πόθος of the Greek sources represents the Semitic *rûaḥ*, which can indeed carry the sense of amorous desire, but is also the divine wind that beats over the dark mass of waters in Genesis 1:2. Its union with ὀμίχλη in Eudemus' account (giving birth to ἀήρ and αὔρα), and with the χάος θολερὸν ἐρεβῶδες in Philo's, is thus parallel to the conjunction of *rûaḥ* and *tehôm* in Genesis. There is a fourth occurrence of the idea in another cosmogony which has been embodied in Philo's narrative in disguise: the Gulf Wind impregnates a woman called Baau, and she gives birth to Aion and Protogonos.[2] Philo interpreted the name Baau as Night, but it is probably related to the (*tōhû* and) *bōhû* of the same verse of Genesis.

Eudemus' Phoenician cosmogony, then, is a genuine Semitic one with a basis in older traditions. Nor is the god Time making an isolated intrusion into those traditions. I have just mentioned the Aion of Philo's second cosmogony. And according to another Sidonian account, from a work by one Mōchos which was adapted into Greek by the Hellenistic writer Laitos, the two first principles were Aither and Aer, and from them arose Ulōmos.[3] Our source adds that certain winds appeared, in an obscure way, even before the birth of Ulōmos, so it looks as if Aither and Aer may be another version of the wind and fog combination. 'Ulōmos' is late Phoenician *'ūlōm*, corresponding to Hebrew *'ōlām*, Remote Time or Eternity. He united with himself, and produced the divine craftsman Chusōros and an egg for him to open; when broken it formed the heaven and the earth. Chusōros is another authentic detail, being recognizable as the K*t*r-and-Ḫss of Ugaritic texts.[4]

Here at Sidon, then, we have not just a god Time, but a creator god Time who, like Pherecydes' Chronos, produces his materials by self-directed sexual activity.

[1] *Forschungen und Fortschritte* 16, 1940, 1 = *Kl. Schr.* ii. 258.

[2] 790 F 2 (Eus. *PE* 1. 10. 7).

[3] 784 F 4 (Dam. loc. cit.).

[4] In the Baal epic he has his palace and workshop in Crete—a notable tribute to Daedalus and his colleagues.

Zurvān

The Zoroastrian cosmogony may next be considered. It is recorded most fully by the Armenian writers Eliše Vardapet and Eznik of Kołb (fifth century A.D.), but the elements that are of interest for the present inquiry can be shown to be much older. In the beginning nothing existed except Zurvān, that is, Time, conceived as a divine agent.[1] He had sexual union with himself,[2] and produced the twin brothers Ohrmazd and Ahriman. Ahriman created the demons and all that is evil, while Ohrmazd created heaven and earth and all that is fair. Further details can be added from the Pahlavi *Bundahišn*, 'Primeval Creation', written in the late ninth century, but based at least in part on the *Dāmdāt Nask*, one of the lost portions of the Avesta, presumably dating from the Achaemenid period. The generation of Ohrmazd and Ahriman from Time is here absent, as generally in the Pahlavi books; instead they are co-eternal with time, and he acts as a sort of supervising genius. Ohrmazd exists in the Beginningless Light, Ahriman in endless darkness, and they are separated by a vacant region. Out of that part of his own essence which is material light, Ohrmazd fashions his creation in the form of a white, round, shining fire, and out of 'time without limit', which is subject to his will, he fashions 'time for long autonomous'. This is a period of twelve thousand years, within which the history of the world plays itself out; at the end all is made perfect and unchanging. For the first three thousand years the creation remains 'in a moist state like semen', but eventually Ohrmazd creates the material world from it. First heaven appears, in the shape of an egg, made of shining metal, reaching up as far as the Beginningless Light. Everything else is created

[1] The common noun in the Avesta means 'time' in general, a period, or a particular appointed time; for details see H. Junker, *Vorträge d. Bibl. Warburg*, 1921/2, p. 129. On the god see R. C. Zaehner's monumental *Zurvan, A Zoroastrian Dilemma* (Oxford, 1955), or the second part of his *DTZ*.

[2] So Eznik: 'Now this is highly ridiculous, that he himself should be both father and mother, and that the same person should have emitted the seed and received it' (Zaehner, *Zurvan*, p. 63). Other sources give Zurvān a separate consort, but are not themselves consistent.

inside it.[1] According to another Pahlavi book, not certainly dated, Ohrmazd's creation was made 'with the blessing of the Infinite Zurvān, for the Infinite Zurvān is unaging and deathless; he knows neither pain nor decay nor corruption'. And by his agency, Ohrmazd and Ahriman arrange to make war on each other for nine thousand years.[2]

How old is all this? In the extant part of the Avesta, dating from about the seventh to perhaps the third century B.C.,[3] Zurvān is little mentioned. But that is only to be expected in books which are mainly of a liturgical nature: he is a god of abstract speculation, not of priestly cult. He is invoked once, as eternal Zurvān, in company with Θwāša and Vayu, roughly Space and Wind,[4] and in one place we meet the distinction between limitless and autonomous Zurvān, which presupposes the temporal framework of the cosmology as it stands in the Pahlavi books.[5] That Zurvān existed as a god by the late sixth century B.C. may be gathered from a theophoric personal name on an Elamite tablet.[6] Attempts to find him earlier have not so far proved successful.[7] Zoroaster himself has a different account of the parentage of Angra Mainyu (= Ahriman): his father was Ahura Mazdāh (= Ohrmazd), and his twin brother was Spənta Mainyu, the Bounteous Spirit.[8]

[1] *Greater Bundahišn* 2. 12–4. 1, 9. 2–10. 8, 11. 2–4, 16. 2–3, 18. 3–9; Zaehner, *DTZ*, pp. 248–58.

[2] *Mēnōk-i-Xrat* 8. 6–9; Zaehner, *Zurvan*, pp. 368–9, *DTZ*, p. 209.

[3] The oldest part consists of the *Gāthās*, hymns by Zoroaster himself. They form a portion of the *Yasna* liturgy. The other main texts are the *Yašts*, a collection of hymns dating from about the fifth century, and, latest of all, the *Vidēvdāt*, containing 'dreary prescriptions concerning ritual purity' and listing 'impossible punishments for ludicrous crimes' (Zaehner).

[4] *Vidēvdāt* 19. 13, 16.

[5] *Yasna* 72. 10; cf. J. Duchesne-Guillemin, *RE* Supp. ix. 1586. In *Vidēvdāt* 19. 9 Ahura Mazdāh is said to have created the *Ašəm vohū* prayer in the limitless *zurvān* (locative), which may imply 'before the material world'.

[6] See Addenda.

[7] The Nuzi tablets mentioned by Duchesne-Guillemin, loc. cit., are now read differently. The recognition of Zurvān in representations on three bronzes from Luristan (ibid.) is highly speculative.

[8] *Yasna* 30. 3, 47. 2–3. Cf. I. Gershevitch, *JNES* 23, 1964, 12 ff. Zoroaster agrees with the *Bundahišn* that heaven and earth were created by Ahura Mazdāh (*Yasna* 44), and the same belief is proclaimed on Achaemenid inscriptions from Darius I down to Artaxerxes III (DNa 1, DSe 1, XPa 1, etc., in R. G. Kent, *Old Persian*, [2]1953; cf. below, p. 196).

This rather scant Iranian evidence is fortunately reinforced by the testimony of Greek writers. Eudemus reported that the Magi and the whole Aryan nation speak of Time or Space, 'from which were separated out either a good god and an evil demon, or, as some say, light and darkness before these'.[1] The second version is apparently that of Aristoxenus, according to whom Pythagoras went to Babylon and learnt from Zaratas that Light and Darkness were the male and female principles from which the world was created; within the world there were two gods, one celestial, the other terrestrial.[2] This version of the cosmology, which also appears in Plutarch (*Is. Os.* 369 f, cf. e), is to be distinguished from that of the New Persian *'Ulemā i Islām* ('The Doctors of Islam'; thirteenth century), in which Zurvān forms Ohrmazd and Ahriman out of fire and water.[3] It is more like the system in the *Bundahišn*, where Ohrmazd and Ahriman exist respectively in the Endless Light and the Endless Darkness. Thanks to Aristoxenus and Eudemus we can see that the idea was current in Iran in much the same form in the fourth century B.C. as in the ninth century A.D.

The 12,000-year duration of Autonomous Time, divided into quarters of 3,000 years and complete with the temporary supremacy of Angra Mainyu and final triumph of Ahura Mazdāh, was certainly established by the fourth century,[4] and can probably be inferred for the fifth. Xanthus of Sardis (765 F 32) dated Zoroaster 6,000 years before Xerxes, apparently by a misunderstanding of the doctrine that Zoroaster's soul was created 6,000 years before his birth, at the time of Ohrmazd's creation. The prophet's birth inaugurated the final trimillennium in which Ohrmazd triumphed over Ahriman. Xanthus wrote sometime after 464; Ephorus (70 F 180) thought he wrote before Herodotus, but that may

[1] Fr. 150 Wehrli, *ap.* Dam. *princ.* 125 *bis* (i. 322. 8 R.).

[2] Fr. 13 Wehrli, *ap.* Hipp. *Ref.* 1. 2. 12, who also names Diodorus of Eretria (unknown) as a source for the story. Zaratas is of course Zoroaster; on the forms of the name see Bidez–Cumont, *Les Mages hellénisés* i. 37.

[3] Zaehner, *Zurvan*, pp. 72 ff., 268, 410. By combining this with Hippolytus, Zaehner attempts to reconstruct a non-Zoroastrian Zurvān-cosmogony.

[4] Theopompus 115 F 65, *ap.* Plut. *Is. Os.* 370 b–c.

have been a guess.[1] Xanthus' evidence does not show that Zurvān as the first father was known in his day, but we can at least say that some of the Magian doctrines reported by the fourth-century writers had been established for a certain time.

Kāla

Zurvān has an Indian parallel in Kāla, which is again a general word for 'time' (a period, a point of time, the right time to act). As a cosmic and cosmogonic power, Kāla first appears in the *Atharvaveda* (the latest of the hymn collections) and the later Upanishads. In a hymn of the *Atharvaveda* he is portrayed as 'thousand-eyed, unaging, possessing much seed'. 'Time generated yonder sky, Time also these earths; what is and what is to be stands out sent forth by Time.' 'The great sky in Time is set.' 'Sent by it, born by it, in it is this (visible world) set firm; Time, becoming the *brahman*, bears the most exalted one. Time generated progeny, Time in the beginning Prajāpati.'[2] In order to generate the world, then, Time became *brahman*, the divine presence that governs it. His firstborn son was Prajāpati, whose name might be literally rendered 'Progenipotens'. He plays the part of a creator.

The *Maitri Upanishad* states the theory thus:

Who reveres Brahman as Time, from him time (i.e. death) withdraws to a very great distance. For thus too did (Maitri) say:

> 'From Time do creatures, flowing, issue,
> From Time they grow and prosper,
> In Time they reach their home (in death):
> Time is formless, (Time) has form!'

There are, certainly, two forms of Brahman,—time and the timeless. That which existed before the sun is the timeless; it cannot be divided into parts. That which begins with the sun, however, is time. And the form of this (time) which has parts is the year. From the year (all) these creatures are born; through the year, once born, they grow,

[1] Herter, *RE* ixA. 1354, puts him about 450; Jacoby in his edition puts him after 425 (with a query).

[2] 19. 53/4, trans. Whitney and Lanman, *Atharva-Veda Saṁhitā*, vol. 2 (Harvard Oriental Series, 8), 1905.

in the year they find their home (in death). So it is that the year is Prajāpati, time, food, the nest of Brahman, and the Self. . . . So it is that Brahman has the sun as its self. One should revere the sun as being synonymous with time.[1]

This is very close to the Iranian doctrine of Autonomous Time that appears out of Limitless Time and at the end is swallowed up in it again.[2]

One of the annoying things about Indian literature is that its chronology is so uncertain; but the *Maitri Upanishad* is put at a very approximate date of 500 B.C.[3] The form of the Kāla-cosmogony that it gives in the passage quoted does not seem to be the oldest form; for in the oldest form Prajāpati will have been a person (like the creator Ahura Mazdāh, or the Phoenician Chusōros), while in the Upanishad he is already interpreted in an abstract sense. In the *Ṛgveda*, Prajāpati is an epithet of Savitṛ, the sun (4. 53. 2), or he is the 'golden embryo' who, once born, generates and upholds earth, sea, and sky (10. 121). He is not yet the offspring of Time, but the Time-cosmogony, it may be conjectured, incorporated him in that early form, the identification with the year being secondary.[4]

Oriental antecedents

We have found the god Time at Sidon, in Iran, and in India, and we have found him behaving with remarkable consistency. In each case he creates out of his seed, without a consort; at Sidon and in Iran he is explicitly said to have had intercourse with himself. In each case he is not himself the builder of the material world, but the progenitor of a divine demiurge.

Pherecydes' Time, like Zurvān and Kāla, always existed. He too creates out of his seed, without a consort, we do not know exactly how. Our world is fashioned not by him but by Zas. Zas, it is true, does not spring from Chronos' seed (as Zeus did

[1] 6. 14–16, trans. Zaehner, *Hindu Scriptures*, 1966, p. 231.

[2] The idea is developed in later literature, cf. *Bhagavad-Gītā* 9. 7, 17, 11. 32; *Vishṇu Purāṇa* i. 2. 14–3. 28.

[3] Zaehner, *DTZ*, p. 197.

[4] In another relatively early text, *Çatapatha Brāhmaṇa* 11. 1. 6 (seventh or sixth century?), he creates the year as a counterpart to himself.

from Kronos'): Pherecydes prefers to say that he too always existed, and that again has Iranian parallels.

Time is not personified by other peoples. Personification of months, seasons, etc., is fairly widespread,[1] but time in the abstract appears as a god only in the regions we are considering. In Greece and perhaps in India it appears in the sixth century B.C. In Iran and at Sidon it is established by the fourth century at latest, and our evidence is so incomplete that there is no difficulty in the idea of its being a couple of centuries older. It appears in all four places in a remarkably similar form. The uniformity is the more remarkable in view of the fact that the progenitor Time appears combined with quite different national traditions: Kāla with the Vedic creator Prajāpati, Zurvān with Zoroaster's creator Ahura Mazdāh, 'Ūlōm with the old Semitic wind and water cosmogony. (We will have to see about Chronos.) Clearly he did not develop independently in these various contexts, but reached them from one common source.

The first steps towards his conception appear to have been taken in Mesopotamia at an early period. A Sumerian genealogy traces the ancestry of Enlil through fifteen divine pairs, the first two being 'Lord and lady Orderliness' and 'Lord and lady Days of Life'; as it were *Κόσμος* and *Θέμις* giving birth to *Αἰών* and *Αἰώνη*.[2] From about 1600 B.C., Duri Dari, 'Ever and ever', appears as a divine pair in Babylonian genealogies, among the primeval gods, and later also Alma and Alama with the same meaning (cf. *'ūlōm/'ōlām*).

In Egypt, Re' the sun-god was from an early period the 'Lord of eternity' or 'traverser of eternity'.

> 'I am the eldest of the Primeval Ones; my soul is the souls of the eternal gods; my embodiment is Eternity, my form is Everlasting; the lord of years, the ruler of eternity.'[3]

[1] Egyptians, Yoruba, Ashanti, Aztecs, etc.; G. Foucart, *ERE* ix. 783; A. H. Gardiner, ibid. 791 f.

[2] T. Jacobsen, *JNES* 5, 1946, 138 f.

[3] *Book of the Dead* (Ani papyrus, *c.* 1320 B.C.), 85. 9–11. Professor Barns has advised me on the translation. Cf. Budge, *Book of the Dead*, p. 550; *ANET*, pp. 365 (iii), 368.

Reʿ is particularly relevant, because he was represented as creating other gods by an act of self-directed *fellatio*.[1]

The Sun of Eternity, Shamash ʿōlām, appears on a Phoenician inscription from Karatepe of the ninth or eighth century B.C., and the Hebrew God can be similarly qualified, as ʾEl ʿōlām.[2] Onomatologically, the ʿŪlōm of Mochos of Sidon is simply a hypostasis from such titles, and the Egyptian evidence suggests that Shamash ʿōlām may have been the direct model. It need not have been in Syria that the self-fertilizing progenitor Time was invented. But somewhere, in about the seventh or sixth century, the old Egyptian myth was refashioned in the more abstract and acceptable form in which it persuaded Iran and India in the east, and in the west Pherecydes.

The five nooks

Chronos creates fire, wind, and water; and he puts them in five nooks where gods appear, the 'five-nook generation' that Damascius is tempted to gloss as the 'five-world' generation. Among the later Iranian accounts of Zurvān's creative activity one is of particular interest here: the Manichaean cosmogony. Two versions of it are to be distinguished. In the more usual version,[3] the realm of light, the kingdom of the highest god (named as Zurvān in the Turfan texts) is invaded by the Prince of Darkness. The highest god sends against him Primal Man (identified with Ohrmazd), who clothes himself with the five elements light, fire, wind, water, and air, like a man putting on armour. But the enemy also possesses five elements, namely smoke, fire, wind, water, and darkness. They are described as 'worlds', κόσμοι or αἰῶνες, Syriac *ālam*, and they occupy different regions of the realm of darkness, regions which Augustine refers to as *quinque*

[1] See Budge, *Book of the Dead*, pp. 267, 379, and *The Gods of the Egyptians*, 1904, i. 310; *ANET*, p. 6; Schwabl, cols. 1500, 1502.

[2] Gen. 21: 33, cf. Isa. 9: 6; E. Jenni, *Zeitschr. f. alttest. Wiss.* 64, 1952, 197–248; 65, 1953, 1–35; Schwabl, col. 1508.

[3] See especially Cumont, *Recherches sur le Manichéisme*, pp. 14 ff., for an account in which the different sources are distinguished; harmonizing accounts e.g. in F. C. Burkitt, *The Religion of the Manichees*, 1925, pp. 24–30; Polotsky, *RE*, Supp. vi. 249 ff.; G. Widengren, *Mani and Manichaeism*, pp. 49–56.

antra tenebrarum.[1] Each has its own Archon, represented as 'son' or 'member' (the Syriac word is ambivalent) of the Prince of Darkness. These five engulf the celestial elements carried by Primal Man; and the rest of history is a long and difficult struggle to undo this mixture of light and dark that constitutes our world.

The other version is reflected in a relatively early source, the Coptic *Kephalaia.*[2] Here Primal Man wears only three elements: fire, wind, and water (p. 153. 27). When swallowed up by the Archontes, they become fire, darkness, and water, but, as it were an antidote to these corrupted elements, the highest god continues to wear fire, wind, and water as his own garments (pp. 83. 20–2, 106. 21 ff.). He poured out the impure elements upon the earth and then swept them away into ditches (φόσσα) at the edge of the firmament, so that the world is surrounded by concentric walls of fire, darkness, and water, with mountains before, between, and beyond them (pp. 86. 18–30, 108. 16–113. 6; cf. 4. 29, 70. 21, 118. 29). But despite all this play with three elements we do not cease to hear about the five (lower) worlds of smoke, fire, wind, water, and darkness (p. 167. 22 ff.). In one place we are told that these five elements came out of five ταμιεῖα in the land of Darkness ('sprudelten aus ihnen hervor', p. 30. 13 ff.). There is no attempt to explain the relationship between the five and the three.

The problem becomes somewhat clearer if we consider Manichaeism in its historical context.[3] Mani lived from A.D. 216 to 274. Though himself of Babylonian origin, his writings were in the Edessan dialect of Syriac, except for one that was addressed to the Persian king. He was a religious leader of unusual education, and the faith that he founded represented an intellectual syncretism of three established religions: Buddhism, Zoroastrianism, and Christianity, by which we must understand the peculiar

[1] *Confess.* 3. 11; cf. *c. epist. fundat.* 18, *haeres.* 46 (both in *Patrol. lat.* 42).

[2] *Kephalaia, Manichäische Handschriften der Staatlichen Museen Berlin*, i, 1940. The papyrus is dated to the fourth or fifth century. The Coptic uses many Greek words, and seems to be a translation from a Greek original, as the title suggests.

[3] See Widengren, op. cit., ch. 1.

kind taught at Edessa by men like Bardaiṣan (Bardesanes). Mani names the Buddha, Zoroaster, and Jesus, in that order, as the three great prophets who came before him. He does not acknowledge any Greek predecessor, and the only Greek influence that can be discerned in his system comes to him indirectly through Christian philosophy.

Bardaiṣan's cosmology is of the most direct importance for Mani. He derived the world from five elements: fire, wind, water, light, and darkness. The first four were situated respectively in the east, west, north, and south, with darkness below and God above. By some chance the stability was destroyed, the elements began to be confounded, and darkness rose and entered them all from below.[1]

Mani identifies the realm of light with that of the highest god and the realm of darkness with that of his enemy, which leaves three elements in between. This is the *Kephalaia* version, in which fire, wind, and water are the King of Light's defences against the King of Darkness. In the other version, of which the *Kephalaia* also shows knowledge, the pentad light–fire–wind–water–darkness is developed into a pair of opposing pentads, to complete the antithesis between (divine) light and (evil) matter.[2] In the 'light' pentad, darkness is replaced by air, while in the 'dark' pentad, light is replaced by smoke.[3]

In combining all this with the Zoroastrian theology, Mani equated the King of Light with Zurvān, and his son Primal Man with Ohrmazd. Why so? According to an ancient Indo-Iranian myth, the world was made from the body of a primeval man, the Vedic Purusha (*Ṛgv.* 10. 90). Alternatively it was the body or clothing of Ohrmazd; the physical elements (cattle, fire, metal, earth, water, plants) were identified with six of the seven Bounteous Immortals, who were emanations from him.[4] So for Mani

[1] H. J. W. Drijvers, *Bardaiṣan of Edessa*, 1966, pp. 96 ff.

[2] Cf. Drijvers, op. cit., p. 226. Similarly the Ophites constructed opposing tetrads.

[3] Smoke was already associated with the world of darkness in Bardaiṣan. Drijvers, op. cit., p. 138.

[4] Gershevitch, *The Avestan Hymn to Mithra*, pp. 10–12, 165 f. Other scattered traces in Duchesne-Guillemin, *RE* Supp. ix. 1585.

the three or five elements are the sons or members of a figure who is both Ohrmazd and Primal Man. Ohrmazd remains the son of the unbegotten god Zurvān as before.

This is all neat and tidy as far as it goes. But there is something unsatisfactory about the idea that this combination was important enough to Mani for him to make old Zurvān, instead of Ohrmazd, the great god of the realm of light who campaigns against the monstrous foe.[1] There is something unsatisfactory, too, about the idea that only as the accidental outcome of this combination does Time operate with those three or five physical elements. For both these motifs—as well as the location of the elements in five cosmic reservoirs—are already present in Pherecydes. Chronos places fire, wind, and water in five nooks. Chronos, not Zas, is the leader of the fight against Ophioneus.

The possibility that Mani was influenced by Pherecydes[2] is remote. Pherecydes was indeed known to at least one second-century gnostic, Isidorus the son of Basilides, and it was from a system related to gnosticism that Mani derived his three or five elements. But he derived his Zurvān and Ohrmazd/Primal Man from Iranian traditions. He cannot have demoted the highest god of the Zoroastrians to subordinate status merely to suit an obscure Greek writer who represented none of the three great religions that he himself recognized.

The alternative is that he drew on other traditions of sufficient antiquity to have influenced Pherecydes. We have seen that the testimony of Greek writers like Theopompus and Eudemus establishes the currency of certain Iranian doctrines centuries earlier than could be assumed from native sources. We need not be terrified of assuming the currency of others in the time of Pherecydes, if we find them appearing in him as if from nowhere.

In the case of the five elements there is supporting evidence

[1] The Manichaean Prince of Darkness combined the forms of the five elemental demons: δαίμων (smoke), lion (fire), eagle (wind), fish (water), δράκων (darkness). *Kephalaia*, p. 30. 33 ff.; C. R. C. Allberry, *A Manichaean Psalm Book*, pp. 57, 15 ff.; An-Nadīm, *Fihrist al-'Ulūm* in G. Flügel, *Mani*, p. 86, K. Kessler, *Mani*, pp. 387 f.

[2] T. Gomperz, *Greek Thinkers* i. 538, who was the first to consider Manichaeism in the context of Pherecydes.

from India. There we find the five 'elements',[1] fire, wind, water, earth, and sky, associated with the creator Time.[2] In Pherecydes, earth and sky are otherwise accounted for, in the form of Chthonie and her bridegroom Zas. The remaining three are represented as the creation of Chronos. Now suppose that a corresponding five-element theory existed in Iran. We know that the antagonism between Ahura Mazdāh and Angra Mainyu came to be seen in metaphysical terms as an antagonism between light and darkness. The conception is ascribed to the Magi or to Zoroaster by fourth-century writers (see p. 32), and Herodotus already knows of the identification of Ahura Mazdāh with 'the circle of the sky' (1. 131). If you combine this polaristic dualism with the five-element theory, light and darkness take the place of sky and earth. Fire, wind, and water remain as physical elements on a lower level between light and darkness; alternatively, all five may be subordinated to the activity of one God. The one view is Bardaiṣan's, the other Mani's.

The theomachy

As Zurvān wars against a monstrous enemy and his bestial sons, who are initially victorious and only overthrown after a long struggle, so Chronos wars against Ophioneus and the Ophionidai, who, it was inferred, enjoyed a period of supremacy before their defeat. But Ophioneus is not a principle of evil, and his power is altogether past. He is the serpent who was banished to the confines of the world, to the stream of ocean and its mansions. We can best appreciate his place in history by looking at a series of myths in which the outer limits of the earth are conceived as a great river or sea and as being occupied by a monstrous figure, or group, sometimes giants, sometimes serpents, sometimes a

[1] The word is unavoidable, but liable to mislead. We must not think of equipollent ingredients in an Empedoclean mixture, but rather of active and passive principles, each with its own character and function.

[2] First implied in *Śvetāśvatara Upan.* 6. 1–2 (a God denied to be Time), dating perhaps from the fifth or fourth century B.C.; then *Mahābhārata* xii. 267. 9; *Vishṇu Purāṇa* i. 2. 14–3. 28; the five elements without mention of Time, Megasthenes (715 F 33) *ap.* Strab. 15. 1. 59 p. 713.

mixture of the two, who rose unsuccessfully against the gods at some past time or do so currently.

Babylonian boundary-stones of the late second and early first millennium often contain, besides inscriptions, pictorial representations of religious and cosmic significance, not all of which can now be understood, but in which the sun, the moon, and Venus are often clearly identifiable in the uppermost register. Associated with them is a huge serpent who rises up from far below, his body sometimes coiling round a good part of the circumference of the stone in a horizontal direction.[1] A possible significance for the serpent is suggested by a notice in a Greek manuscript, according to which the Chaldaeans teach that the zodiac is carried round by a huge serpent who bears six of the signs on his back.[2] For the boundary-stones, 'the zodiac' may be an anachronism; but the serpent of the Chaldaean story might once have had a less sophisticated function. Here is possible evidence for a Babylonian conception of a serpent encircling the world, now rising towards the gods, now turned down again to the surrounding ocean.[3]

Cylinder seals show a similarly huge serpent being attacked by the gods.[4] It is not clear whether Marduk's defeat of Tiâmat should be set in this context. Tiâmat is the goddess of the sea deeps. It has often been maintained that she was conceived as a many-headed 'dragon', but A. Heidel has shown that there is no good evidence for this, and that what evidence there is

[1] See Plate I; L. W. King, *Babylonian Boundary-stones and Memorial-tablets in the British Museum*, 1912, ii, plates i/iv, xviii/xix, xxviii, xliii/xliv/xlvi/xlviii, liii/lxiii–lxvi, lxxvi–lxxviii, lxxxi, xc/xci.

[2] Cumont, *TM* i. 35 n. 1.

[3] A Phoenician cup of the seventh century B.C. (Plate II) shows scenes of various human activities, encircled by a serpent. (*Monumenti* x, pl. xxxi; F. Poulsen, *Der Orient und die frühgriechische Kunst*, 1912, p. 25.) Compare Achilles' and Heracles' shields with their scenes enclosed by the circle of Oceanus. Helbig, who gave the first account of the cup in 1876, quoted Macr. *Sat.* 1. 9. 11–12 *alii mundum id est caelum esse uoluerunt* (*Ianum*) . . . *hinc et Phoenices in sacris imaginem eius exprimentes draconem finxerunt in orbem redactum caudamque suam deuorantem, ut appareat mundum et ex se ipso ali et in se reuolui*. '*Eius*', however, seems to refer to Janus, not *mundus*. For the *ouroboros* as a symbol of Time in late antiquity see Cumont in *Festschr. Benndorf*, 1898, pp. 291 ff.; W. Deonna, *Artibus Asiae* 15, 1952, 163–70; Nilsson, *Gr. Rel.* ii^2. 502.

[4] Plate II; cf. S. N. Kramer, *Sumerian Mythology*, pl. xix facing p. 78.

indicates rather that she had the form of a goat.[1] Heaven and earth were made from her body, so that she has a definite cosmic significance, but cannot very easily be identified with the 'zodiacal' serpent. If we add her to the eleven monstrous beings of her own creation who helped her in the fight,[2] we obtain a set of twelve beasts, certain of whom do resemble certain of the zodia. But we know that the eleven are derived from older accounts of the conquests of Ninurta.

The myths of neighbouring Semitic peoples give a clearer picture. By a detailed examination of the Old Testament allusions to Rahab and Leviathan, Hermann Gunkel was able to reconstruct a cosmological myth with a number of variants.[3] Rahab and Leviathan are both serpents in the sea, described as 'coiling'; in some passages there are references to *R^ehabim* (plural) or to Rahab's helpers or to serpents (plural).[4] They are enemies of Yahweh, destroyed in the beginning, when he divided the waters, made the earth to appear above the flood, and established the sun, moon, and seasons.[5] Or, instead of being killed, Leviathan was fettered, and remains held in check by Yahweh's helpers;[6] his fury manifests itself in the stormy sea.[7] His final overthrow is transferred to the future.[8] His name may mean 'surrounding' (Assyr. *lawû*), and in later times, at any rate, he was imagined as encircling the earth, or as being connected with the zodiac.[9]

1 *The Babylonian Genesis*, 2nd ed., pp. 83 ff. W. G. Lambert takes the same view. May the reason for the goat form be that the myth was brought into connection with a goat-sacrifice?

2 Compared with Pherecydes' Ophionidai by P. Jensen, *Die Kosmologie der Babylonier*, 1890, pp. 303 f.; Gomperz, *Greek Thinkers* i. 538.

3 *Schöpfung und Chaos in Urzeit und Endzeit*, 1895, pp. 30–111.

4 Ps. 74: 13, Job 9: 13.

5 Ps. 44: 19, 74: 12–17, 89: 10–12.

6 Job 3: 8; Gunkel, pp. 59 f.

7 Ps. 89: 9–10.

8 Isa. 27: 1, Ezek. 32: 3 ff.; Gunkel, pp. 87, 315 ff.

9 Rahab's helpers in Job 9: 13 are made into κήτη τὰ ὑπ' οὐρανόν in the Septuagint. 'This crooked Leviathan surrounds the whole earth'—Rashi on Isa. 27: 1 (M. Grünbaum, *ZDMG* 31, 1877, p. 275). 'Behemoth and Leviathan are serpents at the shore of Ocean, and encircle the earth like a ring' (*Vocab. Aethiopicum* in L. Goldschmidt, *Das Buch Henoch*, 1892, p. 83). (Gunkel, p. 47 n. 1.) In the midrashic tradition Leviathan is explicitly the zodiac-bearing serpent (*Sepher Raziel* in S. Karppe, *Étude sur les origines et la nature du Zohar*, 1901, p. 157 n. 1). See also the sixth-century Syriac treatise in *Actes du XIVe Congrès international des Orientalistes* (Alger, 1905), 1907, p. 175, with Kugener's note.

Gunkel regarded the conflict of Marduk and Tiâmat as the prototype of the Hebrew myth. There are some similarities, but they are not close enough for a relationship of direct dependence to be plausible.[1] And we now know that at Ugarit in the second millennium (probably before the composition of *Enûma Eliš*) the Leviathan myth was current in a very similar form to that presupposed in the Old Testament.[2]

The Jewish traditions about giants are also of interest here. Giants lived on earth before the flood; they were the sons of the 'sons of the gods' and mortal women, and they grew powerful and famous, but also wicked. God accordingly decided to destroy them by sending the flood.[3] Only one survived: Og of Bashan (Deut. 3: 11, Josh. 12: 4, 13: 12). A later tradition represented him as the leader of a rebellion against heaven. The influential chronicler Castor of Rhodes (first century B.C.), followed by the shadowy Thallus, explained the legendary Titanomachy and Gigantomachy euhemeristically as a battle that took place in the time of the Assyrian king Belus. He made 'Ogygos' a king of these Titans or Giants, who fled defeated to Tartessus (explanation of 'Tartarus'), and afterwards became king of Attica.[4] The harmless Ogygos or Ogyges of Greek local legend, the earthborn king of Thebes or Athens, has here been identified with a figure of eastern mythology, who (since Ogygos is henceforward associated with a flood) can be none other than Og.[5] The *Book of Enoch*, while it does not name Og, tells of a conflict in which the giants, the sons of the fallen angels, were overthrown by the forces of heaven; and in a dream-vision they are identified with

[1] Cf. Heidel, pp. 110–12.

[2] T. H. Gaster, *Thespis*, pp. 186 f.; Heidel, pp. 107 f.; G. R. Driver, *Canaanite Myths and Legends*, pp. 87, 105; *ANET*, p. 138. Cf. Lambert, *J. Theol. St.* 16, 1965, 290.

[3] Gen. 6: 1–7. Compare the Greek heroes who were born to gods and mortal women, and destroyed by the Trojan War, which Zeus contrived in order to relieve overpopulation (*Cypria*, fr. 1) or to allow him to transfer them to a happier place ([Hes.] fr. 204. 95 ff.).

[4] *FGrHist* 250 F 1, 256 F 2; cf. sch. Hes. *Th.* 806.

[5] F. C. Movers, *Die Phönizier*, 1850, ii. 1. 51 n. 67; K. Müllenhoff, *Deutsche Altertumskunde*, 1870, i. 61. The best study of the traditions and inventions about Ogygos is Jacoby's in his commentary on *FGrHist* 328 F 92.

certain stars (6–10, 19, 21, 55–6, 64, 67–9, 86–8, 90. 20–7). Og's next appearance is in the lost *liber de Ogia* (v.l. *Ogiga*, al.) *gigante, qui post diluvium cum dracone ab hereticis pugnasse perhibetur, apocryphus.*[1] Here he fights with a serpent; but this does not put him on the side of the angels. For in another no longer extant book, which probably used both the *liber de Ogia* and *Enoch*, namely Mani's *Book of the Giants*, it was recorded that 'Ohya' was involved in a fight with Leviathan and Raphael: the three 'lacerated each other, and they vanished'.[2]

Mani's book must have been an important source behind the cosmology of the *Kephalaia*. According to this, there are seven pillars in the great outer sea, in the seven parts of the *κόσμος* (p. 86. 18–30). This sea is inside the *moenia mundi* described above, p. 37; it is the remnants of the impure elements swept out by the highest god that make the waters of the sea bitter. Into these waters the 'giant of the sea' (ⲠⲄⲒⲄⲀⲤ Ⲛ̄ⲐⲀⲖⲀⲤⲤⲀ) has been cast. He was created by a process of 'painting' (*ζωγραφεῖν*). He bears on his body the seal of five 'houses' (*οἶκος*), namely the moments, hours, days, months, and years, as well as the 'impression' (*χαρακτήρ*) of the stars and zodiac; he regulates the wheel of the zodiac, and his breathing causes the tides (pp. 113. 26 ff., 115. 11 ff., 27 ff., 122. 23, 145. 14). His place, like the three ditches for the impure elements, was prepared for him in advance (116. 3 ff.). He is not the only denizen of the outer sea. We also read that 'before the rebels rebelled, there were made for them in the great outer sea seven lodging-places (*πανδοχεῖον*), the places in which they are cast down to the deep and [darkness]'. And for the Egregoroi, before they rebelled, a prison (*φυλακή*) was made under the mountains. And for the impious sons of the Giants, before they were even born, thirty-six townships (116. 31 ff.).

The giant of the sea is in a sense a doublet of the great serpent

[1] *Decretum Gelasianum, Patrol. lat.* 59. 162–3.

[2] The evidence relating to the *Book of the Giants* is collected and discussed by W. B. Henning, *BSOAS* 11, 1943, 52–74; for Ohya see pp. 54, 61, 72, cf. 69. For a comparable Mandaic myth see *Right Ginzā*, pp. 159–67 (W. Brandt, *Mandäische Schriften*, 1893, pp. 172–83).

of the zodiac. The *γίγαντες* in Greek art commonly are serpents below the waist; so that the application of the term *γίγας* to Og (in the Septuagint) and to the Manichaean giant at least permits the hypothesis that they were conceived in this form. The struggle between Og and Leviathan must be regarded in this light: there is not too much difference between a giant wrestling with a serpent and a giant who half consists of a writhing serpent. There is an interesting parallel in the iconography of another later religion of Iranian ancestry, Mithraism. A number of reliefs from Dacia show the sun's chariot rising victoriously over the ocean, and the ocean is represented by a recumbent man entwined in the coils of a large serpent, which raises its head threateningly against the sun.[1]

Another parallel comes from a more remote country. Icelandic myth tells of a great serpent Jǫrmungand, or the Miðgarð-serpent, who girdles the earth. His history is related by the excellent Snorri in *Gylfaginning* 34:

> Yet more children had Loki. Angrboda was the name of a certain giantess in Jötunheim, with whom Loki gat three children: one was Fenris-Wolf, the second Jörmungandr—that is the Midgard Serpent,—the third is Hel. But when the gods learned that this kindred was nourished in Jötunheim, and when the gods perceived by prophecy that from this kindred great misfortune should befall them . . . then Allfather sent gods thither to take the children and bring them to him. When they came to him, straightway he cast the serpent into the deep sea, where he lies all about the land; and this serpent grew so greatly that he lies in the midst of the ocean encompassing all the land, and bites upon his own tail.[2]

The earth is 'ring-shaped without, and round about her without lieth the deep sea; and along the strand of that sea they gave lands to the races of giants for habitation. But on the inner earth they made a citadel round about the world against the hostility

[1] Plate III; M. Vermaseren, *Corp. Inscr. et Monum. Religionis Mithriacae*, 1956–60, nos. 1935, 1958, 1972, 2036, 2038, 2048, 2166, 2291. See Cumont, *TM* i. 177 f. The battle between the gods and the giants also formed part of the Mithraic mythology, see Cumont, *TM* i. 157 f.

[2] A. G. Brodeur, *The Prose Edda*, 1916, p. 42.

of the giants' (*Gylf.* 8). Once Thor pulled up the head of Jǫrmungand in a fishing-contest with the giant Hymi, who panicked and cut the line. Thor hurled his hammer after the sinking serpent, 'and men say that he struck off its head against the bottom; but I think it were true to tell thee that the Midgard Serpent yet lives and lies in the encompassing sea.'[1] At the final cataclysm of Ragnarøk, when the gods of the present world, the Æsir, have to fight against a collection of monsters and demons who escape from their present captivity, Jǫrmungand will again be the special opponent of Thor.[2]

The projection of the battle into the future as well as the past constitutes no obstacle to the comparison with the southern traditions; after all, the defeat of Leviathan alternates between past and future within the Old Testament. The author of an important critical bibliography on the subject of connections between Nordic and southern myth has stated: 'That ideas from the south and from the orient entered the Germanic world in repeated waves from the earliest times to the end of paganism, is now I suppose beyond all doubt. But there are almost insuperable difficulties in distinguishing these different borrowings from each other and in fixing them chronologically.'[3] Scholars have pointed out in this connection that the Ostrogoth empire extended at one time from the Baltic to the Black Sea. We must remember too that the northern isolation of the Icelandic gods is only an appearance: they are the only gods of pagan Europe (apart from Greece) about whose mythology we are at all well informed. The largely aristocratic émigrés who colonized Iceland fortunately managed to develop literary enthusiasms without making them subject to Christianity, a religion which they had adopted rather casually by a vote.

In Egypt we do not find a single encircling snake, but we do find a system that brings us closer to Pherecydes' Ὠγηνοῦ δώματα. When the sun sets in the evening he enters a dark region called

[1] *Gylf.* 48, cf. 47, *Hymiskviða* 23–5, *Ragnarsdrápa* 14–19.
[2] *Vǫluspá* 50, 55–6, *Gylf.* 51. Cf. Axel Olrik, *Ragnarök*, 1922.
[3] E. Olson, *Arch. f. Rel.* 31, 1934, 265. Cf. Eisler, *Weltenmantel*, p. 156 n. 5.

the Dat or Duat, which extends under the earth or round its north side to the place where he is to rise again. He travels by boat along a system of rivers (from which the Nile takes its source). The Dat is also the land of the dead, for they travel with the sun along his dreadful journey, finally to rise with him to heaven if they are lucky. Accounts of the Dat are found in the *Book of the Dead*, the *Book of Gates*, and the *Book of him that is in the Duat*.[1] The way is divided into twelve parts, corresponding to the twelve hours of night. Many of them are occupied by serpents (some winged, or with two or three heads) or other monsters, as well as by souls in various conditions. Some of the serpents assist Reʿ, others are obstructive. When he finally emerges into the sky it is along the body and out of the mouth of the serpent of the twelfth section, Ānkhneteru. The *Book of Gates* takes its name from the gates, each guarded by a serpent, by which the different sections of the Dat are entered. Gates or doors were also a feature of the Field of Reeds, where Osiris ruled over the blessed dead; and, we recall, of Pherecydes' Hades. The Field of Reeds was sometimes identified with the Dat, sometimes made a subdivision of it. It was itself divided into seven 'halls' or 'mansions', each with its appointed door-keeper, look-out, and interrogation officer.[2] Another division was into fifteen 'districts', many of them occupied by serpents and monsters.[3] There is a good deal of inconsistency between the various accounts. But it cannot be denied that there is some similarity between the Dat and the Greek Oceanus. On Oceanus too the sun's vessel sails; from it the rivers of the inner world have their sources; strange creatures dwell by its banks, including the serpent who guards the golden apples; and there the groves of Persephone and the asphodel meadow are found.[4] So when Pherecydes speaks of 'mansions of Ogenos', and populates the river with Ophioneus and his brood, we cannot fail to think of Egyptian as well as of Manichaean cosmography.

[1] See Budge, *The Egyptian Heaven and Hell*, 1905; id. *The Book of the Dead*, pp. 135 ff., 268 ff., 402 ff.; H. Bonnet, *Reallexikon der ägyptischen Religionsgeschichte* s.vv. Amduat and Dat.

[2] *Book of the Dead* (Theban recension), ch. 144.

[3] Ibid., ch. 149.

[4] *Od.* 10. 508 ff., 11. 158, 539, 573.

In an Indian myth the earth is represented as a pillar-shaped mountain, supported below by Vishṇu in the shape of a tortoise, and surrounded by a sea of milk. In the sea the great serpent Vāsuki lies, with his body coiled once round the mountain. The gods pull at his tail and the animal-headed demons at his multiple heads, and as they pull this way and that, the pillar-mountain is made to rotate. This has the effect of churning the milk into butter, and bringing all kinds of things into view.[1] The conception of the serpent in the great sea has survived in the myths of central Asiatic peoples into modern times. In one version he winds three times round the world-mountain and his head is on its summit.[2] The Vedas make frequent reference to the great serpent Vṛtra, 'encompasser', son of Danu 'stream' or 'waters of heaven'. He lay upon a lofty summit, encompassed the water, or the rivers, and prevented them from flowing. But the great god Indra cast him down from his heights, destroying his ninety-nine fortresses, and uncovering the prison of the waters. The escaping waters overflowed the serpent, and he lies enveloped by them at the bottom of the lower air. Indra then produced the sun and set it in the sky. Sometimes the conflict is put in the past, sometimes it is treated as a seasonal event which is repeated constantly.[3]

There are traces of such myths in Greece itself. Kirk has compared the Ophionidai with the family of Typhon and Echidna (Hes. *Th.* 295 ff.). Typhon was a horrible monster who seemed about to become king of the gods, but was blasted by Zeus' thunderbolt and cast into Tartarus or under Etna. But his connections with water are slight;[4] and his strange progeny do not

[1] *Mahābhārata* i. 14. ff.; U. Holmberg, *Der Baum des Lebens*, 1922/3, p. 79. See Plate IV.

[2] Holmberg, *Der Baum des Lebens*, pp. 63 f., 67, 94. Connections between ancient Indian and modern central and northern Asiatic cosmic mythology are proved by correspondences not only of motifs but even of names; see ibid., pp. 40, 63, 67 f.

[3] For details and references see A. A. Macdonell, *Vedic Mythology*, 1897, pp. 58–62, 152, 158–9.

[4] Herodotus and others place him in Lake Serbonis on the border of Egypt, and there was a story that the river Orontes was created by his wriggling into the earth to avoid Zeus' bolts (Strabo 16. 2. 7 pp. 750–1). These represent identifications with local oriental figures. Nicander's tale that when the thunderbolts set him on fire he plunged into the sea and then had Sicily planted on top of him (fr. 59

assist him in his combat with Zeus. The Chimaira is killed by Bellerophon, the Sphinx undone by Oedipus, the Hydra, the Nemean Lion, and the hounds Cerberus and Orthos by Heracles, on separate occasions, and only Orthos lived beyond Oceanus. If there had ever been a myth in which they acted in concert, it lay far back in the past, too far to have conceivably influenced Pherecydes. Then there is Eurynome (see p. 22); but if she had ever been a defeated cosmic serpent, the fact had been forgotten long before Hesiod and Homer. Then again there is Atlas: a baleful, gigantic figure, who, in the version of the *Odyssey*, lives in the sea and supports the columns which hold up the sky (1. 52 ff.). The antiquity of this conception is shown by the parallel of Upelluri in Hurrian–Hittite myth.[1] Atlas was put in his uncomfortable situation by Zeus: Hesiod and Homer say that he was *κρατερόφρων* or *ὀλοόφρων*, and later mythographers make him the leader of the Titan (= Giant?) revolt.[2] He can well be compared with the Manichaean Giant of the Sea, who is also associated with the pillars of heaven. Finally, Theopompus (115 F 75 c) told of a country beyond Oceanus where double-sized men lived.

Such ideas, then, were current in differing forms over a wide area and over a long period. They existed in Greece long before Pherecydes, perhaps as early as the Mycenaean period. But Pherecydes' Ophioneus is so unlike any Greek forms of the myth known at the time that he cannot be derived from native tradition. He must have been taken directly from an eastern source. It is impossible to be more specific about the place of origin; but it may not be out of place to refer back to my suggestion (p. 19) that Pherecydes saw or made a map of the world on which the Mansions of Ogenos were shown. The idea of such a map was new in Greece, but had long been familiar to the Babylonians.

ap. Ant. Lib. 28; cf. Val. Flacc. 2. 26) is nothing but an imaginative development of the idea that he was somehow put beneath Etna.

[1] A. Lesky, *Anz. d. Öst. Ak.* 1950, 148 ff. = *Gesammelte Schr.* pp. 363 ff.; cf. my note on Hes. *Th.* 517.

[2] Hes. *Th.* 509, *Od.* loc. cit., Hyg. *fab.* 150, *Myth. Vat.* 2. 53; cf. Orph. (Rhaps.) fr. 215, Diod. 3. 60.

A specimen in the British Museum, from the Neobabylonian period, shows Mesopotamia surrounded by a circular ocean, round the outside of which are seven triangular areas probably representing mountains.[1] This is much what I imagine Pherecydes' map would have looked like.

The names Ogenos and Zas

This will be the best place to discuss the strange form chosen by Pherecydes as the name of his peripheral river. The least implausible etymology proposed for Ὠκεανός connects it with Aramaic *'ôgānâ*, 'basin', or *'ôgen*, 'rim'.[2] It has been observed that Pherecydes' Ὠγηνός is slightly closer to the foreign word.[3] Since the form Ὠκεανός was firmly established in Hesiod, Homer, and no doubt all other poets who mentioned it, Ogenos must be regarded as a deliberate mutation by Pherecydes. The only credible motive for such a change is the desire to assimilate the name to some other word. No Greek word comes into question; a foreign word, whether or not it was really related to Ὠκεανός, might. Observing that Greeks and barbarians used a similar name, Pherecydes may have postulated a' true' form which had become corrupted.

The question cannot be separated from the problem of the name Zas. If some different explanation of the latter recommends itself, the proposed explanation of Ogenos will be weakened. First it had better be said that there is no question of *Ζάς Ζαντός* being a current form in any Greek dialect. Zeus' name assumes many forms in different dialects, but the -*ντ*- element does not

[1] *Cuneiform Texts in the British Museum*, 1906, xxii, pl. 48; H. and J. Lewy, *Hebrew Union Coll. Annual* 17, 1942/3, 10 ff. See Plate V. The accompanying text says that the transoceanic areas have never been visited, except by certain outstanding persons such as Utnapištim. The circular ocean is called Bitter River.

[2] The once-alleged Sumerian *uginna* 'ring' does not exist (Kirk–Raven, p. 14, make it Hittite!). The name Ὠκεανός is said to be used by many of the barbarians (Favorinus, fr. 82 Barigazzi, from Crates; cf. Diod. 5. 20. 1). Cf. Gisinger, *RE* xvii. 2309.

[3] Gomperz, *Greek Thinkers* i. 538; Eisler, *Weltenmantel*, p. 203. εα was a diphthong in Ionic, hardly if at all distinct from η, so that the only material difference between Ὠγηνός and Ὠκεανός would be the voiced consonant.

and could not occur.[1] Again we have to assume a deliberate mutation by Pherecydes. Secondly it is to be pointed out that we must start from the stem, *Ζαντ-*, to which *Ζάς* is the expected nominative. Interpretations which focus on the nominative and forget the stem are inadequate. Thus the notion of Gomperz and others that a play on the Greek word for 'live' was intended is out of court. For that, Pherecydes might have used the already existing *Ζήν*, *Ζηνός* (= *ζῆν*); *Ζάς Ζαντός* is remote. The same objection must be made to Eisler's reference to men called Zas in lists of priests of Corycian Zeus, for the genitive of that name is *Ζᾶτος*;[2] and to Kirk–Raven, pp. 55 ff.: '*Ζάς* . . . is perhaps intended to stress the element *ζα-* (an intensive prefix), as in *ζάθεος*, *ζαής*; though there is some possibility that the form Zas is intended to link the sky-god Zeus with the earth-goddess Ge, whose Cyprian form is *ζᾶ*.'

Again, Greek has no answer to offer. But in south Asia Minor there was an important god who seems to be what we are looking for: the Luvian Šanta, who lived on in classical Cilicia as Sandes or Sandon. He was equated by the Hittites with their Weather-god,[3] and by the Greeks with Zeus or Heracles.[4] When we consider that the country of the Luvians overlapped the area where Babys and related names occur,[5] the possibility arises that for Pherecydes' father, Zeus was only the Greek name of a god that he had grown up knowing as Šanta. In that case, Pherecydes,

[1] Cf. Collitz, *Bezzenbergers Beiträge* 10, 1885, 52.

[2] *Weltenmantel*, p. 194 n. 1; *Wiener Denkschr.* 44, 1896, 76–7; Zgusta, *Kleinas. Personennamen*, p. 178. Nestle, *Phil. Wochenschrift* 1936, 1302, is in error in saying that Pherecydes' Zas is attested as Pythagorean, for the passages refer to *Ζανὸς πύργος*. A similar confusion in Bechtel, *Gr. Dial.* iii. 132; Kretschmer, *Glotta* 17, 1929, 197. Later Kretschmer became aware of his oversight, but tried to excuse it on the ground that Damascius' *Ζάντα* (really Eudemus') had no support in the text of Pherecydes (*Glotta* 26, 1938, 40). It is true that A 8 is *oratio obliqua* where Pherecydes used *Ζάς*; but it is incredible that Eudemus should have made the accusative *Ζάντα* if this was not the stem-form that Pherecydes used in other places. Herodian attests it too, i. 410. 19 Lentz.

[3] E. Laroche, *Dictionnaire de la langue louvite*, 1959, p. 127.

[4] Cook, *Zeus* i. 593 ff. For the regular change of *nt* to *nd* see Kretschmer, *Einleitung in die Geschichte der gr. Sprache*, 1896, pp. 293–311.

[5] See above, p. 3; on the Luvian-speaking area, Laroche, pp. 8–10. Lycaonia and Isauria are common to both areas.

constructing a 'true' name from which both Greek and barbarian name might be derived, could not have arrived at anything very different from *Ζάς Ζαντός*.

In the century after him, at any rate, Greeks were ready enough to identify their gods with foreign ones, and to argue that whatever they and other peoples had or did in common was likely to be basic and natural, while what was different was thereby exposed as convention. But Pherecydes seems to be doing something bolder: building a new account of the world from Greek and barbarian traditions by subjecting them to a process of crashing syncretism. The Greek elements have not been prominent so far. But we shall see that they were significant.

The wedding

In Greek tradition the most fruitful event in the development of the world was the marriage of Heaven and Earth. (So too in a Graeco-Cilician myth, where Sandes appears as one of the children. Steph. Byz. s.v. *Ἄδανα*.) In Pherecydes, a god Uranos plays no part; Zas is the prime celestial power, and it makes sense that he should be the bridegroom who turns Chthonie into the fecund Earth we know. At the same time, since we have already noted parallelisms with Iranian theologies, we are at liberty to compare a myth of the marriage of Ohrmazd as creator with Spandarmat, Earth, here called 'Queen of Heaven and Mother of Creation'.[1]

The first thing mentioned in the papyrus fragment was the building of a palace. A *θάλαμος* was sometimes newly constructed for a Greek couple,[2] but more than that is involved here: *οἰκία πολλά τε καὶ μεγάλα*, a complex of grand chambers. Schwabl and Walcot have compared the building of a palace for Baal in the Ugaritic Baal and 'Anat cycle:

> Hurry, let a house be built,
> Hurry, let a palace be erected!
> In the midst of the heights of Ṣapân!

[1] Pahlavi *Rivāyat* 8. 2–4 (Zaehner, *Zurvan*, p. 152).
[2] Cf. Gow on Theoc. 18. 3.

A thousand acres the house is to comprise,
A myriad of hectares the palace.[1]

Schwabl also refers to the building of temples for Marduk and the other gods after the defeat of Tiâmat in *Enûma Eliš*, and is perhaps justified in speaking of a 'typically oriental motif'.

The idea of an *anakalypterion*-present given by a god to his bride can be paralleled in certain Greek myths. Sicily was so given by Zeus to Kore. So was Thebes according to another story.[2] For the gift of a robe, Diels and others have referred to a less exalted bridegroom, Cadmus, who gave one to Harmonia.[3] More significant parallels can be found in Sumer and Akkad, where divine brides are given cosmic apparel. In a mythological poem designed to explain the origin of the dazzling planet Venus, it is said that when Anu (Heaven) married Ištar, the gods petitioned him to make her queen of the world. He agreed, gave her the temple Êanna, and 'clothed her form in the mantle of sovereignty, the brilliance of the shining moon; illustrious decoration, divine adornment he caused to shine on her like the day. The royal sceptre, the mighty staff he gave into her arm; the splendent crown like the horn of the moon he set upon her head.'[4] In the Sumerian *Song of Inanna* (= Ištar), it is Enlil her father who gives her her fine clothes (elsewhere An, Heaven, is her father):

The heaven he has set as a crown on my head,
The earth as sandals on my feet,
The shining mantle of the gods he has put about me,
The gleaming sceptre given into my hand.[5]

[1] C. H. Gordon, *Ugaritic Literature*, p. 34, cf. p. 10; Driver, *Canaanite Myths and Legends*, p. 99; Schwabl, *RE* Supp. ix. 1462; Walcot, *CQ* 59, 1965, 79; id. *Hesiod and the Near East*, p. 22.

[2] Diod. 5. 2. 3, Plut. *Timol.* 8; Euphorion, fr. 107 Powell; Diels, *S.B. Berl. Ak.* 1897, 149 = *Kl. Schr.* p. 28.

[3] Apollod. 3. 4. 2. All the gods came to the wedding.

[4] H. Gressmann (ed.), *Altorientalische Texte zum Alten Testament*, [2]1926, p. 254. Compared with Pherecydes by K. Gantar, *Živa Antika* 7, 1957, 237.

[5] A. Falkenstein and W. von Soden, *Sumerische und Akkadische Hymnen und Gebete*, 1953, p. 68; Gantar, p. 238. The mantle is mentioned again in a hymn to Inanna, Falkenstein–Soden, p. 75, where her lover Dumuzi is said to have a similar one. Ninurta too 'wears the heavens on his head like a turban' and 'is shod with the underworld as with sandals' (Lambert, *Orientalia* 36, 1967, 125).

In a hymn to Baba, mother goddess of Lagash, the mantle of the gods is given to her by her father An.[1] The closest approximation to the situation in Pherecydes, however, would seem to be found in the story that when An carried off heaven as his portion, Enlil took the earth, and gave it as a dowry to Ereshkigal, the queen of the lower world, whose name means 'Mistress of the great Below' (*Χθονίη*).[2]

Chthonie's robe is woven by Zas himself. In sixth-century Greece weaving probably was an 'unmasculine task';[3] but what is more important here is the idea of the world as a work of art done by a god. In Greek, Chronos sometimes appears as a craftsman: for Diphilus (fr. 83) he is a *πολιὸς τεχνίτης*, and *χαίρει μεταπλάττων πάντας* (here he takes the place of Prometheus); for Critias (88 B 25. 33) the starry body of heaven is *Χρόνου σοφὸν ποίκιλμα τέκτονος σοφοῦ*. Empedocles (31 B 23) likens the formation of things from elements under the influence of Love and Strife to the mixing of colours by painters, and elsewhere he represents Aphrodite as a moulder of animal forms. Outside Greece we meet the idea of cosmic *weaving*, in particular by the sun, who is given the name 'Weaver' in the Talmud.[4] An Estonian ballad represents the sky with its bright hues of sunrise and sunset as a mantle woven by Tara, the Old Father, the Old and Wise.[5] The idea is more elaborately developed in India. Night and Day weave a web endlessly on six pegs that support the sky. The sun comes and rends apart the dark mantle of night, spreading his own web.[6] Time and space, the whole universe,

[1] Falkenstein–Soden, p. 100; Gantar, p. 238 n. 7.

[2] Jacobsen, *JNES* 5, 1946, 144 f. The earth is not here represented as a mantle, and indeed the idea of earth as a mantle seems to be uncommon. (It was taken up in Orphic verse, cf. frr. 33, 192–3, 196.) The conception of heaven as a mantle is frequent (Greek, Persian, Jewish, etc.); see Lobeck, pp. 379 f., 551; Eisler, *Weltenmantel*, *passim*.

[3] Kirk–Raven, p. 61; cf. the myth of Omphale. Hdt. 2. 35, listing examples of how the Egyptians do everything opposite from the rest of mankind, says that the women trade while the men stay at home and weave. (Hence Soph. *OC* 337 ff.) A little later we hear of male weavers and embroiderers in Greece (Pl. *Phd.* 87 b, *Rep.* 369 d, Aeschin. 1. 97). Cf. Eisler, *Weltenmantel*, pp. 199–201.

[4] Eisler, *Weltenmantel*, p. 226.

[5] F. Kreutzwald and H. Neus, *Mythische und magische Lieder der Ehsten*, 1854, pp. 24 f.

[6] *Atharvaveda* 10. 7. 42 (Zaehner, *Hindu Scriptures*, p. 22), *Ṛgv.* 4. 13. 4.

are woven with a thread of wind or breath. It is the sun that binds the worlds together with this wind-thread, sewing nights and days together and weaving the cloth of the world.[1]

The weaving here is a continuous process, and it must be said of all these parallels that they are too imprecise to be relied on as evidence that Zas' weaving was more than a spontaneous invention by Pherecydes to bring Chthonie's robe into being. The robe itself, however, is probably derived from oriental tradition.

The tree

The Cosmic Tree is another conception that is unfamiliar in Greece but well established in various other places. It appears in different forms.[2] So far as I know it is never said that the world (heaven, earth, etc.) simply *is* a tree. One common Asiatic account is that if you find your way to the central point of the earth, you come to an immense tree which reaches up through all the heavens and extends its roots down to the nethermost regions.[3] Sometimes it grows on the world-mountain, and towers up through the heavens from there. It has as many resting-places in it as there are heavens, and it is the means of communication between the different levels. Among the Altai Tatars, the shaman's ascent from earth to the dwelling of the highest god may be acted out with the help of an actual birch-tree set up inside a kind of tent with its top projecting. Nine steps are notched into its trunk, the shaman mounts from one to the next, hallooing to the gods the while, and finally emerges through the opening at the top.[4] A similar procedure is suggested by certain Indian texts.[5]

[1] *Bṛhadāraṇyaka Upan.* 2. 7. 1, 3. 7. 2, 8. 3, *Çatapatha Brāhmaṇa* 6. 7. 1. 17, 7. 3. 2. 13, 8. 7. 3. 10, 9. 4. 1. 8, 14. 2. 2. 22; Holmberg, *Der Baum des Lebens*, pp. 104 ff.; M. Éliade, *The Two and the One*, 1965, pp. 170 ff.

[2] For a general survey see Éliade, *Patterns in Comparative Religion*, 1958, pp. 265 ff., with bibliography, and *Shamanism*, 1964, pp. 269 ff. Holmberg's *Der Baum des Lebens*, though not so wide-ranging, is a particularly valuable source of more detailed information, and not so much given to universal generalization as Éliade is. E. O. James, *The Tree of Life*, 1966, is a less disciplined study.

[3] Holmberg, *Der Baum des Lebens*, pp. 51 ff.

[4] Ibid., pp. 28, 135 f.; L. Sternberg, *Arch. f. Rel.* 28, 1930, 145 ff.; Éliade, *Shamanism*, pp. 117 ff., 275.

[5] Éliade, *Images and Symbols*, p. 45; id. *Shamanism*, pp. 403–5. The Kasias (Bengal)

The idea of a world-tree in this sense is Babylonian. In the myth of Erra, Marduk complains that Erra has thrown the world into confusion, and asks him, 'Where is the *mes* tree, the flesh of the gods, the adornment of the king of the universe... whose base reaches the bottom of the underworld, in the broad sea a hundred double-hours of water, whose summit... reaches into the heaven [of Anu]?'[1] A sacred tree at Eridu is also described as reaching down to the lower waters.[2] It may or may not be relevant to mention the many scenes in Mesopotamian art where a date-palm, often the object of ceremonial attentions from priests or demon-like figures, rises up to the winged disc of the sun and/or the crescent of the moon, the eight-pointed star of Venus, and other stars.[3] The world-tree of Norse mythology, the ash-tree Yggdrasil, may also come ultimately from the ancient Near East (cf. above, p. 46 n. 3). It covers nine worlds; its top is lost in mist, and one of its three roots reaches down over Hel, the home of the dead, while the other two extend over the land of the Frost Giants and the region inhabited by mankind.[4]

Another kind of mythical tree may be described as the 'Tree of Destinies'. Egyptian funerary art portrays the divine scribe Thoth, with Sekhet and Atum, carefully writing on the leaves of a luxuriant tree, while the dead king sits by. The same idea is found in modern Asia. The Osmanli Turks tell of a great tree in the middle of heaven with a million leaves, on each of which

think the stars are men who climbed to heaven up a tree that has since been felled; the Mbocobis of Paraguay hope after death to climb up the Llagdigua tree that binds heaven and earth. (E. B. Tylor, *Primitive Culture*, [4]1903, i. 291; *Researches into the Early History of Mankind*, [3]1878, p. 358.)

[1] Gressmann (see p. 53 n. 4), p. 218. Mr. Lambert has advised me on the translation.

[2] P. Dhorme, *Choix des textes religieux assyro-babyloniens*, 1907, p. 99; S. Langdon, *Journal of the Royal Asiatic Soc.* 1928, 843 ff. Cf. Lambert, *Babylonian Wisdom Literature*, 1960, p. 327.

[3] Hélène Danthine, *Le palmier-dattier et les arbres sacrés dans l'iconographie de l'Asie occidentale ancienne*, 1937, i. 94–7, 144–6, 160–1; ii, figs. 31, 40, 169, 268, 278, 329, 333, 345, 363, 371–2, 406, 425–47, 459, 471, 576, 1124, etc. Cf. Éliade, *Patterns*, pp. 272 f.; G. Widengren, *The King and the Tree of Life* (1951).

[4] *Vǫluspá* 2, 19, *Grímnismál* 29–35, *Gylfaginning* 15–16; J. A. MacCulloch, *Eddic Mythology*, 1930, pp. 331–6; E. O. G. Turville-Petre, *Mythology and Religion of the North*, 1964, pp. 279 ff.

a human fate is written, and when the leaf falls, the man dies. The Ostyaks and the Bataks have a similar belief.[1] The associations between the Tree of Destinies and the World-Tree are easily understood. The powers that determine fates naturally station themselves at the centre of things, where all the channels of knowledge meet. The shaman uses his cosmic tree to obtain knowledge of the future from heaven. Beneath Yggdrasil's ash flows a prophetic spring, and there sit the three Norns, Past, Present, and Future, commanding the world's destinies.[2] The Biblical Tree of Knowledge belongs in this context. And the mythical tree has its real counterpart in the oracular tree from whose leaves the decrees of fate may be ascertained.[3]

Next to the Tree of Knowledge in the garden of Eden stands the Tree of Life. The idea of the tree that provides life-giving or rejuvenating fruit or juice has wide currency, and it is commonly the same as the cosmic tree. In central Asiatic accounts the tree is noted for its everlasting freshness, and very often it is associated with a spring, or it stands in water, or on the bank of a river or beside a sea. The Minusinsk Tatars tell that its leaves and bark are golden, and the pool at its foot is filled with the water of life, guarded by Tata the ancestor of the race. According to a Yakut poem, a divine yellow juice flows down from the top of the tree to refresh the weary and satisfy the hungry. These themes go back to Indo-Iranian antiquity. The Vedic gods sit in the Aśvattha tree in the third heaven, and yellow *soma* drips down its leaves; with them is Yama, the first man, taking care of our ancestors.[4] In the lake Vourukaša, the source of all the world's rivers according to the Persian world-picture, stands the wondrous tree Gaokərəna, with the evil lizard that Ahriman created lurking below it, trying to get at the white *haoma* that confers immortality.[5] This reptile has parallels in the serpent under the

[1] U. Harva (formerly Holmberg), *Die religiösen Vorstellungen der altäischen Völker*, 1938, pp. 72, 172 f.; J. Warneck, *Die Religion der Batak*, 1909, pp. 49 f.

[2] Cf. Holmberg, *Der Baum des Lebens*, p. 66.

[3] 2 Sam. 5: 24; Dodona (cf. H. W. Parke, *The Oracles of Zeus*, 1967, pp. 27 ff.); compare the loose leaves in the Sibyl's cave, and A. Dieterich, *Abraxas*, p. 98 n. 2.

[4] *Ṛgv.* 10. 135. 1, *Atharvav.* 5. 4. 3, *Chāndogya Upan.* 8. 5. 3.

[5] *Yašt.* 1. 30, *Sīh rōčak* 2. 7, *Vidēvdāt* 20. 4, *Bundahišn* 18, 27. 4.

Tree of Life in Eden (that tree too is associated with the first man); in the serpent Niðhǫgg who gnaws at the foot of Yggdrasil; and in the serpent who lurks in the pool at the bottom of the world-tree, or coils round its trunk, in several of the Asiatic myths.[1]

The tree of life is a feature of the Egyptian paradise, the Field of Reeds, to which every man hopes to gain admittance after his death. The gods eat from it and feed the deified dead from it, besides giving them the cool water to drink.[2] Illustrations in funerary papyri and reliefs show the man kneeling before the tree, which grows up from a reservoir of water, and an arm reaching out from the tree and pouring water into his cup.[3] Elsewhere, too, the bounteous spirit of the tree of life shows a tendency to manifest herself in partial human form. Yakut tradition has it that the first man approached the tree, and suddenly a female being appeared growing from its trunk, and offered him her breast. He drank, and felt his strength grow a hundredfold.[4]

Traces of this complex of ideas can be found in early Greek poetry and myth. Hesiod and others speak of the 'roots' of the earth and sea, though it seems to be a dead metaphor, and they have no real conception of a world-tree.[5] Large trees are sometimes described as reaching up to heaven or down towards Tartarus;[6] it is a possibility, but hardly more, that a description of a world-tree was the prototype for which such expressions were coined.[7] Homer's famous comparison of human lives to leaves[8] is perhaps an echo of the belief in a 'tree of destinies'. The

[1] Holmberg, *Der Baum des Lebens*, pp. 63 f., 67; id. *Finno-Ugric and Siberian Mythology*, pp. 356 ff.

[2] See below, p. 65.

[3] Cf. Plate VI; W. Max Müller, *Egyptian Mythology*, p. 36; *Annales du Service* 29, 1929, facing p. 88.

[4] Holmberg, *Der Baum des Lebens*, pp. 57–9, cf. 69.

[5] Hes. *Th.* 728 with my note.

[6] *Il.* 14. 288, *Od.* 5. 239, Virg. *G.* 2. 291–2.

[7] Q.S. 5. 49–56, 14. 196–200 sets a tree on top of Hesiod's hill of Virtue, and represents man as having to climb up it to heaven. This looks like a late development influenced by the Asiatic conception of the tree on the world-mountain leading up to heaven. Allegorical use of the primitive tree-image is found, for example, in the Upanishads and the Manichaean *Kephalaia*, and is extremely common in Christian and Mohammedan writings.

[8] *Il.* 6. 146–9, cf. Mimn. 2. 1–3, [Sim.] fr. 85 Bergk, 'Musaeus' 2 B 5.

idea that the trees flowed with honey in the Golden Age[1] is surely related to the Tree of Life that feeds the first men; and the Tree of Life is clearly recognizable in the tree of the Hesperides, with its golden apples and coiling serpent, sometimes located in the far west, sometimes in the underworld, but always close to Atlas the supporter of heaven. It is there that Euripides places the κρῆναι ἀμβρόσιαι.

But these are only traces, echoes of a forgotten cosmography. No one will pretend that the conception of a world tree, of any of the types described, was really alive in Greece in Pherecydes' time. There is therefore an initial presumption that he derived it, like so much else, from the orient, where it retained a powerful hold on men's minds then and for a long time afterwards. The presumption is strengthened when we observe how many of the characteristic features of the Asiatic tree he reproduces in his.

1. Because of its wings, we guess that it was a self-supporting frame to which heaven, earth, and the other parts of the world were attached; in other words, it connected the different levels of the cosmos.
2. It has the robe on it; in other words, earth and Ogenos are round it, it is in the centre.
3. By the same token, it is surrounded by the serpent who lurks in the waters.
4. The robe is at the same time Chthonie's; in other words, the tree changes place with a goddess—the bounteous Goddess-within-the-earth, the universal mother.
5. This tree-world contains a spring of ambrosia, on which the gods feed, and (if this is not the same) an 'outflow' (from the base of the tree-trunk?) which gives new life to the dead.

Pherecydes' tree is unique in being winged. It has been thought that the idea was suggested by Assyrian representations of the holy tree with the winged disc of the sun hovering immediately

[1] Directly attested only late (Virg. *E.* 4. 30, *G.* 1. 131, Hor. *epod.* 16. 47 f., Tib. 1. 3. 45 f., Ov. *M.* 1. 112), but suggested by Hes. *Op.* 233, where the rewards of the righteous city are described in Golden-Age terms; the honey and fruit of the mythical oaks are rationalized as bees and acorns.

above it.[1] The possibility cannot be excluded; but the wings must have had a significance for Pherecydes as appendages of the tree, and that being so, there were enough precedents in Greek art and fancy for him to invent them on his own initiative.[2] They imply that the tree-world supports itself in space. ('Space' is not an ideal word to use here, but it is better than 'void' or 'air', two things which were not differentiated till the fifth century.) Perhaps Pherecydes thought of the winds that blow about Tartarus, where the Harpies and Thyella are, as upholding the whole world.[3]

The wind had long been considered by the Egyptians and others as the raiser or supporter of the sky. The extension of the idea to the support of the earth was new, and, so far as I know, Greek. We shall see it shortly in Anaximenes. Only later do we find parallels in oriental philosophy.[4]

Metempsychosis

Implicit in the idea of a Tree of Life is the possibility of escape from death. In Egypt the tree feeds the man who enters upon eternal life in the company of the gods; in the Greek gold plates, drinking from the water that springs up below the cypress tree is the beginning of immortality; and the tree or the water of life continues to be promised to the virtuous by Jewish, Christian, and Mohammedan writer.[5] It may also be the source that enables

[1] Jacobi, *Theol. Studien*, 1851, i. 212; Eisler, *Weltenmantel*, p. 591. I need not repeat from *CQ* 57, 1963, 168 my criticisms of Eisler's further speculations.

[2] The sun's horses, bed, etc.; cf. Wilamowitz, *Glaube* ii. 7; Nilsson, *MMR*, p. 507; in most detail S. Eitrem, *RE* viA. 886 f.

[3] Cf. Eisler, *Weltenmantel*, p. 455 n. 6.

[4] Job 26: 7 (fourth century B.C.?): 'God spreads the canopy of the sky over chaos | and suspends earth in the void.' A rabbinical discourse quoted by Eisler, *Weltenmantel*, p. 325 n. 1, teaches that the world rests on pillars, the pillars rest on water, the water on mountains, the mountains on wind, the wind on the storm, the storm on the arm of God—a remarkable concatenation of primitive cosmological conceptions. A sixth-century Syriac treatise (see p. 42 n. 9) says, 'Sous la terre, se trouve la mer redoutable des eaux nombreuses; sous les eaux, le feu; sous le feu, le vent; sous le vent, les ténèbres; sous les ténèbres, ne cherche rien' (p. 177).

[5] 2 Esd. 2: 12–19, 1 Enoch 24–5, 2 Enoch 8–9, Test. Levi 18. 11; Rev. 2: 7, 21: 6, 22: 1–3, 17; *Koran*, Surah 18. 30 ff., 37. 39–47, 56. 12–39, 67. 16 ff., 75. 12–22.

men to enter on earthly life in the first place. We have seen that it sometimes feeds the first men. Altai Tatars say that when a child is to be born, the god Yayutši draws its life from the lake of milk in paradise.[1] The parallelism between human lives and leaves on the Tree of Destinies may be relevant here.

Pherecydes taught that souls enter a succession of bodies, and I have argued that before a new incarnation they drink from the 'outflow'. There is no direct evidence that he believed in interchange between animal species, but as this was the form in which the theory of metempsychosis was current among the Pythagoreans, there is a presumption that he did. The idea that human souls enter animals after the death of the man is held in a simple form by a great many primitive peoples all over the world.[2] But these peoples do not seem to think further than the existence which is to succeed the present one. They do not develop elaborate speculative systems which account for the soul's progress through many thousands of years. That is something found, outside Greece, only in India; and it is found there in a form strikingly like the Pythagorean. Briefly, 'those endowed with Goodness reach the state of gods, those endowed with Activity the state of men, and those endowed with Darkness ever sink to the condition of beasts; that is the threefold course of transmigrations'.[3] And as in the primitive religions it is necessary to abstain from eating the particular species of animal that men become after death, the Indian says: 'Meat can never be obtained without injury to living creatures, and injury to sentient beings is detrimental to the attainment of heavenly bliss; let him therefore shun meat.' 'Me he will devour in the next (life), whose flesh I eat in this.'[4]

[1] W. Radloff, *Aus Sibirien* ii. 11.

[2] Frazer, *GB* viii, ch. 16; xiii, ch. 59. Little reliance can be placed on statements that transmigration was taught by some Thracians (Mela 2. 2. 18; from Hdt. 4. 94–6?) or by the Gallic Druids (Caes. *BG* 6. 14. 5, Diod. 5. 28. 5–6; from Posidonius?).

[3] *Laws of Manu* 12. 40. 'Activity' is marked by delight in undertakings, want of firmness, and sensuality; 'Darkness' by covetousness, sloth, cruelty, etc. (ibid. 32–3).

[4] *Manu* 5. 48, 55. Certain sacrifices are excepted. For the Indian equivalents of the later Greek expressions 'wheel of birth', 'wheel of time', see Eisler, *Mysteriengedanken*, pp. 89 ff.

Only the primitive form of metempsychosis-theory is attested in the Vedas.[1] The developed theory first appears in the *Çatapatha Brāhmaṇa* and the Upanishads. It was commonly accepted in the time of Buddha (died *c.* 480 B.C.), and must go back to about the seventh century. Like the doctrine of the creator Time, then, it appears in India at an epoch not very far removed from its appearance in Greece. In the case of the Time-god it was judged probable that this coincidence was a result of the diffusion from a common centre of a renovated Egyptian myth. Can we similarly assume a common source for metempsychosis, or are we to postulate independent development along the same lines from a substrate of primitive belief?

Egypt again has a stake in the game. For Herodotus, metempsychosis as taught by Pythagoras was at home in Egypt (2. 123). The Egyptians certainly believed that the soul is immortal, and can transform itself into different animal shapes;[2] this can be regarded as a variant of the primitive form of transmigration-theory described above. The developed theory is not attested by native sources of any period. But Herodotus' testimony is not to be rejected lightly. He had personal knowledge of the people he was talking about, his statement of what they believe is explicit and detailed, and while it obviously never attained general or lasting currency, we should accept that it was maintained at least for a short period by some Egyptian theologians. Herodotus' evidence relates to an epoch not far removed (on a large view of history) from that at which metempsychosis came to India and to Greece.

Ambrosia in the moon

The case for a historical connection is strengthened by a remarkable parallel of detail. Pherecydes said that the moon produces ambrosia daily, and that the gods feed on it there. In certain of the Vedic hymns, but more commonly and more clearly in the Brāhmaṇas, Upanishads, and Purāṇas, we find the idea that the moon is the vessel from which the gods drink *soma*,

[1] See A. A. Macdonell, *History of Sanskrit Literature*, 1899, p. 329.
[2] Cf. Budge, *Book of the Dead*, pp. 304 ff.

the divine liquid that gives them immortality. During the second part of the month the gods are drinking the moon up, and so it wanes; then it goes in to the sun, and is refilled during the first part of the next month, at the same time feeding the spirits of the dead.[1] As the drink of immortality, *soma* is called *amṛta*, which is the equivalent of *ἀμβροσία*, etymologically as well as in sense. At the same time, *soma* is the juice pressed from a terrestrial plant and drunk at religious ceremonies.

The moon is a place of special importance for the Indian theory of metempsychosis. According to the *Kaushītakī Upanishad* (sixth century B.C.?),

> Everyone who departs from this world, comes to the moon. In the first fortnight (the moon) waxes on their breath-souls (*prāṇa*), while in the latter half it prepares them to be born (again); for the moon is the gateway of the heavenly world. Those who answer it, it allows to pass on, but those who do not answer are turned into rain and (the moon) rains them down on earth. (Then) they are born again here in different places (in a form) which accords with their (former) deeds (*karma*) and knowledge,—as worms or moths, fish or birds, tigers or lions, boars or rhinoceros, or as men or some other (animal).
>
> When a man reaches (the moon, the moon) asks him, 'Who are you?' He should answer:
>
> 'From (the moon) far-seeing, fifteenfold produced,
> From the world of the fathers, ye seasons, semen was produced.
> Speed me then forth into a male who fashions (offspring),
> And by (this) fashioning male into a mother pour me.'
>
> (Or else:)
>
> 'I am he who is born and is reborn
> Like the twelfth or thirteenth month
> Of a father who has twelve or thirteen parts.
> This do I know, this do I understand. O seasons,
> Lead me to (the land of) immortality!
>
> 'Through this truth, through this ascetic fervour, I am a season, a son of the seasons.'

[1] See A. Hillebrandt, *Vedische Mythologie* i². 297 ff.; Macdonell, *Vedic Mythology*, pp. 112 f.

'Who art thou?' (asks the moon).

'I am thou.'

It lets him pass on.

(And so) reaching that path (called) the 'way of the gods' he comes to the worlds of (the fire-god) Agni, of (the wind-god) Vāyu, of Varuna, of the sun, of Indra, of Prajāpati and of Brahman. In this world of Brahman there are the lake Āra, the moments Yeshtiha, the river Vijarā ('ageless'), the tree Ilya, the public place Sālajya, the residence Aparājita ('unconquered'), the door-keepers Indra and Prajāpati, the palace Vibhu ('extensive'), the throne Vicakshanā ('far-seeing'), the couch Amitaujas ('of boundless strength'), the dearly beloved Mānasī ('mental') and her counterpart Cākshushī ('visual'). (It is these two who weave the worlds out of flowers.) (There too are) the nymphs (*apsaras*) (called) 'mothers' and 'nurses', and the rivers Ambayā.

He who knows about this comes to this (world). To him Brahman says: 'Run on: by my glory this one has reached the river Vijarā, he will never (more) grow old.'[1]

A somewhat more detailed account is given in the *Bṛhadāraṇyaka* (6. 2. 13–15) and *Chāndogya* (5. 8. 1–10. 8) Upanishads. Both works are generally agreed, on grounds of language and content, to be considerably earlier than the time of Buddha. The rain produces plants, and these, when consumed by animals, are converted into semen and so into new animal bodies.

The moon has no such role in Egypt. But the dialogue that the Indian soul conducts with the moon, in its function as guardian of paradise, must be compared with the 58th chapter of the *Book of the Dead*. The scribe Ani wishes to enter Khert-Neter ('divine subterranean place'), and to breathe the fresh air and drink the water there. The vignette in the papyrus shows 'the scribe Ani and his wife Tutu standing up to their knees in a canal or arm of the Nile, scooping up water into their mouths with their right hands. Ani holds in his left hand a sail, symbolic of air or wind, and Tutu holds in her left hand a fan. By the side of the water two young palms and a large mature palm are

[1] 1. 2–3, trans. Zaehner (*Hindu Scriptures*, pp. 149 f.).

growing, and from the leafy crown of the large palm hang two clusters of ripe dates' (Budge, p. 284). The text begins:

> Speech by the Osiris Ani: 'Open to me!'—'Who, pray, art thou? What art thou? Where didst thou come into being?'—'I am one of you.'

He thus declares that he is one of the gods and entitled to pass. At the end of the chapter he demands milk, cakes, bread, and meat. The rubric of the 72nd chapter speaks of him entering the Field of Reeds:

> Barley and emmer (shall be) given to him therein; he shall be flourishing as when he was upon earth, and he (shall) keep doing what he pleases, even as this divine Ennead which is in the Dat.

According to Pyramid text 1216 a–e, the deceased 'went to the great island in the midst of the Marsh of Offerings, on which the gods cause the swallows to alight. The swallows are the imperishable stars. They give to him the tree of life whereof they live, that he may, at the same time, live thereof' (S. A. B. Mercer, *The Pyramid Texts*, 1952, i. 202).

Exactly the same dialogue-motif occurs in Greek, in the gold plates.[1] There we read that there are two springs in Hades, one on the left, which is to be avoided, the other on the right, with cool water flowing from the Lake of Memory. By one of the springs stands a cypress—the right-hand spring according to most copies.[2] This spring is guarded, and a dialogue takes place there.

> 'Who art thou? Whence art thou?'
>
> 'I am a child of Earth and Heaven, and of heavenly birth, you know it yourselves. But I am parched with thirst, I perish: give me quickly to drink of the unfailing spring on the right by the cypress-tree.'

They do so, and he is admitted to the company of the heroes, to the 'holy meadows and groves of Phersephoneia'. In another series of texts he says, 'I come pure and from the pure, O queen

[1] Cf. p. 26 n. 1.

[2] Fr. 32b I–III; Ἀρχ. Ἐφ. 89/90, 1950/1, 99 (here it is the right-hand spring that is to be avoided); 1953/4, 57, 58. Only in fr. 32a is the cypress on the left.

of the chthonians, Eukles, Eubouleus, and you other immortal gods: for I claim to be of your blessed stock also, and I have paid my penalty for all unrighteousness.'[1] There is good reason to think in terms of a direct Egyptian connection here, for the very idea of providing the dead man with such documents has its only parallel in the *Book of the Dead*,[2] and the longing for cool water is especially appropriate to an Egyptian.

Further parallels between Greek and Indian eschatology appear in Pythagorean theory. The famous taboo on eating beans was understood, at least by some, to be because souls return to the light by way of beans:[3] this recalls the doctrine of the early Upanishads (above, p. 63), that souls return from the moon by way of rain and plants.[4] On both sides, repeated animal incarnation is combined with the possibility of final escape to a paradise. And the comparison gains in sharpness when we take into account the old Pythagorean *σύμβολον* that says the sun and moon are the Isles of the Blessed.[5]

The idea of the sun and moon as resorts of the dead, especially of departed kings or priests, is found among a number of primitive peoples. The Natchez of Mississippi and the Apalaches of Florida say that chiefs and braves go and dwell in the sun. Similar beliefs are reported from Mexico and Peru. The Saliva Indians of South America regard the moon as a paradise with the particular advantage of freedom from mosquitoes. The Guaycurus reserve it for chiefs and medicine-men.[6] The Eskimos and others also think of a lunar Hades.[7] Especially interesting is the belief on Tokelau that while some men after death become stars,

[1] Fr. 32d–e, cf. c and g.

[2] S. Morenz in *Aus Antike und Orient* (Festschr. Schubart), 1950, pp. 65–71.

[3] See Burkert, *WW*, p. 165.

[4] Admittedly, on the Indian theory it would help the souls if we ate as many beans as possible (as Aristoxenus asserted that Pythagoras did: Burkert, *WW*, p. 96). The true origin of the taboo is certainly different.

[5] Iambl. *VP* 82 = DK 58 C 4. 'The planets are the hounds of Persephone' (Clem. *Strom.* 5. 50, Porph. *VP* 41 = DK 58 C 2), so Persephone is in heaven (Burkert, *WW*, p. 299). See below, p. 215. For the sun and moon in later Greek eschatological speculation see Cumont, *Symbolisme*, pp. 177–203.

[6] Tylor, *Primitive Culture*, ii⁴. 69 f.

[7] References in Roscher, ii. 999, 2769; Cumont, *Symbolisme*, p. 177 n. 1.

others, principally kings and priests, go to the moon; and that the moon wanes because its inhabitants are eating it, and then grows again in the other half of the month.[1] A popular fancy of this sort evidently underlies the Indian and Pythagorean eschatologies. But its combination in both cases with an elaborate theory of animal reincarnation and final escape—and, in the version of the *Kaushītakī Upanishad*, with a 'who are you?' 'I am of you' dialogue that has close Egyptian and Greek parallels—makes the hypothesis of independent development implausible, to say the least.

Iran makes a gap in our picture, but perhaps not an unbridgeable gap. Zoroastrianism had no place for metempsychosis; it preferred the single and final to the cyclical.[2] But it too maintained the theory of the good soul's ascent to the kingdom of God via the moon and sun. In a lost portion of the Avesta it was said that 'when they sever the consciousness of men it goes out to the nearest fire, then out to the stars, then out to the moon, and then out to the sun'.[3] The journey of the soul to the stars, from there to the moon and then the sun, and finally to the 'Beginningless Light' which is the abode of Ohrmazd, is a fixed doctrine which is often mentioned in the Pahlavi books.[4] Its appearance in the *Dāmdāt Nask* shows that it is ancient in Persia, but also that it is of non-Zoroastrian origin. For the original form of the theory must have been the one we find in the Upanishads, that it is the flame of the funeral pyre that sends the soul up to the heavenly fires.[5] The Zoroastrians abhorred cremation

[1] R. W. Williamson, *Religion and Cosmic Beliefs of Central Polynesia*, 1933, i. 117.

[2] In Greece and India we find the idea of a recurring 'great year', 10,800 years in Heraclitus (below, p. 156), 120,000 in 'Orpheus' (fr. 250), 12,000 in India; whereas in Persia the same period of 12,000 years (likened to a year with its seasons by Zātspram 34. 21–8 (Zaehner, *Zurvan*, p. 350)) is a single, non-recurrent span of time (above, p. 30). Cf. B. L. van der Waerden, *Hermes* 80, 1952, 147 ff.; 81, 1953, 481–3.

When Porphyry ascribes belief in metempsychosis to the Magi (*abst.* 4. 16), he is apparently using a recent writer on the Mithraic mysteries, in which there was an element of Platonism.

[3] *Dāmdāt Nask* in *Šāyast Lā-Šāyast* 12. 5, trans. West (*SBE* v. 341 f.).

[4] Below, p. 89.

[5] *Bṛhadāraṇyaka Upan.* 6. 2. 14–15, *Chāndogya Upan.* 5. 10. 1–3.

and (at least from the time of Herodotus) practised exposure of the dead, a primitive custom found among other peoples.[1] Hence the less natural doctrine that the soul makes its own way to the nearest fire.

The seed of the bull that was killed by Angra Mainyu was carried up to the moon and purified by its light, and gave birth to the first male and female of every animal species on earth.[2] We have here a certain parallel to the Indian cycle of mortality, animal–moon–rain–plants–animal. It has been argued by H. Lommel that the *haoma*, the drink of immortality, like the Indian *soma*, was identified with the moon.[3]

All that is attested for Pherecydes is metempsychosis and a moon that produces ambrosia for the gods. But when we reflect that these doctrines of his were part of a system that has to be explained almost throughout from oriental (and in some cases Indian) thought—the cosmic progenitor Time, the three elements and the five, the nooks, the banishment of a great serpent to the outer waters, the Mansions of Ogenos, the robe of Chthonie, the world tree, and the water of life—only the most obstinate agnostics among us will decline to believe that these features too came from abroad and not from Pherecydes' fantasy. This conclusion does not, unfortunately, help us to reconstruct the details of his eschatology.[4]

The theomachy paralleled in Greek cult

The oriental motifs just listed are known to us from various regions, Egypt, Palestine, Mesopotamia, Iran, India, or inner Asia. Their currency was clearly wide, and studying their

[1] *ERE* iv. 420 f.; in southern Anatolia *c.* 6000 B.C., see J. Mellaart, *Çatal Hüyük*, 1967, p. 204.

[2] *Bundahišn* 10. 2, 14. 3, supported by allusions in the Avesta, as *Yašt* 7. 0–7, 12. 33, *Sīh rōčak* 1. 12, etc.

[3] *Wörter und Sachen* 19, 1938, 250 ff., *Numen* 2, 1955, 196–205. I have not seen his discussions in *Paideuma* 3, 1949, 209–18, and *Symbolon* 4, 1965, 159 ff.

[4] He appears not to have spoken of men who shared in the lunar feast, for then Plutarch would just have said 'as old Pherecydes thinks' without adding 'that the gods themselves feed'. Cf. p. 24. The text is uncertain, however, and we cannot exclude e.g. σιτεῖσθαι αὐτούς ⟨τε καὶ τοὺς⟩ θεούς.

geographical distribution does not enable us to pin-point a single place from which Pherecydes received them. What appears to us in our ignorance to have been Indian may often have been Indo-Iranian, what seems to us Iranian or Jewish may have been Babylonian or Egyptian. The most precise indication of where Pherecydes' learning came from, and of how, was given by our analysis of the name Zas (p. 51). It was suggested that Pherecydes set out to reconcile a barbarian theology learned from his parents, or his father, with the traditions of the country he lived in. The name Ogenos yielded to the same method of interpretation.

Pherecydes' interest in Greek religion was not exclusively linguistic. He gave an aition for the *anakalypteria*; and there are other things in his narrative that seem to be related to observances of Greek cult. First, the battle of the gods, in which it is arranged that each side shall try to push the other into the surrounding water of Ogenos. Granted that Pherecydes is explaining how the Ophionidai came to be in Ogenos, he has chosen to do so in a way that differs from all the parallel myths, and one that suggests a ritual contest. Ritual battles are an institution found in many parts of the world, and in a number of places in ancient Greece.[1] There is one such battle that resembles Pherecydes' theomachy in its topographical setting and in its aim: the battle of the ephebi at Sparta.[2] It was said to have been established by Lycurgus. The ephebi who were to take part sacrificed to Achilles, and on the night before the battle they repaired to Phoibaion near Therapne, where they sacrificed a puppy to Enyalios. They were apparently already divided into two parties. Following the sacrifice they made a pair of gelded boars fight; the party whose boar was victorious was supposed to win the contest on the following day, and generally did. We are also told that they drew lots during this night, as a result of which one party became the party of Heracles, the other that of

[1] Cf. Lobeck, pp. 679 ff.; Frazer, *GB* ix. 173 ff.; Nilsson, *Gr. Feste*, pp. 402 ff.; Allen–Halliday on *H. Dem.* 265–7. Attempts to find the same significance in all of them have come to nothing.

[2] Described by Paus. 3. 14. 8–10, cf. 20. 2 and 8; Lucian, *Anacharsis* 38; cf. Cic. *Tusc.* 5. 77. Compared with Pherecydes by Eisler, *Weltenmantel*, p. 532 n. 8.

Lycurgus. The battle took place at Platanistas, an area thickly grown with tall planes and surrounded by a circular moat.[1] Two bridges led on to it, one bearing a statue of Heracles, the other one of Lycurgus. Shortly before midday the ephebi went into the artificial island by the appropriate bridges and a fierce free-for-all ensued. They punched, they kicked, they bit and scratched at each other's eyes; but their common objective was to force the enemy party into the moat. Once this was achieved they stopped.

The victor's crown

After defeating the Ophionidai, Chronos was given a crown or wreath. This is an unexpected detail in a mythical narrative about the gods, and again points to the usages of real life. There was at least one Greek festival in which the slaying of a mythical serpent was followed by the wearing of crowns: the Stepterion (or Septerion) celebrated every eight years at Delphi. A wooden booth was erected in the likeness of a royal palace. A procession carrying firebrands approached it in stealthy silence, led by a boy whose parents were living, set fire to it, overturned a table, and immediately fled through the doors of the temple. The ritual was associated with a procession of boys away to Tempe. There they made sacrifice and performed such actions as do people seeking to free themselves from *μηνίματα δαιμόνων οὓς ἀλάστορας καὶ παλαμναίους ὀνομάζουσιν* (Plut. *def. or.* 418 bc), and returned to Delphi with wreaths of the sacred bay, accompanied by a piper. The burning was understood to represent Apollo's defeat of the Python, and the journey to Tempe his eight-year servitude. It is clear that the Python did not appear, and the interpretation is only intelligible if this was the season of Apollo's return to Delphi after his winter absence. The bringing of the bay confirms this; Callimachus says expressly that it was brought *ἐπὴν τὰ τὠπόλλωνος ἶρ' ἀγινῆται* (fr. 194. 36). The date of Apollo's return was Bysios 7th, early in the spring (Plut. *qu. Graec.* 292 e). It would seem that the *theoroi* left for Tempe some time earlier: Apollo's flight

[1] On its location cf. Bölte, *RE* iiiA. 1369 f.

was not equated with their departure (as would be natural if they left after the burning), but with the dash through the doors of the temple; and his arrival was understood as his return from a journey undertaken eight years before. If it was possible to take the burning as the killing of Python, Apollo must already have been present. It was therefore the return of the *theoroi* that coincided with the burning; and that explains why the burning-festival was called Stepterion, for the boys brought wreaths of bay with them, and probably ended their journey by garlanding the shrine.

This springtime ritual has its place in the context of European Lent festivals, in which not only is the lighting of bonfires very frequent, but it is common for an effigy of straw or other material, variously named 'Death', 'Carnival', or 'Shrove Tuesday', to be 'killed' and ceremoniously buried, burned, or thrown into water, sometimes amid merriment and jollification, sometimes amid lamentation and proper funeral formalities.[1] 'Death' is usually disposed of by the children of the district; in some cases, having rid their hands of him, they turn and run away with all haste.[2] 'The carrying out of Death is generally followed by a ceremony, or at least accompanied by a profession, of bringing in Summer, Spring, or Life.'[3] This is represented by a young tree, suitably decorated, or by branches.[4] All these typical features, it will be noted, are found in the Delphic Stepterion. It cannot be doubted that the Python supposedly burned in the booth corresponds to the figure of Death destroyed in the modern festivals, while the bay of Apollo that the boys brought in corresponds to the tree or branches that herald spring.

The defeat of winter is a common theme in ritual battles;[5] and it is possible that the Spartan battle that so resembles

1 Frazer, *GB* iv. 220–65; x. 119–20. A particularly close parallel to the burning of the 'palace', and to the burning of straw booths in spring and autumn at nearby Tithorea (Paus. 10. 32. 13–17), comes from Rhenish Prussia, where a 'hut' or 'castle' of straw and brushwood was burned (Frazer, *GB* x. 115 f.).

2 Ibid. iv. 236, 239.

3 Ibid. 233.

4 Ibid. 246 ff.

5 Ibid. 254 ff. But Usener was wrong to generalize this explanation of mock battles (cf. above, p. 69 n. 1).

Pherecydes' theomachy once had such a significance. The ostensible issue, a conflict between Heracles and Lycurgus, makes no mythological sense and must be secondary. The two heroes have simply been adopted as mascots.

Apollo killed Python when he arrived at Delphi, and he then had to go away and be purified for eight years. Similarly when Cadmus arrived at Thebes, he killed a great serpent that guarded the spring of Ares, and had to go and serve Ares for eight years (Apollod. 3. 4. 1–2). Frazer (on Paus. 9. 10. 4) is probably justified in connecting the myth with the festival celebrated at Thebes every eight years, the Daphnaphoria, at which a procession brought a '*kopo*' to the precincts of Apollo Ismenios and Chalazios or Galaxios. The *kopo* was an olive-stock decorated with bay and assorted flowers, with 365 purple ribands attached to it, and at the top a bronze globe, from which other smaller globes hung. These were said to represent the sun, moon, and stars.[1] The lower end was wrapped up in a saffron-dyed cloth. A boy whose parents were alive led the procession. Next came his closest relative (presumably his brother, or if he had none, a cousin), carrying the *kopo*. Next came the *daphnaphoros*, a boy of good family and physique, with hair hanging free, dressed in a magnificent long robe, a golden crown and wreath of bay, and fancy shoes. In the wake of this trio came a chorus of girls with branches.[2] If Frazer's combination is accepted, the Daphnaphoria are parallel to the Stepterion: a bringing of a 'maybranch' to Apollo by children, at eight-year intervals, associated with the slaying of a mythical serpent and the wearing of crowns.

The tree and the robe

The robe of Chthonie, Goddess-within-the-earth, is 'the robe on the tree'. In terms of cult—and only in terms of cult—this

[1] Cf. ibid. ii. 63: 'It appears that a hoop wreathed with rowan and marsh marigold, and bearing suspended within it two balls, is still carried on May Day by villagers in some parts of Ireland. The balls, which are sometimes covered with gold and silver paper, are said to have originally represented the sun and moon.' Cf. the same page and p. 65 for the use of gilt eggshells.

[2] Proclus *ap.* Phot. *Bibl.* p. 321 a–b Bekker = Arethas on Clem. *Protr.* 2. 10 (i. 298 St.); Nilsson, *Gr. Feste*, pp. 164 f.

makes good sense, and takes its place in the same seasonal context as the rituals we have just been considering. Decoration of a tree with cloths and ribbons is a widespread European custom at the beginning of summer. In Russia, for example, there is or was a Whitsuntide custom of dressing up a young birch-tree in woman's clothes.[1] There is a story that Xerxes decorated a plane-tree with precious vestments and trinkets.[2] In Greece tree-trunks may have been fashioned into images of Dionysus and clothed accordingly.[3]

A cult-tree might be regarded as a goddess. We hear of a festival of Persephone in which a tree was formed into the shape of a girl, brought into the town, lamented for forty nights, and then burned.[4] This brings us close to the idea of a tree who was ἡ *Χθονία*. At Plataea there was a festival, the Daidala, at which an oak was cut down and made into the image of a girl, dressed as a bride, and escorted along in a wagon in a mock wedding. No bridegroom was in evidence. It was said that Zeus had once contrived the wooden bride to trick Hera out of a sulk; or that Hera was the bride.[5] Another tree-wedding of a chthonic or vegetation goddess took place in Sparta, perhaps close by Platanistas where the ephebi used to have their battle. It was the wedding of Helen, the Laconian counterpart of Kore. A large company of girls went to their Dromos beside the Eurotas to make garlands, one or all of which were hung on Helen's holy plane-tree. Oil was also poured on the tree.[6] The tree may have been near or even on Platanistas, marked by its name as 'where the planes are'; Pausanias mentions a shrine of Helen not far from it, beside the tomb of Alcman (3. 15. 3). Elsewhere (3. 19. 10) he records a *Ἑλένη δενδρῖτις* worshipped at Rhodes, so it is natural to suppose that at one stage the Spartan tree too was treated as the living body of the goddess.

1 Mannhardt, *Feld- und Waldkulte* i. 157 f.; Frazer, *GB* ii. 64.
2 Hdt. 7. 31, Ael. *VH* 2. 14.
3 On the so-called Lenaia vases (Nilsson, *Gr. Rel.* i³. 587 n. 8) his image is made on a pillar, but this looks as if it has taken the place of a tree.
4 Firm. Mat. *err.* 27. 1.
5 Paus. 9. 2. 7–3. 8, Eus. *PE* 3. 1. 6; Nilsson, *Gr. Feste*, pp. 50 ff.
6 All this is inference, but safe inference, from the eighteenth poem of Theocritus.

Finally, I may mention what Cadmus did after killing the serpent and serving out his eight years with Ares. He was installed as king of Thebes and given Harmonia to marry. He then gave her a robe and a necklace (cf. p. 53). We have seen in discussing the Stepterion that the octennial ritual comprised not only actions corresponding to those of Apollo on his first arrival, when he killed Python, but also actions corresponding to his return eight years later. By the same token, the wedding of Cadmus, as well as his killing of the serpent, may have been part of the aetiology of the octennial Theban Daphnaphoria. As the newly installed king he would correspond to the noble-born and noble-featured *daphnaphoros* with his splendid attire. If we ask where Harmonia was, the rituals described in the preceding paragraph will suggest that she was the mythical prototype of the *kopo*, and therefore that she was only a step away from her husband. The legendary robe and necklace would correspond to the saffron-dyed cloth and the other ornaments with which the *kopo* was decorated. We know that Harmonia ranked as a goddess (Hes. *Th.* 975). The fact that she could appear as a snake (Eur. *Bacch.* 1330 ff.) suggests a chthonic connection, and there was a Samothracian festival at which she was sought, like a seasonal deity.[1]

Pherecydes the syncretist

The bulk of our information about Greek local festivals comes from comparatively late authors. There must have been many that they failed to record, and no doubt some that existed in Pherecydes' time but had lapsed by theirs. So it would be rash to assume that he was familiar with a group of festivals in, say, Sparta, on the strength of the material presented above and the biographical tradition that links him with Sparta (pp. 3 f.). There may have been other places—perhaps his own island of Syros—where it was possible in the sixth century to observe a ritual battle like that of the Spartan ephebi, crowns worn after a simulated serpent-slaying, and the wedding of a tree-goddess,

[1] Sch. Eur. *Phoen.* 7, perhaps from Ephorus (70 F 120); cf. Lobeck, pp. 677 ff.

possibly one named Chthonie. That he knew such customs from somewhere is clear.

By combining them extensively with oriental cosmological and eschatological conceptions, which he may have inherited from his parents, he created a novel theology; and by taking the trouble to set it down in writing he enabled it to become known to later antiquity and (however imperfectly) to us. In spite of some similarities with the ideas of the Pythagoreans, it was destined to remain uninfluential, a literary curiosity; it failed to catch the Greeks' imagination. We might understand the reasons better if we had the book. But it may be suspected that Pherecydes' mistake was to give the Greeks myths unsupported by reasoning, just at the time when they were beginning to demand the opposite. It was not that the *theologos* now had to abandon the arena to the *physiologos*. Few Greek thinkers, after all, had a greater following than Pythagoras and Plato. But their poetic fancies had a coherent theoretical backing which, we may surmise, those of Pherecydes lacked. He was not, in the sense that we shall later attempt to define, a philosopher.

3

ANAXIMANDER AND ANAXIMENES

NOT long before or after Pherecydes, Anaximander of Miletus wrote a discourse of a rather different kind;[1] different enough, at any rate, to ensure him a place in all histories of early Greek philosophy, while many of them say nothing of Pherecydes. The separation goes back to Aristotle, and there can be no doubt that it was justified. But when we put the two Ionian cosmologists in contrasted categories, there is a danger that we may be obscuring what they have in common and giving false emphasis to the

[1] For the chronology cf. p. 1. If it is true that Anaximander recorded his own age as 64, he anticipated by many decades Simonides, who recorded his age in 476 (fr. 77 Diehl), Xenophanes who did so in 473 (DK 21 B 8), and Sophocles who did so in 441 (fr. 2 Diehl). In the fifth century we can understand this phenomenon as a consequence of the growth of an interest in the biography of older poets, and the regret that they did not give more information about themselves. Theagenes was the first writer we know of who concerned himself with the date of Homer, in the time of Cambyses. He came from Rhegium, and it was probably in Sicily that Simonides and Xenophanes were writing; there too, perhaps, that Pindar recorded his birth in the year of a Pythian festival (fr. 193). Anaximander falls outside this circle. But in view of the interest in numbers that his cosmology reveals, may he not have thought it of interest to say that he had just completed the ninth hebdomad of the ten described by Solon (fr. 19 Diehl), and wished to postpone no longer the written statement of his opinions? This might have suggested Apollodorus' statement that he died soon afterwards.

A slight problem is presented by Aelian's statement that Anaximander led the colony that settled at Apollonia. If he wrote his book after that, he would have called himself Anaximander of Apollonia; if before it, a position that called for an active man at the height of his abilities was entrusted to a man of over 64 who thought he might not have long to live. But perhaps he never went. Ps.-Scymnus gives the foundation-date of the colony as 610, which coincides with Apollodorus' date for Anaximander's birth. Aelian, finding the two events registered under one epoch, may have confusedly made a connection between them. Jacoby, *Apollodors Chronik*, p. 192, thinks that Ps.-Scymnus knew the connection but got the wrong foundation-date by reading off Anaximander's birth-year instead of his acme; this seems less likely. Pottery from Apollonia goes back to about 600 (J. Boardman, *The Greeks Overseas*, p. 255). Wilamowitz (*ap.* Jacoby) thought the story was invented to make a link between Anaximander and Diogenes of Apollonia; but it would have been much more fitting to make Anaximenes go. Diogenes no doubt did owe much to tradition brought directly from Miletus.

distance between them. For Aristotle himself the contrast was not absolute: Pherecydes was a θεολόγος, but of an intermediate sort who did not say everything in mythical language (above, p. 14). We can still see that Anaximander for his part was no rigorous rationalist. He allowed divinity an important place in his universe, major parts of his system had a visionary rather than a logical foundation, and he explained certain cosmic changes in terms of 'injustice', 'retribution', 'ordinance', language which Simplicius calls 'rather poetic' (DK 12 B 1) but which it is more meaningful to classify as theological. We are not in a position to judge how far his style differed from Pherecydes'. Diogenes says that he made a 'summary exposition' of his opinions (2. 2), but it is possible that a doxographer's analysis was mistaken for the original.[1] A certain pretension is suggested by the information that Empedocles, in 'cultivating a vain theatricality and adopting imposing costume', emulated Anaximander.[2] Another link with theology lies in the assertion that Anaximander was one of those whom Pythagoras heard (Apul. *Flor.* 15, Porph. *VP* 2). This comes from a disreputable source, Apollonius of Tyana; but it has been observed that Apollodorus' dating of Anaximander's 'age 64' to 547/6 puts his birth in or near the fortieth year before that of Pythagoras.[3] The more obvious and usual idea of Anaximander's influence was that he taught Anaximenes, who passed the tradition on to Diogenes of Apollonia and Anaxagoras. But we shall see that there were respects in which Pythagoras might seem to an ancient investigator to have been influenced by Anaximander as well as by Pherecydes.[4] And we shall see that Anaximander, like Pherecydes, was himself deeply influenced by the conceptions prevailing in

[1] Suggested by Kirk–Raven, p. 101.

[2] Diodorus of Ephesus (περὶ Ἀναξιμάνδρου γράφων) *ap.* D.L. 8. 70 = DK 12 A 8. Cf. below, p. 214 n. 1.

[3] Jacoby, p. 190; Kirk–Raven, p. 100. Anaximander's birth would come in 612/11 or 611/10, depending whether he was 64 at the beginning or end of 547/6; Hippolytus gives 610/9. Pythagoras' birth was put in 572/1.

[4] Cf. Burkert, *WW*, p. 271 n. 91: 'Wäre Anaximandros nicht unstreitig älter als Pythagoras, er wäre in einem Maße "pythagoreisch" wie kein anderer Denker (vollkommene Kreise, Rolle der Neunzahl, kosmische Dike).'

his time among the peoples of the east. The attribution to him of achievements like the production of a map of the world, and the invention of the *gnomon* (something in the nature of a sundial), must not be relied on as historically exact, but it cannot be without significance that such operations, which derive from Babylonian science, are firmly linked by tradition with him and his fellow Milesians.[1] These are external considerations and I mention them only as a preliminary; but mentioned they must be.

The Boundless

Anaximander derived the world from a source for which he used the term ἀρχή.[2] In later philosophy this came to be a technical term, but in Anaximander it must have had its simple non-technical sense of what has first place. If, like Pherecydes and Anaxagoras, he opened his work with a statement of the original state of things, he may well have started, 'The beginning of all things was . . .'[3] The primacy connoted by ἀρχή need not, however, be purely temporal; Terpander (?) addressed Zeus as πάντων ἀρχά, πάντων ἁγῆτορ, and Anaximander's Boundless 'steers everything' as well as being its origin.

ἀρχὴ πάντων (χρημάτων)—what? Hardly τὸ ἄπειρον without preparation. Greek writers do not present new concepts in such a way.[4] τὸ ἄπειρον is Aristotle's and Theophrastus' summary name for Anaximander's first principle, but Theophrastus also referred to it more vaguely as φύσις τις ἄπειρος or φύσις τις τοῦ ἀπείρου.[5] When I try to envisage something that Anaximander might have said, I find it easiest to do so on such lines as these:

τῶν ὑπὲρ γῆς καὶ τῶν κάτω γῆς ἐόντων πείρατα μὴ δίζεο, ἀλλὰ ἐς

[1] Cf. U. Hölscher, *Hermes* 81, 1953, 415 f. (= *Begriffswelt*, p. 172); Kahn, *Anaximander*, pp. 83 f., 91 f.; Burkert, 'Iranisches', pp. 102 f.; van der Waerden, *AA*, pp. 254 f.

[2] A 9, 11, + Simpl. *Phys.* 150. 23. This is certainly what Theophrastus meant, see Kahn, pp. 30–2.

[3] Cf. Burkert, 'Iranisches', p. 132 n. 100.

[4] Cf. Burkert, ibid., who suggests ἀρχὴ πάντων ἄπειρον ('das Neutrum des Adjektivs als Prädikat')· ἐκ δὲ τοῦ ἀπείρου . . . But 'something boundless' seems hardly more satisfactory.

[5] A 9, 11, cf. Cic. *Ac. pr.* 2. 118 (A 13) *infinitatem naturae* (read *infinitam naturam*?).

ἄπειρον ἱκνεῖται πάντῃ, καὶ ἐξ ἀπείρου ξυνέστη τὰ πρῶτα. αὕτη γὰρ ἀρχὴ πάντων ἐγένετο, αὐτὸ δὲ ἀρχὴν οὐκ ἔχει οὐδὲ πέρας, ἀλλὰ ἀΐδιόν ἐστι καὶ ἀγήρων, καὶ πάντα ἐν ἑωυτῷ ἔχει καὶ πάντα κυβερνᾷ.[1]

Of course such guesswork has little chance of absolute success, and, to quote Xenophanes, *εἰ . . . καὶ τὰ μάλιστα τύχοι τετελεσμένον εἰπών, αὐτὸς ὅμως οὐκ οἶδε*. But it is essential to make the effort to translate the linguistic and conceptual idiom of the Peripatos into that of sixth-century Miletus.

When Simplicius says, of Anaximander's *ἀρχή*, *λέγει δ' αὐτὴν μήτε ὕδωρ μήτε ἄλλο τι τῶν καλουμένων εἶναι στοιχείων, ἀλλ' ἑτέραν τινὰ φύσιν ἄπειρον*, he imports a false antithesis, and one that results from over-schematic classification of early thinkers. Theophrastus' version was less misleading: 'He does not say what the boundless is, whether air or water or earth or some other corporal entity.'[2] But it is still barking up the wrong tree. *τὸ ἄπειρον* is not a material,[3] or a denial of other materials, it is a denial of limits. In a cosmological context, it is a denial of the kind of limits that other people had talked about in cosmological contexts: the *πείρατα* of earth, sea, sky, and Tartarus, which were intimately linked with their 'sources'. Anaximander says that they have their sources in a boundless Beyond, inexhaustible and imperishable. The ancients were in error in treating him as a monist in the mould of Thales.

[1] Hes. *Th.* 736 ff. *ἔνθα δὲ γῆς δνοφερῆς καὶ ταρτάρου ἠερόεντος | πόντου τ' ἀτρυγέτοιο καὶ οὐρανοῦ ἀστερόεντος | ἑξείης πάντων πηγαὶ καὶ πείρατ' ἔασιν.* Xenoph. 21 B 28 *γαίης μὲν τόδε πεῖρας ἄνω . . . τὸ κάτω δ' ἐς ἄπειρον ἱκνεῖται.* For *ἀΐδιον . . . κυβερνᾷ* cf. A 11, 15, + Arist. *Phys.* 207a19 f.; Jaeger, *Theology*, pp. 29 f., 202; F. Solmsen, *Arch. f. Gesch. d. Phil.* 44, 1962, 109 ff.; Kirk–Raven, pp. 114–17. Hippolytus' *ἀΐδιον καὶ ἀγήρω(ν)*, coming from Theophrastus, is more likely to be correct than Aristotle's *ἀθάνατον καὶ ἀνώλεθρον*, for three reasons: Aristotle is not speaking of Anaximander alone but also of *οἱ πλεῖστοι τῶν φυσιολόγων*; he is in general an inaccurate quoter; and Anaximander, in echoing the epic *ἀθάνατος καὶ ἀγήραος*, might have preferred *ἀΐδιος* to *ἀθάνατος* for the non-personal subject while retaining the easier metaphor *ἀγήρων*. Melissus 30 B 4 says *ἀρχήν τε καὶ τέλος ἔχον οὐδὲν οὔτ' ἀΐδιον οὔτ' ἄπειρόν ἐστι*, cf. B 7. Diogenes B 7–8 couples *ἀΐδιον καὶ ἀθάνατον*, of the cosmic Air, and Eur. fr. 910 has *ἀθανάτου καθορῶν φύσεως κόσμον ἀγήρων*. See also Arist. *de cael.* 283b27 ff.

[2] D.L. 2. 1 (A 1) + Aet. 1. 3. 3 (A 14).

[3] Rightly W. Kraus, *Rh. Mus.* 93, 1950, 365, 378; Seligman, pp. 31, 54.

Worlds

It seemed obvious to Aristotle, and it may seem obvious to us, that the Boundless is full of matter in some form, even if Anaximander chose to say nothing about its nature, and called it by a name that has no material reference. This is to attribute to Anaximander, perhaps too hastily, a straightforwardly physical world-view. Pythagorean thought was capable of generating a world from a purely mathematical *ἄπειρον* (Arist. *Metaph.* 1091ᵃ15 ff., probably Philolaus), in other words, of concentrating exclusively upon the formal aspect of cosmogony and ignoring the material. Anaximander's thought certainly did not reach that degree of abstraction; but are we in a position to say that he was as sophisticated a materialist as they were formalists? The specific substances from which our world is composed appeared, according to him, when our world was formed. Had he a concept of matter apart from them? If so, why did he not attempt to explain it to his less enlightened audience, whether in terms of mixture, similarity, or negative characteristics?

What he did say about the Boundless was that it is everlasting and ageless, encompasses and steers all things,[1] and is in eternal motion.[2] In it, in consequence of the eternal motion, worlds come into being and pass away.[3] Ours is one of them; the existence of others is beyond the reach of observation, but it is unreasonable that our temporary world should be a unique creation of the Boundless. Whatever the processes involved, they must have produced numberless other worlds elsewhere and at different times.[4] The assumption of universal processes is a hallmark of the

[1] These are predicates suitable for a divinity, but Anaximander may not have said explicitly that the Boundless was divine. Aristotle in A 15 seems to infer it from the predicates.

[2] A 9, 11, 12, 17. Cf. Arist. *de an.* 405ᵃ29 ff. (Alcmeon A 12) *φησὶ γὰρ αὐτὴν (τὴν ψυχὴν) ἀθάνατον εἶναι διὰ τὸ ἐοικέναι τοῖς ἀθανάτοις· τοῦτο δ' ὑπάρχειν αὐτῇ ὡς ἀεὶ κινουμένῃ· κινεῖσθαι γὰρ καὶ τὰ θεῖα πάντα συνεχῶς ἀεί, σελήνην, ἥλιον, τοὺς ἀστέρας καὶ τὸν οὐρανὸν ὅλον.*

[3] As the frequent English use of 'world' for 'the earth' (and by extension sometimes for 'planet') occasionally causes confusion, let me say that in this chapter, at least, I shall use 'world' and 'cosmos' consistently to mean this 'set-up' comprising earth, sky, and celestial luminaries, or any similar set-up that may exist elsewhere.

[4] Cf. Metrodorus of Chios 70 A 6.

scientific approach. Anaximander did not, however, leave his worlds to appear and vanish at random. He said that they were equidistant,[1] and endured for a fixed period.[2] His Boundless had a fine sense of symmetry.

In speaking of Anaximander's worlds, Theophrastus used a curiously precise expression, *οἱ οὐρανοὶ καὶ οἱ ἐν αὐτοῖς κόσμοι*.[3] This seems to contain something of Anaximander's terminology. He probably did not speak of *κόσμοι*, for doxographers say that Pythagoras was the first to use *κόσμος* for 'world'.[4] But if, as would be likely enough, he used *οὐρανοί* for the shells enclosing the worlds from the Boundless, the words *καὶ οἱ ἐν αὐτοῖς κόσμοι* would be a very natural explanatory addition by Theophrastus.[5] These shells are fiery, to judge from the account of our world's emergence in A 10;[6] and they are gods.[7]

Time's ordinance

Simplicius quotes two sentences of Anaximander almost verbatim. In their original form they may have run: *ἐκ τῶν δὲ ἡ*

[1] Aet. 2. 1. 8 (A 17). Those who hold that Anaximander believed in only one world existing at any one time have to suppose, against Aetius, that Anaximander meant 'equidistant in time' (Zeller–Nestle i[6]. 311 n. 4), or that there was a confusion influenced by the equidistant luminary rings (Cornford, *CQ* 28, 1934, 12).

[2] Hipp. *Ref.* 1. 6. 1 (A 11), see below, pp. 82 f.

[3] Simplicius in A 9, Hippolytus in A 11 (as emended by Ritter; cf. Kahn, p. 34); distorted by [Plut.] in A 10, *τούς τε οὐρανοὺς . . . καὶ καθόλου τοὺς ἅπαντας ἀπείρους ὄντας κόσμους*. Cf. Aet. 1. 7. 12 (A 17) *ἀπεφήνατο τοὺς ἀπείρους οὐρανοὺς θεούς* ~ Cic. (ibid.) *natiuos . . . deos . . . innumerabilis esse mundos*.

[4] Burkert, *WW*, p. 68 n. 152: 'Die Pythagoras-Tradition hätte sich kaum durchsetzen können, wäre das Wort bei Anaximandros in diesem Sinn belegt gewesen, zumal aus Anaximandros Theophrast die erste Verwendung des Terminus *ἀρχή* registriert.'

[5] Cornford's idea that *οὐρανοί* might have been used of the rings of fire that we see as the fixed stars (*CQ* 28, 1934, 10; we do not know in fact that Anaximander assumed thousands of rings, a separate one for each star, cf. p. 86) is accepted by Guthrie, *HGP* i. 112, but seems to me fantastic. It might be used of the three levels, stars, moon, sun (Zeller–Nestle i[6]. 307; Kahn, p. 50), but then they were not *ἄπειροι*. If people would simply accept the well-attested fact that Anaximander believed in innumerable coexistent worlds there would be no problem, and no need to think with Burkert ('Iranisches', p. 103) of the use of plural 'heavens' in Semitic.

[6] Aet. 2. 11. 5, however, says that Anaximander's heaven was constituted *ἐκ θερμοῦ καὶ ψυχροῦ μίγματος*. (Achilles, *Isag. in Arat.* p. 35. 1 Maass, turns this into *γήινον* (so Maass, for *πτηνόν*), *πυρὸς μετέχοντα*.) Cf. p. 84.

[7] Aet., above, n. 3, clearly more accurate than Cicero's *mundos*.

γένεσίς ἐστι τοῖς ἐοῦσι, καὶ ἡ φθορὴ ἐς ταῦτα γίνεται κατὰ τὸ χρεών. διδοῖ γὰρ δίκην καὶ τίσιν ἀλλήλοισι τῆς ἀδικίης κατὰ τὴν Χρόνου τάξιν.[1] The things that perish into what they came from, paying the penalty to each other for their unrighteousness, are sometimes taken to be worlds, sometimes elements or opposites within our world.[2] Let us read the fragment in context and beside the parallel report in Hippolytus. (Hippolytus has excerpted his source clumsily; I have inserted a shorter version of the quotation, for the last sentence is a commentary on it. χρόνον, γενέσεως, οὐσίας, φθορᾶς, pick up χρόνου, γένεσις, οὖσι, φθοράν.)

SIMPLICIUS	HIPPOLYTUS
ἀρχήν τε καὶ στοιχεῖον εἴρηκε τῶν ὄντων τὸ ἄπειρον . . . λέγει δ' αὐτὴν . . . τινὰ φύσιν ἄπειρον, ἐξ ἧς ἅπαντας γίνεσθαι τοὺς οὐρανοὺς καὶ τοὺς ἐν αὐτοῖς κόσμους.	οὗτος ἀρχὴν ἔφη τῶν ὄντων φύσιν τινὰ τοῦ ἀπείρου, ἐξ ἧς γίνεσθαι τοὺς οὐρανοὺς καὶ τοὺς ἐν αὐτοῖς κόσμους (τὸν . . . κόσμον: corr. Ritter), ταύτην δ' ἀΐδιον εἶναι καὶ ἀγήρω· ἣν καὶ πάντας περιέχειν τοὺς κόσμους. ⟨ἐξ ὧν δὲ ἡ γένεσίς ἐστι τοῖς οὖσι, καὶ τὴν φθορὰν εἰς ταῦτα γίνεσθαι κατὰ τὴν τοῦ χρόνου τάξιν.⟩
ἐξ ὧν δὲ ἡ γένεσίς ἐστι τοῖς οὖσι, καὶ τὴν φθορὰν εἰς ταῦτα γίνεσθαι κατὰ τὸ χρεών· διδόναι γὰρ αὐτὰ δίκην καὶ τίσιν ἀλλήλοις τῆς ἀδικίας κατὰ τὴν τοῦ χρόνου τάξιν, ποιητικωτέροις οὕτως ὀνόμασιν αὐτὰ λέγων.	λέγει δὲ "χρόνον", ὡς ὡρισμένης τῆς γενέσεως καὶ τῆς οὐσίας καὶ τῆς φθορᾶς.

Two things may reasonably be affirmed. First, Anaximander was not thinking specifically of worlds (as entities) coming from the Boundless. He would not have called them τὰ ἐόντα. Nor was he thinking of a specific list of opposites. The statement is quite general: things that change into other things also change back again.[3] Second, Theophrastus quoted it with application to

[1] On the authenticity of the wording in the first sentence see Kahn, pp. 173–8, especially 177; Seligman, pp. 66–71.

[2] For the first view see, e.g., G. Vlastos, *CPh* 42, 1947, 170 ff.; H. Fränkel, *D. u. Ph.* pp. 304 f.; Seligman, p. 79; for the second, Kirk–Raven, pp. 118 f.; Kahn, pp. 167 f.; Guthrie, *HGP* i. 81.

[3] Cf. Epicharmus, fr. 245 (DK 23 B 9) συνεκρίθη καὶ διεκρίθη κἀπῆλθεν ὅθεν

world-systems.[1] Aristotle appears to assume the same connection, for Anaximander's formula seems to be the model for *Metaph.* 983^{b}8: ἐξ οὗ γὰρ ἔστιν ἅπαντα τὰ ὄντα, καὶ ἐξ οὗ γίγνεται πρώτου καὶ εἰς ὃ φθείρεται τελευταῖον . . . τοῦτο στοιχεῖον καὶ ταύτην ἀρχήν φασιν εἶναι τῶν ὄντων—that is, in Anaximander's case, the Boundless.

The connection was probably made by Anaximander himself. He must have treated the dissolution of worlds into the Boundless as a particular example of the universal principle enunciated in the fragment. The expression τὰ ἐόντα does not denote worlds, but it certainly includes them. So long as we do not limit its reference to worlds, we need not be troubled by the difficulties that have been felt over the plurals ἐξ ὧν, εἰς ταῦτα (contrast Aristotle's formulation), and over the idea of the Boundless being involved with the worlds in issues of unrighteousness and retribution.

The passing away of that which comes to be, whether it is a world or something within a world, is regulated by the decree of Time.[2] This must mean, as Hippolytus says, that each thing has a natural existence of fixed duration. Not only moons and seasons, leaves and lives, but all cosmic change, even the birth and death of worlds, has its appointed time. And as in Pherecydes, Time itself is a divine agent.

The formation of the present world

The formation of worlds is due to the eternal motion in the Boundless (A 9, 11, 12). The formation of our world is described by [Plut.] *Strom.* in A 10. The stages are as follows.

ἦλθεν πάλιν, γᾶ μὲν εἰς γᾶν, πνεῦμα δ' ἄνω, [Hp.] *nat. hom.* 3, Pl. *Phd.* 70 c ff.; J. B. McDiarmid, *Harv. Stud.* 61, 1953, 140 n. 48.

1 Kirk–Raven, p. 118. Hence also Aetius 1. 3. 3 (A 14).

2 F. Dirlmeier, *Rh. Mus.* 87, 1938, 376–82 = *Begriffswelt*, pp. 88–94, made a spirited but unsuccessful attempt to show that the words κατὰ τὴν τοῦ χρόνου τάξιν, although immediately followed by ποιητικωτέροις οὕτως ὀνόμασιν αὐτὰ λέγων, did not belong to Anaximander but reflected Peripatetic interpretation. See McDiarmid, op. cit., pp. 141 f.; Kirk–Raven, pp. 117, 118; Kahn, pp. 171 f. Time as a judge appears in Solon 24. 3 Diehl, Pind. *Ol.* 10. 53, Soph. *OT* 1213 f.; cf. the apophthegm of Aeschylus recorded in Ath. 347 e–f: ἡττηθεὶς ἀδίκως ποτέ . . . ἔφη Χρόνῳ τὰς τραγῳδίας ἀνατιθέναι, εἰδὼς ὅτι κομιεῖται τὴν προσήκουσαν τιμήν.

1. φησὶ δὲ τὸ ('fort. τι' Diels, *Doxogr.* 579) ἐκ τοῦ ἀιδίου γόνιμον θερμοῦ τε καὶ ψυχροῦ . . . ἀποκριθῆναι. From the Eternal, which here seems to take the place of the eternal Boundless, something capable of generating the contrasted powers of heat and cold became marked off. [Plutarch], i.e. Theophrastus, must have had a special reason for not saying simply τὰ ἐναντία, or θερμόν τε καὶ ψυχρόν, but γόνιμον θερμοῦ τε καὶ ψυχροῦ. The first thing to appear was a unit, not a pair; a generative unit. γόνιμον is probably Theophrastus' word, not Anaximander's, and we must not read too much into it (Kirk–Raven, p. 132); it is possible, however, that Anaximander spoke of a σπέρμα, or of an egg-like formation. ἀποκρίνεσθαι may have been his own word. It says nothing about the mechanics of the event: the unit simply became marked off.

2. καί τινα ἐκ τούτου φλογὸς σφαῖραν περιφυῆναι τῷ περὶ τὴν γῆν ἀέρι, ὡς τῷ δένδρῳ φλοιόν. From the unit, a sphere of flame grew, enclosing the space round the earth, like bark round a tree. The flame and the space enclosed by it are the θερμὸν καὶ ψυχρόν of Theophrastus. Anaximander spoke neither of these nor of 'the opposites'.[1] There is no reason to think that 'opposites' as such played a part in his thought.

Earth materialized in the centre, covered by the sea; all around was a spacious region which Theophrastus refers to as the ἀήρ (anachronistically? cf. p. 60); and it was enclosed by a shell of fire. The process was one of growth. φλοιός was a more natural word to think of than 'bark' would be for us, because it was a less specific word (see Guthrie, *HGP* i. 91). But tree-bark is specified here, and we must ask why. It seems to have the following possible points of relevance: it is an example of the spontaneous formation of a protective rind at the outer limits of an organism; the ability of trees to grow rings inside their trunks, as it were

[1] It is Aristotle who, in his own context, makes them 'the opposites' (*Phys.* 187^{a}20; Simpl. *Phys.* 24. 24; both in A 9). He must first have translated them into 'hot and cold'. The same process of double generalization is seen in 188^{a}19 (cf. *Metaph.* 986^{b}34), πάντες δὲ τἀναντία ἀρχὰς ποιοῦσιν . . . καὶ γὰρ Παρμενίδης θερμὸν καὶ ψυχρὸν ἀρχὰς ποιεῖ, ταῦτα δὲ προσαγορεύει πῦρ καὶ γῆν. Again in Anaximenes A 7 § 3 it is only an interpretation by Theophrastus that makes hot and cold τὰ κυριώτατα τῆς γενέσεως.

inwards from the bark, may have seemed to Anaximander a parallel for the development of luminary rings from the outer fire (below); and if we may discount the word *σφαῖρα*, a cylindrical cosmos would suit the drum-like shape of his earth.[1]

3. *ἥστινος ἀπορραγείσης καὶ εἴς τινας ἀποκλεισθείσης κύκλους ὑποστῆναι τὸν ἥλιον καὶ τὴν σελήνην καὶ τοὺς ἀστέρας*. I have been assuming that the rings do not use up all the outer fire, but leave an unbroken envelope of flame at the outer extremity of the cosmos. It would hardly be necessary to introduce the envelope if it was not going to be a permanent feature; it was not an obvious way of getting rings.

The arrangement of the rings. The earth

The sun and moon are explained as rings of fire somewhat like carriage-wheels, each enclosed in *ἀήρ* except for an orifice (*στόμιον*, *ἐκπνοή*) through which the fire shows, as the fire in a crucible shows through the holes provided for the insertion of bellows.[2] Eclipses and the phases of the moon are caused by the partial or total closing of these apertures, resulting from the twisting of the tubes of *ἀήρ*. The rings lie aslant (Aet. 2. 25. 1); this was probably the basis for Pliny's statement that Anaximander discovered the obliquity of the ecliptic (*NH* 2. 31 = A5), and the same interpretation is assumed by a number of modern writers. Without qualification, however, 'lying aslant' naturally refers to the more obvious fact that the circles lie oblique to the plane of the earth's surface. The other interpretation is only possible on the assumption that Anaximander himself was confused. For the sun's circle in his system does not correspond to the ecliptic but to the path of its daily revolution. The seasonal changes in its altitude cannot be accounted for by the tilting of this ring: it must rise and sink as a whole, while its angle of

[1] W. A. Heidel, *Proc. Amer. Acad. of Arts* 48, 1913, 686. But the analogy with bark here breaks down, for the fire surely seals off the top and bottom of the cosmos as well as the sides. Leucippus combined a spherical world with a drum-shaped earth, A 22, 26.

[2] *ὥσπερ διὰ πρηστῆρος αὐλοῦ* Aet. 2. 20. 1, 25. 1 (A 21–2), cf. Hipp. 1. 6. 4 (A 11). For the bellows-holes cf. my note on Hes. *Th.* 863.

inclination remains the same. The ecliptic is a more sophisticated abstraction, which was already known to the Babylonians (below, p. 109), but has no counterpart in Anaximander's system.[1]

The stars are similarly accounted for by rings of fire. Hippolytus speaks of rings in the plural, and certainly a single ring would hardly suffice; but there need not have been a separate one for each of the several thousand stars that are visible in a clear sky. A few broad bands would do (see Kahn, p. 89). There is no good evidence that Anaximander made separate provision for the planets (see Kahn, p. 61); he may have been content with the popular threefold division into sun, moon, and stars,[2] and his rings seem all to have been accommodated at one of three distances. The sun is equal in size to the earth, and its ring is 27 times the size (diameter or circumference) of the earth; the moon is nearer, its ring being 18 times the size of the earth; the stars nearer still, presumably in rings of size 9.[3]

[1] According to Eudemus, its obliquity was discovered by Oinopides (41 A 7). Burkert, *WW*, p. 285 n. 42, and Guthrie, *HGP* ii. 360, interpret this to mean that Oinopides first *measured* the obliquity.

[2] *Il.* 18. 484 ff., Alcm. 5 fr. 2 ii. 25 ff.?, Parm. B 11, Anaxagoras B 12, etc. Cf. pp. 237 f.

[3] This series 27:18:9 represents the usual reconstruction, based on A 11, 18, 21, 22. Hippolytus and Aet. 2. 21. 1 agree on the figure 27, which is thereby guaranteed as what Theophrastus reported; but Aet. 2. 20. 1 + 25. 1 gives 28 for the sun and 19 for the moon. The figures 18 and 9 are conjectural. Attempts have been made to reconcile the discrepancies by supposing that 27 and 28 represent an inner and outer measurement of the solar ring. But this involves the assumption that the figure given is for the ring's radius (cf. D. O'Brien, *CQ* 61, 1967, 423 ff.), which *κύκλος ὀκτωκαιεικοσαπλασίων τῆς γῆς* really cannot mean. Besides, it is unlikely that Anaximander or Theophrastus would trouble to give two figures, or that Aetius would copy one in one place and the other shortly afterwards, in neither case specifying the inside or outside of the ring. Kahn, p. 62, supposes that the figure 28 is corrupt. I believe that this is correct, but we then have to explain the coincidence that the figure 19 for the moon is also too great by one. It can be explained, as follows. In 2. 20 Aetius gives the opinions of philosophers on the nature of the sun, and in 2. 25 opinions on the nature of the moon. The description of Anaximander's rings, with the comparison to a carriage-wheel, is duplicated in the two sections. In the source, clearly, the material was not distributed under subject-headings in this way. There was one account which dealt with sun, moon, and stars together, and the aberrant figures 28 and 19 stood close together in that context. Suppose that the original version ran *εἶναι δὲ τὸν τοῦ ἡλίου κύκλον ἑπτακαιεικοσαπλασίονα τῆς γῆς, τὸν δὲ τῆς σελήνης ὀκτωκαιδεκεπλασίονα, τοὺς δὲ τῶν ἄστρων ἐννεαπλασίονας*. Suppose that a scribe wrote *ἐννεα-* instead of *ὀκτω-καιδεκαπλασίονα*, his eye running on to *ἐννεαπλασίονας*. *οκτω* was

The earth is drum-shaped, its depth a third of its diameter. It is possible that its upper and lower faces are concave, and that there are antipodes inhabiting the opposite side from ourselves (see Kahn, pp. 55 f., 84 f.). At any rate it is unsupported below, and anyone who was on the far side would see the sun, moon, and stars as we do, their day being our night.[1]

Oriental elements in Anaximander's world-model

If it is true that Anaximander described the earth's surface as concave, he would seem to be modernizing a mythical scheme of geography according to which the earth was surrounded by a ring of mountains. This is not a Greek scheme: it is oriental. The Babylonian map which shows seven great mountains arranged round the earth, beyond the circle of the Bitter River, has already been mentioned (p. 50), and we recall that Anaximander himself was familiar with the idea of making such a map (cf. pp. 19, 78). Diodorus (2. 31. 7) knows not only that the Chaldaeans have the most individual notions about the earth, saying that it is hollow like a bowl, but also that they are not lacking in plausible arguments to support their belief.[2]

In Iranian cosmology, besides the idea of a polar mountain (below, p. 106), we find the idea that the earth is surrounded by Mt. Elbrus; the Caucasian mountain is extended sideways into a complete ring, and upwards to connect with the sky. There are special holes for the sun to pass through, 180 in the east and the same number in the west.[3] The idea of a surrounding mountain is also found in Egypt, and here it has its most natural origin in terms of real geography.[4]

then written in the margin as a correction, but mistakenly substituted for ἑπτα- in ἑπτακαιεικοσαπλασίονα.

[1] Simplicius *in cael.* 532. 13 says that Anaximander held the earth to be supported by aer as well as by its central position. But Aristotle not only omits him from the list of those who used aer in this way (*de cael.* 294^{b}13) (Kahn, p. 55), he explicitly distinguishes him from them (295^{b}10 ff.).

[2] For other Babylonian evidence cf. B. Meissner, *Babylonien und Assyrien*, 1925, ii. 107–12.

[3] *Bundahišn* 5. 3 ff., 12. 1 ff.

[4] H. Schäfer, *Ägyptische und heutige Kunst, und Weltgebäude der alten Ägypter. Zwei Aufsätze*, 1928, pp. 88 f.; J. A. Wilson in H. Frankfort and others, *Before Philosophy*, pp. 49, 54. Cf. Eisler, *Weltenmantel*, pp. 622 ff.

Now let us look up from the earth. Before Anaximander, the sun and the other heavenly bodies had been treated as detached, self-contained entities moving free from earth to heaven and back again. Anaximander attaches them to invisible wheels running right round the earth. He has become aware of a luminary's orbit as a real thing in itself, controlling the luminary and making its regular revolution a physical necessity.

Ezekiel the priest, the son of Buzi, has described two grandiose visions in which he saw in the sky the throne of God supported by four Cherubim. They ran and returned continually, up from the earth and down upon it; their appearance was as if burning coals or torches were darting among them. As for the likeness of their faces, each had the face of a man and the face of a lion on the right side, and the face of an ox and the face of an eagle on the left side. There have been many proposals to relate these creatures to points on the zodiac.[1] If you say the man is Aquarius, you come to Taurus three signs further on, and Leo three signs further still; then, looking for an eagle in the tenth place, you encounter a scorpion. It does not quite work; but it is a tempting line of approach. Granted that a prophet's vision of God is not the same thing as a session in a planetarium, Ezekiel's account does look as if it is related in some way to an astronomical model. There are many obscurities of detail, but the pattern is visible.

Each cherub was attached to a wheel which revolved with a rushing sound. The wheels were apparently concentric, all alike, glinting like topaz. They were so high that they were dreadful, and full of eyes round about the four cherubs. When the cherubs went up from the earth the wheels went up. Wherever they went, the wheels went, for their spirit was in the wheels. There was fire between the wheels.[2]

[1] See F. Dornseiff, *Antike und alter Orient*, p. 372.

[2] Ezek. 1 : 5–24, 3 : 13, 10 : 8–22. Eisler, *Weltenmantel*, p. 202 n. 1 (q.v., with Nachtrag, p. 761) adduced both this and the zodiacal wheel of the mythical Manichaean cosmology (above, p. 44; cf. also the serpent on p. 41). The more abstract wheels that appear in India—the wheel of the year (*Ṛgv.* 1. 164. 11, *Atharvav.* 10. 8. 4), the wheels of Time's chariot, identified with all beings (ibid.

We are told where and when Ezekiel saw these things: near Babylon, in 593 and 592 B.C. There, in Anaximander's youth, the invisible machinery of heaven revealed itself to an astonished priest. Within half a century the Milesian saw it too; and we may imagine that it struck him with much the same awe.

We are not in a position to say that the wheel-theory was specifically Babylonian, and we had better fall back on 'oriental'. From another point of view Anaximander's astronomy presents a distinctly Iranian appearance. He placed the stars nearest the earth, then the moon, then the sun. He is almost the only Greek known to us who arranged the heavenly bodies in that order;[1] but it is the standard Persian conception.[2] In the Avesta, stars, moon, sun, and the Beginningless Lights are regularly named as a series. In at least three places it is certain that that represents the order from earth outwards. One is a fragment of the *Dāmdāt Nask* that has already been quoted in another context.[3] A second is a fragment preserved in the Pahlavi *Dēnkart* (7. 2. 3 West, *SBE* xlvii):

As it is said in revelation: . . . from the light which is endless it (the divine glory) fled on, on to that of the sun; from that of the sun, it fled on, on to the moon; from that of the moon it fled on, on to those stars; from those stars it fled on, on to the fire which was in the house of Zôis (the grandfather of Zoroaster, who was about to be born).[4]

The third is *Yašt* 12. 9–37, where the spirit of righteousness Rašnav is invoked:

even if, o holy Rašnav, you are in the region of Arəzahī . . . (there follows a long series of possible places on earth where he may be,

19. 53. 1, cf. *Mahābh.* xiv. 1160, 1243–4)—may reflect an older, non-astronomical idea, like περιτελλόμενοι ἐνιαυτοί.

1 Aet. 2. 15. 6 ascribes the same view to Metrodorus of Chios and Crates. The usual order was moon, sun, stars, though Leucippus (A 1 § 33) preferred moon, stars, sun; Empedocles (A 50) put the sun at the edge of the cosmos, and Parmenides (A 40 a) is said to have put only Venus above it. See also p. 238, and D. O'Brien, *JHS* 88, 1968, 117 n. 24.

2 First noted by Eisler, *Weltenmantel*, p. 90 n. 3; in most detail Burkert, 'Iranisches', pp. 103 f., 106 ff., cf. id. *WW*, p. 288 n. 64.

3 Above, p. 67; overlooked by Burkert.

4 Quoted by Burkert, who however overlooked the introductory words 'As it is said in revelation': this is a formula meaning 'As it is said in the Avesta'.

ending with the summit of Mt. Haraitī, about which 'stars, moon and sun circle'); even if, o holy Rašnav, you are in the Mazdāh-created star Vanant . . . (there follows a series of other stars); even if, o holy Rašnav, you are there in the moon, where the ox has its origin, we invoke, we seek to propitiate the powerful Rašnav . . . even if, o holy Rašnav, you are in the swift-horsed sun, we invoke (etc.) . . . even if, o holy Rašnav, you are in the beginningless self-created lights, we invoke (etc.) . . . even if, o holy Rašnav, you are in the best existence of the faithful, the bright place of every delight, we invoke (etc.) . . . even if, o holy Rašnav, you are in the bright house of praise, we invoke (etc.).[1]

In the Pahlavi books the journey of the soul after death to the stars, moon, sun, and Beginningless Lights, as in the *Dāmdāt Nask*, is a fixed doctrine. As in Anaximander, the distances between each are equal; in one place it is specified as 34,000 parasangs.[2] In the Persian texts, both Avestan and Pahlavi, the scheme is particularly associated with eschatological theory, and this is probably its original context. The order stars, moon, sun is not derived from any scientific considerations—if speeds of revolution are compared, the moon cannot be intermediate between stars and sun—but on a religious conception of gradations of fiery purity as one ascends from earth to heaven. From this point of view the smallness and relative faintness of the stars is a reason for placing them nearest to the earth instead of furthest from it as common sense might argue. Burkert is probably right to assume a shamanistic background for the system.[3]

[1] Burkert quotes this and other Avestan passages (*Yasna* 1. 16, 22. 18, 71. 9; *Yašt* 13. 57; *Gāh* 3. 6, where 'the Beginningless Lights' are followed by 'and the goodly dwelling-place of the blessed'; *Vidēvdāt* 11, where the series fire, water, earth, cow, plant, man, woman is continued with stars, moon, sun, Beginningless Lights). We may further add *Vidēvdāt* 7. 52: '"Stracks gehe weiter zum Paradies" (so) werden ihn, o Zaraθuštra, willkommen heißen die Sterne und der Mond und die Sonne' (trans. F. Wolff, *Avesta*, 1910).

[2] *Rivāyat* on *Dātastān-i-Dēnīk* in Zaehner, *Zurvan*, p. 365. In *Bundahišn* 12. 1 the growing mountain Elbrus reaches each station after 200 years. These and other passages are set out by Burkert.

[3] 'Iranisches', pp. 110 f. He refers to the gates of the sun in *P. Mag.* 4. 575 ff., 620 ff. The sun is the 'gate of going-out of the soul' in the *Kephalaia*, p. 158. 31. So in the *Maitri Upan.* 6. 30, one reaches the world of Brahmā by breaking through the door of the sun. Cf. above, pp. 63 f., 66, and Holmberg, *Der Baum des Lebens*, p. 136. It is possible that such ideas made it easier for Anaximander to

He has further pointed out that the 'Beginningless Lights', which constitute the heavenly paradise and the throne of Ohrmazd, correspond, at least in position, to Anaximander's Boundless. The adjective translated 'beginningless', *anaγra-*, means 'having no *aγra*': *aγra* is 'the first, highest, the culmination, beginning', corresponding quite closely to Greek ἀρχή. Anaximander said that his Boundless was the ἀρχή of all things, and he might well have said at the same time that it had itself no ἀρχή. It is not unharmonious that the other epithet applied to the Beginningless Lights is *χ^vaδāta-*, 'self-created' or 'autonomous'.

The order stars–moon–sun is not Babylonian;[1] the Babylonians put the stars on the furthest heaven that we can see.[2] But it is interesting that this heaven, which is made of jasper, is the lowest of three, there being two higher ones that we cannot see;[3] and that in a more scientific account it is divided into three zones, that of Anu, a band about 33° wide lying round the celestial equator, that of Enlil in the northern sky, and that of Ea in the southern.[4] This may be relevant to Anaximander's division of the stellar sphere into rings, and the combination of Babylonian and Persian conceptions may help to account for the most awkward feature of his system, stellar rings wrapped in mist that do not obstruct our view of the moon and sun beyond.

The dimensions of his cosmos perhaps betray another Babylonian element. Commentators speak in general terms of the sacred significance of the numbers three and nine that play such an evident role in his system. But there may be something more to it. If the stars' wheels are nine times the size of the earth, the

arrive at the thought that what we see as the sun, moon, and stars are in fact holes through which we get glimpses of a vaster brilliance (cf. Burkert, p. 126). The Yakuts regard the stars as holes through which the light of heaven shines (Holmberg, p. 22).

1 As Hölscher suggests, *Hermes* 81, 1953, 415 (= *Begriffswelt*, p. 172); refuted by Burkert, p. 103 n. 20.

2 It has been suggested that they assumed different levels for each of the planets, with the moon lowest, as early as the Old Babylonian period: O. Neugebauer, *The Exact Sciences in Antiquity*², p. 100.

3 A. Jeremias, *Handbuch d. altorient. Geisteskultur*², 1929, pp. 137 f.

4 Van der Waerden, *JNES* 8, 1949, 16 f.; id. *AA*, p. 69. The zones are so divided that the sun passes from one zone to the next at equal intervals of time.

moon's wheel eighteen, and the sun's twenty-seven, the outer οὐρανός will be thirty-six, whether diameters or circumferences are being compared. The Egyptians from early times selected 36 stars from the circumference of the sky (we call them decans, δεκανοί: ten degrees), so that their risings should correspond to the ten-day 'weeks' into which they divided their months. Each decan was presided over by a god, who enjoyed formidable power for the ten days of his validity, so that the 36 decans came to be considered more and more as powers of fate.[1] The Babylonians too had a division of the sky and the year under 36 stars, though it was not the same as the Egyptian until the systems were assimilated in the Hellenistic period. Originally, the three stars rising each month were assigned to the three regions Elam, Akkad, and Amurru. Lists are extant giving the twelve stars of Elam, the twelve stars of Akkad, and the twelve stars of Amurru. It may be guessed that they were the stars whose appearance in each month was of special portentous significance for the respective countries. There was also another system in which the three stars of each month belonged to the three zones of Anu, Enlil, and Ea, being arranged according to their northern or southern positions in the sky.[2] It seems possible that there is some connection between these apportionments and Anaximander's formula 'heaven = 36'. Given the Egyptian idea that each of the 36 stars was capable of holding in its sway not a single country but the whole earth, it might be argued that its part of the sky must be commensurate with the earth, and the whole circumference of heaven 36 times greater.

However Anaximander arrived at his figures, the fact that he even attempted to measure the dimensions of the sky places him far in advance of his Greek predecessors. Hesiod had said it was equal to the earth, and indicated its height by saying that an anvil would take nine days to fall (*Th.* 126, 722 f.). Only the Babylonians, so far as is known, had a precise figure for its

[1] Detailed treatment in W. Gundel, *Dekane und Dekansternbilder*, 1936 (Stud. Bibl. Warburg, 19), pp. 16 ff., 226 ff.; O. Neugebauer and R. A. Parker, *Egyptian Astronomical Texts* i, 1960; van der Waerden, *AA*, pp. 17–28.

[2] Van der Waerden, art. cit. 13, cf. id. *AA*, pp. 56 ff.

circumference: 360 × 1,800 *bêru*, a *bêru* being a double-hour's journey of about 6⅔ miles.[1]

Oriental elements in the cosmogony

Anaximander's cosmos comes into being out of the eternal and unaging Boundless, and at the end, after a life of fixed duration, vanishes back into it, according to the decree of Time. So in the Iranian cosmogony the world is created by the god of the Beginningless Lights, out of that part of his essence which *is* light. It is created with the blessing of Time without limit, 'for he is unaging and deathless', and concurrently 'Time for long autonomous' is created out of Time without limit. A duration of 12,000 years is appointed, after which this world of change comes to an end, and all is made perfect and unchanging. For details see p. 30.

In Indian philosophy too, at least as early as Anaximander, we meet the idea that worlds come out of the infinite and perish back into it.

'What is the goal of this world?' said (Śīlaka Śalavatya). 'Space', said (Pravāhana); 'for all these contingent beings originate from space, and to space do they return. For space is greater (and more ancient) than they: space is the final goal. This is the supremely desirable (manifestation of) the syllable Oṁ: (and) it is infinite.'
(*Chāndogya Upanishad* 1. 9. 1–2, trans. Zaehner, *Hindu Scriptures*, p. 84)

In the beginning this (world) was Brahman, the One unbounded,—unbounded to the east, unbounded to the south, unbounded to the west, unbounded to the north, (unbounded) above and below, unbounded in every direction. East and west, north and south, do not enter into his (mode of) conception, nor yet do across, above and below.

Inconceivable is this All-Highest Self, uncircumscribed, unborn, beyond all logic and discursive thought, unthinkable! Space is his

[1] Van der Waerden, *AA*, p. 76. The figure is actually for the circumference at about 36° north of the equator, but probably A. Kopff, *Zeitschr. f. Assyriol.* 28, 1914, 361, is right in thinking that no larger figure was assumed for the equatorial circumference. On the other hand, we need not suppose that they consciously thought of a cylindrical heaven.

self; and He, the One, alone remains awake when all things fall to ruin. Out of this space he causes all that consists of thought alone to awaken. By this He thinks (into existence) this (material world) and into Him it disappears.

(*Maitri Upanishad* 6. 17, trans. Zaehner, *Hindu Scriptures*, p. 231)

For a thousand ages lasts
  One day of Brahmā,
And for a thousand ages one such night:
This knowing, men will know (what is meant by) day and night.

At the day's dawning all things manifest
Spring forth from the Unmanifest;
And then at nightfall they dissolve again
In (that same mystery) surnamed 'Unmanifest'.

(*Bhagavad-Gītā* 8. 17–18, trans. Zaehner, *Hindu Scriptures*, p. 284)

In the late *Vishṇu Purāṇa* (*c.* A.D. 500?) there is even a doctrine of infinite worlds, forming and dissolving periodically in a boundless continuum without form or colour. They proceed from Vishṇu considered as Time, and at the end he swallows them up again. At the formation of a world the five elements (cf. p. 40) combine and form an egg, which expands like a bubble in water, and Vishṇu becoming Brahman makes it his home. His life as Brahman, and the life of that world, is a hundred Brahman-years, each day of which is equivalent to a thousand *mahāyugas*. A *mahāyuga* is the old period of twelve thousand solar years.[1] The egg of the nascent world is surrounded by spheres of water, air, fire, sky-stuff, as well as of Egotism, Intelligence, and the Unmanifest.[2] Here, at any rate, some influence from Greek (Stoic) philosophy is probable;[3] there was certainly Greek influence in Indian astronomy by this period. But the doctrine of innumer-

[1] Cf. p. 67 n. 2. Originally the *mahāyuga* represented the whole duration of a world to its dissolution. Though its length is the same as that of the non-recurrent Iranian Long-autonomous Time, it is differently divided up. Instead of being 12 × 1,000 or 4 × 3,000 years, it is made up of four *yugas*, or world ages, of decreasing length, 4,000, 3,000, 2,000, and 1,000 years, the total made up to 12,000 by the artificial expedient of augmenting each *yuga* by a 'dawn' and a 'dusk' of one-tenth of its length, thus 400 + 4,000 + 400, 300 + 3,000 + 300, and so on.

[2] *V.P.* i. 2–3 + ii. 7. The standard translation is by H. H. Wilson, 2nd ed., 1864.

[3] Cf. D.L. 7. 137, *SVF* ii. 180.

able worlds is not Stoic, and was not dominant in Greek thought at the time of Greek influence on India (though upheld by Epicurus). Like the extravagant figure for the duration of the world, it is fully explicable from the generous non-empiricism of oriental speculation. We know that the Time-god and the five elements go back to older Indian doctrines with cognates that came to Greece in Anaximander's time. The possibility is not to be excluded that the same is true of the idea of many worlds.[1]

The process by which Anaximander's cosmos is initiated can again be compared with the Iranian accounts.[2] The appearance of what Theophrastus described as the *γόνιμον θερμοῦ τε καὶ ψυχροῦ*, from which sprang a shell of flame that is our heaven, resembles Ohrmazd's creation 'in the form of a fire, bright, white, round, and visible from afar', which begins 'in a moist state like semen', and then forms the shining egg of heaven, contiguous with the Beginningless Lights; the things inside are created last.

It was suggested above that Anaximander's bark-simile may have had a connection with the idea of rings breaking away inwards from the heaven. It would be reasonable to imagine that the original unit was something smaller than the present cosmos, and that it grew like a tree-trunk, leaving rings behind it. Aristotle perhaps has Anaximander in mind (so Kahn, pp. 66 f.) in *Meteor*. 355^{a}21 ff.: *τὸ δ' αὐτὸ συμβαίνει καὶ τούτοις ἄλογον καὶ τοῖς φάσκουσι τὸ πρῶτον ὑγρᾶς οὔσης καὶ τῆς γῆς καὶ τοῦ κόσμου τοῦ περὶ τὴν γῆν ὑπὸ τοῦ ἡλίου θερμαινομένου ἀέρα γενέσθαι καὶ τὸν ὅλον οὐρανὸν αὐξηθῆναι, καὶ τοῦτον (τὸν ἀέρα) πνεύματά τε παρέχεσθαι καὶ τὰς τροπὰς αὐτοῦ (τοῦ ἡλίου) ποιεῖν*. Alexander on an earlier passage of the *Meteorologica* (353^{b}5 ff.), where the same doctrine is mentioned, but without the initial expansion of the heaven, says that Theophrastus recorded it from Anaximander (= A 27) and Diogenes (64 A 9), and there is other evidence that it agrees with Anaximander's view

[1] The Indian doctrine is mentioned by Seligman, p. 129, as an independent parallel to Anaximander.

[2] Cf. Burkert, 'Iranisches', pp. 124–6.

of the origin of the sea and of winds (Hippolytus in A 11, Aetius in A 24, 27). Anaximander may have envisaged the growth of the cosmos, then, as a three-stage process, first the stellar wheels being deposited by the fiery shell as the rising aer enlarged it, then the moon's wheel, then the sun's. We can compare an Iranian account recorded by Plutarch (*Is. Os.* 370 a). After creating the world egg, Oromazes 'enlarged himself three times, removing himself as far from the sun as the sun is from the earth, and arrayed the heaven with stars'. 'One is inclined to connect the god's threefold growing with the three heavenly regions of Iranian cosmology; that Plutarch puts the sun in the middle between heaven and earth would then have to be secondary, perhaps Hellenistic adaptation.'[1]

Anaximander the debtor

In Chapter 2 it was shown that the Iranian cosmogony, although mainly known from late sources, is of early origin; that it has significant affinities with the cosmogonies of other peoples of the ancient east; and that it and other Iranian traditions have to be adduced in order to explain much of Pherecydes. Now we find that it is no less relevant to Anaximander. And whereas before, although it was the Iranian version that seemed closest to the Greek, we could not feel sure that the things involved were purely Iranian, here we seem to be on firmer ground. The wheels and their measurements may perhaps show Babylonian inspiration. But the order of the heavenly bodies is peculiar to the Persians among the peoples who come into question. They cannot have got it from the Greeks, since Anaximander is almost the only Greek who believed in it, and it is against all reason that a philosopher who was hardly read by his own people should have supplied the standard world-picture to the Persians. Besides, his cosmology is in several respects more sophisticated than theirs; and it was remarked that the eschatological context in which they

[1] Burkert, 'Iranisches', p. 125, with references to C. Clemen, *Die griech. u. lat. Nachrichten über die persische Religion*, 1920, pp. 165 ff.; E. Benveniste, *The Persian Religion according to the Chief Greek Texts*, 1929, pp. 95 ff. For the world as the body of Ohrmazd see p. 38. Anaximander's *οὐρανοί* are gods too.

set it appears to be primary. Coincidence is excluded. Anaximander's conceptions cannot be derived from Greek antecedents, and to suppose that they chanced to burgeon in his mind without antecedents, at the very moment when the Persians were knocking at Ionian doors, would be as preposterous as it was pointless.

Meteorology

At the same time, Anaximander inherited an established Greek tradition of materialistic meteorology. The further he goes outside our earth, the more his explanations become theological and non-Greek in inspiration; the nearer he is to earth, the more they are physical and follow native lines of thought. Wind and rain are caused by vapours drawn up from earth by the heat of the sun. (This evaporation is a continual process; the sea is all that remains of a mass of water that originally covered the whole earth, and one day all will be dry.) Thunder and lightning are caused by the splitting of clouds from the force of winds shut up inside them.[1] Theories of this sort remained standard throughout antiquity, for there was no obvious way of improving on them. It would be a mistake to suppose that they originated with the Milesians. Passing allusions in Hesiod show that his ideas were not very different. Aer draws up moisture from the rivers, is carried hither and thither by wind, and may turn into rain or remain as a wind.[2] Thunder, lightning, earthquakes are caused by Zeus or Poseidon, but can at the same time be spoken of as inflated by winds.[3]

Anaximander's dependence on this tradition is shown most clearly by his reliance on vapours drawn up by the sun. In the early Greek view the sun was so close to the earth that its position could be defined by specifying a region on the earth's surface. In winter it 'goes to visit the country of the black men, and shines more tardily for the Greeks' (Hes. *Op.* 527 f.). It rises and sets at Ocean's stream, at the edge of the earth, hard by the Aithiopes (*Od.* 1. 23–4); Circe's island is at its risings (*Od.* 12. 4). Its

[1] See Kahn, pp. 63–71, 98–113.

[2] *Op.* 548 ff., cf. Kahn, pp. 145 f.

[3] *Th.* 706 f.; see my commentary.

seasonal turning-places, *τροπαί*, are geographically fixed too: one of them is at the 'island of Syria' (*Od.* 15. 404). The stars, similarly, set in Oceanus (*Od.* 5. 275, *al.*); Sirius, when in the sky, is 'over men's heads' (Hes. *Op.* 418). For people who thought on this scale, as most probably still did in Anaximander's time, it was reasonable to speculate in terms of vapours rising under the sun, varying according to the part of the earth that the sun was passing over, and themselves affecting the sun's behaviour. Thus Xenophanes, who postulated a whole battery of suns and moons moving across different regions of his infinitely wide earth, explained them as incandescent clouds fed by vapours from below, and suffering eclipse when they chanced to pass over an arid region.[1] For Heraclitus the sun is a small object, the size of a man's foot,[2] consisting of a bowl in which exhalations from below are collected in fiery form. Half a century later, Herodotus (2. 24–6) describes the winter sun being driven by storms towards the south of Libya, instead of 'the middle of the sky'; it dries up the waters in whatever region of the earth it visits. Anaximander used the same framework of ideas. He explained rain as coming from 'vapour given up by the parts below the sun'.[3] From this evaporation he also accounted for solstices;[4] presumably he was here thinking on the same lines as Anaximenes and Anaxagoras, who allowed the sun and moon to be physically pushed aside by a concentration of aer (13 A 15, 58 A 42 § 9). But these doctrines do not suit a cosmos of the design and proportions of Anaximander's. It is inappropriate to speak of 'parts of the earth below the sun' when you have put the sun $13\frac{1}{2}$ earth-diameters away and your earth is flat; and it is hard to imagine the vapour streaming away from the earth sideways at such an

[1] 21 A 32, 33, 40, 41a; P. J. Bicknell, *Eranos* 65, 1967, 73–7.

[2] Fr. 57 = 22 B 3 *εὖρος ποδὸς ἀνθρωπείου*. This may mean that the width of the sun equals the length of a man's foot, since it is normally the length of a foot that is used as a unit of measurement. (The measurement is paraphrased as *ποδιαῖος* by some sources.) The apparent diameter of the sun's disc, half a degree of arc, corresponds to the apparent length of my foot at a distance of thirty metres.

[3] Hipp. 1. 6. 7 (A 11) *ἐκ τῆς ἀτμίδος τῆς ἐκ γῆς, ἀναδιδομένης ἐκ τῶν ὑφ' ἥλιον* MSS.: *ἐκ τῆς ἀτμίδος τῆς ἐκ τῶν ὑφ' ἥλιον* (v.l. -ου) *ἀναδιδομένης* Cedrenus.

[4] See Kahn, pp. 65–7.

angle as to come anywhere near the solar and lunar wheels, even though it is the sun that is drawing it towards itself. It does not seem possible that the vapour theory was first formulated for this cosmology.

Anaximenes' Aer

This contrast between two contributory traditions, Greek rationalism and barbarian theology, is at its most open and unresolved in Anaximander's system. In the cosmology of his younger fellow citizen Anaximenes it has already become blurred; the inevitable processes of assimilation and integration are at work. The materialistic principle has been extended beyond the confines of the visible world, so that instead of a mysterious Boundless we have boundless Aer.

However, we shall not understand Anaximenes by imagining that he started with Anaximander's system and went forward from there. Presocratic thought was not like a boat steered by a succession of pilots, each trying to correct his predecessors' errors. Anaximenes certainly heard (or read) the views of Anaximander, but he seems to have been less influenced by them than by the more conventional assumptions of Greek cosmology. At the same time he has assimilated certain foreign ideas independently of Anaximander.

Everything that exists comes, according to him, from a single substance: *ἀήρ*, not exactly our 'air', but close to it; seen as mist, vapour, or not at all; felt in wind, breath, or changes of temperature. The idea of a basic constituent was not new. Hesiod's Pandora was made of earth and water (*Op.* 61, cf. 70, *Th.* 571), and there is other evidence from Homer and later poets for the idea that these are the physical constituents of man.[1] We are not in a position to follow the steps that led from this primitive piece of analysis to the systematic monism that we first hear of in connection with Thales.[2] But we can assume that they were

[1] See Kahn, p. 155, and my note on Hes. *Th.* 571.

[2] He was *ὁ τῆς τοιαύτης ἀρχηγὸς φιλοσοφίας* (Arist. *Metaph.* 983^{b}20), i.e. *τῶν εἰς ἐπίσκεψιν τῶν ὄντων ἐλθόντων καὶ φιλοσοφησάντων περὶ τῆς ἀληθείας* (^{b}2), the first of whom mostly recognized only material *ἀρχαί* (^{b}6).

gradual. Anaximenes is following a tradition with a long history. He modifies it by taking aer for his basic substance, and by giving it the qualities of Anaximander's Boundless. He makes it unbounded in extent all round the world, eternal, perpetually in motion, and divine, or at least the father of gods.[1]

Aer is indeed animate, being the stuff of breath and the soul. This may have been one reason why he made it his universal element. He did illustrate its cosmic importance from the importance of the soul in the body, not attempting to establish the concept of a 'soul of the world', but to fortify the proposition that aer *surrounds* the world: ἡ ψυχὴ ἡ ἡμετέρα ἀὴρ οὖσα συγκρατεῖ ἡμᾶς, καὶ ὅλον τὸν κόσμον πνεῦμα καὶ ἀὴρ περιέχει.[2] In another fragment we find Anaximenes using the affinity of aer and soul for a further end, and no less artificially: to show that the aer is infinite. ἐγγύς ἐστιν ὁ ἀὴρ ⟨τῆς ψυχῆς⟩ [τοῦ ἀσωμάτου], καὶ ὅτι κατ' ἔκροιαν τούτου (ταύτης?) γινόμεθα, ἀνάγκη αὐτὸν καὶ ἄπειρον εἶναι καὶ πλούσιον [διὰ τὸ μηδέποτε ἐκλείπειν].[3] When children are begotten, soul comes forth as if from an unfailing spring; soul is much the same as aer (in Aetius' version of B 2 it *is* aer);

[1] Hippolytus (A 7 § 1) and Augustine (A 10) say that gods arose out of the aer, Cicero and Aetius (ibid.) that the aer was a god.

[2] 13 B 2. The wording has suffered modernization in the source, see Reinhardt, *Kosmos und Sympathie*, p. 210; Vlastos, *AJP* 76, 1955, 363 n. 55; Kirk–Raven, p. 159; Kerschensteiner, *Kosmos*, pp. 72–83; J. Longrigg, *Phronesis* 9, 1964, 1–4. πνεῦμα καὶ ἀὴρ περιέχει may be original. Anaximander's (?) πάντα περιέχει καὶ πάντα κυβερνᾷ would give good sense. The soul of the world is wrapped round outside it, as well as being put inside it, in Pl. *Tim.* 34 b. Xenophanes is said to have written of his cosmic god that it sees and hears as a whole, but *does not breathe* (D.L. 9. 19): someone must have said it did, perhaps Anaximenes.

[3] B 3. Diels branded the quotation as "gefälscht', and modern commentators have ignored it. His grounds were (1) the 'schwindelhafter Charakter' of the source (Olymp. *de arte sacra lapidis philos.*). But he quotes it elsewhere (Xenophanes A 36, Melissus A 13); its offerings must be treated on their merits. (2) ἀσώματος: certainly a post-Anaximenean word, but what follows suggests that it is a gloss on ψυχή. Diels thought the statement derived from Arist. *Phys.* 212ᵃ12 ὁ ἀὴρ δοκῶν ἀσώματος εἶναι, but the resemblance is superficial. (3) πλούσιος. But this is a sign of earliness, not lateness. (4) διὰ τὸ μηδέποτε ἐκλείπειν, which Diels derived from Arist. *Phys.* 203ᵇ19, 208ᵃ8; it is probably an explanatory addition. In favour of authenticity are (1) the parallel with B 2, (2) the simple classical ἐγγύς expressing natural affinity, (3) the doubling of ἄπειρον by πλούσιον. For κατ' ἔκροιαν γινόμεθα cf. Heraclitus 28 (DK 22 B 80) γινόμενα πάντα κατ' ἔριν; Powell, *Lexicon to Herodotus* s.v. κατά B III 7.

therefore aer is infinitely abundant. A puerile argument, and evidently a preconceived conclusion.

Aer's progeny

Aer is connected with begetting in another way. Although it turns into other things by thickening or rarefying, Anaximenes seems to have chosen to describe its changes in genealogical language. According to Hippolytus, he said that boundless aer was the first principle, *ἐξ οὗ τὰ γινόμενα καὶ τὰ γεγονότα καὶ τὰ ἐσόμενα καὶ θεοὺς καὶ θεῖα γίνεσθαι, τὰ δὲ λοιπὰ* (!) *ἐκ τῶν τούτου ἀπογόνων.*[1]

The first thing to be produced was the earth (A 6). It is flat and very broad, like a table, and is supported by the aer beneath it (A 6, 7, 20). It forms the floor of the whole of our world. From it the sun, moon, and stars came into being, terrestrial vapours becoming rarefied and converted into fire. They are flat and two-dimensional, like paintings, which enables them to ride the aer like leaves.[2] Among them, but invisible to us, move certain earthy bodies (A 7 § 5 *γεώδεις φύσεις*, A 14 *γεώδη σώματα*). Their function was probably to account for eclipses, since Anaxagoras, although he knew that the earth's shadow causes lunar eclipses, believed in invisible bodies like those of Anaximenes that could do the same.[3]

[1] 1. 7. 1 = A 7, clearly echoing phrases of the original. Cf. Kahn, pp. 156, 174 f., adding Democr. A 39, Orph. fr. 167. 6. Later Hippolytus uses *γεννᾶσθαι* thrice, of the origin of winds, clouds, and rainbows, whereas in reporting Anaximander and Anaxagoras he has *γίνεσθαι*. Cf. also A 6, 21; Anaximander A 14, and his '*γόνιμον*' (p. 84); Xenoph. 21 B 30. 5.

[2] Achilles, *isag.* p. 40. 20 Maass *τινὲς δὲ πετάλοις ἐοικέναι (τοὺς ἀστέρας) ἐκ πυρός, βάθος οὐκ ἔχοντας ἀλλ' ὥσπερ γραφὰς εἶναι*; cf. Aet. 2. 14. 4 discussed below.

[3] Arist. *de cael.* 293^{b}21 ff. mentions a similar Pythagorean theory; see Burkert, *WW*, pp. 321 f.; O'Brien, *JHS* 88, 1968, 117 f. Diogenes 64 A 12 used the idea of invisible bodies—correctly—to account for the meteorite that fell at Aegospotami in 467. Kirk–Raven claim that Anaxagoras' dark bodies must have had the same function, and that Anaximenes, since he lived before 467, did not speak of dark bodies at all: 'the theory was probably projected on to him from his assumed follower Diogenes.' This is untenable. Anaxagoras' dark bodies moved below the stars, some of them below the moon, and Theophrastus explicitly related them to eclipses (59 A 77, cf. 42 §§ 6, 9). The meteorite fell from the outer firmament, being one of the stones that are held there by centrifugal force and seen by us as the stars (59 A 12, cf. 71).

The stars, though fiery, give no heat, because of their distance from us (A 7 § 6); the seasons are produced not by them but solely by the sun (A 14, end). Anaximenes here seems to be attacking the simple view, as seen in Hes. *Op.* 416–19, 587, and in the sixth century in [Hes.] *Sc.* 153, that Sirius is responsible for the heat of summer.[1] Parmenides (B 11. 3) still speaks of the ἄστρων θερμὸν μένος.

The motion of the heavenly bodies

Hippolytus says that all the stars were fiery and aerborne. But there is a confused notice from Aetius to the effect that they were fixed like nails in the firmament. It stands in different places in the two sources from which Aetius is reconstructed. (1) In the pseudo-Plutarchean *Placita* it comes in the section on the shape of the stars: Ἀναξιμένης δὲ ἥλων δίκην καταπεπηγέναι τῷ κρυσταλλοειδεῖ. ἔνιοι δὲ πέταλα εἶναι πύρινα ὥσπερ ζωγραφήματα (2. 14. 3–4). It is certain that the leaves belong to Anaximenes, so something has gone wrong. One manuscript gives καθάπερ for ἔνιοι δέ. Heath, *Aristarchus*, p. 42, conjectured ἐνίους δέ (sc. ἀστέρας; it should in the context have been ἔνια δέ (ἄστρα)), taking these to be the planets in contradistinction to the fixed stars. (2) In Stobaeus it comes in the preceding section, on the nature of the stars: Ἀναξιμένης πυρίνην μὲν τὴν φύσιν τῶν ἄστρων, περιέχειν δέ τινα καὶ γεώδη σώματα συμπεριφερόμενα τούτοις ἀόρατα. ἥλων δὲ δίκην καταπεπηγέναι τὰ ἄστρα τῷ κρυσταλλοειδεῖ (2. 13. 10, but Diels transfers the second sentence to 2. 14. 3). The leaves do not appear here. At the corresponding place in the *Placita* there is nothing on Anaximenes, but a notice that Empedocles held

[1] Cf. Manil. 5. 207 *latratque Canicula flammas* | *et rabit igne suo, geminatque incendia solis*, Plin. *NH* 18. 269–70; Frazer, *GB* vii. 307 f.: 'According to a writer, whose evidence on other matters of Australian beliefs is open to grave doubt, some of the aborigines of New South Wales denied that the sun is the source of heat, because he shines also in winter when the weather is cold; the real cause of warm weather they held to be the Pleiades, because as the summer heat increases, that constellation rises higher and higher in the sky' etc. (J. Manning, *Journal and Proceedings of the Royal Soc. of N.S.W.* 16, 1883, 168).

the fixed stars συνδεδέσθαι τῷ κρυστάλλῳ. Stobaeus has this more logically with the earlier notice of Empedocles in the same section, following 2. 13. 2.

It is impossible to be sure what has happened here. It may be that the nails and the κρυσταλλοειδές (probably originally intended as 'icelike') have been accidentally transferred from Empedocles or another. There are, however, two considerations which *might* support their attribution to Anaximenes. Firstly, a solid sky covering the space over the earth was a feature of the traditional world-picture, and it has a counterpart in most (though not all) Presocratic cosmologies; even the atomists assumed a membrane enclosing the world from the surrounding infinite. We would expect Anaximenes not to deny the existence of this sky (and surely if he had denied it, the fact would have been recorded), but to tell us what it is made of; it would not be surprising if he said it was of aer, frozen like ice. Secondly, he taught that the heavenly bodies do not go under the earth but round it, 'as a felt cap goes round our head' (A 7 § 6; cf. A 1, 14). They disappear from view because the earth is higher to the north of us.[1] For Anaximenes the heavenly bodies are small in relation to the earth, and his earth was perhaps too broad for them to get beyond it. It is usually assumed that they moved in two planes, rising upwards in the east, sinking down in the west, and then levelling out to pass round the north. But there is no need to postulate such awkward orbits. Xenophanes taught that the sinking of the sun is an optical illusion: it is really proceeding westwards in a straight line at a constant altitude. So in Anaximenes' view it is hidden 'not because it goes under the earth but because it is covered by the higher parts of the earth, *and because of its increasing distance from us*' (loc. cit.). This suggests that the heavenly bodies actually revolve horizontally round the mountain, and that it is this motion that Anaximenes wished to illustrate by the cap image. But the simile is less naturally applied

[1] Cf. Arist. *Meteor.* 354a28. This has sometimes been interpreted to mean that the whole plane of the earth's surface slopes from north to south. Against this see Kirk–Raven, p. 157; J. D. P. Bolton *Aristeas of Proconnesus*, p. 188.

to a collection of detached leaves of fire than to a vaulted structure covering the whole.[1]

Anaximenes' affinities

Anaximenes' boundless Beyond may show the influence of Anaximander, but the same cannot be said of his cosmos, which stands in the older tradition. The earth floats on aer as in Thales' system it had floated on water. It is as broad as the sky; the sun and moon are much smaller, are constantly above it, and may reasonably be represented as affected by vapours rising from it (see above, p. 98). Anaximander's orbit-wheels are ignored. Aetius 2. 1. 3 (DK 12 A 17) names Anaximenes in a list of those who believed in infinite worlds, but Simplicius (*Phys.* 1121. 14 = DK 13 A 11) links him with Heraclitus, Diogenes, and the Stoics as a believer in one world periodically destroyed and replaced, so that this may be another respect in which he fails to share Anaximander's novel vision.

Yet it would be wrong to represent him as a stalwart conservative hardly touched by new and foreign currents of thought. There are certain things that link him too with eastern and specifically with Iranian speculation.

In connection with his aer that surrounds the world and also, as the soul, possesses us, Burkert[2] refers to the Iranian wind-god Vayu, who is represented as the vital breath both of the world and of man. I am doubtful, however, whether this is a significant parallel. Nothing of the sort is said of Vayu in the extant part of the Avesta, although there are several references to him, some extended.[3] A single Pahlavi text seems to be in question.

> He who quickens the world and is the life (the breath-soul) of living things is Vāy.... Similarly what quickens the body of man is the fiery wind which is life (the breath-soul).[4]

[1] Cf. Kirk–Raven, loc. cit. Boll (*ap.* Kopff, above, p. 93 n. 1) took the hat to have straight sides, and compared the Babylonian heaven as it might be imagined (cf. the same note on p. 93).

[2] 'Iranisches', p. 127 n. 86.

[3] *Yasna* 25. 5, *Yašt* 15. 43 ff., *Aogemadaēčā* 77 ff. (Zaehner, *Zurvan*, p. 84, *DTZ*, p. 149).

[4] *Dēnkart*, p. 278. 14 Madan (Zaehner, *Zurvan*, p. 85).

A better parallel is the basic doctrine of all the Upanishads, that Brahman, the changeless life-soul of the world, is identical with Ātman, the individual self, in other words, our personal awareness of being alive is only a local and imperfect observation of a universal reality. Often the Brahman is identified with breath (*prāṇa*). In a hymn to Prāṇa in the *Atharvaveda* (11. 4; Zaehner, *Hindu Scriptures*, p. 27), the whole universe is said to obey it. The thunder and the rain come from it; it is the sun and moon, Prajāpati, animals and plants. It takes living creatures as its garment, it is what quickens the embryo. Some call it the wind. All things are based on it: in it is what is past and what is yet to be. Elsewhere, wind or breath is represented as a thread with which living things and worlds are woven and held together. A man dies when that thread is broken, and that is why it is said that his limbs are unstrung (cf. λύθεν δέ οἱ ἅψεα πάντα).[1] So in Anaximenes the aer-soul holds us together (συγκρατεῖ in the report), and aer and wind encompass the whole world. If it was he who propounded the doctrine of divine respiration denied by Xenophanes (see p. 100 n. 2), it is appropriate to refer here to another passage in the *Atharvaveda* (10. 7. 34; Zaehner, *Hindu Scriptures*, p. 21), where the wind is identified with the breathing in and breathing out of Skambha, the mighty figure who supports the universe.

The reference in the Prāṇa hymn to what is past and what is yet to be recalls another detail in Anaximenes (cf. p. 101). This way of describing 'everything' in a cosmological context appears again in the *Bṛhadāraṇyaka Upanishad* 3. 8. 3:

> She said: 'Yājñavalkya, that which is above the sky, which is below the earth, which is between sky and earth,—that which men speak of as past, present and future: on what is that woven, warp and woof?'

The great mountain in the north, about which Anaximenes' sun, moon, and stars circle, is perhaps a slightly incongruous feature of an earth conceived as being flat and broad like a table,

[1] *Bṛhadāraṇyaka Upan.* 3. 7. 1–2; cf. *Çatapatha Brāhmaṇa* 6. 7. 1. 17, 7. 3. 2. 13, 8. 7. 3. 10; Éliade, *The Two and the One*, pp. 170 ff.

and able to float on air because of its flatness and thinness. Mythical geography knew of a great mountain in the north, Rhipe, from which the blast of Boreas came.[1] Belief in the existence of Rhipe no doubt helped Anaximenes towards his theory. But in the ordinary man's world-picture, Rhipe was a place the sun never visited ('Hp.' *aer.* 19). Anaximenes seems to be influenced by the primitive conception, widespread in Asia, of a world-mountain. At the centre of the world, it is believed, there is a great mountain, often represented as terraced; it may assume various fantastic shapes, and Holmberg has argued that the Babylonian Ziggurat and the pagoda of the Far East were conceived as imitations of it.[2] It rises, in Asiatic and Indian accounts, not towards the zenith but towards the pole star,[3] which implies that the heavenly bodies revolve round it. It is related to the idea of a heavenly pillar in the middle of the world, to which the stars are attached by threads.[4] In the Avesta the world-mountain is called Harā or Haraitī, and it is said explicitly that the stars, moon, and sun circle round it.[5] The belief continued to assert itself in the Near East against the much truer concepts of Hellenistic astronomy, and in the sixth century of our era Cosmas Indicopleustes makes it a cornerstone of his *Christian Topography*. The sun sets, he declares, because it is hidden behind the higher parts of the earth in the west and north (2. 34 p. 89 c, 4. 12 p. 188 a). Some of his diagrams, carefully copied in the extant manuscripts, are well suited to illustrate Anaximenes' cosmology (see Plate VII). The theory in question is criticized by Philoponus (*de opificio mundi* 3. 10 p. 138. 3 Reichardt), writing a little earlier than Cosmas. He is arguing against doctrines of the Syrian Christians of whom Theodorus of Mopsuestia had

[1] Bolton, *Aristeas*, pp. 39 ff.

[2] *Der Baum des Lebens*, pp. 33–51. See also P. Jensen, *Kosmol. d. Babylonier*, 1890, pp. 201–12; F. von Andrian, *Der Höhencultus asiat. u. europ. Völker*, 1891, p. xxv; W. Gaerte, *Anthropos* 9, 1914, 956–79; Jeremias, op. cit. (p. 91 n. 3), pp. 130 ff.

[3] Holmberg, *Der Baum des Lebens*, p. 41.

[4] Ibid., p. 23, cf. 43.

[5] *Yašt* 12. 25, see p. 90; cf. *Vidēvdāt* 21. 5. There Mithra has his abode; there is neither night nor darkness, cold or heat, sickness or impurity; no mists rise from it (*Yašt* 10. 50).

been the outstanding figure a century before. Theodorus and other Syrian writers are named by Cosmas as his principal sources, besides the Babylonian Mar Aba, and it looks as if the northern mountain was part of their oriental heritage. It will not be suggested that they formed their views under the influence of Anaximenes.[1]

In some cases the Asiatic world-mountain is topped by the world-tree.[2] Possibly some popular fancy saw the stars as leaves on the world-tree, as it also attached them to the world-pillar by means of threads: Turkic peoples had the idea that each man lives so long as his leaf remains on the tree (above, pp. 56 f.), and the idea that he lives so long as his star remains in the sky.[3] It would then be conceivable that Anaximenes' image of fiery leaves borne on the aer was suggested by such a conception.[4] On the other hand he may simply have been impressed by the ability of flat thin things like leaves to ride on the breeze, and invoked it to account for the flight of the heavenly bodies (though other thinkers were content to say that fire naturally rises and has no need of support from below). His hat simile too need be no more than a homely illustration which he thought of himself.[5]

It can hardly be a coincidence, however, that his explanation of eclipses as being caused by dark bodies circulating below the sun and moon is identical with the belief of the Persians.

1 See further Eisler, *Weltenmantel*, pp. 253, 622 ff.

2 Holmberg, *Der Baum des Lebens*, p. 52, cf. above, p. 55, and p. 58 n. 7.

3 Ibid., pp. 109 f.

4 Cf. W. Schultz, *Altjonische Mystik*, p. 338 n. 1; Eisler, *Weltenmantel*, p. 32 n. 1. If the paintings simile needs external inspiration, compare the Manichaean giant of the sea (p. 44), and other manifestations of the idea of cosmic art by the gods (p. 54; Eisler, *Weltenmantel*, p. 110 n. 3).

5 Eisler, *Weltenmantel*, p. 64 refers to Jensen, *Kosmol. d. Bab.* 17, where a name of a star or constellation that Jensen identifies with the pole of the ecliptic is interpreted as 'Königsmütze'; and to the star-spangled cap of Attis, interpreted as the visible heaven by Jul. *Or.* 165 b (cf. 171 a), as heavenly power by Sall. *de dis* 4. In Mithraic iconography the Phrygian cap symbolizes the air, according to Cumont, *TM* i. 116.

For the 'icelike' firmament see Ezek. 1 : 22. Eisler refers to a rabbinic doctrine that the heaven is made of hail (p. 94 n. 4). Zoega, *Abhandlungen*, p. 220, inferred from Orph. fr. 237. 1 (*Βακχικά*) *τήκων αἰθέρα δῖον* that the poet of the verses thought of the *αἰθήρ* as 'dicht und erfroren'.

Two dark progeny of the primeval ox move and are made to revolve from far below the sun and moon, and whenever, during the revolution of the celestial sphere, they make one pass below the sun, or below the moon, it becomes a covering which is spun over the sun, and it is so when the sun or moon is not seen. Of each of those two progeny of the primeval ox—one of which is called 'the head', and one 'the tail'—the motion is specified among astronomers.

(*Dātastān-i-Dēnīk* 69. 2–3, trans. West, *SBE* xviii)

Et deux Druj très puissantes, qui sont les adversaires planétaires du soleil et de la lune, se meuvent en opposition, sous le rayonnement des deux luminaires.

(*Škand-Gumānīk Vičār* 4. 46, trans. P. J. de Menasce, 1945)

The eclipsing bodies were also called the 'dark sun' and 'dark moon' (*Greater Bundahišn*, p. 57. 7 Anklesaria, trans. in Zaehner, *Zurvan*, p. 160). They appear only in the Pahlavi books, but one would not expect to find a theory of eclipses in the Avesta, and it is reasonable to assume that such a crude explanation was not introduced at a late date in place of something cruder still, but had been handed down from antiquity. There is no question of its having been taken from the Greeks, for the Greeks discovered the true causes both of solar and of lunar eclipses in the fifth century, and soon forgot about dark bodies. Nor is it likely that Anaximenes thought of the explanation himself. Given his view of the sun and moon as being like leaves, and Anaximander's theory that eclipses were caused by the twisting-over of the outer tubes of their wheels, it would have been natural for Anaximenes to say that eclipses occurred when the leaves turned over.[1] The dark bodies are foreign to the logic of his system. Are we to suppose that they, like the luminaries, arose from terrestrial vapours? If so, why did they not likewise turn into fire? Like the mountain of the north, they must be accounted for as concepts accepted from barbarian speculation, and not really suited to Ionian physics. In the Ionian tradition we can discern the unspoken aim to explain the observed world from itself, without invoking additional factors beyond the reach of observation. The invisible

[1] Heraclitus used this idea with his solar and lunar bowls.

things in Anaximenes' and Anaximander's systems—the dark bodies, the mountain of the north, the celestial wheels, the Boundless, and the countless other worlds that are in it—all come from abroad.

Finally, the recognition that the sun alone causes the alternation of the seasons appears to have been anticipated at Babylon. In a text of which the oldest copy is dated to 687 B.C., the sun's path through the sky is divided into the four equal sections that fall in the zones of Enlil (summer), Anu (spring and autumn), and Ea (winter), and directly linked with the corresponding weather:

From the first day of the twelfth month to the thirtieth day of the second month, the sun stands on the way of Anu: wind and storm. From the first day of the third month to the thirtieth day of the fifth month, the sun stands on the way of Enlil: harvest and heat. From the first day of the sixth month to the thirtieth day of the eighth month, the sun stands on the way of Anu: wind and storm. From the first day of the ninth month to the thirtieth day of the eleventh month, the sun stands on the way of Ea: cold.[1]

Whether Anaximenes was the first Greek to deny the stars' heat, we cannot tell, but it was probably a new idea. Xenophanes and Heraclitus repeat it.[2] When in the fifth century it was discovered that the sun was also the source of the moon's light—and according to some the source of *all* light—it is not surprising that he was hailed in some circles as king and father of all the gods.[3] Anaximenes is still some way from this.

Anaximander and Anaximenes have traditionally been considered members of a clearly-defined 'Milesian school', characterized above all by monism. We have seen that this is misleading. Anaximenes was a monist as Thales had been; Anaximander was nothing of the sort. They were both exposed to similar influences: a native tradition of materialist meteorology and physics, and an oriental tradition of metaphysical speculation. But they

[1] Van der Waerden, *AA*, pp. 78, 230.
[2] Xenoph. A 42; Heraclitus, D.L. 9. 10, cf. fr. 60 (= B 99).
[3] *οἱ σοφοί ap.* Soph. fr. 752 P. (= 1017 N.[2]), cf. *OT* 660.

differed greatly in the weight they allowed to these traditions. Schwabl rightly remarks (col. 1521): 'As thinkers, Anaximander and Anaximenes are two quite different individuals, and their relationship is certainly more obscured than correctly characterized by the assumed teacher–pupil relationship.' Anaximander's thick, solid earth resting in contented equipoise amid its vast wheels of fire and mist is truly an inspiring vision beside Anaximenes' floating raft and his thin, wafery luminaries blown round above it like leaves in an autumn gust. One might well say of Anaximenes' cosmology, 'Why, they're nothing but a pack of cards!'

4

HERACLITUS (1): ΦΥΣΙΚΟΣ ΛΟΓΟΣ

What was Heraclitus?

PHERECYDES gave a mythical account of the world with moral implications; the Milesians made much more serious attempts to interpret the structure of the universe in real terms, and did not, as far as we know, make their theories the basis for ethical conclusions. It is customary to associate Heraclitus with the latter tradition rather than the former. It is agreed that he is a Philosopher, and that a chapter in our history of Philosophy must be devoted to him. We duly discuss his date, the biographical material, and his cosmology; we also note that he had views on religious and political matters, and we try to estimate how much he owed or gave to the other Philosophers.

Plato and Aristotle started it. Heraclitus did have a certain amount to say about cosmology, and it was natural for them to take an interest in it and compare it with what others said.[1] Theophrastus followed their lead, and dealt with Heraclitus in his comprehensive work on the *δόξαι τῶν φυσικῶν*. Later doxographers excerpted Theophrastus, and so gave further emphasis to the idea of Heraclitus as a cosmologist among many.

Yet Theophrastus was forced to report that Heraclitus' account was very defective. He complained that he wrote *τὰ μὲν ἡμιτελῆ, τὰ δὲ ἄλλοτε ἄλλως ἔχοντα*, and that in his account of cosmic change he explained nothing clearly.[2] He was silent on specific points of some importance: the nature of the surroundings of the cosmos, the shape of the earth and its mode of support, and the

[1] It had already drawn the attention of late-fifth-century 'Heracliteans' such as Cratylus. Plato had an early association with this school (Arist. *Metaph.* 987ᵃ32). Cf. Pl. *Crat.* 440 c, *Theaet.* 179 d–e, Arist. *Metaph.* 1010ᵃ11, [Arist.] *Probl.* 908ᵃ30, 934ᵇ34, D.L. 9. 6.

[2] D.L. 9. 6, 8.

origin and substance of the bowls in which he held the sun's and moon's fires to be collected (D.L. 9. 9, 11). Evidently he was not interested in these questions; and if he was not interested in these questions, he cannot have been very interested in physical cosmology in the Milesian manner at all.

In fact, Diogenes states that his book had 'Nature' for its unifying theme, but was divided into three discourses: *περὶ τοῦ παντός*, *πολιτικός*, and *θεολογικός* (9. 5). I may quote Burnet's sensible comment (*EGP*, p. 132): 'It is not to be supposed that this division is due to Herakleitos himself; all we can infer is that the work fell naturally into these three parts when the Stoic commentators took their editions of it in hand.' (Only I see no justification for talk of 'editions'; and Stoics were not the first to distinguish politics and theology as branches of study.) The cosmology, then, was only a beginning, leading to a disquisition concerning public institutions and religion. There is other, independent evidence that it was not central in Heraclitus' thought. Of those who published interpretations of him, most were philosophers. The only one described as a *γραμματικός*, Diodotus by name, wrote that the work was not about nature but *περὶ πολιτείας*, and that the natural philosophy it contained was there by way of illustration (D.L. 9. 15). He called it 'a true piece of helmsmanship to the line of life'.[1] Sextus Empiricus (*adv. math.* 7. 5–7), after listing the Milesians, Empedocles, Parmenides, and Heraclitus as physical philosophers, qualifies this by saying that Empedocles and Parmenides, according to Aristotle, began rhetoric and dialectic, *ἐζητεῖτο δὲ καὶ περὶ Ἡρακλείτου εἰ μὴ μόνον φυσικός ἐστιν ἀλλὰ καὶ ἠθικὸς φιλόσοφος*. These testimonia have often been despised or ignored by scholars.[2] Yet the conclusion

[1] D.L. 9. 12 *ἐπιγράφουσι δ' αὐτῷ (τῷ βιβλίῳ) οἱ μὲν Μούσας* (from Pl. *Soph.* 242 d), *οἱ δὲ Περὶ φύσεως* (the standard title for Presocratics' works), *Διόδοτος δὲ* "*ἀκριβὲς οἰάκισμα πρὸς στάθμην βίου*" (from Diodotus' criticism of the standard title—hence the intrusion of the verse in the list of titles)· *ἄλλοι* †*Γνώμην ἠθῶν τρόπου κόσμον ἑνὸς τῶν ξυμπάντων*.† (Perhaps *Γνώμην ἠθῶν* (fr. 90 = B 78), *Τρόπου κόσμον* (Ael. *VH* 6. 12), *Ἓν ἀντὶ ξυμπάντων* (fr. 95 = B 29); or *Γνώμην ἠθῶν τρόπου, Κόσμον ἕνα τὸν ξυνὸν πάντων* (fr. 24 = B 89, 51 = B 30). See also Marcovich, *Estudios*, pp. 53–5.

[2] See e.g. Kirk, *HCF*, pp. 7 and 11. Kirk is right to observe that for Heraclitus

to which they point was drawn from the fragments themselves by the most penetratingly original of modern students of Heraclitus. He wrote that Heraclitus' philosophy 'has a religious end-purpose', and that Heraclitus 'offers just so much physical explanation as he needs for the comparison of the microcosm with the macrocosm; the rest is valueless to him'.[1]

A conjectural opening sequence of fragments

Apart from the general division into three parts mentioned by Diogenes, it is difficult to get much idea of the structure of Heraclitus' book. There is no prospect of determining the original order of more than a very few fragments. Not that it is difficult to arrange most of the remainder in plausible sequences; on the contrary, the trouble is that it is easy.[2] Like the pretty bits in a kaleidoscope they slide together all too readily in intriguing new patterns. We shall only delude ourselves if we approach the task with the optimism of a Schuster.

On the other hand we cannot afford the total resignation of a Diels. I think it is possible at least to suggest how the discourse began.

1 = B 1 ⟨Ἡράκλειτος Ἐφέσιος τάδε λέγει.⟩ τοῦ δὲ λόγου τοῦδε ἐόντος αἰεὶ ἀξύνετοι γίνονται ἄνθρωποι καὶ

all branches of knowledge were interconnected, and that a strict disposition of material under three subject-headings is not to be assumed for him. But a shift of emphasis in the course of the book is likely enough. Kirk thinks that the 'book' may have been from the start a 'collection of sayings' (*HCF*, p. 7, Kirk–Raven, p. 185). This is unlikely; no other early book took such a form, and Walzer in his edition notes that fr. 1, and particularly διηγεῦμαι, 'non indica una raccolta di aforismi, ma piuttosto uno scritto diegematico'. Many of the fragments have a gnomic character, but then, so have many of the fragments of Euripides. Kirk then supposes a second collection, published in Alexandria (why?), in which the tripartite arrangement appeared. Similarly Kranz.

[1] Reinhardt, *Parmenides*, pp. 193, 201. Though he is often cited on details, Reinhardt's general insight into Heraclitus' purpose, in relation to the questions of his time, has had less influence than might have been expected, probably because it was associated with the unorthodox thesis (recently revived by Hölscher) that Heraclitus wrote after Parmenides and was influenced by him. The opposite view is well stated by Vlastos, *AJP* 76, 1955, 341 n. 11. My own view is that Parmenides may well have been the earlier writer, even if the younger man, but that there is no sufficient reason to suppose that either knew anything of the other.

[2] Cf. Fränkel, *D. u. Ph.* p. 422.

πρόσθεν ἢ ἀκοῦσαι καὶ ἀκούσαντες τὸ πρῶτον.
γινομένων γὰρ πάντων κατὰ τὸν λόγον τόνδε
ἀπείροισιν ἐοίκασι πειρώμενοι καὶ ἐπέων καὶ ἔργων
τοιούτων ὁκοίων ἐγὼ διηγέομαι κατὰ φύσιν διαιρέων
ἕκαστον καὶ φράζων ὅκως ἔχει· τοὺς δὲ ἄλλους
ἀνθρώπους λανθάνει ὁκόσα ἐγερθέντες ποιοῦσιν,
23(*a*) = B 114 ὅκωσπερ ὁκόσα εὕδοντες ἐπιλανθάνονται. ξὺν νῷ
λέγοντας ἰσχυρίζεσθαι χρὴ τῷ ξυνῷ πάντων,
ὅκωσπερ νόμῳ πόλις, καὶ πολὺ ἰσχυροτέρως·
τρέφονται γὰρ πάντες οἱ ἀνθρώπειοι νόμοι ὑπὸ ἑνὸς
τοῦ θείου· κρατεῖ γὰρ τοσοῦτον ὁκόσον ἐθέλει καὶ
23(*a*) *bis* = B 2 ἐξαρκεῖ πᾶσι καὶ περιγίνεται. τοῦ λόγου δὲ ἐόντος
ξυνοῦ ζώουσιν οἱ πολλοὶ ὡς ἰδίην ἔχοντες φρόνησιν.
24 = B 89 ⟨In this too they are like sleepers, for⟩ the sleeping turn away each to a private κόσμος (set of appearances), but those awake share one common κόσμος.

51 = B 30 κόσμον τόνδε, τὸν αὐτὸν ἁπάντων, οὔτε τις θεῶν
οὔτε ἀνθρώπων ἐποίησεν, ἀλλ' ἦν αἰεὶ καὶ ἔστι καὶ
ἔσται· πῦρ ἀείζωον, ἁπτόμενον μέτρα καὶ ἀπο-
53 = B 31 σβεννύμενον μέτρα. πυρὸς τροπαὶ πρῶτον θάλασσα,
θαλάσσης δὲ τὸ μὲν ἥμισυ γῆ, τὸ δὲ ἥμισυ πρηστήρ.
καὶ ἡ μὲν διαχεῖται καὶ μετρεῖται ἐς τὸν αὐτὸν λόγον
ὁκοῖος πρόσθεν ἦν ἢ γενέσθαι γῆ· ⟨πρηστὴρ δέ . . .
54 = B 90 In this way⟩ πυρὸς ἀνταμοιβὴ τὰ πάντα καὶ πῦρ
ἁπάντων, ὅκωσπερ χρυσοῦ χρήματα καὶ χρημάτων
33 = B 60 χρυσός· ὁδὸς ἄνω κάτω, μία καὶ ἡ αὐτή.

Fragment 1 (B 1)

We are told that this fragment came at the beginning of Heraclitus' book: Arist. *Rhet.* $1407^{b}16$ ἐν τῇ ἀρχῇ αὐτοῦ τοῦ συγγράμματος, S.E. *adv. math.* 7. 132 ἐναρχόμενος τῶν περὶ φύσεως. These expressions do not exclude a few words preceding, and the initial δέ implies that. It has been plausibly conjectured that what preceded was something like Ἡράκλειτος Ἐφέσιος τάδε λέγει.[1]

[1] The δέ is only found in Hipp. *Ref.* 9. 9. 3, omitted by Aristotle and Clem.

A man speaking of ὁ λόγος ὅδε at the beginning of a book must in any case be understood to mean 'this discourse of mine'.[1] What is said about it in the rest of the fragment fully confirms this interpretation. It is something that other men hear, and might but do not understand. Everything that happens, happens in accordance with ὁ λόγος ὅδε, but men's reactions belie their acquaintance with such things as ἐγὼ διηγέομαι κατὰ φύσιν διαιρέων ἕκαστον καὶ φράζων ὅκως ἔχει. The parallelism is unmistakable. Everything happens in accordance with my account: κατὰ τὸν λόγον τόνδε differs from κατάπερ ἐγὼ λέγω only in the detachment with which the writer speaks of his own discourse as if it had a being of its own, a phenomenon that we also meet in Herodotus.[2] When Heraclitus says τοῦ λόγου τοῦδε ἐόντος αἰεὶ ἀξύνετοι γίνονται ἄνθρωποι, etc., he means that men show no understanding of what I say, either before or after they have heard it (i.e. as little understanding after as before), although it stands throughout (whether they have heard it or not, and whether they understand it or not).[3]

There is another way of construing the sentence which we know to have been considered by the time of Aristotle (*Rhet.* loc. cit.), and which has been preferred in modern times by Reinhardt, Kirk, and others.[4] That is to take αἰεί with ἀξύνετοι and τοῦ λόγου τοῦδε ἐόντος as 'the λόγος (or my discourse) being such'. But that would have been expressed more fully, by

Strom. 5. 111. 7, but the omission is natural, the addition unlikely (Zeller–Nestle i⁶. 792). Sextus begins with the word λόγου. See Gigon, p. 1; Kirk, *HCF*, p. 36; above, p. 9.

1 So Ion of Chios 36 B 1 ἀρχὴ δέ μοι τοῦ λόγου πάντα τρία, Diog. Apoll. 64 B 1 quoted on p. 117; 'Pythagoras' *ap.* D.L. 8. 6 and *ap.* Iambl. *VP* 146. Cryptic though he is, Heraclitus would not seek to baffle his student at the outset with a novel sense of λόγος; if he had explained the use of the word in a preceding sentence, Sextus and Hippolytus would not have omitted it in quoting, if they had known it (cf. Verdenius, *Mnemos.*³ 13, 1947, 271).

2 e.g. 1. 95. 1 ἐπιδίζηται δὲ δὴ ἐνθεῦτεν ἡμῖν ὁ λόγος τόν τε Κῦρον ὅστις ἐὼν τὴν Κροίσου ἀρχὴν κατεῖλε, 4. 30. 1.

3 ὁ ἐὼν λόγος means 'the real story', Hdt. 1. 95. 1, 116. 5, Ar. *Ran.* 1052–3 (cf. *Il.* 20. 254 v.l.); in τοῦ λόγου ἐόντος αἰεί, where the participle is predicative I feel that 'being true' is too strong a translation, but there is doubtless a suggestion that the λόγος is true. Hence my rendering.

4 See Kirk, *HCF*, p. 34.

something like τοῦ λόγου ἐόντος τοιούτου ὁκοῖον ἐγὼ ἀποδείκνυμι.[1] τοῦ λόγου τοῦδε ἐόντος would mean rather 'here is the discourse, but . . .'. I find this less satisfactory. In the following sentence we have τὸν λόγον τόνδε meaning simply 'this λόγος', and it seems natural to take τοῦ λόγου τοῦδε in the same way. Then in fr. 23(*a*) *bis* = B 2, which followed fr. 1 after a short interval, Heraclitus says τοῦ λόγου δὲ ἐόντος ξυνοῦ ζώουσιν οἱ πολλοὶ ὡς ἰδίην ἔχοντες φρόνησιν, a sentence strikingly and perhaps intentionally parallel in structure.[2] ἐόντος ξυνοῦ surely suggests that the predicate in the earlier sentence is ἐόντος αἰεί, not τοῦδε ἐόντος. Nor is the second interpretation helped by the fact that αἰεί leads up to and includes the following alternatives, 'both before and after they have heard it'. It does so whichever way it is taken. It makes no difference to its force whether we have 'it stands throughout, but they are devoid of understanding both before and after' or 'it is so, but they are devoid of understanding all the time, both before and after'.

At the end of the fragment, other men are criticized for ignorance of what they *do*, not simply for their opinions about the world at large. This corresponds to the criticism in fr. 23 that they ζώουσιν ὡς ἰδίην ἔχοντες φρόνησιν. Their non-comprehension is compared to that of the sleeper. ἐπιλανθάνονται does not here mean 'forget' things they were aware of while sleeping, for fr. 24 = B 89 shows that Heraclitus does not hold that sleepers have knowledge of a real world which they forget when they wake up; it is the personal verb equivalent to the preceding λανθάνει, 'they are unmindful of, have no consciousness of'.[3] The reference is to bodily movements which they make while dreaming.[4]

[1] Cf. below, τοιούτων ὁκοίων ἐγὼ διηγέομαι; Hdt. 7. 16β. 2 ἐνύπνια . . . τοιαῦτά ἐστι οἷά σε ἐγὼ διδάξω. (γ. 1) εἰ δ' ἄρα μή ἐστι τοῦτο τοιοῦτον οἷον ἐγὼ διαιρέω.

[2] Reinhardt, *Parmenides*, p. 61; W. Capelle, *Hermes* 59, 1924, 200 f.

[3] Gigon, p. 6. I follow Kirk (*HCF*, p. 44) and Marcovich in thinking that Marc. Ant. 4. 46 (= B 73) is merely an allusion to the present fragment. Cf. also Lucr. 3. 1047 f.

[4] Arist. *parv. nat.* 456ᵃ24 κινοῦνται δ' ἔνιοι καθεύδοντες καὶ ποιοῦσι πολλὰ ἐγρηγορικά, οὐ μέντοι ἄνευ φαντάσματος καὶ αἰσθήσεώς τινος . . . τὰ μὲν ἐνύπνια μνημονεύουσιν ἐγερθέντες, τὰς δ' ἐγρηγορικὰς πράξεις οὐ μνημονεύουσιν.

I translate the fragment, accordingly:

'And of this my account, which stands throughout, men prove uncomprehending, both before they hear it and once they have heard it. For though everything goes on in accordance with this my account, they seem unacquainted with it, acquainted as they are both with the language I use and with such facts as I explain, as I judge[1] each thing according to its real nature and indicate the truth about it, while the rest remain as unaware of what they do when they are awake as they are of what they do when they are asleep.'

Fragment 23(a) (*B 114 and 2*)

Heraclitus has chosen to begin his discourse with a manifesto-type preface. A statement of principle such as ἰσχυρίζεσθαι χρὴ τῷ ξυνῷ πάντων is in place here; compare especially Diog. Apoll. 64 B 1 λόγου παντὸς ἀρχόμενον δοκεῖ μοι χρεὼν εἶναι τὴν ἀρχὴν ἀναμφισβήτητον παρέχεσθαι. As a number of scholars have seen, the ἰσχυρίζεσθαι fragment fits very well before τοῦ λόγου δὲ ἐόντος ξυνοῦ, which, Sextus tells us, followed fr. 1 after a short interval. If ξὺν νῷ λέγοντας followed directly on fr. 1, the emphatic opening phrase would stand in antithesis to the senseless rest who have just been castigated; they will include senseless speakers.[2]

A sensible speaker must take his stand on what is common to all, as a city on its law and custom, and much more so; for the (manifold) laws of men's cities all branch off from, and are inferior to, a single divine law (and so are common to all only on the local view). There is a latent implication that an intelligent man may be capable of improving on the city's established usages; at any rate, their absolute validity is subject to qualification.

[1] Cf. Powell, *Lexicon to Herodotus*, s.v. (Kirk, *HCF*, p. 41).

[2] Cleanthes, a keen student of Heraclitus who wrote a commentary on him in four books, and drew comparisons between his views and Zeno's (Eus. *PE* 15. 20. 2, *SVF* i. 117. 20), gave Zeno's σπερματικὸς λόγος a Heraclitean turn by identifying it with the κοινὸς καὶ θεῖος νόμος which people obey σὺν νῷ (*Hymn to Zeus* 21–5, cf. 2, 12, 39; Chrys. *ap.* D.L. 7. 88, *SVF* iii. 4. 3 (wrongly printed also under Zeno, i. 43. 2)). If the three fragments of Heraclitus belonged together in the way here accepted, it is obvious how Cleanthes arrived at this combination.

The following fragment, like fr. 1, is quoted by Sextus, in a passage where he is trying to demonstrate that Heraclitus' criterion for truth was the *κοινὸς λόγος*, in other words, that what commended itself to the minds of men generally was true, while the private opinions of individuals were false. Heraclitus actually believed the precise opposite: that the mass of men were deluded, and that he alone saw the truth. By *ἰσχυρίζεσθαι τῷ ξυνῷ πάντων* he did not mean 'follow the general opinion' but 'take one's stand on universal principles' (such as the identity of opposites). We can see that Sextus is trying to read his epistemological theory into fragments which mean something altogether different. After a long general account (fr. 116 = A 16), he quotes fr. 1, and reads into its harmless 'discourse' a theory of participation by men in a Divine Reason:

διὰ τούτων γὰρ ῥητῶς παραστήσας ὅτι κατὰ μετοχὴν τοῦ θείου λόγου πάντα πράττομέν τε καὶ νοοῦμεν, ὀλίγα προσδιελθὼν ἐπιφέρει· διὸ δεῖ ἕπεσθαι τῷ κοινῷ· ξυνὸς γὰρ ὁ κοινός· "τοῦ λόγου δὲ ἐόντος ξυνοῦ ζώουσιν οἱ πολλοὶ ὡς ἰδίαν ἔχοντες φρόνησιν."

This is fr. 23(*a*) *bis* (B 2). It is usually assumed that something is wrong with the text, the words *διὸ δεῖ ἕπεσθαι τῷ κοινῷ* being part of the fragment and requiring emendation to *διὸ δεῖ ἕπεσθαι τῷ ξυνῷ* (*ξυνὸς γὰρ ὁ κοινός*) (Schleiermacher), or *τῷ* ⟨*ξυνῷ, τουτέστι τῷ*⟩ *κοινῷ· ξυνὸς γὰρ ὁ κοινός* (Bekker). I agree with Bywater that they are not part of the fragment. There are linguistic objections to them as Heraclitus' own words:

1. *διό* is very rare in early prose. Herodotus has it only twice in the whole of his work (the two instances are close together, 7. 6. 4 and 7. 8*a*. 2), Thucydides only five times. It cannot be ruled out for Heraclitus, but it is suspect.
2. We expect Heraclitus to say *χρή*, not *δεῖ*. Cf., besides *ἰσχυρίζεσθαι χρή*, frs. 7(?), 28, 102, 103 (B 35, 43, 44, 80). Marc. Ant. 4. 46 (B 73, 74) is paraphrase, not verbatim quotation.
3. *ἕπεσθαι* in Heraclitus could mean 'conform to' (cf. Hdt.

5. 18. 2; Kirk, *HCF*, p. 60), but hardly 'rely on' for understanding of the truth;[1] in Sextus it easily can, because his whole discussion is epistemological.

The sentence seems in fact to be a paraphrase of *ἰσχυρίζεσθαι χρὴ τῷ ξυνῷ πάντων*. Perhaps it had displaced it in Sextus' source, or perhaps it has displaced it in his manuscript tradition. It is at any rate incredible that, if Sextus knew that *ἰσχυρίζεσθαι κτλ.* stood here, he should deliberately pass over ("*ὀλίγα προσδιελθών*") something so ideally suited to his argument.[2]

Sextus' interpretation of *λόγος* is obviously no more in place here than in fr. 1. There Heraclitus had said *τοῦ δὲ λόγου τοῦδε ἐόντος αἰεὶ ἀξύνετοι γίνονται ἄνθρωποι*, and meant 'Whereas this my account stands throughout, men prove uncomprehending.' If shortly afterwards he says *τοῦ λόγου δὲ ἐόντος ξυνοῦ ζώουσιν οἱ πολλοὶ ὡς ἰδίην ἔχοντες φρόνησιν*, he must have meant something corresponding: 'And whereas my account is public, they live mostly as though they had a private understanding.' Heraclitus' account is 'valid for all', 'of general concern', like the city's law. It is the antithesis of the miscellany of *λόγοι* over which the *βλὰξ ἄνθρωπος ἐπτοῆσθαι φιλεῖ* (fr. 109 = B 87). Yet people do not live in the way that it calls for.

Fragment 24 (B 89)

The contrast between the *ξυνὸς λόγος* and *ὡς ἰδίην ἔχοντες φρόνησιν* is closely paralleled by the contrast in fr. 24 (not a verbatim quotation) between the *εἷς κοινὸς κόσμος* of the waking world and the *ἴδιος κόσμος* to which each sleeper turns away. In fr. 1 the uncomprehending hearers of the *λόγος ἐὼν αἰεί* were scornfully likened to men asleep; it strengthens the parallelism already noted between frs. 1 and 23 if the disunited hearers of the *λόγος ἐὼν ξυνός* are shown to be like men asleep in a different respect. If the association was already in Heraclitus' mind at the

[1] It is a variant for *πείθονται* in fr. 101 = B 104.

[2] If he quoted it after *ὀλίγα προσδιελθὼν ἐπιφέρει*, I should of course have to abandon the suggestion that it followed straight after fr. 1.

end of fr. 1, the transition from the sleepers there to ἰσχυρίζεσθαι χρὴ τῷ ξυνῷ πάντων becomes more significant.

Plutarch casts the fragment in indirect speech, and opinions vary on the extent to which he has reworded it. Elsewhere in Heraclitus, wakers and sleepers are twice contrasted as ἐγερθέντες and εὕδοντες,[1] twice as ἐγρηγορώς and (καθ)εύδων;[2] 'common' and 'private' are ξυνός and ἴδιος.[3] κόσμος must be Heraclitus', from the way Plutarch picks it up with his own τῷ δὲ δεισιδαίμονι κοινὸς οὐδεὶς ⟨οὐδ' ἴδιός⟩ ἐστι κόσμος. The use of the word for a subjective world, or set of appearances, is unparalleled, but perhaps more likely at an early period, when κόσμος still had its full sense of 'arrangement', than later.[4]

Fragments 51 (B 30), 53 (B 31), 54 (B 90), 33 (B 60)

There is another advantage in putting fr. 24 here. As soon as the manifesto-preface is complete, Heraclitus will begin his exposition. The first section, which we know to have been περὶ τοῦ παντός, would naturally start with the question of the world's origin (cf. p. 78). That is dealt with once and for all in fr. 51, which begins κόσμον τόνδε, τὸν αὐτὸν ἁπάντων.[5] This must be a reference to the distinction between the one real world that is the same for all and the many worlds of delusion.[6] Such a reference would be natural if (and perhaps only if) the fragment followed close after fr. 24 where the distinction was made.[7]

Fr. 53 followed immediately, or at any rate closely, after 51, as Clement's words τὰ ἐπιφερόμενα show. Taking the two

[1] Fr. 1 = B 1, 49 = B 21; cf. Pl. *Tim.* 46 a, 52 c.

[2] Fr. 41 = B 88, 48 = B 26; cf. Pl. *Tim.* 85 b.

[3] Fr. 23. ἕνα καὶ κοινόν may be Plutarch's expansion; but cf. perhaps above, p. 112 n. 1.

[4] Cf. Melissus B 7. 3, Emp. B 26. 5, Anaxag. B 8; Reinhardt, *Parmenides*, pp. 174 f. Heraclitus' κόσμον τόνδε (fr. 51 = B 30; cf. Diog. Apoll. B 2) may be translated 'this world', but it is only a step beyond τάδε πάντα. Cf. Kahn, p. 228; below, p. 196.

[5] Gigon, pp. 52 f.: 'Wir haben hier sozusagen einen zweiten Anfang, den kosmogonischen Anfang der Milesier mit der Nennung der physischen ἀρχή. Frg. 30 mag den kosmologischen Teil des Werkes eröffnet haben.' For the genuineness of the words τὸν αὐτὸν ἁπάντων see Marcovich, ed. pp. 268–70.

[6] Vlastos, *AJP* 76, 1955, 345 n. 18.

[7] Cf. Kirk–Raven, p. 199.

fragments together, we see that Heraclitus is being very brisk and methodical:

1. The world is an everlasting fire with measured changes.
2. The first change is into sea.
3. The sea's change is half into earth, half into πρηστήρ.
4. The earth is dispersed.

It is easy to guess that the next sentence explained what happened to the πρηστήρ.

Once the cycle of changes was fully stated, a restatement of the primacy of fire would be in place, on the principle of ring composition, and in fr. 54 we appear to have such a restatement. It is here too that, if I were Heraclitus, I would feel compelled to blurt out my idea of the 'way up and down' that is one and the same (fr. 33). There is strong evidence that this 'way up and down' had a cosmological significance, and referred to the changes of fire. It had better be set out, because some scholars have denied it.

1. The late-fifth-century Heracliteans were particularly taken with Heraclitus' remark that the river you step into twice is not the same (fr. 40 = B 12, 49a, 91). It had probably been intended to illustrate that a thing's substance can be changing without affecting its shape and measurements; but they altered the emphasis, and made it appear the cardinal doctrine of Heraclitus that all things are fluid and transient, and that there is no stability in the world.[1] It was from this angle that they saw Heraclitus' theory of cosmic change. For Plato, the phrase ἄνω καὶ κάτω was associated with it, and characterized the flux as alternating, first running one way and then reversed.

> *Phaedo* 90 c (οἱ περὶ τοὺς ἀντιλογικοὺς λόγους διατρίψαντες) τελευτῶντες οἴονται σοφώτατοι γεγονέναι καὶ κατανενοηκέναι μόνοι ὅτι οὔτε τῶν πραγμάτων οὐδενὸς οὐδὲν ὑγιὲς οὐδὲ βέβαιον οὔτε τῶν λόγων, ἀλλὰ πάντα τὰ ὄντα ἀτεχνῶς ὥσπερ ἐν Εὐρίπῳ ἄνω κάτω στρέφεται καὶ χρόνον οὐδένα ἐν οὐδενὶ μένει.

[1] See the passages from Plato and Aristotle set out by Kirk, *HCF*, pp. 14 ff., Marcovich, ed. pp. 194 ff., and cf. above, p. 111 n. 1.

Phileb. 43 a ἀλλὰ γὰρ οἶμαι τόδε λέγεις, ὡς ἀεί τι τούτων (pleasure and pain) ἀναγκαῖον ἡμῖν συμβαίνειν, ὡς οἱ σοφοί φασιν· ἀεὶ γὰρ ἅπαντα ἄνω τε καὶ κάτω ῥεῖ.—Λέγουσι γὰρ οὖν, καὶ δοκοῦσί γε οὐ φαύλως λέγειν.—Πῶς γὰρ ἄν, μὴ φαῦλοί γε ὄντες;

(In *Cratylus* 413 e–414 a, on the other hand, the word ἀνδρεία is interpreted as ἀν-ῥεία, ἡ ἄνω ῥοή, that is, running against a (wrongful) current, for if all things are a flux, then battle is in reality a simultaneous two-way flux.[1])

Plato, then, habitually associates the idea 'up and down' with the Heraclitean theory of cosmic change as he conceives it. We know that Heraclitus used the phrase: here is our earliest source apparently alluding to it in the specific context of cosmology.

2. [Hp.] *vict.* 1. 5, in a section full of Heraclitean echoes, writes: χωρεῖ δὲ πάντα καὶ θεῖα καὶ ἀνθρώπινα ἄνω καὶ κάτω ἀμειβόμενα· ἡμέρη καὶ εὐφρόνη ἐπὶ τὸ μήκιστον καὶ ἐλάχιστον, ἥλιος καὶ σελήνη ⟨ἐπὶ⟩ τὸ μήκιστον καὶ ἐλάχιστον, πυρὸς ἔφοδος καὶ ὕδατος ἐπὶ τὸ μακρότατον καὶ βραχύτατον. This text probably dates from the mid fourth century.[2] πάντα χωρεῖ is exactly Plato's formulation of Heraclitus' teaching in *Crat.* 402 a. Again the idea is of constant alternation, and ἄνω καὶ κάτω is used to express it. The author seems to have known Plato's work, but he also had some direct knowledge of Heraclitus, and may be an independent witness at least to the fifth-century interpretation. His ἀμειβόμενα recalls Heraclitus' πυρὸς ἀνταμοιβὴ τὰ πάντα, although he applies it to alternations such as day and night.

3. Aristotle (*Meteor.* 347ᵃ2 ff.) likens the meteorological cycle of rising evaporation, condensation, and precipitation to a ποταμὸς ῥέων κύκλῳ ἄνω καὶ κάτω, and goes on to suggest that if the ancients meant their river Oceanus as an allegory, this might have been what they meant. He must have been familiar

[1] There is possibly an echo of the Heracliteans in Eur. *Med.* 410 f. ἄνω ποταμῶν ἱερῶν χωροῦσι παγαί, καὶ Δίκα καὶ πάντα πάλιν στρέφεται.

[2] See Kirk, *HCF*, pp. 26–9. Kahn, p. 189 n. 2, seems to ascribe it to Herodicus of Selymbria, the teacher of Hippocrates, but I cannot believe in such an early date. 1. 18 seems to me to presuppose Pl. *Symp.* 187 a (cf. Arist. *Eth. Eud.* 1235ᵃ25, [Arist.] *de mundo* 396ᵇ15; Kirk, *HCF*, pp. 209, 243; Marcovich, ed. p. 124).

with the allegorical account of Oceanus twice put forward (in jest?) by Plato (*Crat.* 402 b–c, *Theaet.* 152 e), who connects it with Heraclitus' universal flux. It is possible that his train of thought was simply 'circulation of elements: river flowing round and round: Oceanus', but on the whole it seems more likely that it was 'circulation of elements up and down: Heraclitus' river: Oceanus'.

4. Theophrastus, who had the text of Heraclitus in front of him and was striving to formulate a clear and faithful account of the cosmology contained in it, stated that Heraclitus called the interchange of elements 'the way up and down'. The change fire–water–earth was the way down, and the change earth–water–exhalation was the way up (D.L. 9. 8–9). I do not think that Heraclitus was as explicit as this, and I think that Theophrastus has got the details wrong (see below); but I cannot see any reason to suppose that he read 'way up and down' out of context and gave it an arbitrary interpretation.

5. The Stoics were by no means dependent upon Theophrastus for their knowledge of Heraclitus; they studied him directly. But they understood the way up and down in the same way as Theophrastus.[1]

Some authors transferred Heraclitus' famous phrase to other contexts—the mutability of fortune, and so on (see Kirk, *HCF*, p. 106). This is understandable, and does not throw doubt on the interpretation indicated by all the good and early sources. The fact that Hippolytus quotes the fragment verbatim merely as an example of Heraclitus' belief in the identity of opposites does not mean that that was its only point in the original; he is collecting all the examples of that belief that he can find in Heraclitus, and this clearly is one.[2]

[1] Cf. Lucr. 1. 788, Cic. *ND* 2. 84 (and 3. 31); Philo *de aetern. mundi* 109 (quoted on p. 136); Epict. fr. 8 p. 460 Schenkl; Marc. Ant. 6. 17; Cleomedes *de motu circ. corp.* 1. 11 (61) p. 112. 1 Ziegler (from Posidonius, according to Reinhardt, *Poseidonios*, p. 200, *Hermes* 77, 1942, 17 = *Vermächtnis*, p. 59). So also Max. Tyr. 41. 4 p. 481 Hobein.

[2] Kirk, *HCF*, p. 109 quotes also [Hp.] *nutr.* 45, where ὁδὸς ἄνω κάτω μία is appended to a denial of absolute good and bad in conditions of the blood, and seems to be used just as a relativistic motto; and Luc. *vit. auct.* 14 (a cento of

No 'Logos-doctrine' in Heraclitus

I shall now abandon the attempt to follow the order of Heraclitus' thoughts, and enlarge upon some of the themes connected with the fragments I have discussed.

Firstly, it will have been noticed that in frs. 1 and 23 (B 1, 2) I insisted that the word *λόγος* referred to Heraclitus' discourse and nothing else. Almost all students of Heraclitus have supposed that in these and some other fragments—or in Heraclitus' thought considered without reference to particular fragments—he used *λόγος* in some larger sense of his own: the truth behind the discourse, divine reason, the 'formula of things', the Logos, and so on. It seems to me that there is no foundation for this notion, but two reasons for its persistence, one general and one specific: the power of exegetical tradition, whose mists can deceive even the clear-sighted (the Neoplatonists were not all born stupid); and inadequate recognition of the way in which Ionian writers tend to refer to their discourses as self-activated autonomous beings.[1] Those scholars who have attempted a struggle against the first difficulty have generally been defeated by the second.[2] Two exceptions known to me deserve to be named with honour: Burnet, and H. W. J. Surig, the author of a dissertation entitled *De betekenis van Logos bij Herakleitos volgens de traditie en de fragmenten* (Nijmegen 1951).

Surig points out that neither Plato nor Aristotle breathes a word about a 'Logos-doctrine'; that there is no mention of it in either the long or the short account of Heraclitus' teaching

Heraclitean phrases) *ἔστι τωὐτὸ τέρψις ἀτερψίη, γνῶσις ἀγνωσίη, μέγα μικρόν, ἄνω κάτω*, where however he ought in fairness to have given the next words too, *περιχωρέοντα καὶ ἀμειβόμενα ἐν τῇ τοῦ Αἰῶνος παιδιῇ*. Kirk further argues that Aristotle's complaint in *Phys.* 253^b9, that those who say everything is in perpetual movement do not explain its direction, is 'surprising if Heraclitus himself had defined cosmic motion in terms of what might appear to be absolute "up" and "down"'. But firstly, Heraclitus' up and down were one and the same—Aristotle could hardly accept that; secondly, *ἄνω κάτω* can mean simply 'to and fro'.

[1] Above, p. 115 n. 2; below, p. 127 and n. 2.

[2] Cf. Reinhardt, *Parmenides*, p. 217 n. 1; A. Busse, *Rh. Mus.* 75, 1926, 203 ff.; Gigon, pp. 4–19; E. L. Minar, *CPh* 34, 1939, 323 ff.; Verdenius, *Phronesis* 11, 1966, 81 ff.; U. Hölscher, in *Varia Variorum* (Festgabe Reinhardt), 1952, pp. 69 ff., and *Anfängliches Fragen*, 1968, pp. 130 ff.

that Diogenes derived from Theophrastus; and that no reliance can be placed on the epistemological theory attributed to Heraclitus by Sextus Empiricus and supported by the quotation of fragments 1 and 23, that we are rational through contact with the *θεῖος καὶ κοινὸς λόγος*.[1] In the rest of the doxographical tradition, *λόγος* is mentioned only by Aetius, who says that Heraclitus explained *εἱμαρμένη* as the *λόγος* which runs through and shapes all things: 1. 7. 22 *λόγον ἐκ τῆς ἐναντιοδρομίας δημιουργὸν τῶν ὄντων*, 1. 28. 1 *λόγον τὸν διὰ οὐσίας τοῦ παντὸς διήκοντα . . . καὶ περιόδου μέτρον τεταγμένης*. The thought and language are obviously Stoic.[2] Contrast Diogenes, who says *πάντα δὲ γίνεσθαι καθ' εἱμαρμένην καὶ διὰ τῆς †ἐναντιοτροπῆς ἡρμόσθαι τὰ ὄντα* (9. 7, cf. 8), but not a word about *λόγος*.

This leaves the fragments themselves. They must be discussed individually. (I am not here attempting to summarize Surig's work, but presenting the case as it appears to me.) Fragments 1 and 23 have already been dealt with; three other fragments containing the word *λόγος* in obviously ordinary senses can be set aside.[3]

Fr. 4 (B 72): Marc. Ant. 4. 46 *μεμνῆσθαι δὲ . . . καὶ ὅτι ᾧ μάλιστα διηνεκῶς ὁμιλοῦσι, λόγῳ τῷ τὰ ὅλα διοικοῦντι, τούτῳ διαφέρονται, καὶ οἷς καθ' ἡμέραν ἐγκυροῦσι, ταῦτα αὐτοῖς ξένα φαίνεται.*

[1] See above, p. 118. In writing *πρὸς λογικούς* Sextus naturally speaks in terms of *λόγος*, not only in dealing with Heraclitus but in dealing with other philosophers from Thales on: *adv. math.* 7. 89 ff.

[2] Zeno, *SVF* i. 24. 31 *διὰ ταύτης δὲ (τῆς ὕλης) διαθεῖν τὸν τοῦ παντὸς λόγον, ὃν ἔνιοι εἱμαρμένην καλοῦσι*, D.L. 7. 149 (on Zeno, Chrysippus, and Posidonius) *ἔστι δὲ εἱμαρμένη . . . λόγος καθ' ὃν ὁ κόσμος διεξάγεται*, Marc. Ant. 5. 32 *τὸν δι' ὅλης τῆς οὐσίας διήκοντα λόγον καὶ διὰ παντὸς τοῦ αἰῶνος κατὰ περιόδους τεταγμένας οἰκονομοῦντα τὸ πᾶν*, Clem. *Strom.* 5. 89. 3 *ἀλλ' οἱ μὲν (Στωικοὶ) διήκειν διὰ πάσης τῆς οὐσίας τὸν θεόν φασιν*. Aetius' next entry in 1. 28, claiming to give Plato's view of *εἱμαρμένη*, again imports the Stoic *λόγος*: *Πλάτων λόγον ἀΐδιον καὶ νόμον ἀΐδιον τῆς τοῦ παντὸς φύσεως.*

[3] 83 = B 108 *ὁκόσων λόγους ἤκουσα*, 109 = B 87 *βλὰξ ἄνθρωπος ἐπὶ παντὶ λόγῳ ἐπτοῆσθαι φιλεῖ*, 100 = B 39 *Βίας . . . οὗ πλέων λόγος ἢ τῶν ἄλλων* (cf. Pind. *N.* 7. 20 *πλέον' ἔλπομαι λόγον 'Οδυσσέος ἢ πάθαν διὰ τὸν ἁδυεπῆ γενέσθ' Ὅμηρον*, Hdt. 8. 10. 3 *Ἀθηναίων γὰρ αὐτοῖσι λόγος ἦν πλεῖστος ἀνὰ τὰ στρατόπεδα*).

The initial position of *ἐν Πριήνῃ* in the Bias fragment is striking. Did it come from a passage in which Heraclitus passed judgement on a series of *σοφοί*? These would be 'the others' who were of less account than Bias.

The latter part may be an echo of fr. 3 (B 17) *οὐ γὰρ φρονέουσι τοιαῦτα πολλοὶ ὁκοίοις ἐγκυρέουσιν κτλ.*; the first part may be a paraphrase of the same, or represent a separate fragment. As elsewhere, Marcus is adding comment of his own, and the phrase *λόγῳ τῷ τὰ ὅλα διοικοῦντι* is evidently added by him as an explanation of what it is, as it at present strikes him, that men most constantly consort with and are at variance with.[1] Diels and Walzer attribute only *τῷ τὰ ὅλα διοικοῦντι* to Marcus and *λόγῳ* to Heraclitus. What is the *λόγος* then, and in what sense do they consort with it most? Are there others that they consort with less? *λόγος ὁ τὰ ὅλα διοικῶν* is an indivisible phrase, and unmistakably Stoic.[2]

Fr. 26 (B 50): Hipp. *Ref.* 9. 9 *Ἡράκλειτος μὲν οὖν φησιν εἶναι τὸ πᾶν διαιρετὸν ἀδιαίρετον, γενητὸν ἀγένητον, θνητὸν ἀθάνατον, λόγον αἰῶνα, πατέρα υἱόν, θεὸν δίκαιον· "οὐκ ἐμοῦ ἀλλὰ τοῦ δόγματος ἀκούσαντας ὁμολογεῖν σοφόν ἐστιν ἓν πάντα εἰδέναι". καὶ ὅτι τοῦτο οὐκ ἴσασι πάντες οὐδὲ ὁμολογέουσιν, ἐπιμέμφεται ὧδέ πως·* (fr. 27 = B 51.)

The words *λόγον αἰῶνα*, like the remainder of what precedes *οὐκ ἐμοῦ*, are Hippolytus' own elaboration of the Heraclitean idea of the unity of opposites.[3] The verbatim quotation is confined to the corrupt words *οὐκ ἐμοῦ . . . εἰδέναι*. Bernays's *λόγου* is a generally accepted emendation of *δόγματος*, a word whose intrusion was invited by Hippolytus' subject-matter, and one occurring (in the genitive plural) shortly before. The end of the fragment must be discussed in the next chapter; we are for the moment only concerned with the meaning of *λόγος*.

It is said that a contrast between the speaker and his discourse is bizarre,[4] and that *λόγος* must therefore mean something else.

[1] So Bywater; Burnet, *CR* 15, 1901, 423.

[2] Cf. in Marcus himself, 6. 1 *ἡ τῶν ὅλων οὐσία εὐπειθὴς καὶ εὐτρεπής· ὁ δὲ ταύτην διοικῶν λόγος* . . ., 6. 5 *ὁ διοικῶν λόγος*, 6. 42 *ὁ τὰ ὅλα διοικῶν*, 7. 25 *ἡ τὰ ὅλα διοικοῦσα φύσις*, 11. 18. See also Chrysippus *ap.* D.L. 7. 87 (*SVF* iii. 4. 7) and *ap.* Philod. *π. εὐσ.* 11 (*SVF* ii. 315. 4), Alex. Aphrod. *de fato* p. 192. 26 (*SVF* ii. 273. 26), Clem. *Strom.* 5. 104. 4, Hipp. *Ref.* 9. 10. 7.

[3] Cf. Kirk, *HCF*, p. 66; Marcovich, *Studia Patristica* 7, 1966, 255 ff., and ed. p. 113.

[4] Kirk, *HCF*, p. 67: 'especially for Heraclitus, who shows no signs of wishing

But the contrast has a point, the harder for us to grasp because we cannot easily make it in English. 'Don't listen to me but to what I'm saying' makes puzzling advice. But we must bear in mind firstly that *ἀκούω* often contains the idea of *attending* to what is said (hence *obeying*, etc.), secondly that Heraclitus does not say *τὸν λόγον* but *τοῦ λόγου*. *ἀκοῦσαι τὸν λόγον* would be the same as *ἀκοῦσαι Ἡρακλείτου*, but *ἀκοῦσαι τοῦ λόγου* is something that can be distinguished from it. *λόγος* is something that can be heard, just as in fr. 1, and it can influence the hearer to *ὁμο-λογεῖν*, to say the same.[1] It is still, in fact, Heraclitus' discourse; but it is being treated as something that speaks, instead of something that is spoken.[2] Heraclitus is telling men that they should be persuaded not by his personal authority but by the autonomous authority of his argument. He said elsewhere that they should not listen 'like children to their parents'.[3] Fools are excited whatever you tell them. (Fr. 109 = B 87.) It is important to know how to listen: fr. 1(*g*) = B 19 *ἀκοῦσαι οὐκ ἐπιστάμενοι οὐδ' εἰπεῖν ⟨ὀφείλουσι⟩*.[4] Uncomprehending hearers are like deaf men: fr. 2 = B 34 *ἀξύνετοι ἀκούσαντες κωφοῖσιν ἐοίκασι*. They hear, and do not hear: they hear Heraclitus, but are deaf to the argument.

to subdue his own personality in the pronouncement of the truth'. But this overshoots the mark; by saying *οὐκ ἐμεῦ ἀλλά* . . . Heraclitus is 'subduing his own personality', whatever the meaning of *λόγος*.

1 Kirk's attempt to interpret *ὁμολογεῖν* on the assumption that *λόγος* means 'something far beyond "word" ' (*HCF*, p. 68) is a characteristic example of the oddities and complexities that that assumption always brings in its train.

2 Cf. above, p. 115 n. 2; Hdt. 9. 122. 1 *Ἀρτεμβάρης . . . ὁ Πέρσῃσι ἐξηγησάμενος λόγον, τὸν ἐκεῖνοι ὑπολαβόντες Κύρῳ προσήνεικαν, λέγοντα τάδε*, 5. 90. 2 *οἱ χρησμοὶ λέγοντες* . . ., etc.; Pl. *Gorg*. 523 a *ἄκουε δή, φασί, μάλα καλοῦ λόγου*, *Tim*. 20 d; Arist. *Metaph*. 1012a24 *ὁ Ἡρακλείτου λόγος λέγων πάντα εἶναι καὶ μὴ εἶναι*, *Eth. Nic*. 1179b26 *οὐ γὰρ ἂν ἀκούσειε λόγου ἀποτρέποντος οὐδ' αὖ συνείη ὁ κατὰ πάθος ζῶν*, Luc. *Hermot*. 66 *μὴ ἐμέ, ὤγαθε, ἐρώτα, ἀλλὰ τὸν λόγον αὖθις αὐτόν. καὶ ἴσως ἂν ἀποκρίναιτό σοι ὅτι κτλ*.

3 Marc. Ant. 4. 46 (fr. 89 = B 74) *καὶ ὅτι οὐ δεῖ ⟨ἀκούειν ὡς⟩ παῖδας τοκεώνων, τουτέστι κατὰ ψιλόν* ('without evidence', cf. LSJ *ψιλός* IV. 1), *καθότι παρειλήφαμεν*. with Apul. *apol*. 39 *an de dis immortalibus patri et matri credere?*

4 The addition of *ὀφείλουσι* gives a much improved sense; the word could easily have dropped out before *ὠφεληθείς*, which immediately follows in Clement. Cf. in general fr. 110 = B 109 *κρύπτειν ἀμαθίην κρέσσον ἢ ἐς τὸ μέσον φέρειν*, Democr. B 86 *πλεονεξίη τὸ πάντα λέγειν, μηδὲν δὲ ἐθέλειν ἀκούειν*.

Fr. 47(*c*) (B 62): Clem. *Paed.* 3. 2. 1 ὀρθῶς ἄρα εἶπεν Ἡράκλειτος· ἄνθρωποι θεοί, θεοὶ ἄνθρωποι· λόγος γὰρ ὡυτός.

The form ὡυτός could have been introduced by scribes if they thought it part of the fragment, cf. the impossible ὡυτή in fr. 33 (Hippolytus). λόγος γὰρ ὁ αὐτός is likely to be Clement's, but if it should be Heraclitus' (Gigon, p. 124), it will mean no more than 'the principle is the same'.[1]

Fr. 53 (B 31) μετρεῖται ἐς τὸν αὐτὸν λόγον ὁκοῖος πρόσθεν ἦν means 'it is measured to the same amount as was there before'. The idea of a given quantity seems to be present also in two fragments which speak of a λόγος of the soul:

Fr. 67 (B 45) ψυχῆς πείρατα οὐκ ἂν ἐξεύροις πᾶσαν ἰὼν ὁδόν· οὕτω βαθὺν λόγον ἔχει.[2]

Fr. 112 (B 115) (Σωκράτους·) ψυχῆς ἐστι λόγος ἑαυτὸν αὔξων.[3]

If the soul's λόγος is related to its πείρατα, and can 'increase' and be 'deep', it must be quantitative, as in fr. 53, a 'measure' or 'account'. It is a property of the soul, not something with a separate existence, a 'Logos'.

Our review of the evidence therefore leads to the conclusion that Heraclitus uses λόγος only in the ordinary senses of the word attested in and before the fifth century,[4] and that the Logos can

[1] Cf. Hdt. 1. 134, 186, 7. 95; 'Hp.' *aer.* 14, 18, 23; Epich. fr. 170 b Kaibel (23 B 2. 12); Pl. *Theaet.* 158 d, *Parm.* 136 b.

[2] For the text see Wilamowitz, *Hermes* 62, 1927, 276 f. = *Kl. Schr.* iv. 432. ἐξεύροις, which he prints without comment, is more idiomatic than the middle read by Diels (ἐξεύροι ὁ mss.). Cf. the echo in the *Enchiridion Sexti* 403 (= fr. 67(*c*)) σοφοῦ ψυχῆς μέγεθος οὐκ ἂν ἐξεύροις μᾶλλον ἤπερ καὶ θεοῦ.

[3] Marcovich (*Phronesis* 11, 1966, 29 = *Estudios* p. 28; ed. p. 569) rightly draws attention to the suspicious resemblance to Xenocrates' definition of the soul as ἀριθμὸς ἑαυτὸν κινῶν (fr. 60–8 Heinze); Stobaeus' Σωκράτους might in theory be a mistake for Ξενοκράτους. But I think that Hense's ascription of the fragment to Heraclitus is more likely, in view of fr. 67 = B 45, and the double divergence from Xenocrates' statement (which many authors quote). Admittedly one can build a bridge over the gap by quoting Plotinus 6. 5. 9, who mentions people who say that the soul is an ἀριθμὸς ἑαυτὸν αὔξων, and 3. 6. 1, 5. 1. 5, Andronicus *ap.* Themist. *paraphr. Arist. de an.* p. 32. 25 Heinze (Comm. in Arist. gr. V. 3), where ἀριθμός is linked with λόγος in this context.

[4] Illustrated and discussed by Guthrie, *HGP* i. 420–4, who refers also to H. Boeder in *Arch. f. Begriffsgeschichte* 4, 1958, 82–112.

Boundary-stone of Gula-Eresh. Twelfth century B.C.

PLATE II

a. Assyrian cylinder seal

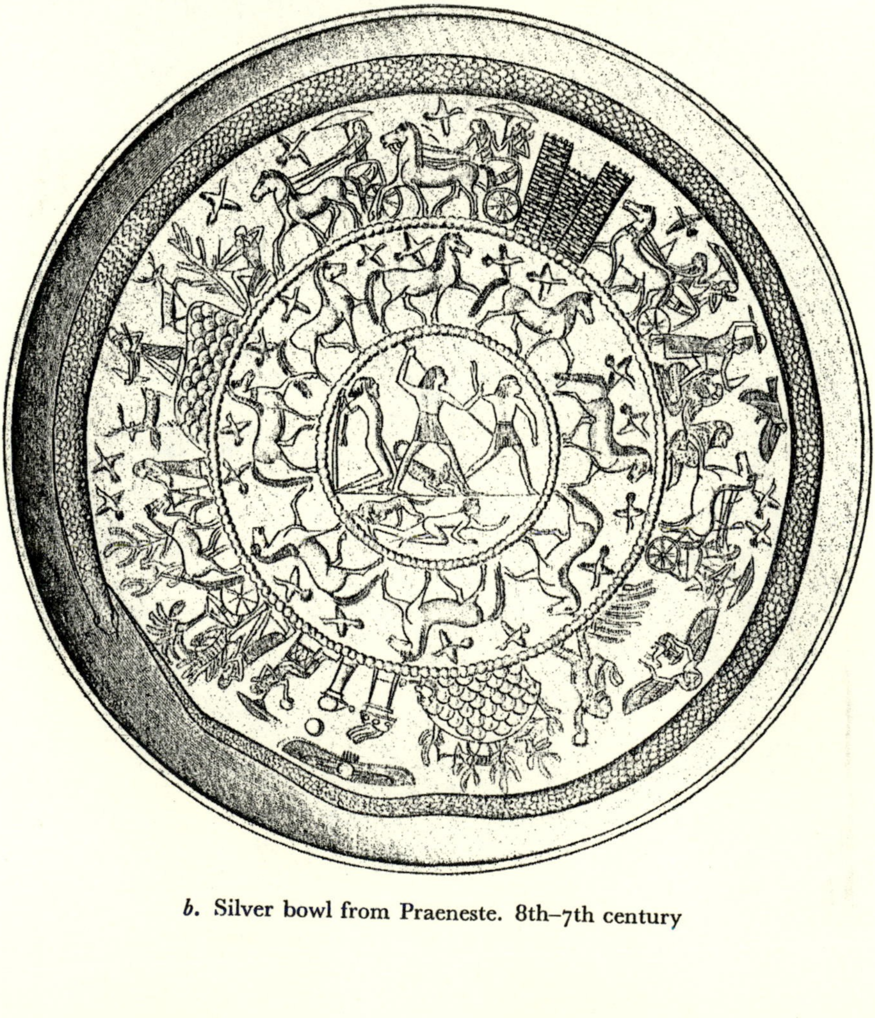

b. Silver bowl from Praeneste. 8th–7th century

Mithraic reliefs from Dacia and Moesia. Compare the representations of ocean in the lower right corners

PLATE IV

Central part of relief at Aṅkor Wāt, Cambodia.
Twelfth century A.D.

Babylonian map of the world

PLATE VI

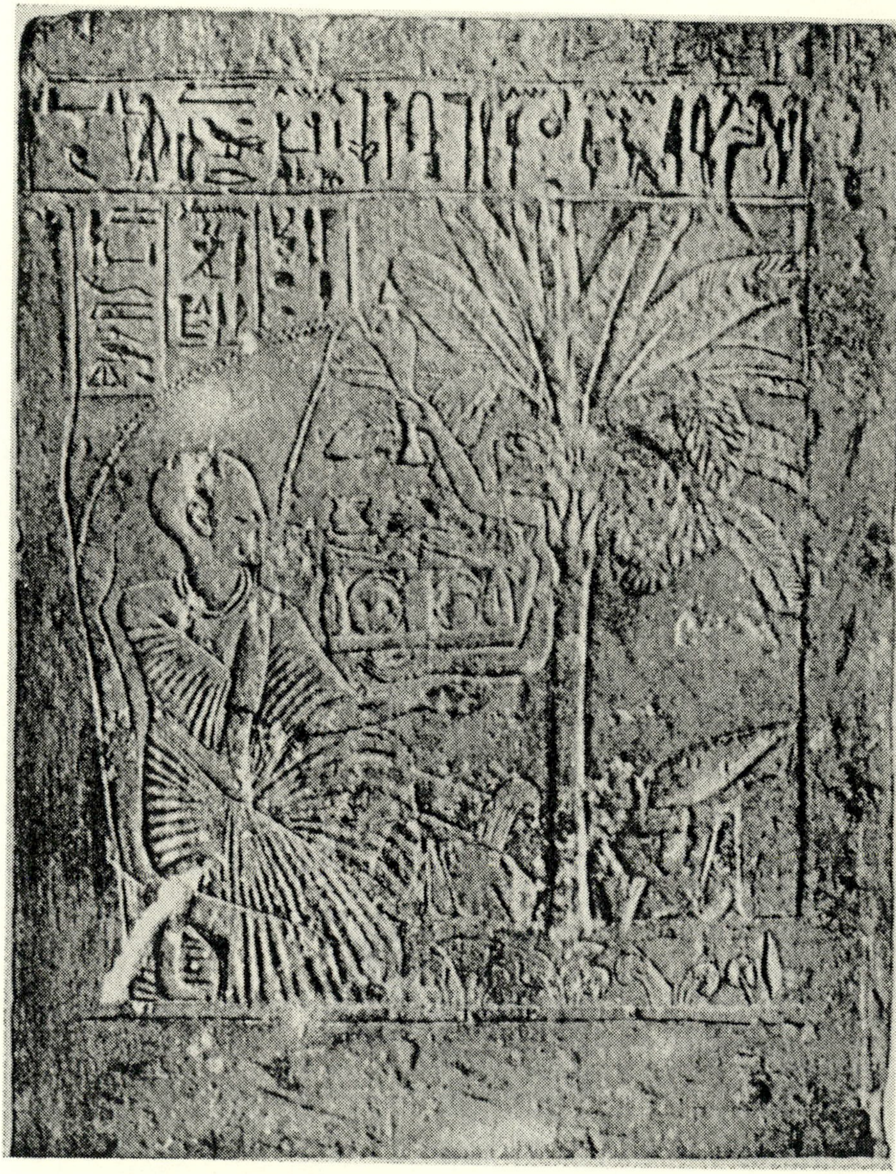

Relief from Abusir. 19th–20th Dynasty

PLATE VII

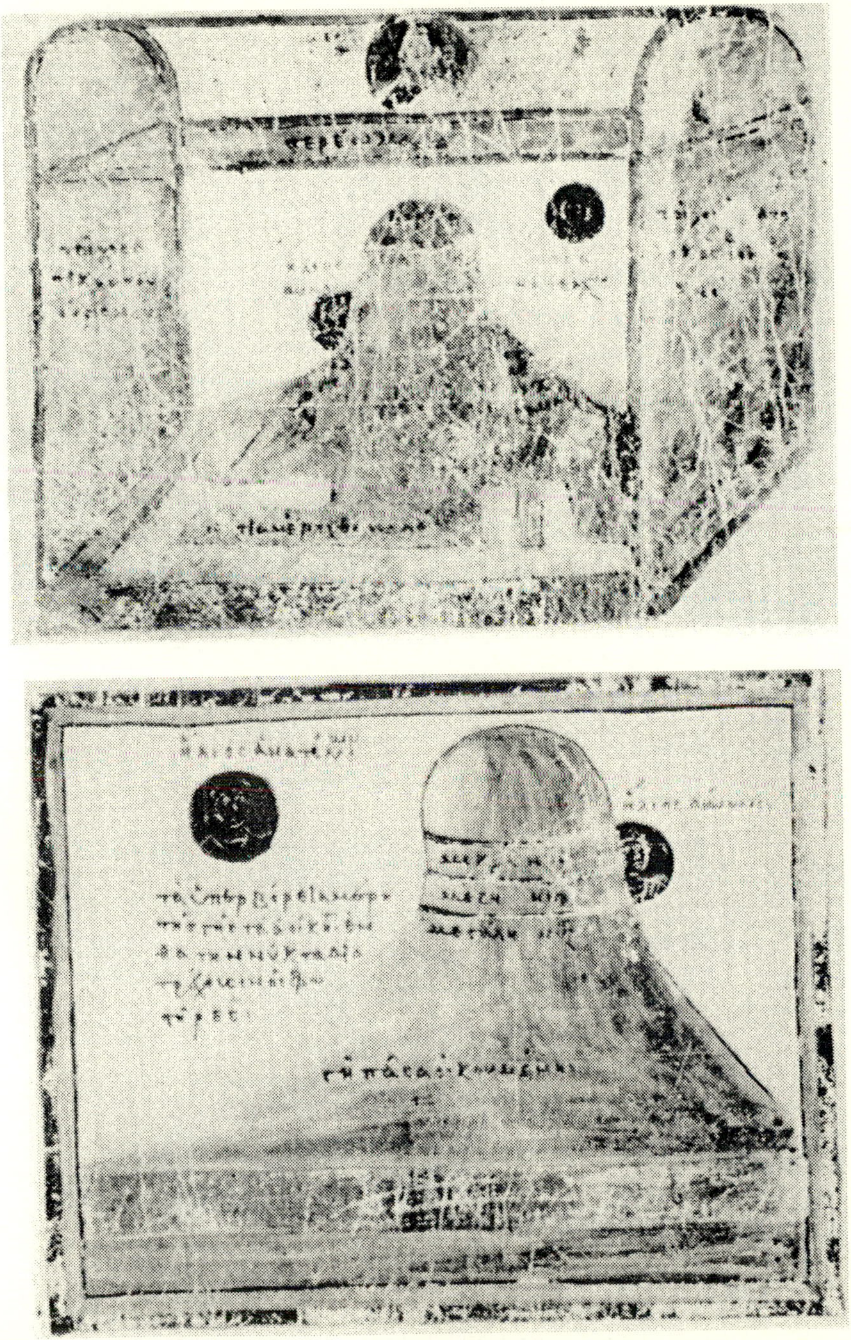

Cosmas' conception of the world
(MS. Laur. Plut. 9. 28)

PLATE VIII

a. Median tomb-relief of 600–550 B.C. showing a fire-altar

b. Sketch and plan of fire-altar found at Kūh i Khwāja. Arsacid period

be banished from our account of his philosophy. And good riddance. It would indeed have been surprising to find an Ionian philosopher explaining the world in terms of a metaphysical entity that no one else had heard of before him and no other philosopher was to use for a good two centuries after him. However much our histories of philosophy may emphasize the individual features of each thinker's teaching, we must never forget to what an extent they were using and adapting stock conceptions, or how difficult and slow the birth of a new concept is.

The world a fire (frs. 51 = B 30, 54 = B 90)

This 'world', this set-up that we all see about us, was always and is and will be. It did not develop from some more primitive state, it is stable in its present form. It is a fire, never extinguished, though not all parts of it are alight at once: 'kindling in measures and going out in measures'. The parts that are not alight exist as other things, which appear 'in exchange' for fire, as goods for gold.

Thus Heraclitus believes in a cyclical interchange of different substances. Why does he pick out one stage in the cycle, fire, and exalt its importance? Why does he regard it as more significant to say that water is mutated fire than to say what is equally true, that fire is mutated water? Clearly he was influenced by the established idea that the multiplicity of appearances in the world should be related to a single underlying factor. Anaximenes made a connection between his basic substances (fire, aer, cloud, water, earth, stones) by assuming a single kind of change, condensation/rarefaction, but not content with that, chose one of them to be the basic and original substance, the progenitor of the rest (cf. pp. 99 f.). Heraclitus is doing something similar. Theophrastus erred, of course, in attributing to him Anaximenes' theory of change.[1] He did not think of fire as a stuff that could be compressed or rarefied into other things. His conception of change was derived from the nature of fire itself. Fire, more

[1] D.L. 9. 8–9, Aet. 1. 3. 11, Simpl. *Phys.* 23. 33 ff.; J. B. McDiarmid, *Harv. Stud.* 61, 1953, 94 f.

obviously than water or earth, is as much a process as a material. Heraclitus saw in it a 'coin' into which other things can visibly be converted, an active, living force with its own sense of direction and purpose, involving ceaseless flow but marked by an inherent stability. The fuel going into it is balanced by the loss at the other end, and the flame itself, though in perpetual upward motion, remains more or less constant. The process does not end at the point where the flame disappears, but continues throughout the world.[1] It is in this sense that all things are (living or dead) fire: this is their unity.

The changes of fire (*fr. 53 = B 31*)

'The changes of fire are, first, sea, then from sea half earth and half *πρηστήρ*. The one is dispersed, and measured to the same amount as before it became earth.'

Theophrastus' next mistake was to take these as successive stages of the world. The changes are really concurrent, and continue all the time.[2]

Heraclitus says sea and earth, not water and earth; he is thinking not of elements as such, but of world-masses. The sea, he says, comes directly from fire. Where is this fire? We shall see that it is at the western horizon; it is the fire of the setting luminaries.

Half the sea turns to earth and half to *πρηστήρ*.[3] This makes most sense if we assume the earth to float on sea, as in Thales and perhaps still in the popular view. *πρηστήρ* will represent what the sea turns into at its upper surface where it does not turn into earth, and the half-and-half division is based on the

[1] Cf. Arist. *Meteor.* 357b26 ff. *καὶ δὴ καὶ περὶ οὗ ἀπορῆσαι πρότερον ἀναγκαῖον, πότερον καὶ ἡ θάλαττα ἀεὶ διαμένει τῶν αὐτῶν οὖσα μορίων ἀριθμῷ ἢ τῷ εἴδει καὶ τῷ πόσῳ μεταβαλλόντων ἀεὶ τῶν μερῶν, καθάπερ ἀὴρ καὶ τὸ πότιμον ὕδωρ καὶ πῦρ· ἀεὶ γὰρ ἄλλο καὶ ἄλλο γίνεται τούτων ἕκαστον, τὸ δ' εἶδος τοῦ πλήθους ἑκάστου τούτων μένει [καθάπερ τὸ τῶν ῥεόντων ὑδάτων καὶ τὸ τῆς φλογὸς ῥεῦμα].*

[2] Reinhardt, *Hermes* 77, 1942, 14 ff. = *Vermächtnis*, pp. 56 ff. Theophrastus probably followed Aristotle; see Kirk, *HCF*, pp. 319 ff.

[3] The syntax is anacoluthic. Heraclitus has said *πυρὸς τροπαί* with the whole series of changes in view, but then treats the second change as a change of sea, the genitive *θαλάσσης* taking over from *πυρός*. *τὸ μὲν ἥμισυ, τὸ δὲ ἥμισυ* are adverbial accusatives.

assumption that sea and earth are equal in surface area—an example of the isometric principle often seen in early Greek cosmology and geography.[1]

Next Heraclitus dealt with the death of earth.[2] According to Theophrastus' interpretation, which was followed by the Stoics (and incorporated in the text of the fragment by Burnet's conjecture), earth turns back into water. This is only intelligible, however, on the false view that the changes are consecutive. Earth and sea cannot be simultaneously passing into each other, for the whole area of the earth's underside corresponds to that half of the sea which is turning into earth; it is all becoming-earth, and none of it can be ceasing-earth. The fire theory implies something much more straightforward: the dispersion of the earth at its upper surface. The sea turns into πρηστήρ, which, whatever it is, is normally invisible; the earth either turns into the same, or into something analogous, measured out to the same amount as before it became earth, so that the balance is preserved and the earth remains constant in size.

The 'exhalations'

The structure of the fragment has led us to expect that an account of the πρηστήρ's fortunes must come next; and here is how Theophrastus' interpretation, as reproduced by Diogenes, proceeds: (πάλιν τε αὖ τὴν γῆν χεῖσθαι, ἐξ ἧς τὸ ὕδωρ γίνεσθαι·) ἐκ δὲ τούτου τὰ λοιπά, σχεδὸν πάντα ἐπὶ τὴν ἀναθυμίασιν ἀνάγων τὴν ἀπὸ τῆς θαλάσσης. . . . γίνεσθαι δὲ ἀναθυμιάσεις ἀπό τε γῆς καὶ θαλάσσης, ἃς μὲν λαμπρὰς καὶ καθαράς, ἃς δὲ σκοτεινάς κτλ. These 'exhalations' are then made to account for the heavenly bodies, the alternation of day and night, summer and winter,

[1] Cf. Vlastos, *CPh* 42, 1947, 169.

[2] That earth is the subject of διαχεῖται is clear from ὁκοῖος πρόσθεν ἦν ἢ γενέσθαι γῆ, from Theophrastus' interpretation (D.L. 9. 9) πάλιν τε αὖ τὴν γῆν χεῖσθαι, and from Chrysippus' modernization, *SVF* ii. 136. 23. Clement's θάλασσα is usually emended by the insertion of γῆ before it (Burnet). But if Heraclitus had meant 'earth turns back into sea'—which I do not believe—would he not have said γῆ πάλιν θάλασσα γίνεται? After γῆ θάλασσα . . ., διαχεῖται seems too carefully chosen. It is as simple to suppose that θάλασσα is a mistaken gloss on καὶ ἡ μέν.

and meteorological phenomena. But that must be the σχεδὸν πάντα that were explained from the sea exhalation: Theophrastus seems to have been in some uncertainty whether it was the sea-exhalation alone that was involved, or exhalations from both land and sea.

The reason for his embarrassment may be guessed. Heraclitus had said that the sea becomes πρηστήρ, and more vaguely that the earth διαχεῖται. Theophrastus interpreted the πρηστήρ—perhaps not too inaccurately—as some kind of ἀναθυμίασις.[1] He misunderstood the statement about the earth, taking it to mean that earth became sea again, and so he found no explicit mention of exhalation from the earth, which however seemed to be implied in what followed.

Heraclitus' later disciples, too, put more trust in the sea-exhalation. [Arist.] *Probl.* $934^{b}33$ says of some (or one) of them that they held stones and earth to be solidified from fresh water (i.e. the water directly under the earth, that comes out of springs), but the sun to be 'exhaled' from the sea.[2] Zeno adapted Heraclitus as follows:

	Stob. I. 17. 3 (from Arius Didymus) (*SVF* i. 28. 16)
πυρὸς τροπαὶ πρῶτον θάλασσα·	ὅταν ἐκ πυρὸς τροπὴ εἰς ὕδωρ δι' ἀέρος γένηται,
θαλάσσης δὲ τὸ μὲν ἥμισυ γῆ,	τὸ μέν τι ὑφίστασθαι καὶ γῆν συνίστασθαι,
τὸ δὲ ἥμισυ πρηστήρ.	ἐκ τοῦ λοιποῦ δὲ τὸ μὲν διαμένειν ὕδωρ, ἐκ δὲ τοῦ ἀτμιζομένου ἀέρα γίνεσθαι·

[1] Arist. *de an.* $405^{a}26$ already refers to an ἀναθυμίασις from which Heraclitus derives τἆλλα. That the πρηστήρ was identical with the doxographers' ἀναθυμίασις was seen by Gigon, pp. 66–8, cf. 83; Walzer, *Eraclito*, p. 72 n. 3; Reinhardt, *Hermes* 77, 1942, 16 = *Vermächtnis*, p. 57. Gigon points out that Heraclitus' explanation of the heavenly bodies stands in the tradition represented by Anaximenes and Xenophanes. Perhaps others before him had used the name πρηστήρ for a hypothetical substance that can be set alight in heaven (Reinhardt suggested that the term was Milesian). With the abandonment of this view of the heavenly bodies, it became obsolete.

[2] 'Da sind naturwissenschaftliche Herakliteer, die mit Kratylos kaum etwas zu tun haben dürften. . . . Für die Zeit zwischen dem alten Heraklit und der Stoa ist dies nicht ohne Interesse' (Gigon, p. 84).

⟨πρηστήρ . . . ἥλιος κτλ.⟩	λεπτυνομένου δὲ τοῦ ἀέρος πῦρ ἐξάπτεσθαι. *Et. Gud.* s.v. ἥλιος (*SVF* i. 35. 2) (τὸν ἥλιον) ἄναμμα νοερὸν ἐκ τοῦ θαλάσσης ⟨ἀναθυμιάματος⟩.

Note three modifications which remain standard for the Stoics: the changes are made successive in time, as in Theophrastus' interpretation; 'sea' is generalized as 'water', as by Theophrastus; and air is slipped in between fire and water. Chrysippus' version is virtually identical.[1]

In Anaximenes' and Xenophanes' accounts, however, the exhalation that sustained the sun came from the earth as a whole, except perhaps for certain particularly arid spots.[2] It seems likely that Heraclitus regarded the effluence from the earth's surface as being of the same kind as that from the sea's. It is true that Theophrastus distinguished two different kinds of exhalation in Heraclitus. But they vary with times and seasons, and although one sort increases heat and the other moisture, it is not said or implied that the one comes from the land and the other from the sea. Kirk has shown that Theophrastus' interpretation is here influenced by Aristotle's theory of two exhalations, a moist one (ἀτμίς) and a nameless dry one, both rising from the earth.[3] Aristotle himself spoke of a single ἀναθυμίασις in Heraclitus, of the same nature as the soul, and the source of many other things (above, p. 132 n. 1).

But Theophrastus distinguishes the exhalations not as dry and moist (as in Aristotle), but as bright and dark. He had Heraclitus' book before him, and his dual-exhalation interpretation, however Aristotelian, must have been an interpretation of something in the book. The question is complicated by the fact that in the actual fragment that speaks of the nature of day and night and winter and summer, they are explained as changes in God.

1 In the verbatim fragment, *SVF* ii. 179. 30; Arius Didymus (ibid. 136. 20) attributes to him the more schematic sequence fire–air–water–earth–water–air–fire.

2 13 A 7 § 5; p. 98 n. 1.

3 *Meteor.* 341b8 ff., etc.; Kirk, *HCF*, pp. 271–6.

Fr. 77 = B 67 ὁ θεὸς ἡμέρη εὐφρόνη, χειμὼν θέρος, πόλεμος εἰρήνη, κόρος λιμός· ἀλλοιοῦται δέ, ὅκωσπερ ⟨ ⟩ ὁκόταν συμμιγῇ θυώμασιν ὀνομάζεται καθ' ἡδονὴν ἑκάστου.[1]

The problem is to unravel Theophrastus' knitting. In fr. 51 = B 31, and what followed it, he found a periodic alternation between διακόσμησις and ἐκπύρωσις. In fr. 28(*c*) = A 22 and fr. 29 = B 53, he found Eris and Polemos lauded as essential to the preservation of the world order, and on this, no doubt influenced by his memory of Empedocles' Φιλία and Νεῖκος (cf. Gigon, p. 49), he founded the interpretation reproduced in D.L. 9. 8 τῶν δὲ ἐναντίων τὸ μὲν ἐπὶ τὴν γένεσιν ἄγον καλεῖσθαι πόλεμον καὶ ἔριν, τὸ δὲ ἐπὶ τὴν ἐκπύρωσιν ὁμολογίαν καὶ εἰρήνην.

War and peace appear in the fragment about God. In Stoic-influenced writers, and in Hippolytus, we find two of the other pairs from fr. 77, deficiency/satiety and winter/summer, identified with the διακόσμησις and the ἐκπύρωσις.[2] This must go back to a Theophrastean interpretation of the fragment. Since Hippolytus says that it was the fire that Heraclitus called deficiency and satiety, we may infer that Theophrastus understood ὁ θεός, who changed 'like fire (?) mixing itself with different incenses', to be the world fire. πόλεμος εἰρήνη and κόρος λιμός he took to be metaphors for the differentiation-period and the ecpyrosis. Day

[1] I hesitate between Diels's ⟨πῦρ⟩ and Fränkel's ⟨ἔλαιον⟩. See Kirk, *HCF*, pp. 191–7. The idea that scent is a superficiality is implied in fr. 75 = B 92 if ἀμύριστα belongs to Heraclitus. (ἀγέλαστα at least suits his later reputation: Luc. *vit. auct.* 14, *Epist.* 5 p. 73. 6, 7 p. 74. 20 Bywater.) In *Epist.* 7 p. 75. 11–12 he is made to deplore the waste of oil in perfume.

In the allusion to the fragment in Philodemus (77(*c*)), read ἀποφ]αίνει δὲ κα[ὶ τἀ]ναντία θε[ὸν ε]ἶναι, νύκτα [ἡμέραν κτλ.

[2] Philo, *de spec. leg.* 1. 208 (v. 50. 8 C.–W.); Plut. *de E* 389 c; Hipp. *Ref.* 9. 10. 7–8. (Fr. 55(*a*, *b*[1], *c*).) (Fränkel's transpositions in the Hippolytus passage seem irresistible at first sight, but I have come to the conclusion that they are mistaken. See Reinhardt, *Parmenides*, pp. 163–8; Kirk, *HCF*, pp. 351–2.)

These writers agree in substituting the more abstract χρησμοσύνη for λιμός, which may have seemed unsuitable for cosmology. That their χρησμοσύνη καὶ κόρος really comes from fr. 77, and is not a separate fragment (55 = B 65), is perfectly clear from Hippolytus' words. After saying that these terms signify the διακόσμησις and ἐκπύρωσις, he decides to quote the relevant section (κεφάλαιον) because it contains the whole of Heraclitus' personal doctrine, which is also that of the heretic Noetus; and fr. 77 it is.

and night, winter and summer, were likewise alternations of the fire.

His exhalations cannot have been based solely on this. The bright ones we can account for from what we know; they are Heraclitus' *πρηστήρ* which feeds the sun and stars. Daylight is simply sunlight (fr. 60 = B 99). Hence D.L. 9. 11 *τὴν μὲν γὰρ λαμπρὰν ἀναθυμίασιν φλογωθεῖσαν ἐν τῷ κύκλῳ τοῦ ἡλίου ἡμέραν ποιεῖν*. The dark ones must be based on something more than we know. They are connected with winter, night, wind, and rain. What can Heraclitus have mentioned in connection with all these phenomena? I know of only one answer: it is a surprising one, and it must be reserved for a later context.

The cycle completed

Concentrated in the bowls of heaven, *πρηστήρ* becomes fire again, and we see it as the sun, moon, and stars. They cross the sky, day after day, night after night, and are extinguished in the sea.[1] This must mean that they become sea, for fire does not go out without turning into something new. In the case of the sun, at least, we can watch its fire flooding out into the Aegean, but the other luminaries too make a substantial contribution in the course of twenty-four hours. A little reflection confirms that in aggregate they contain exactly the right amount of fire to maintain the sea; for they represent a concentration of all the substance rising from the surface of sea and earth, which was the substance of the sea in the first place. The fire that turns to sea, then, is all visible to us, and Heraclitus does not ask us to believe in some extra-mundane fire, for example below the sea.[2] *ὅσων ὄψις ἀκοὴ μάθησις*, he said, *ταῦτα ἐγὼ προτιμέω* (fr. 5 = B 55). Theophrastus' complaint that he said nothing about *τὸ περιέχον* is justified.

The reversion of fire to sea completes the cycle, and everything proceeds as before: a way up and down, never turning back, one way and the same. *καθάπερ γὰρ αἱ ἐτήσιοι ὧραι κύκλον*

[1] Fr. 58 = B 6, especially testimonia *b*[3], *c*, *g*. Cf. p. 98.

[2] Similarly in Empedocles, fire as a world-mass is represented by the sun. See p. 234 n. 1.

ἀμείβουσιν ἀλλήλας ἀντιπαραδεχόμεναι πρὸς τὰς ἐνιαυτῶν οὐδέποτε ληγόντων περιόδους, τὸν αὐτὸν τρόπον καὶ τὰ στοιχεῖα τοῦ κόσμου ταῖς εἰς ἄλληλα μεταβολαῖς, τὸ παραδοξότατον, θνήσκειν δοκοῦντα ἀθανατίζεται δολιχεύοντα ἀεὶ καὶ τὴν αὐτὴν ὁδὸν ἄνω καὶ κάτω συνεχῶς ἀμείβοντα (Philo, *de aetern. mundi* 109 (vi. 106. 4 C.–W.)).

5

HERACLITUS (2): GODS AND MEN

Dike and Eris

ACCORDING to Theophrastus, the regular changes of the physical world happened *καθ' εἱμαρμένην*, or *κατά τινα εἱμαρμένην ⟨καὶ⟩ ἀνάγκην*.[1] Heraclitus cannot have used the noun *εἱμαρμένη*; he seems, however, to have used somewhere the participial *εἱμαρμένα*, and there is no reason why he should not somewhere else have spoken of *ἀνάγκη*.[2] He had no very firm preference for one word in this area. In fr. 28(*ab*) = B 80 he says that everything comes to pass *κατ' ἔριν καὶ χρεών*, 'by way of discord and necessity'. Apportionment, compulsion, necessity: we can find logical distinctions between the concepts, but they were evidently not important to Heraclitus.

From what cosmic power did these constraints emanate? Again, there was no single answer. In fr. 52 = B 94 the sun's measures are maintained, through the Erinyes, by Dike, and since the sun's measures cannot be isolated from the measures of the world fire at large, it must be possible to say that Dike governs the whole process.[3] So in fr. 28: everything comes to pass *κατ' ἔριν καὶ χρεών*, and at the same time *ἔρις* is *δίκη*. One element in Heraclitus' theology, then, corresponds to Anaximander's concept of world changes occurring *κατὰ τὸ χρεών* and

[1] Testimonia under fr. 28(*d*–*d*[1]) = A 1 §§ 7–8, 5, 8; cf. Cic. *de fato* 39. *εἱμαρμένη ἀνάγκη*, 'apportioned compulsion', is an unlikely concept; Usener proposed to delete *ἀνάγκην*. The insertion of *καί* is suggested by Aet. 1. 27. 1 *Ἡράκλειτος πάντα καθ' εἱμαρμένην, τὴν δ' αὐτὴν ὑπάρχειν ἀνάγκην* (v.l. *καὶ ἀνάγκην*).

[2] Fr. 28(*d*[1]) = B 137; Kirk, *HCF*, pp. 303–5.

[3] Cf. Pl. *Crat.* 412 d–e (below, p. 143), and, for interest, *Epist.* 5 p. 72. 32 Bywater *ἰάσομαι ἐμαυτόν, μιμήσομαι θεόν, ὃς κόσμου ἀμετρίας ἐπανισοῖ ἡλίῳ ἐπιτάττων*. Similarly Parmenides: Dike controls the alternation of Day and Night (1. 14), and holds all Being in fetters (8. 14); in both roles she alternates with Ananke (8. 30, 10. 6, cf. A 32, 37).

by way of justice and retribution (p. 82). But at the same time he thinks of them as occurring *κατ' ἔριν*, and he can elevate Eris to equal status with Dike. He picked on Achilles' line in *Iliad* 18. 107,

ὡς Ἔρις ἔκ τε θεῶν ἔκ τ' ἀνθρώπων ἀπόλοιτο,

and expressed his own violent dissent.[1] Eris is an indispensable goddess; Eris and Dike are the same, in other words they perform the same service of apportioning to each quarter of the world its due.

> Fr. 29 = B 53 *Πόλεμος πάντων μὲν πατήρ ἐστι, πάντων δὲ βασιλεύς, καὶ τοὺς μὲν θεοὺς ἔδειξε, τοὺς δὲ ἀνθρώπους, τοὺς μὲν δούλους ἐποίησε, τοὺς δὲ ἐλευθέρους.*

Here is Polemos exalted as the great ruling power. Heraclitus is not fussy about names; Polemos here suits the examples. In fr. 28 we cannot mistake the parallelism between *πόλεμος* and *ἔρις*: *εἰδέναι χρὴ τὸν πόλεμον ἐόντα ξυνὸν καὶ δίκην ἔριν*. All receive their portions in war without discrimination; *ὁ πόλεμος ξυνός* echoes another memorable Homeric tag from the same book as Achilles' damnation of Eris.[2]

Opposites

For Heraclitus the ordering of the world depends on correct apportionment (*μέτρα, Δίκη, εἱμαρμένα*). The result and the purpose of apportionment, the actual and the desirable state of the world, is differentiation (which can also be regarded as the result of Eris, hence Eris = Dike). Heraclitus' attitude towards differentiation shows in three respects the influence of current modes of thought.

[1] Fr. 28(*c*), partly in DK 22 A 22. Cf. Kirk, *HCF*, pp. 168–9, 242–4; Marcovich, ed. pp. 140–2.

[2] *Il.* 18. 309 *ξυνὸς Ἐνυάλιος· καί τε κτανέοντα κατέκτα*. The idea of *δίκη* is very near at hand here. Cf. Archil. fr. 98 Tarditi *ἐτήτυμον γὰρ ξυνὸς ἀνθρώποις Ἄρης*.

A third connection between Heraclitus and *Iliad* 18 would be given by fr. 63(*a*) = B 105 if genuine, but I agree with Bywater, pp. viii–ix, and Kirk, *HCF*, pp. 158 f., that it is not.

1. He treats differentiation as the central problem of cosmology.
2. He sees it in terms of opposites. He is familiar with the tetrad hot/cold, wet/dry (fr. 42 = B 126), but he does not himself recognize a fixed canon of opposites: he finds examples everywhere.
3. He is concerned to show that behind all this differentiation there is unity (cf. p. 129). Besides relating the physical πολλά to the fire's ἕν, he never tires of demonstrating that apparent opposites are somehow the same, or that the gap between them can be bridged.[1]

Hot, cold, wet, dry, are not absolutes: cold things warm up, a hot thing cools, a wet thing dries, a dry thing gets wet (fr. 42). Living and dead, awake or asleep, young and old, the same thing persists therein, for these by changing become those and those by changing become these (fr. 41 = B 88).[2] Some 'opposites' are present simultaneously in the same object: straight and crooked in the fuller's roller (or whatever it is, fr. 32 = B 59), beginning and end on a circle (fr. 34 = B 103), drinkable and undrinkable in the sea (fr. 35 = B 61), *ΒΙΟΣ* and *ΘΑΝΑΤΟΣ* in the bow (fr. 39 = B 48), torture and benefit in surgery (fr. 46 = B 58), handsome and ugly in an ape (fr. 92(*b*) = B 82).

Heraclitus sometimes liked to say that the opposites which he linked in these or other ways were 'one' or 'one and the same'; for instance, Hesiod was wrong about day and night, because they are one. Heraclitus does not mean that their alternation is an illusion, as Parmenides would say. The point is that day *changes* to night and night to day, in other words we have one thing changing, not two separate things.[3] What is this one thing?

[1] Philo, *quis rer. div. heres* 214 (iii. 48. 19 C.–W.), says of the connection of opposites, 'Is this not what the Greeks say their celebrated Heraclitus put at the head of his philosophy and boasted of it as a new discovery?'

[2] Cf. Pl. *Phd.* 70 e ff., Arist. *parv. nat.* 453^{b}24 ff. From this point of view the transformations of fire are not magic but natural. Each thing has its natural life: fr. 56(*b*) = B 84 b κάματός ἐστι τοῖς αὐτοῖς μοχθεῖν καὶ ἄρχεσθαι. Cf. Arist. 454^{a}24 ff.; [Hp.] *vict.* 1. 5. 2, 8. 1.

[3] Heraclitus comes nearest to Parmenides when he says (fr. 91 = B 102, perhaps not a verbatim quotation) that to God all things are fair and good and right, but men have supposed some things to be wrong, others right; Parmenides' poem

It is not itself either night or day, but something more fundamental. In the remarkable fragment mentioned at the end of the last chapter (p. 134), it is called God. This is not to say that all opposites are God. The eight things named in the fragment are all large powers affecting human life; six of them are personified in Hesiod.[1] If they are represented as manifestations of God, it does not mean that God is present in a wet shirt that becomes dry, in the circumference of a circle, or in a handsome ape. These have their own unifying factor.

τὸ σοφόν

The expression *ὁ θεός* recurs in no other reliable fragment.[2] We hear of a 'single divine law' (fr. 23(*a*) = B 114) that feeds and surpasses all laws of men, and of a *θεῖον ἦθος* (fr. 90 = B 78) which possesses wisdom denied to men. This leads us naturally to consideration of fr. 84 = B 32, *ἓν τὸ σοφόν· μοῦνον λέγεσθαι οὐκ ἐθέλει καὶ ἐθέλει Ζηνὸς ὄνομα.*[3]

Instead of a divinity that claims wisdom, we here have a Wisdom that claims divinity. It 'does and does not want to be called by the name of Zeus alone'. It deserves a single name, but 'Zeus' is only partly appropriate; it has some of Zeus' traditional characteristics but not others.[4] The proposition that 'the wise

announced to mankind that the differentiations apparent to them disappear in the god's-eye view. So in B 8. 57–8, men wrongly accept two opposites, one of which is the same as itself throughout and not the same as the other. This cleft is just what Heraclitus too wants to see abolished.

[1] *Νύξ* and *Ἡμέρη*: *Th.* 123–4, 748 ff., etc. *Πόλεμος*: *Op.* 161. *Εἰρήνη*: *Th.* 902, *Op.* 228. *Κόρος*: *Th.* 593. *Λιμός*: *Th.* 227, *Op.* 299, 302.

[2] For fr. 91 see above, p. 139 n. 3. The unarticled *θεός* in Diels's B 83 belongs to Plato, not Heraclitus, cf. Marcovich, ed. pp. 488 f. The *δαίμων* in fr. 92(*a*) = B 79 is grammatically parallel to *ἀνήρ* in the second phrase, and need not be a unique being.

[3] Rightly punctuated, I think, by Hölscher, *Anfängliches Fragen*, p. 133 n. 10. Without the anaphora *ἕν . . . μοῦνον*, the connection is very abrupt, but I do not rule out Schuster's *ἓν τὸ σοφὸν μοῦνον· λέγεσθαι κτλ.* I do rule out making the whole fragment one sentence; *ἓν τὸ σοφὸν μοῦνον* cannot be one noun phrase.

[4] For the 'yes-and-no' form cf. fr. 25 = B 10, 40(c^2) = B 49a; Anacreon, *Melici* 428 *ἐρέω τε δηὖτε κοὐκ ἐρέω, καὶ μαίνομαι κοὐ μαίνομαι*; fifth-century examples in Vlastos, *AJP* 76, 1955, 341 n. 10. For *λέγεσθαι ἐθέλει* cf. Fraenkel on Aesch. *Ag.* 160; also Arist. *Eth. Nic.* 1110^{b}30 *τὸ δ' ἀκούσιον βούλεται λέγεσθαι οὐκ εἴ τις ἀγνοεῖ τὰ συμφέροντα*; Pl. *Crat.* 422 d, 426 d; R. Rödiger, *Glotta* 8, 1917, 18–20.

(clever, competent, skilful) is one' seems to recur in three other fragments.

83 = B 108 ὁκόσων λόγους ἤκουσα, οὐδεὶς ἀφικνεῖται ἐς τοῦτο ὥστε γινώσκειν ὅτι σοφόν ἐστι πάντων κεχωρισμένον.

The absence of the article with σοφόν suggests that this fragment came first in order. σοφόν ἐστιν ⟨ἕν,⟩ is suggested by Apollonius of Tyana *ap*. Eus. *PE* 4. 13. 1 (= fr. 83(*b*) Marcovich) θεῷ . . . ἑνί τ' ὄντι καὶ κεχωρισμένῳ πάντων.

D.L. 9. 1 (fr. 85 = B 41) εἶναι γὰρ ἓν τὸ σοφόν, ἐπίστασθαι γνώμην †οτεη κυβερνῆσαι πάντα διὰ πάντων.

The text is corrupt, and Diogenes himself seems to have been confused. The original quotation surely said that 'τὸ σοφόν is ἕν, and it knows that knowledge that steers everything through the world'.[1]

26 = B 50 οὐκ ἐμέο ἀλλὰ τοῦ λόγου ἀκούσαντας ὁμολογεῖν †σοφόν ἐστιν ἓν πάντα εἰδέναι†.

Again the text is corrupt. Hippolytus seems to represent Heraclitus as saying 'it is wise to admit that all things are one'. But he does not usually tell men that *it is wise* to admit, simply 'it must be realized'.[2] It is tempting to conjecture that the original quotation said 'it is necessary to admit that the wise is one'.

The words οὐδεὶς ἀφικνεῖται ἐς τοῦτο in fr. 83 suggest that some of those whose discourses Heraclitus had heard made approaches towards the idea of the Wise that is single and aloof. Pythagoras is alleged to have reserved the term σοφός for God.[3] Xenophanes

[1] That the γνώμη is something possessed by the σοφόν is shown by fr. 90 = B 78 ἦθος γὰρ ἀνθρώπειον μὲν οὐκ ἔχει γνώμας, θεῖον δὲ ἔχει; Epicharmus and Anaxagoras quoted on p. 142; Cleanthes, *Hymn to Zeus* 34 f. δὸς δὲ κυρῆσαι / γνώμης, ᾗ πίσυνος σὺ Δίκης μέτα πάντα κυβερνᾷς; Plut. *Is. Os.* 382 b ἡ δὲ ζῶσα καὶ βλέπουσα καὶ κινήσεως ἀρχὴν ἐξ ἑαυτῆς ἔχουσα καὶ γνῶσιν οἰκείων καὶ ἀλλοτρίων φύσις κάλλους τ' ἔσπακεν ἀπορροὴν καὶ μοῖραν ἐκ τοῦ φρονοῦντος ὅπως κυβερνᾶται τό †τε σύμπαν καθ' Ἡράκλειτον.

[2] Fr. 28 = B 80 εἰδέναι χρή, Democr. B 6 γινώσκειν χρή, [Hp.] *morb. sacr.* 17, *nat. hom.* 9, 12, 15. Cf. Philostr. *VA* 1. 17. σοφόν (ἐστι) with inf. first in Eur. *Hec.* 228?

[3] Heraclides Ponticus *ap*. D.L. 1. 12, cf. Pl. *Phdr.* 278 d; Gigon, p. 140; Burkert, *Hermes* 88, 1960, 159 ff.

tells of one god, greatest among gods and men, who moves everything by thought (21 B 23, 25). The uniqueness of τὸ σοφόν is comically disputed by Epicharmus, fr. 172 Kaibel (DK 23 B 4):

> Εὔμαιε, τὸ σοφόν ἐστιν οὐ καθ' ἓν μόνον,
> ἀλλ' ὅσσαπερ ζῇ, πάντα καὶ γνώμαν ἔχει κτλ.

Anaxagoras' Nous is αὐτοκρατὲς καὶ μέμικται οὐδενὶ χρήματι ἀλλὰ μοῦνος αὐτὸς ἐπ' ἑωυτοῦ ἐστιν . . . καὶ γνώμην γε περὶ παντὸς πᾶσαν ἴσχει καὶ ἰσχύει μέγιστον. Of particular relevance is Diogenes of Apollonia. He considers that all the differentiated things in the world must be differentiated (ἑτεροιοῦσθαι, cf. Heraclitus' ἀλλοιοῦται in fr. 77 = B 67) ἀπὸ τοῦ αὐτοῦ, καὶ τὸ αὐτὸ εἶναι. They are not different in their real nature, but τὸ αὐτὸ ἐὸν μεταπίπτει (cf. Heraclitus fr. 41 = B 88) πολλαχῶς καὶ ἑτεροιοῦται (64 B 2). He further considers that the measured apportionment of winter and summer, day and night, rain, wind, and serenity, presupposes the activity of νόησις (B 3). He then proceeds to identify τὸ τὴν νόησιν ἔχον (compare Heraclitus' neuter σοφόν) with air: this is what steers and rules all, this is God, arranging everything and present in everything in different ways, becoming hotter and colder, drier and wetter, and suffering countless other variations (B 5). We are naturally prompted to ask, had Heraclitus too identified his intelligent divine principle, which produced summer and winter and day and night by changing itself, with his 'material ἀρχή'?

The thunderbolt

The closest connection that I can find between fire and God is in fr. 79 = B 64, given by Hippolytus as τάδε πάντα οἰακίζει κεραυνός.[1] οἰακίζω is equivalent to κυβερνῶ (though the latter is usual in cosmological contexts), so that κεραυνός becomes parallel to τὸ σοφόν or its γνώμη in fr. 85 (above). τὸ σοφόν is 'Zeus'; and Philodemus quotes fr. 79 as κεραυνὸς π[άντα οἰη]κίζει καὶ Z[εύς.

The thunderbolt is exactly what is needed to hold together

[1] τάδε (Boeder) is likelier than τὰ δέ, cf. p. 196.

the rival concepts, Zeus and a world fire. It is the traditional instrument of Zeus' will. It distinguishes itself from ordinary fire by its ferocious power, its driving purposefulness. It is in what it accomplishes that it differs from ἀστραπή, which is merely something seen. Of all manifestations of fire, it is the most fitted to 'steer all things'. If Heraclitus gave thought to its relationship with the world-fire, we may perhaps imagine it as being like a single strong current running through an open sea from end to end, or from end to beginning.

It would be interesting to know whether Heraclitus was the originator of this idea of a divine will darting through the world (unlike Xenophanes' unmoved mover). Something like it appears in Empedocles B 134: God is not anthropomorphic,

> ἀλλὰ φρὴν ἱερὴ καὶ ἀθέσφατος ἔπλετο μοῦνον,
> φροντίσι κόσμον ἅπαντα καταΐσσουσα θοῇσι.[1]

The late-fifth-century Heracliteans (ὅσοι ἡγοῦνται τὸ πᾶν εἶναι ἐν πορείᾳ) held that the moving body of the world was traversed by something much faster and subtler which administered everything (ἐπιτροπεύει) and brought all things to pass (Pl. *Crat.* 412 d). Socrates says he has been told that this δια-ιόν is τὸ δίκαιον, and also Zeus, because things happen *ΔΙΑ* it. Beyond this, he says, there is disagreement. One says it is the sun, but another scoffs at this answer, asking if there can be no δίκαιον after sunset, and giving fire as his own answer (412 e–13 c). Here, at any rate, Plato is not reporting a post-Heraclitean dispute, but echoing a point settled by Heraclitus himself: fr. 81 = B 16 τὸ μὴ δῦνόν ποτε πῶς ἄν τις λάθοι; must have followed an attack on Homer's ἥλιος πανόπτης (*Il.* 3. 277, etc.). Plato evidently understood τὸ μὴ δῦνόν ποτε to be fire.[2] It ought to be something that has (or can engage) the power of punishment, and we think of Dike

[1] In Homer a man's mind darts (ἀΐσσει) from place to place when he imagines himself elsewhere (*Il.* 15. 80).

[2] This elemental interpretation of Heraclitus, or a similar fourth-century theory, is echoed in Philemon fr. 91 Kock (DK 64 C 4), where Air, 'whom one could also call Zeus', says he knows absolutely everything that god or man does, because he is everywhere at once.

who καταλάψεται ψευδέων τέκτονας καὶ μάρτυρας,[1] and who controls the sun itself. We cannot tell whether Heraclitus said anything about the relationship between Dike and the thunderbolt.[2]

God and fire not the same

To sum up the main considerations relevant to the identity or otherwise of God and fire:

There is a divine intelligence, 'Zeus', which πάντα κυβερνᾷ, and a 'thunderbolt' which πάντα οἰηκίζει with Zeus.

The divine intelligence cannot be identical with the world-fire, for it is πάντων κεχωρισμένον, and it must have more to govern than itself. This does not positively exclude its being identical with the parts of the world-fire that are alight, i.e. what we ordinarily call fire, but it is doubtful whether Heraclitus would have regarded that as πάντων κεχωρισμένον.

There is no good evidence that either the world-fire as a whole or what we call fire is sentient.[3]

God changes into day and night, winter and summer, war and peace, satiety and starvation. Theophrastus, as we saw, took this God to be the world-fire, but that only makes the utterance stranger.

Other gods

The Wise is one; but there is not only one god. War 'makes some gods and others men' (fr. 29 = B 53). 'And they pray to

[1] Fr. 19 = B 28. Not to be combined with fr. [82] = B 66 τὸ πῦρ . . . καταλήψεται, which is Christian interpretation based on πάντα οἰηκίζει κεραυνός (sc. κατευθύνει, sc. κρίνει). Reinhardt, *Parmenides*, pp. 163–8; Kirk, *HCF*, pp. 359–61.

[2] Cleanthes (cf. p. 117 n. 2) hymns Zeus as governing everything with Dike, and as guiding the world with his ever-living thunderbolt (10 ἀειζώοντα, cf. Heraclitus' πῦρ ἀείζωον)—especially the κοινὸς λόγος, ὃς διὰ πάντων / φοιτᾷ μειγνύμενος †μεγάλων μικροῖσι φάεσσι (-οις μικροῖς τε Brunck, -ῳ μικροῖς τε Diels). In verse 11 I suggest πάντ' ἔργα ⟨νομεύεις⟩, *cl.* Hclt. fr. 80 = B 11.

[3] Reinhardt, *Hermes* 77, 1942, 25–7 = *Vermächtnis*, pp. 68–70, argues that Hippolytus' λέγει δὲ καὶ φρόνιμον τοῦτο εἶναι τὸ πῦρ (9. 10. 7) should be treated as a fragment, but Kirk, *HCF*, pp. 352–4 shows that it is likely to be Stoic. In any case, τοῦτο τὸ πῦρ in the context should be the κεραυνός. Sextus Empiricus' account of Heraclitus' epistemology (*adv. math.* 7. 127 ff. = fr. 116 = A 16; from Aenesidemus), according to which we enjoy sense through contact with τὸ περιέχον, like coals glowing when brought near a fire, is valueless, being spun out of fragments 1, 13, 23 (B 1, 2, 107); cf. pp. 118 f.; Marcovich, *RE* Supp. x. 268, 316, ed. p. 583; Hölscher, *Anfängliches Fragen*, pp. 153–4.

these images, as if one were to hold conversation with a house, not recognizing what gods or heroes are.'[1] According to D.L. 9. 7, Heraclitus believed *πάντα ψυχῶν εἶναι καὶ δαιμόνων πλήρη*,[2] and in an anecdote told by Aristotle (*part. an.* 645ᵃ17), some friends calling on Heraclitus found him 'warming himself by the stove',[3] and hesitated to advance, but he said to them: 'Come in, don't be afraid—there are gods even here.'

At least some of the names men give the gods are valid: Zeus (partly), Dike, the Erinyes, Dionysus, Hades.[4] About the last two, however, they are not enlightened.

> Fr. 50 = B 15 *εἰ μὴ γὰρ Διονύσῳ πομπὴν ἐποιέοντο καὶ ὕμνεον ᾆσμα αἰδοίοισιν †ἀναιδέστατα εἴργασται†· ὡυτὸς δὲ Ἀίδης καὶ Διόνυσος, ὅτεῳ μαίνονται καὶ ληναΐζουσι.*

I think Wilamowitz (*Glaube*, ii. 207 n. 1) is right in supposing that there is a lacuna, and that *ᾆσμα* would not have been brought into the phrase except to carry an adjective (sc. *ἀναιδές*, deliberately juxtaposed with *αἰδοίοισιν*). I propose two alternative interpretations.

1. 'If they were not making procession to Dionysus, and they sang a shameless song to the shameful parts,[5] ⟨their conduct would be most reprehensible. *νῦν δὲ οὐδὲν ἀναιδὲς*⟩ *εἴργασται*, (and the ritual has a sense, though one that they do not understand,) because Dionysus is really *Ἀίδης* (and not *ἀναιδής*).'

[1] Fr. 86 = B 5. The images are at best 'houses' which the gods may sometimes fill but never be wholly contained in. The idea is rhetorically expanded in *Epist.* 4, p. 71. 22 ff. Bywater.

[2] This idea is also attributed to Thales (Arist. *de an.* 411ᵃ7, D.L. 1. 27, etc.) and Pythagoras (D.L. 8. 32). Cf. Pl. *Lg.* 899 b. 'Everything is full of' is idiomatic: Aesch. *Pers.* 603 *πάντα μὲν φόβου πλέα*; Hdt. 8. 4. 1 *ὡς εἶδον νέας τε πολλὰς καταχθείσας ἐς τὰς Ἀφέτας καὶ στρατιῆς ἅπαντα πλέα*; cf. 132; Antiphon B 49 *φροντίδων ἤδη πάντα πλέα*; Xen. *Hell.* 2. 3. 44, 3. 4. 18.

[3] D. S. Robertson, *Proc. Camb. Phil. Soc.* 1938, 10, makes it probable that this is a euphemism for 'in the lavatory'.

[4] In referring to Apollo as *ὁ ἄναξ οὗ τὸ μαντεῖόν ἐστι τὸ ἐν Δελφοῖσιν*, fr. 14 = B 93, Heraclitus may have wished to avoid as inappropriate a name which suggested destruction (cf. Fraenkel on Aesch. *Ag.* 1081). But he needed to mention the oracle, and that may explain the periphrasis.

[5] That is, probably, to Phales, as in Ar. *Ach.* 237 ff. Cf. in general Hdt. 2. 48; Nilsson, *Gr. Feste*, pp. 263 ff.; Wilamowitz, *Glaube* ii. 77.

2. 'If they were not making procession to Dionysus, and they sang a shameless song to the shameful parts, ⟨*παραφρονεῖν ἂν ἐδόκεον πάντως· νῦν δὲ ἀφρονέσ*⟩*τατα εἴργασται κτλ.*' (Cf. fr. 86 = B 5: a man would be thought mad to talk to a house, but the religious institution is equally mad.) On this view, Dionysus' being Hades makes things worse, not better.

In fr. 69 = B 117, Heraclitus explains that a man who is drunk has his faculties impaired because his soul has become damp. In fr. 68 = B 118, quite consistently, he declares that a dry soul is wisest and best.[1] Evidently he deplored drunkenness and regarded it as a serious danger to man's soul. And in fact he says explicitly in fr. 66 = B 36, *ψυχῇσι θάνατος ὕδωρ γενέσθαι*. But in fr. 66(d^1) = B 77[a], Porphyry cites Heraclitus as saying that it is not only death but delight for souls to become wet.[2] Heraclitus seems to have acknowledged that while it is death for souls to become wet, they enjoy dying.[3] If we now turn back to fr. 50 we can see what he must be getting at. Men acclaim Dionysus, the god of intoxication, with ecstatic rejoicing: in so doing, they are acclaiming death.[4] Besides the god ostensibly worshipped in these processions, the god that men are aware of, there is another god whose presence they are not aware of; or rather not another god, but a larger, more universal god of whom Dionysus is only one aspect. Heraclitus regards it as more significant to call the god Hades than to call him Dionysus.

We have no right to assume that in calling him Hades Heraclitus was speaking allegorically, or dressing up his real meaning

[1] To the passages collected by Marcovich add (at his a^{10}) Philostr. *VA* 8. 7. 30.

[2] Both *τέρψιν* and *θάνατον* are guaranteed by the context; Porphyry adds fr. 47 = B 62 specially to show that 'death' means birth. Kranz's *καί* for *μή* seems the easiest solution to the textual difficulty.

[3] Cf. fr. 56(*a*) = B 84a *μεταβάλλον ἀναπαύεται*. The idea that the fulfilment of desire goes together with expenditure of soul is more clearly expressed in fr. 70 = B 85 *θυμῷ μάχεσθαι χαλεπόν· ὅτι γὰρ ἂν χρῄζῃ γίνεσθαι, ψυχῆς ὠνεῖται*. Cf. fr. 71 = B 110 *ἀνθρώποισι γίνεσθαι ὁκόσα ἐθέλουσιν οὐκ ἄμεινον*.

[4] It has long been customary to explain Dionysus here as 'god of life', identified by Heraclitus with his opposite. But no one in antiquity ever spoke of Dionysus as the 'god of life'.

in poetic terms so as to sound more like the Delphic oracle; to assume, more precisely, that in his private thoughts he did not contemplate a theological proposition about Dionysus and Hades, but only a psycho-physiological proposition about alcoholic liquids and the human soul. The thinkers of the sixth and fifth centuries were not concerned to eliminate the gods from the world, but to locate them. By formulating 'natural' principles of motion and change and seeing how far the working of the world could be explained by reference to them, it became possible to say more exactly where the 'divine' (super-natural) sources of motion and creation lay, what they did, and at what stages in the cosmogonic process. If conflicting powers were manifest in the working of the world, then different gods could be identified.

The living soul is σοφωτάτη—most like the Wise, 'Zeus'—when it is driest. It is rational that a different god should be made responsible for its death through wetness, and no more fitting name for such a god can be imagined than Hades.

Sleep

Diogenes of Apollonia had a similar theory about the effect of moisture on intelligent thought. We think by means of air that is pure and dry, and we think less well when it is made damp.[1] As circumstances in which this occurs he mentioned, besides intoxication, sleep. Heraclitus refers to sleep in a number of fragments, and this will be the best occasion to discuss them.

He agrees with Diogenes that sleep represents an inferior mental state. His uncomprehending hearers are scornfully compared to men asleep (fr. 1 = B 1, 73). He includes dreaming with sleeping: sleepers turn aside each to his private world (fr. 24 = B 89), which is the contrary of what is necessary for apprehension of the truth (fr. 23 = B 114).

Fr. 49 = B 21 θάνατός ἐστιν ὁκόσα ἐγερθέντες ὁρέομεν, ὁκόσα δὲ εὕδοντες ὕπνος.

[1] 64 A 19 § 44. Vlastos, *AJP* 76, 1955, 364 n. 56, finds in Diogenes' theory a pointer to Miletus (specifically to Anaximenes). Cf. R. B. Onians, *The Origins of European Thought*, pp. 30 ff., for its popular background; 'Hp.' *morb. sacr.* 17 f.

It is not clear what point Heraclitus is here making about sleep. 'What we see when awake is death' implies that the most accurate available view of the world shows it to be characterized by essential change. Possibly the second clause means simply that it is no use looking to dreams for an alternative insight, for that is mere sleep. In that case, *θάνατος* and *ὕπνος* would not be logically parallel but chosen for the sake of a verbal antithesis.

Still more puzzling is fr. 48 = B 26:

ἄνθρωπος ἐν εὐφρόνῃ φάος ἅπτεται ἑωυτῷ {ἀποθανών}, ἀποσβεσθεὶς ὄψεις· ζῶν δὲ ἅπτεται τεθνεῶτος εὕδων {ἀποσβεσθεὶς ὄψεις}, ἐγρηγορὼς ἅπτεται εὕδοντος.

There is probably some interpolation—the words *ἑαυτῷ, ἀποθανών, ἀποσβεσθεὶς ὄψεις* in both places, and *εὕδων* have all been condemned by someone—and the punctuation is uncertain too. The first part surely refers to dreaming. In the night a man's eyes, which in waking life light things up for him, are extinguished, and he kindles a light for himself. Then follows a pair of statements in intentional parallelism: living–dead, waking–sleeping. In fr. 41 = B 88 these things are parallel in that something enduring through the change connects living with dead, making it the same, and similarly waking with sleeping. Here too the idea of continuity seems inherent in *ἅπτεται*, whether it is to be translated 'kindles from', 'adjoins', or 'partakes in the nature of'. The chief difficulty is to find the connection between the two parts of the fragment.

Pindar fr. 131 b Snell is probably relevant:

σῶμα μὲν πάντων ἕπεται θανάτῳ περισθενεῖ,
ζωὸν δ' ἔτι λείπεται αἰῶνος εἴδωλον, τὸ γάρ ἐστι μόνον
ἐκ θεῶν· εὕδει δὲ πρασσόντων μελέων, ἀτὰρ εὑδόντεσσιν ἐν πολλοῖς ὀνείροις
δείκνυσι τερπνῶν ἐφέρποισαν χαλεπῶν τε κρίσιν.

Here is a faculty, of divine origin, that sleeps when we are awake, is awake when we are asleep, and remains alive when we are dead. If we regard Heraclitus' dreamlight in similar terms, but describe it as 'dead' during the day instead of 'sleeping', we might read ζῶν (neut.) δὲ ἅπτεται τεθνεῶτος εὕδων, ἐγρηγορὼς ἅπτεται εὕδοντος, 'and this living light he kindles from dead in his sleep, while in waking he kindles (his eyes' light) from sleeping'. In other words, both dreamlight and eye-light spring in their turn from a state of extinction.

Alternatively, if ζῶν is masculine (as one's first reaction would suggest), the sense might be 'though living, he is in contact with death, as he sleeps; in waking he is in contact with sleep'. In other words, sleep is a half-way house between life and death, and on the other hand is linked by continuity to waking; so that even in life there is a bridge connecting the full waking state with death.

The soul

In Homer the ψυχή does nothing but animate the body. When seen on its own, in Hades, it is revealed as a mere ghost that darts about like a shadow or a dream, void of intelligent thought and articulate speech except when poetic convenience demands otherwise. It is the θυμός in the φρένες, the breath-spirit in the lungs, that is the centre of consciousness, feeling, emotion, and understanding, and the νόος, also in the φρένες, that is responsible for reasoned thought and deliberation.[1] By Heraclitus' time, the position has changed. νόος is not very different; it may generally be translated 'sense' or 'intelligence' where it occurs in the fragments.[2] The great change that has taken place is the usurpation by the ψυχή of many of the functions of the Homeric θυμός. θυμός has been narrowed down to the seat of strong, anti-rational emotions, especially anger and desire. So in Heraclitus: θυμῷ μάχεσθαι χαλεπόν· ὅτι γὰρ ἂν χρῄζῃ γίνεσθαι, ψυχῆς ὠνεῖται (fr. 70 = B 85). The ψυχή has become the seat of feeling, and the entity of which moral and intellectual qualities are predicated.[3] In

[1] Onians, op. cit., pp. 23 ff.; B. Snell, *The Discovery of the Mind* (*Die Entdeckung des Geistes*), ch. I.

[2] 16 = B 40; 23 = B 114; 101 = B 104.

[3] The early fifth century provides many examples of ψυχή in its wider senses, e.g. Pind. *Ol.* 2. 70, *P.* 1. 48, 3. 61, *N.* 9. 32, 39, *Isth.* 3. 71 b, Bacch. 11. 48, Aesch. *Pers.* 28, 442, 841. (All before 470?) There is not much sixth-century evidence, but cf. Anacreon, *Melici* 360.

Heraclitus it appears as the organ of understanding that interprets the information received by the senses.

Fr. 13 = B 107 *κακοὶ μάρτυρες ἀνθρώποισιν ὀφθαλμοὶ καὶ ὦτα βαρβάρους ψυχὰς ἐχόντων.*[1]

Fr. 69 = B 117 *ἀνὴρ ὁκόταν μεθυσθῇ ἄγεται ὑπὸ παιδὸς ἀνήβου σφαλλόμενος, οὐκ ἐπαΐων ὅκῃ βαίνει, ὑγρὴν τὴν ψυχὴν ἔχων.*

Fr. 68 = B 118 *αὔη ψυχὴ σοφωτάτη καὶ ἀρίστη.*

It has a deep and increasing measure (p. 128). It is still the part of man that survives in Hades: it retains the faculty of smell (fr. 72 = B 98).

This last item, as well as the ability to exist in a damp state, suggests an airy rather than a fiery soul. The late testimonies that Heraclitus said the soul was of fire[2] cannot reflect an explicit statement by him, since Aristotle in *de an.* 405ᵃ26 (= fr. 66(f^1)) has to infer the equivalence of soul with the *ἀρχή* from its equivalence with *ἡ ἀναθυμίασις ἐξ ἧς τἆλλα συνίστησι*; he adds that it was *ἀσωματώτατον δὴ καὶ ῥέον ἀεί.* He evidently has no doubt that the *ἀναθυμίασις* is soul, and that means that, somehow or other, soul is rising from earth to heaven. It is natural to think in this connection of fr. 67 = B 45: if you cannot find the soul's limits *πᾶσαν ἰὼν ὁδόν*, perhaps it really does reach up into the sky. Strange as the idea may seem, it is supported by Orph. fr. 226:

ἔστιν ὕδωρ ψυχῇ †θάνατος δ' ὑδάτε⟨σ⟩σιν ἀμοιβή†,
ἐκ δ' ὕδατος ⟨πέλε⟩ γαῖα, τὸ δ' ἐκ γαίας πάλιν ὕδωρ,
ἐκ τοῦ δὴ ψυχὴ ὅλον αἰθέρα ἀλλάσσουσα.

[1] Cf. Diog. 64 A 19 § 42 *ὅτι δὲ ὁ ἐντὸς ἀὴρ αἰσθάνεται μικρὸν ὢν μόριον τοῦ θεοῦ, σημεῖον εἶναι διότι πολλάκις πρὸς ἄλλα τὸν νοῦν ἔχοντες οὔθ' ὁρῶμεν οὔτ' ἀκούομεν.* Epich. fr. 249 Kaibel (DK 23 B 12) *νοῦς ὁρῇ καὶ νοῦς ἀκούει, τἆλλα κωφὰ καὶ τυφλά.*

[2] Theodoretus and Tertullian in fr. 66(f^4). Macrobius ib. says it was a *scintilla stellaris essentiae.* I suspect that he has got this from Porphyry's commentary on the myth of Er. At 621 b Er sees the souls flying away to be reborn, *ᾄττοντας ὥσπερ ἀστέρας.* Porphyry may have cited *Il.* 4. 75 ff. *οἷον δ' ἀστέρα ἧκε Κρόνου πάϊς ἀγκυλομήτεω / ἢ ναύτῃσι τέρας ἠὲ στρατῷ εὐρέϊ λαῶν, / λαμπρόν· τοῦ δέ τε πολλοὶ ἀπὸ σπινθῆρες ἵενται,* commenting, e.g., *διὰ τούτων δὲ αἰνίττεται ὁ ποιητὴς τὴν εἰς γένεσιν πτῶσιν· σπινθῆρες γὰρ ἀστρικῆς οὐσίας αἱ ψυχαὶ ἡμῶν, ὡς καὶ Ἡράκλειτος ὁ φυσικὸς δηλοῖ ἐν οἷς φησιν "αὐγὴ ξηρὰ ψυχή"* (fr. 68 = B 118). This fragment is twice quoted by Porphyry (once with *αὐγή*), and Galen refers to the dry, rayed light of the stars as a parallel supporting the statement that such a soul is wise (fr. 68(a^8); cf. Cic. *ND* 2. 42).

The verses are modelled on Heraclitus fr. 66(*a*) = B 36: ψυχῇσιν θάνατος ὕδωρ γενέσθαι, ὕδατι δὲ θάνατος γῆν γενέσθαι· ἐκ γῆς δὲ ὕδωρ γίνεται, ἐξ ὕδατος δὲ ψυχή. The poet seems to have been a pre-Stoic 'Heraclitean', and the phrase ὅλον αἰθέρα ἀλλάσσουσα must be taken to express a doctrine of Heracliteans. Another fragment (228 a) says

ψυχὴ δ' ἀνθρώποισιν ἀπ' αἰθέρος ἐρρίζωται.

The Stoics, after introducing air into the Heraclitean physical scheme (p. 133), identified soul and air,[1] constructed a 'soul of the world',[2] and transferred the 'deaths' of the soul-cycle to the cosmic elements.[3] We can neither be surprised nor enlightened to learn that the Stoics and 'certain Heracliteans' held the soul to be an ἀναθυμίασις from bodily moisture, and attributed the same doctrine to Heraclitus (fr. 66(f^{2-3})).

Birth and death

Souls come from water which (unlike the water of the sea) comes from earth, and they die when they become such water again. It is legitimate to suppose that water and earth may stand here for liquid and solid.[4] The obvious liquid for the soul to come from is semen;[5] semen might be thought of as coming from food or from the solid parts of the body. This would account for the second part of fr. 66.

The first part, 'it is death for souls to become water', is more obscure. At least some souls survive the death of the body, since they retain the faculty of smell 'in Hades' (fr. 72 = B 98), and men are awaited after death by things they do not expect (fr. 74 = B 27). The body itself becomes a revolting thing, not fit to be

1 See Philo, *de aetern. mundi* 111 (vi. 106. 16 C.–W.) (fr. 66(*b*) Marcovich).

2 Aet. 4. 3. 12 (fr. 66(f^3) = A 15).

3 See the passages in fr. 66(e^{1-4}) = B 76, with Marcovich, ed. p. 360.

4 See p. 99, [Hp.] *hebd.* 18, and Marcovich, ed. p. 363.

5 So Hippon, DK 38 A 3. The view that the father alone contributes to the substance of the child was common, cf. Hippon A 13, Anaxagoras 59 A 107, Diogenes 64 A 27, Aesch. *Eum.* 658 ff.; A. E. Taylor, *Comm. on Plato's Timaeus*, pp. 637 f.; Erna Lesky, *Abh. Mainz* 1950 (19), 1225–1425.

burned or buried but only to be cast out.[1] According to Aetius (4. 7. 2 περὶ ἀφθαρσίας ψυχῆς, DK 22 A 17), souls on leaving the body go to join 'the soul of the world', being of like nature to it; but this all follows from (and presupposes) the Stoic interpretation of fr. 66 recorded above. Nor is it possible to accept Olympiodorus' statement (*in Phaed.* p. 57. 27 Norvin = fr. 117) that uneducated souls perish quickly, while those of the wise and virtuous survive to the ecpyrosis. That was the doctrine of Chrysippus (D.L. 7. 157), and in Aetius loc. cit. it is distinguished as the Stoic view from that of Heraclitus.

However, several fragments indicate that there were distinctions between the fates of different souls—as indeed we might expect to be told by a θεολόγος.

Fr. 96 = B 24 ἀρηϊφάτους θεοὶ τιμῶσι καὶ ἄνθρωποι.

Fr. 97 = B 25 μόροι γὰρ μέζονες μέζονας μοίρας λαγχάνουσι.

Theodoretus took these two fragments to be related, and this is supported by Pl. *Crat.* 398 b λέγει οὖν καλῶς καὶ οὗτος (Hes. *Op.* 121–3) καὶ ἄλλοι ποιηταὶ πολλοὶ ὅσοι λέγουσιν ὡς ἐπειδάν τις ἀγαθὸς ὢν τελευτήσῃ, μεγάλην μοῖραν καὶ τιμὴν ἔχει καὶ γίγνεται δαίμων κατὰ τὴν τῆς φρονήσεως ἐπωνυμίαν (sc. δαίμων – δαήμων), together with *Rep.* 468 e–9 b, where it is proposed that the good man who dies in battle shall be deemed to be of the golden race, and worshipped as a δαίμων in accordance with Hesiod's words; and the same honour will be accorded to men of pre-eminent virtue however they die.[2] All this makes us think of the Heroes

[1] Fr. 76 = B 96 νέκυες κοπρίων ἐκβλητότεροι, usually taken to mean that the body is no use for anything once the soul has left it ('as worthless now as dung', Kirk, *HCF*, p. 342). But dung is not a symbol of the useless but of the offensive and contaminating. Why should Heraclitus quarrel with the normal methods of disposal (burial was commoner than cremation in sixth-century Ionia) for something that was merely useless?

[2] The special mention of those slain in battle arises naturally out of Plato's argument. On the popular tendency to glorify and even heroize fallen warriors cf. Rohde, *Psyche* (Eng. ed.), p. 528. Polemos, we remember, makes some gods and others men (cf. Gigon, p. 119). Fr. 95 = B 29 αἱρέονται ἓν ἀντὶ ἁπάντων οἱ ἄριστοι, κλέος ἀέναον θνητῶν, κτλ., may also refer to death in battle, but need not. Fr. 96(*b*) = B 136, ψυχαὶ ἀρηΐφατοι καθαρώτεραι ἢ ἐνὶ νούσοις, does not come from any 'metrical version' of Heraclitus but from the Chaldaean Oracles, see *CR* 82, 1968, 257 f.

of fr. 86 = B 5: 'men do not understand what gods or heroes are.' That they are in fact souls of men that have left their bodies seems to follow inescapably from fr. 47 = B 62 ἀθάνατοι θνητοί, θνητοὶ ἀθάνατοι, ζῶντες τὸν ἐκείνων θάνατον, τὸν δ' ἐκείνων βίον τεθνεῶτες. (A number of testimonia substitute θεοὶ θνητοί, ἄνθρωποι ἀθάνατοι, but Hippolytus' text is probably correct.) Mortal and immortal are thus unified on the same continuity-principle as night and day, young and old, wet and dry, alive and dead (p. 139). Yet Heraclitus can hardly have held that all gods die and become mortals, or that all mortals after death become heroes or gods. The whole scheme is difficult to reconcile with the birth and death of souls from water.

After quoting fr. 47 Hippolytus goes on to quote a fragment to show that Heraclitus spoke of a resurrection of the flesh, brought about by God.

> Fr. 73 = B 63 †ἔνθα δεόντι† ἐπανίστασθαι καὶ φύλακας γίνεσθαι ἐγερτὶ ζώντων καὶ νεκρῶν.

God is missing in the fragment as it stands, and I would suggest changing the corrupt opening phrase to ἐν θεοῦ δέοντι, 'at God's need'.[1] γίνεσθαι means 'act as' rather than 'become', as the adverb shows. ζώντων καὶ νεκρῶν will be an elevated expression for 'mortal men', since νεκροί as such need no watching. The φύλακες recall Hesiod's φύλακες θνητῶν ἀνθρώπων, mentioned once as the good *daimones* who are the men of the golden race of old (*Op.* 123), once as invisible police spirits who observe men's righteous and unrighteous behaviour (ib. 248–55). One wonders whether Heraclitus' guardians have any punitive powers, like the Erinyes who will punish irregular behaviour by the sun (fr. 52 = B 94).[2]

Hippolytus' interpretation—a general resurrection at the Last Trump—is out of court. Heraclitus did not believe in an end of the world; those who rise up in the fragment become the guardians

[1] The change is minimal: ΕΝΘΟΥ > ΕΝΘΑ.

[2] It may be worth noticing *Epist.* 9 p. 77. 29 Bywater πολλαὶ Δίκης Ἐρινύες, ἁμαρτημάτων φύλακες. Ἡσίοδος ἐψεύσατο τρεῖς μυριάδας εἰπών· ὀλίγαι εἰσίν, οὐκ ἀρκοῦσι κακίᾳ κόσμου.

of others who are still enjoying the ordinary life of mortals; and the present tense of the infinitives implies a recurrent process, not a single once-for-all event. But ἐπανίστασθαι does mean to stand up or rise up, and seems to signify some kind of selective resurrection as a cosmic institution.

The cycle of generation

It still remains hard to see in what circumstances after death souls can become water. Perhaps we should turn our attention rather to their condition during life. A man's way of life, Heraclitus said, may determine his fate.[1] The θυμός is prepared to buy what it wants at the expense of soul.[2] We have seen one example of this in the drunkard who courts Hades by wetting his soul. Now there is another obvious way in which the soul may turn to liquid during life, producing pleasure but also death: procreation.

> Fr. 99 = B 20 γενόμενοι ζώειν ἐθέλουσι μόρους τ' ἔχειν· καὶ παῖδας καταλείπουσι μόρους γενέσθαι.

The only natural interpretation of this fragment is that a man's children are his μόροι, being successors to his life, and that nevertheless he wishes to have children. Obviously they are not complete deaths—a man does not die on becoming a father—but each child reduces the deep measure of his father's soul.[3] That gives a possible sense to the soul-cycle of fr. 66:

soul	soul	my father
water	semen	
earth	body	me
water	semen	
soul	soul	my son.

[1] Fr. 94 = B 119 ἦθος ἑκάστῳ δαίμων. To the parallels collected by Marcovich add *Epist.* 8 p. 76. 27–8 Bywater; Democr. B 171; Xenocrates, frs. 81–3 Heinze.

[2] Fr. 70 = B 85. ψυχῆς ὠνεῖσθαι was or became a semi-proverbial phrase (to the passages cited by Marcovich add Isoc. 6. 109); but Heraclitus will not have used the word ψυχή carelessly.

[3] Zeno held the semen to be πνεῦμα μεθ' ὑγροῦ, ψυχῆς μέρος καὶ ἀπόσπασμα καὶ τοῦ σπέρματος τοῦ τῶν προγόνων κέρασμα καὶ μεῖγμα τῶν τῆς ψυχῆς μερῶν συνεληλυθός (Eus. *PE* 15. 20. 1, *SVF* i. 36. 3).

It must be granted that this does not represent the whole truth: I have a soul as well as a body, and my father and son have bodies as well as souls.

There is other evidence of Heraclitus' preoccupation with the generative cycle, and in particular with the number of years it takes to complete. He determined that it took thirty years, and called this period a γενεή.[1] We are given conflicting explanations of the figure: Philo accounts for it as the interval from a boy's birth to the birth of his grandson, Plutarch and Censorinus as that from a son's birth to a grandson's. Most recent scholars rightly accept the second, which fits the conventional age for men to marry in archaic Greece.[2] But puberty seems to have a place in the scheme: Aet. 5. 23 (πότε ἄρχεται ὁ ἄνθρωπος τῆς τελειότητος) Ἡράκλειτος καὶ οἱ Στωικοὶ . . . περὶ τὴν δευτέραν ἑβδομάδα, περὶ ἣν ὁ σπερματικὸς κινεῖται ὀρός κτλ.[3]

The great year

Aetius and Censorinus name Heraclitus among a number of people who believed in a 'great year', which both writers understand to be the time that the sun, moon, and planets take to return to their original positions; Censorinus adds that it has a winter consisting of an all-engulfing deluge and a summer consisting of an ecpyrosis.[4] This astronomical great year cannot be traced earlier than Plato's *Timaeus* (39 d, 22 c–d),[5] and it is clear

[1] Fr. 108 = A 19.

[2] Hes. *Op.* 696, Solon 19. 9–10 Diehl; Fränkel, *AJP* 59, 1938, 89–91 = *W. u. F.*, pp. 251 f.; Reinhardt, *Hermes* 77, 1942, 231 = *Vermächtnis*, p. 78 = *Begriffswelt*, p. 185; Kirk, *HCF*, pp. 298 f. Marcovich, however, cleaves to Philo.

[3] Fr. 108(*c*) = A 18. There is a risk that the notice is mere inference from the definition of a generation, on the basis of the (Stoic?) interpretation followed by Philo. On the other hand, it is something that Heraclitus certainly could have said; cf. Solon 19. 3–4 Diehl.

[4] Fr. 65 = A 13. Aetius says that Diogenes of Babylon (*SVF* iii. 215. 22) based his great year on Heraclitus', multiplying it by 365. Reinhardt (*Parmenides*, pp. 188 f., *Hermes* 77, 1942, 234 = *Vermächtnis*, p. 82 = *Begriffswelt*, p. 190) plausibly conjectures that Diogenes was the source for Aetius and Censorinus, as well as for Plut. *def. or.* 415 f, where the Stoic ecpyrosis is mentioned as spreading into Heraclitus and others.

[5] On Tzetzes' ascription of such a year to Meton see p. 237. In Philolaus 44 A 18 (Aet. 2. 5. 3), φθοράν is corrupt for τροφήν, see Galen in Diels, *Doxogr.* 622. 5. The error comes from what precedes.

that the periods listed by Aetius and Censorinus were variously intended by their devisers.

Heraclitus' year is given as 10,800 (Censorinus) or 18,000 (Aetius) solar years. Censorinus' figure is generally and rightly preferred. One cannot see how 18,000 years could have been arrived at,[1] whereas 10,800 years is arithmetically transparent: it is 360 × 30 years. We know the significance that the period of 30 years had for Heraclitus.

It follows that Heraclitus' 'great year', whether or not he called it that, really was a *year*; and that his view of the human generative cycle had led him to see it as a day in a year. When we compare his account of that cycle with his account of the daily cycle, we see the parallel.

Dawn.	Sea turning into 1. earth, 2. πρηστήρ . . . sun.	*Birth.*	Semen converted into 1. body, 2. soul.
Day.	Sun progresses steadily through day.		Soul grows steadily without setback.
Sunset.	Sun turns back to sea.	*15th year, Puberty.*	Soul converted to semen.
Night.	Appearance of numerous small fires, constantly turning back to sea.		Intermittent conversion of soul to semen.
Dawn.	A new sun (νέος ἐφ' ἡμέρῃ, fr. 58 = B 6).	*30th year, Marriage.*	A new soul thrown off.

Again, this is not the whole picture—the parallelism of earth and the body soon breaks down—but it must be something like the part of the picture that Heraclitus was looking at. It is indeed surprising that it occurred to him to look for a similarity

[1] Van der Waerden, *Hermes* 80, 1952, 136, 150, and *AA*, p. 211, explains it as five Babylonian Sars of years. (A Sar is not a period or cycle, it is the number 3,600. The Sar of years is a unit used in king-lists; there were 120 of them before the flood. Kirk, *HCF*, p. 300, is vague and inaccurate.) But what could they have meant to Heraclitus, and why should he take five of them together?

between the day and the generation. But he must have done so, or he could not have arrived at his great year.

The daily suns do not follow exactly the same path throughout the year. In summer they rise higher and burn hotter and longer, in winter they are lower and weaker and turn sooner into sea. For there is the larger cycle of 360 days in which the balance between sea and fire shifts to and fro. The zones of the sky marked out in fr. 62 = B 120 may belong in this context. They define the ἠοῦς καὶ ἑσπέρης τέρματα, the limits of the sun's movement in declination. The 'boundary of Zeus Aithrios' is the base-line behind which the sun never retreats.[1] These are the μέτρα appointed by Dike, which the sun will not transgress; or if he does, the Erinyes will find him out. Now this same regularity, governed by the cosmic number 360, must, Heraclitus argued, be found also in the long succession of human generations. The solar year of 360 days must be matched by a life-soul year of 360 generations.

This does not mean that the individual soul survives or passes through a cycle of changes over that immense period, as some have supposed.[2] Their interpretation destroys the parallelism with the solar year, which is our only guide to Heraclitus' meaning. The true counterpart of the solar year is a cycle of alternation between world ages of contrasted moral character. In summer the weather remains dry, the sun burns brighter and survives longer before his inevitable watery death. So there must be periods of the world at which souls are drier (= wiser), purer, and longer-lasting; such as the time of Hesiod's golden race, who lived long without the signs of age, and became the *daimon*-guardians of mankind; the time of the great heroes who died in battle, or πρόωροι, before marrying, and are venerated as demigods. In winter the weather is wet, the sun weak, low, and short-lived. So there are periods of the world at which souls are stupider and weaker and succumb more easily to liquefaction,

[1] Cf. [Hp.] *vict.* I. 5 (quoted on p. 122) and I. 3, and Addenda.

[2] Reinhardt, *Parmenides*, pp. 192 ff.; *Hermes* 77, 1942, 234 = *Vermächtnis*, p. 82 = *Begriffswelt*, p. 189; Kirk, *HCF*, p. 302, cf. Kirk–Raven, p. 202.

notably through drink and sexual excess; such as the time of Hesiod's short-lived iron race, and the time of the prophet himself.

The connection between physical cosmology and ethical 'psychonomics' is strengthened by the operation of the same gods in both spheres. It is Dike who supervises the movements of the sun, and Dike who will overtake artificers and witnesses of falsehood (fr. 19 = B 28). It is to Zeus' boundary that the winter sun retreats: Zeus as the Wise is linked with the wise dry soul, as Hades with the sodden one. This might point to a standing conflict between Zeus and Hades, for which sentences in the *de victu* can be quoted as possible echoes.[1]

Aion

Day and night, summer and winter, war and peace, satiety and starvation, are all manifestations of ὁ θεός (fr. 77). We have seen that Theophrastus understood this God to be the world-fire (p. 134). I have taken the view that it was really the divine intelligence, 'Zeus' (pp. 142, 144).

The alternations of the soul's cycle are parallel to those of the sun's cycle. If day and night, summer and winter, represent changing conditions of 'Zeus', are the alternations of soul and semen, or of better and worse ages of the world, likewise aspects of a single divinity? If so, are these also 'Zeus', or perhaps the same divine principle under a different name?

There was a very suitable name available to Heraclitus in Aion. Where it is found before his time, *αἰών* always refers to a man's lifetime, or to the spinal marrow that was thought (at least by some) to be the source of the semen.[2] Soon after him it is being used (*a*) of the very long or endless life of the gods,[3] (*b*) of Life or Time as a changer of fortunes.[4]

[1] 1. 4 *νομίζεται δ' ὑπὸ τῶν ἀνθρώπων τὸ μὲν ἐξ Ἅιδου ἐς φάος αὐξηθὲν γενέσθαι, τὰ δ' ἐκ τοῦ φάεος ἐς Ἅιδην μειωθέντα ἀπολέσθαι* . . . (5) (after the passage quoted on p. 122) *πάντα ταὐτὰ καὶ οὐ ταὐτά· φάος Ζηνί, σκότος Ἅιδῃ, φάος Ἅιδῃ, σκότος Ζηνί.*

[2] Taylor on Pl. *Tim.* 91 a 2–4; Onians, *Origins of European Thought*, pp. 200 ff.

[3] Simon. *Melici* 584; Aesch. *Supp.* 574 (cf. 582); Emp. B 16.

[4] Pind. *Ol.* 2. 10 (476 B.C.), *N.* 2. 8 (485?), *Isth.* 3. 18 (474?), 8. 14 (478); Eur. *Hipp.* 1109, *Hcld.* 900; cf. *Χρόνος* in id. fr. 304.

We know that Aion, personified for the first time, actually did appear in Heraclitus; and Clement identifies him with Heraclitus' 'Zeus'.

Fr. 93 = B 52 *Αἰὼν παῖς ἐστι, παίζων, πεσσεύων· παιδὸς ἡ βασιληίη.*

Clem. *Paed.* 1. 22. 1 *τοιαύτην τινὰ παίζειν παιδιὰν τὸν ἑαυτοῦ Δία Ἡράκλειτος λέγει.*

What is Heraclitus talking about? He represents Aion as a king, and this surely means as a god (cf. fr. 29, Polemos as 'king of all'). We gather that there is a power in the world that controls certain things in the same way as a child moves draughts.[1] That might mean 'capriciously, unpredictably', but caprice and hazard seem out of keeping with the strict regularity, necessity, compulsion (*μέτρα, χρεών, ἀνάγκη, εἱμαρμένα*) that we hear of elsewhere in Heraclitus. The more likely sense is that what appears at the receiving end as the exercise of compelling power in fact requires little effort or attentiveness on the part of the divine agent. This suits the emphasis added by the word *παίζων*, and the way in which child's-play comparisons are used in Homer, Alcman, and Anacreon.[2]

Aion must be something higher and more universal than an individual man's life (which is ruled by his *ἦθος*, according to fr. 94 = B 119). The best sense would be that suggested by the passages under (*b*) (p. 158 n. 4). Here as there, Aion's special association is apparently with human aspirations. If we press the metaphor *πεσσεύων*, individual souls may be understood as the pieces pushed about in Aion's vast carefree game.

[1] Not dice, as Marcovich, ed. p. 494, prefers. *πεσσεύειν* is *not* the same as *ἀστραγαλίζειν*.

[2] In *Il.* 15. 361 ff. Apollo knocks down the Achaean wall as easily and thoughtlessly as a child kicks in a sand-castle. Alcman, *Melici* 58 *Ἀφροδίτα μὲν οὐκ ἔστι, μάργος δ' Ἔρως οἷα ⟨παῖς⟩ παίσδει, / ἄκρ' ἐπ' ἄνθη καβαίνων (ἃ μή μοι θίγῃς) τῶ κυπαιρίσκω.* Anacreon, *Melici* 398: the furious passions that convulse men are the childish playthings of Eros, *ἀστραγάλαι δ' Ἔρωτός εἰσιν μανίαι τε καὶ κυδοιμοί.* The idea of man as a plaything of the gods recurs in Plato, *Lg.* 644 d–e, 803 c–4 b.

Consequences for morality

If Heraclitus' theory of the soul leads to the conclusion that alcoholic and sexual excess are evils to be avoided, he is of course not simply following abstract reasoning whithersoever it may lead, he is rationalizing a preformed moral attitude. We cannot say just how severe his teaching was on these subjects. He can hardly have called for total abstinence from sexual intercourse, but he may have held that it should be kept to a minimum, and directed strictly towards procreation. This would be in keeping with his theory (wasted semen would mean a permanent diminution of soul) as well as being a likely position for a moralist to adopt. A prophet of our own times has written in similar vein:[1]

> I use 'gonorrhoea' not in the accepted sense of 'one of the venereal diseases' but in its original and proper meaning of 'a discharge of semen' or rather 'a morbid addiction to the discharging of semen in ways and on occasions that are biologically meaningless' . . . this morbid addiction involves the destruction of God.
>
> The function of the prostate is to extract life from the body in order to pass it on to the offspring. . . . it is absolutely certain that when life is not being removed from the body *via* the prostate, the man enjoys a quality of life incomparably superior to that of the normal sexual addicts who regard themselves as men . . . they not only enjoy freedom from fear, freedom from pain, freedom from disease and innumerable other freedoms, but their intelligence is greatly enhanced, intuition takes the place of reason, they have power to penetrate the past and the future and to communicate with their fellow men telepathically and they enjoy divine inspiration . . . these powers are simply the attributes of God.

The opinion that sexual intercourse is invariably debilitating is expressed in an apophthegm attributed to Pythagoras, and one of the books written in his name stated that the seasons of the year differ in suitability for it: *ἀφροδίσια χειμῶνος ποιέεσθαι, μὴ θέρεος· φθινοπώρου δὲ καὶ ἦρος κουφότερα. βαρέα δὲ πᾶσαν*

[1] J. M. Wyllie ('the Barras Seer'). The pamphlet quoted is headed 'An Advance Specimen of the Forthcoming Part Four of *The Great Betrayal* or *The Failure of Science*', and dated 9 May 1968.

ὥρην καὶ ἐς ὑγιείην οὐκ ἀγαθά.[1] This doctrine clearly has something to do with the Hesiodic description of high summer as the time when women are sexiest and men weakest.[2] But it might also reflect a Heraclitean association between the cycles of soul and sun. A syncretism of Pythagorean with Heraclitean thought is not without parallel. We do not know enough about the teaching of Hippasus of Metapontum, the early Pythagorean whom Aristotle links with Heraclitus as one who chose fire for his ἀρχή (DK 18). But Scythinus of Teos is certainly a Heraclitean in part, besides describing a cosmic lyre in Pythagorean terms.[3] The Heraclitizing 'Orphic' fragments quoted on pp. 150 f. perhaps come from the context of the Pythagorean metempsychosis-theory as it was expounded in one of the poems that contributed to the Rhapsodic theogony (cf. frs. 223–4, 228, 231, 291).

All this may belong in the fifth century. If we want a firmer case of the confluence of Heraclitean and Pythagorean theory, we need look no further than Plato. Plato may indeed preserve a reflection of Heraclitus' theory of the great year. His ideal state is ruled by Guardians, persuaded that they are of the golden race, and fully trained to live up to this conviction (*Rep.* 414–15). Plato is adapting the Hesiodic myth of races, but we have noted that the heroization of ἀρηΐφατοι (468 e–9 b) recalls Heraclitus.[4] When in Book VIII he comes to discuss the ways in which the political order may be corrupted, he writes (546 a–d):

A city which is thus constituted can hardly be shaken; but seeing that everything which comes into being also perishes, even this constitution will not last for ever, but will be dissolved. And this is its dissolution: Not only in plants that grow in the earth, but also in

[1] D.L. 8. 9; Thesleff, *Pythagorean Texts*, p. 171; before 200 B.C., cf. Burkert, *Philol.* 105, 1961, 24.

[2] *Op.* 586, echoed by Alc. fr. 347. 4. See Addenda.

[3] DK 22 C 3, A 1 § 16. Scythinus' date is uncertain between the late fifth and early third century (cf. Jacoby on *FGrHist* 13; Kirk, *HCF*, p. 11). I incline to the higher limit. Note the similarity of the Stobaeus fragment to Hermippus, fr. 4 Kock, and the coincidence of the Kylikranes appearing in both writers (Scyth. 13 F 1, Hermippus, fr. 70).

[4] p. 152. On Plato's use of Hesiod cf. F. Solmsen, *Fondation Hardt Entretiens*, vii. 173–96.

animals that move on the earth's surface, fertility and infertility of soul and body occur when revolutions complete circles for each, short orbits for short-lived ones, the contrary for the contrary. But your race's fertilities and infertilities all the wisdom and education of your rulers will not attain by calculation or observation, and they will bring children into the world when they ought not. Now that which is of divine birth has a period which is contained in a perfect number, but the period of human birth is comprehended in a number in which — (There follows a complex formula.) Now this number represents a geometrical figure which has control over superior and inferior procreations. When your guardians are ignorant of them, and unite brides to bridegrooms out of season, children will not be well-formed or well-endowed.

The number itself comes out as 12,960,000, which in all probability represents the number of days in a great year of 36,000 solar years.[1] This is most simply and plausibly explained as 360 × 100 years, which makes it strikingly like Heraclitus' great year, the thirty-year *γενεή* being replaced as the unit by the hundred-year period which appears later in the *Republic* (615 b) as the span of human life. It can hardly be coincidence that a cosmic period so similarly constructed governs the alternation of better and worse world ages and brings times when sexual concourse were better avoided.[2]

It is significant for Heraclitus' puritan mentality that the particular festival of Dionysus that he picks out for condemnation is one involving sexual symbols and indecent singing. When he criticizes praying to images, and blood-purifications,[3] he affects

[1] See Adam's commentary, especially ii. 208 and 301 ff. Rees in the introduction to the reprinted edition (1965) reviews the development of opinion since Adam.

[2] See also the myth of the *Politicus*, 268 e ff., where it even appears as a feature of the rule of Kronos that the dead lying in the earth rise up and come to life (hence the myth of earthborn men) (271 b). Other fourth-century echoes of Heraclitus' great year are doubtful. When Aristotle couples him with Empedocles as believing in periodic *φθοραί* (*de cael.* 279^b14 = fr. 51(b^1) = A 10), and when Theophrastus says *ποιεῖ δὲ καὶ τάξιν τινὰ καὶ χρόνον ὡρισμένον τῆς τοῦ κόσμου μεταβολῆς κατά τινα εἱμαρμένην ⟨καὶ⟩ ἀνάγκην* (*Phys. Op.* fr. 1 = fr. 28(*d*) Marcovich = A 5), both seem to have in mind the changes of fire in fr. 53 = B 31. See Kirk, *HCF*, pp. 318 ff.

[3] Fr. 86 = B 5. For the rite involved cf. Eur. *IT* 1223, 'Hp.' *morb. sacr.* 4, sch. [Pl.] *Min.* 315 c; Rohde, *Psyche*, pp. 194 n. 77, 296.

to be doing so on the ground of their comic illogicality. But fr. 87 = B 14 *τὰ νομιζόμενα κατ' ἀνθρώπους μυστήρια ἀνιερωστὶ μυέονται*, shows that he had his own ideas of what was proper and holy, and that they determined his attitude towards current rituals. If it is true that he resigned to his brother the hereditary kingship of Ephesus,[1] the reason may have been that it entailed officiation at the rites of Eleusinian Demeter.[2] It may have been the purveyors of mysteries and purifications that he branded as *ψευδέων τέκτονες καὶ μάρτυρες* whom Dike would overtake;[3] with them he may have included Pythagoras the chief of charlatans.[4] A true purification, he said, is a rare occurrence (fr. 98(*g*) = B 69).

By the law of God, the laws of men are sustained (fr. 23 = B 114); and Heraclitus is a fervent upholder of *εὐνομίη*.

Fr. 103 = B 44 *μάχεσθαι χρὴ τὸν δῆμον ὑπὲρ τοῦ νόμου ὅκωσπερ τείχεος*. The law, as much as the wall, is the city's defence, and it is noteworthy that this is the simile Heraclitus thinks of to support his epistemological principle (fr. 23) *ἰσχυρίζεσθαι χρὴ τῷ ξυνῷ πάντων ὅκωσπερ νόμῳ πόλις*.

Fr. 102 = B 43 *ὕβριν χρὴ σβεννύναι μᾶλλον ἢ πυρκαϊήν*, is exactly parallel. A fire may destroy the city wall, but violence and disorder will destroy the law. Law is to obey the will of one (fr. 104 = B 33): as Homer put it, *οὐκ ἀγαθὸν πολυκοιρανίη, εἷς κοίρανος ἔστω*. The Wise is one, one is worth ten thousand if he is *ἄριστος*, the Ephesians have cast out Hermodorus saying 'let us have no one best man'.[5]

This is no longer Philosophy, it is political exhortation in a live situation. And when a man speaks of the honour that death in

[1] Antisthenes 508 F 10 *ap.* D.L. 9. 6.

[2] Strabo 14. 1. 3 p. 633. Cf. Kirk, *HCF*, pp. 8 f.

[3] Fr. 19 = B 28. Cf. Clem. *Protr.* 22. 2 (= B 14 a) *τίσι δὴ μαντεύεται {'Ηράκλειτος} ὁ 'Εφέσιος; νυκτιπόλοις, μάγοις, βάκχοις, λήναις, μύσταις· τούτοις ἀπειλεῖ τὰ μετὰ θάνατον, τούτοις μαντεύεται τὸ πῦρ.* The Judgement Fire is a product of Christian interpretation (cf. p. 144 n. 1), and the list of those in danger is probably Clement's compilation from hints like *ληναΐζουσι* fr. 50, *μυστήρια* fr. 87 (Marcovich, ed. pp. 465–7). But the passage makes the link with fr. 19, where again Clement finds the cleansing by fire.

[4] Fr. 18 = B 81; Gigon, p. 128.

[5] Fr. 98 = B 49, 105 = B 121.

battle wins from gods and men, it is usually the case either that he is making a funeral oration, or that he is rousing his audience to defend their country.[1] The praise of Polemos in fr. 29 = B 53 shows an enthusiasm greater than one would expect an abstract cosmic principle to inspire, and the reminder that it divides the slaves from the free may be pointed. We shall not say, with Diodotus (p. 112), that Heraclitus' book as a whole was political and not about nature. But we shall do well to remember that it was not so much the changes of fire that roused his blood as the doings of gods and men.

[1] It was in the latter context that Heraclitus' fellow citizen Callinus, 150 years before, had written *λαῷ γὰρ σύμπαντι πόθος κρατερόφρονος ἀνδρὸς / θνήσκοντος ζώων δ' ἄξιος ἡμιθέων*. Cf. Tyrt. 6. 1–2, 9. 23–34 Diehl.

6

HERACLITUS AND PERSIAN RELIGION

Quaestio perpetua

Two letters of late Hellenistic composition represent Darius as being interested by Heraclitus' book and inviting him to come and give instruction at the court, and Heraclitus as declining.[1] Different views may be taken about the likelihood of such an incident; but even as a fiction it suggests that a stronger connection with the Persian religion was seen in the case of Heraclitus than in the case of other philosophers. Certainly Clement, in attributing to Heraclitus a doctrine of purification by fire of those who have led evil lives, says that he took it from 'barbarian philosophy',[2] and he was no doubt thinking of the doctrines of the Magi made known to educated Greeks by such writers as Theopompus and Eudemus.[3] Christian charges that the Greeks derived their wisdom from the east are of course common and uncritical, and cannot serve as a serious basis for discussion. But with Heraclitus the dispute about possible connections between his philosophy and the Persian religion has enjoyed a long span of renewed life in modern times. In the words of a recent writer: 'The problem, seriously studied by the moderns, has often been negatively solved by the great historians of Greek philosophy: but it seems, nevertheless, repeatedly to rise anew like the Phoenix from its ashes, as though the temptation to compare the two traditions and discover a bond of interdependence between them periodically became irresistible.'[4]

[1] *Epist.* 1–2, *ap.* D.L. 9. 13–14.

[2] *Strom.* 5. 9. 4.

[3] Theopompus 115 F 64–5, Eudemus, frs. 89 and 150 Wehrli; cf. Nigidius Figulus, fr. 67 Swoboda.

[4] J. Duchesne-Guillemin, *East and West*, N.S. 13, 1962, 198 = *Hist. of Religions* 3, 1963, 34.

The question was already raised at the beginning of the last century by that pioneer of Heraclitean studies, Friedrich Schleiermacher, and I should not be surprised to learn that it had been raised earlier. At the end of his collection and discussion of the fragments of Heraclitus,[1] Schleiermacher writes that important investigations remain to be made, and one of those that he mentions is whether 'persische Weisheit' exercised any formative influence on the Ephesian's teaching. The idea is cautiously formulated; more so than in the next work in which it appears, Friedrich Creuzer's *Symbolik und Mythologie der alten Völker*.[2] In this imposing and once influential book, Creuzer attempted to show that Greek religion was based on the profound wisdom of the east, which recognized that light in all its forms was the true object of worship. Any physical creature or object that appeared in myth or ritual was symbolic of some elemental essence. In Heraclitus, 'a servant of pure fire', Creuzer found an important link between eastern elementalism and Greek rationalism. He declared that Heraclitus thought and taught in the spirit of Zoroaster, only penetrating what he had taken from the east with the shafts of clear Hellenic logic, and reducing it to a coherent system so as to make it acceptable to his people.

The same view of Greece's innate superiority was presupposed in the first serious attempt to follow up these dicta. In a series of monographs, the first of which was published in 1841, and in a more comprehensive work of 1852,[3] August Gladisch expounded the theory that the earlier Greek philosophers, one after another, took over the religious world-pictures of different peoples of antiquity, and made them into self-consistent philosophical systems. Pythagoras took the Chinese world-picture, Heraclitus the Persian, Xenophanes and the Eleatics the Indian, Empedocles the Egyptian, Anaxagoras the Israelite; and finally Plato,

[1] *Museum d. Alterthumswiss.* 1, 1808, 315–533 = *Sämmtliche Werke*, 3. Abtheilung, 2. Band (1838), 3–146.

[2] 2nd ed., 1819–21, ii. 192–9; 3rd ed., 1840, ii. 595–601. I have not seen the first edition of 1810–12.

[3] *Die Religion und die Philosophie in ihrer weltgeschichtlichen Entwickelung und Stellung zu einander*, Breslau.

absorbing all these foreign influences, brought native Hellenic thought and religion to its final consummation. Greek philosophy was thus revealed as the crown of early man's intellectual endeavours, incorporating, transfiguring, and superseding the combined wisdom of China, India, Persia, Egypt, and Israel.

Heraclitus was dealt with in *Herakleitos und Zoroaster: eine historische Untersuchung* (Leipzig, 1859). This begins with a reference to 'all the other amazing facts which I have discovered'—the sort of language often used by hopeful cranks whose earlier works have not been taken very seriously. But *Herakleitos und Zoroaster* is by no means a work of fantasy. It is a serious and conscientious study of a question which, as Gladisch points out, others had raised. He knew Greek well enough to discuss the text of the fragments of Heraclitus without appearing irresponsible by 1859 standards. But he laboured under handicaps that no Hellenist of his time could very well have avoided. Zoroastrian literature had not been understood as well or made so generally available as it has been since. He did not himself know Avestan or Pahlavi, and the secondary works on which he had to rely, such as Anquetil du Perron's *Zend-Avesta* (1769–71) and Thomas Hyde's *Historia religionis veterum Persarum* (1710, 1760), sometimes gave inaccurate or misleading information. His evaluation of the Greek sources, as he had not the benefit of Diels's analysis of the doxographical tradition, appears very uncritical today. Lassalle did no better in his monumental two-volume work on Heraclitus,[1] published after Gladisch's *Religion und Philosophie* (which he refers to without praise) but just before *Herakleitos und Zoroaster*. He discusses the Persian question with enthusiasm and a certain limited sobriety. He is conscientious in acknowledging the difference between Zoroastrian dualism and Heraclitean unitarianism, a difference which Bernays a few years earlier had represented as a grave obstacle to what he called the 'Parsification' of Heraclitus.[2] It is to Lassalle's credit that he does not

[1] *Die Philosophie Herakleitos des Dunkeln*, Berlin 1858, i. 351–73.

[2] *Rh. Mus.* 7, 1850, 93 ff. = *Gesammelte Abhandlungen*, 1885, i. 40 ff.

minimize the difference but accepts it, without attaching to it the decisive importance that it seemed to Bernays to possess.

Before the century was out, half a dozen other scholars had joined the hunt for foreign influences, not only Persian, but Egyptian, Phoenician, and Indian.[1] None of them impressed by the kind of evidence they adduced, and the best-qualified interpreters of Heraclitus were much more inclined to be guided by the voice of Bernays. The negative reaction was most eloquently and influentially represented by Zeller, who repeated and elaborated Bernays's criticisms.[2] E. Wellmann, in the 1912 Pauly–Wissowa article on Heraclitus, dismisses the matter in a sentence with a reference to Zeller. Confidence in the φιλοβάρβαροι was by no means strengthened by Eisler's *Weltenmantel und Himmelszelt* (1910). Eisler was a prime illustration of the principle πολυμαθίη νόον οὐ διδάσκει. Not that he was a dullard; on the contrary, he had a brilliant combinatorial intelligence, and I have several times in this book cited him as the first author of an important idea, besides drawing on the vast stores of learning to be found in his writings. But he had no idea when to stop. For example, following the lead of Wolfgang Schultz,[3] he found particular satisfaction in calculating and comparing the arithmetical values of Greek words and names, and he did not hesitate to attribute this pastime to the ancient philosophers. His discussion of Heraclitus is entirely given up to the detection of isopsephisms such as this:

λόγος (62) + Ζεύς (49) = 111.
πῦρ ἀείζων (53 + 58) = 111.

I need not stress what a lack of historical sense it indicates that such relationships should even be looked for.

Since the First World War, Babylon has been brought into

[1] E. Röth, *Gesch. unserer abendländischen Philosophie*, 1846–58, i. 436 f.; G. Teichmüller, *Neue Studien zur Gesch. der Begriffe*, 1878, ii. 103 ff.; A. Chiappelli, *Atti dell'Acc. di Scienze morali e politiche della Soc. Reale di Napoli*, 1887; O. Gruppe, *Culte und Mythen* i. 653 f.; R. Garbe, *Philos. Monatsheft*, 29, 1895, 513–30; R. Oldenberg, *Deutsche Rundschau* 22, 1898, 193–225.

[2] Zeller–Nestle i⁶. 935 n. 1. Cf. above, p. 28.

[3] *Studien zur antiken Kultur*, i (1905), ii (1907).

the ring;[1] India, after a period of neglect, has revived;[2] Egypt has all but lapsed;[3] Persia remains irrepressible.[4] The writers include four ladies and three orientals (including one oriental lady). More significantly, they have recently for the first time included leading Iranists. S. Wikander reviewed the question at a colloquium held in Strasbourg. His conclusions are published only in the form of a two-page summary,[5] but it appears that his attitude, though sceptical, is not completely negative. J. Duchesne-Guillemin has stated his views more fully (and repetitively).[6] Here, of course, we find a mastery of the Iranian material such as none of the older writers had; but the treatment of Heraclitus is not rigorous or detailed enough, and Duchesne-Guillemin has an easygoing habit of choosing between rival interpretations to suit his needs. We see also the distorting influence of Dumézil's theories of Indo-European social structure.

The writers of standard works on Heraclitus, however, remain aloof. Neither in Kirk–Raven nor in Kirk's 400-page book on Heraclitus do we find a word to suggest that the Hellenic purity of his thought has ever been questioned. In Marcovich's 75-column Pauly–Wissowa article, as in Wellmann's, a single sentence suf-

[1] A. Levi, *Riv. di filos. neoscolastica* 1, 1919; L. A. Stella, *Rendiconti della Reale Acc. naz. dei Lincei*, Classe di Scienze morali, storiche e filologiche, Ser. VI. iii, 1927, 571–602; Y. Nakahara, *L'Idée babylonienne à l'origine de la doctrine héraclitéenne du Logos* (*Tetzugaku-Kenkyu* 1932 (4)); van der Waerden, *Hermes* 80, 1952, 129–55, and *AA*, pp. 209 f. I have not seen Levi or Nakahara.

[2] Sri Aurobindo, *Heraclitus*, 1941, 1947; P. Masson-Oursel, *La Philosophie en Orient*, 1941, p. 15; E. Paci, *Acme* 2 (1/2), 1949, 189; A. Somigliana, *Influenze vediche nel pensiero eracliteo*, Milan 1953; *Sophia* 27, 1959, 87–94; *Monismo indiano e monismo greco nei frammenti di Eraclito*, Catania 1961.

[3] P. Tannery, *Pour l'histoire de la science hellène*, ²1930, pp. 179–86.

[4] A. Stöhr, *Heraklit*, Vienna 1920; Stella, op. cit.; J. Przyluski, *Rev. hist. rel.* 122, 1940, 85–101; C. Ramnoux, *Revue de la Méditerranée* 19, 1959, 329–64; R. M. Afnán, *Zoroaster's Influence on Greek Thought*, New York 1965. I know of Stöhr's essay only through the work of his disciple J. M. Cleve, *The Giants of Pre-Sophistic Greek Philosophy*, 1965, i. 31–129, who says he follows the outlines of Stöhr's interpretation. Cleve is a confident believer in the principle that the understanding of Heraclitus does not call for a 'philologist' so much as for a 'philosopher', by which he seems to mean a man of poetic imagination.

[5] *Éléments orientaux dans la religion grecque ancienne*, Paris 1960, pp. 57–9.

[6] *The Western Response to Zoroaster*, 1958; *East and West*, N.S. 13, 1962, 198–206; *Filosofia* (Turin) 13, 1962, 549–61; *La Religion de l'Iran ancien*, Paris 1962, pp. 221 f.; *Hist. of Religions* 3, 1963, 34–49.

fices for dismissal (Supp. x. 294. 56). In the 90-page chapter on Heraclitus in Guthrie's *History of Greek Philosophy* we find only a brief note which explains that this 'has been omitted because in fact there is no sure evidence of contact or affinities, but only a field for speculation and conjecture'. 'Those interested' are referred to Wikander's summary mentioned above. It seems to be expected that only a few seekers after curious lore are likely to be interested in a question of fundamental importance to our assessment of Heraclitus' thought and the autonomy of early Greek philosophy.

Pitfalls

It is understandable that it should be the most scholarly scholars, so to speak, who show the least interest in non-Greek material. They are used to operating with texts whose language and background they have learned to understand at the cost of much effort. In a foreign field they feel incompetent, and especially where fools have rushed in, they fear to tread. It is easiest to put up the barriers, and to persuade themselves that what they know and can manage is all they need to know and manage. Besides, scepticism is always respectable in a scholar; it is thought better to disbelieve something that may turn out to be true than to believe something that may turn out to be false.

Fear is not called for; but circumspection is. Heraclitus' Logos, for example, has played a prominent part in the debate; it was not difficult to find Indo-Iranian parallels for a concept at once so abstract and so elastic. We have now seen that it is a concept which Heraclitus did not have. Another nice Zoroastrian element was his belief in a fire of judgement at the end of the present world. Again, it is only realistic to admit that Heraclitus was innocent of any such notion.

Fire

Another danger is vagueness. Fire is conspicuous in Zoroastrianism and in Heraclitus, and since Creuzer it has seemed one of the most obvious links between them. But it is not enough to say that fire is very important for both parties; it is necessary to analyse the nature of its importance.

The Zoroastrians have always been famous for the holiness they attach to fire. To extinguish it is a sin; to defile it is worse, and to defile it by burning rather than exposing a corpse is a horror for the perpetration of which the *Vidēvdāt* repeatedly threatens the direst punishments. Fire is a god that can be prayed to under the name Ātar. He is closely associated with Ahura Mazdāh, indeed he is constantly called his son.

As fire you are the joy of Mazdāh Ahura, as holiest spirit you are his joy. Whichever of your names is the most beneficial, O Ātar, son of Mazdāh Ahura, with it (on our lips) let us approach you.

(*Yasna* 36. 3)

The *Vahrhān* fire, the fire preserved in the most sacred shrines, was addressed in a quite lengthy prayer, the fifth *Nyāyišn* of the Avesta. The priest prayed to it for fortune, protection, life; knowledge, holiness, quickness of tongue, comprehension; unfailing memory, manly courage, healthy progeny. Strabo says that whatever god the Persians are sacrificing to, they pray to the fire first (15. 3. 16 p. 733).

In one place it is declared that it is said by revelation that a man is to go as much as possible to the abode of fires, and the salutation of fire is to be performed with reverence; because three times every day the archangels form an assembly in the abode of fires, and shed good works and righteousness there; and then the good works and righteousness shed there, become more lodged in the body of him who goes much thither, and performs many salutations of fire with reverence.

(*Šāyast Lā-Šāyast* 20. 1–2, trans. West, *SBE* v)

These passages will serve as an indication of the status of fire in religious cult. One or two others give us an idea of its cosmological significance.[1] There occur at one place in the Avesta the following words:

Thee, Ātar, the son of Ahura Mazdāh, we honour:—the *Bərəzisavah*-

[1] For what follows cf. Duchesne-Guillemin's last article listed in n. 6 on p. 169.

fire we honour, the *Vohufryāna*-fire we honour, the *Urvāzišta*-fire we honour, the *Vāzišta*-fire we honour, the *Spəništa*-fire we honour.

(*Yasna* 17. 11)

Explanations of these five fires and their functions are given in the *Bundahišn* (17. 1–9) and in the *Selections of Zātspram* (11. 3–5, *SBE* v). *Bərəzisavah* shines before Ohrmazd the Lord; it comes from the rocks and other natural sources, and when properly prepared and sanctified makes the *Vahrhān* fire. *Vohufryāna* is in the bodies of men and animals; it is responsible for the brightness of the eyes, digestion of food, and the warmth of sleep. *Urvāzišta* (named also in *Yašt* 13. 85) is in the earth and in plants, warming the waters and producing fragrance and bloom. *Vāzišta* exists in cloud, to fight against the *daēva* Spənjaγrya (*Vidēvdāt* 19. 40). *Spəništa* is ordinary workaday fire.

This ancient classification implies a much wider conception of fire than the one natural to us. It not only presupposes the common pre-scientific assumption that fire must exist in things like clouds and rocks because it can be struck forth from them;[1] it sees fire wherever there is warmth, brightness, and growth.[2] According to Zātspram:

Then Ohrmazd projected creation in bodily form on to the material plane, first the sky, second water, third earth, fourth plants, fifth cattle, sixth man; and fire permeated all six elements, and the period for which it was inserted into each element lasted, it is said, as much as the twinkling of an eye.

(1. 25, trans. Zaehner, *Zurvan*, p. 342)

This is by no means the same as Heraclitus' theory. Earth for him has not got fire in it, it is fire that has gone out and so changed its substance. Yet the difference conceals a similarity. The parts of the world that are not fire nevertheless retain the vital forward

[1] Cf. my note on Hes. *Th.* 563.

[2] Duchesne-Guillemin compares *Chāndogya Upan.* 5. 4–8 (≏ *Bṛhadāraṇyaka Upan.* 6. 2. 9–13), where the heaven, the storm, the earth, man, and woman, are all seen as fires. (Cf. below, p. 187.) In the *Bhagavad-Gītā* 15. 12–14, Krishna says he is the splendour in the sun, moon, and fire, he penetrates the earth and causes all plants to grow, he becomes the digestive fire and dwells in the bodies of all that breathe.

flow of fire. Fire makes a link between apparently widely separate cosmic districts: this is the essential thought that Heraclitus had to think before he could make use of fire in his cosmology in the way described on p. 130. The question is how he came to think it. From some histories of philosophy one would suppose that he was more or less bound to. Thales had based his cosmology on water, Anaximenes on air, and so it was only natural that Heraclitus should turn to fire! But that presupposes an explicit assumption common to Ionian thinkers, 'everything must be reducible to one of the (Empedoclean) elements, but it is less certain which'. I believe that Heraclitus would not naturally have turned to fire without some particular stimulus. Such a stimulus could have been given by observation of the extraordinary status accorded by the Persians to fire. Besides the theory of fire pervading earth, plants, and animals, it is in place to recall the doctrine of the soul's ascent from earthly fire to the fires of heaven (pp. 67, 89 f.).

The interchange of elements

It is because of the universal process of change that the world is called a fire. For the same reason, I supposed (p. 148), Heraclitus said that everything we see is death. The death of fire itself is the birth of water. These remarkable thoughts are paralleled in a verse of the *Bṛhadāraṇyaka Upanishad* (3. 2. 10):

'Yājñavalkya', said (Jāratkārava Ārtabhāga): 'Since all things are food for death, which is the natural phenomenon of which death is the food?'

'Death is fire and the food of water. (Whoso knows this) overcomes repeated death.'

A theory of interchange between fire and other elements is found elsewhere in the *Upanishads*.

It is the wind that consumes all; for when a fire blows out, it simply goes to the wind; when the sun sets, it too goes to the wind; and when the moon sets, it also goes to the wind. When water dries up, it goes to the wind; for it is the wind that consumes all these. So much for natural phenomena.

(*Chāndogya Upanishad* 4. 3. 1–2, trans. Zaehner, *Hindu Scriptures*, p. 91)

In India, then, before the time of Heraclitus, there is a version of the Prāṇa-theory (see p. 105) in which the wind is regarded as taking over the vital essence of fire, sun, moon, lightning, water, wherever one of these entities dies. At the same time there is a line of transmission from fire to sun, sun to moon, moon to lightning, lightning to wind:

Now we come to the cyclic death of natural phenomena.

This Brahman shines when the fire blazes, and dies when it stops blazing: its virtue goes to the sun, its breath of life to the wind.

This Brahman shines when the sun can be seen and dies when it can no longer be seen: its virtue goes to the moon, its breath of life to the wind.

This Brahman shines when the moon can be seen and dies when it can no longer be seen: its virtue goes to the lightning, its breath of life to the wind.

This Brahman shines when the lightning flashes and dies when it no longer flashes: its virtue goes to the wind, its breath of life to (that same) wind.

So all these natural phenomena enter the wind and die in the wind, but they do not congeal [*or* lose consciousness], for they rise up again from it.

(*Kaushītakī Upanishad* 2. 12, trans. Zaehner, *Hindu Scriptures*, p. 152)

This looks like a development from the eschatological theory mentioned on p. 67 (cf. 89 f.) as common to the Upanishads and the Avesta. Instead of just a path for the ascending soul, we now have to do with a more general system of mutation and transference of elements. As fire in Heraclitus, so wind in this cosmology might be described as the common coin into which other things are changed. In another place, it is said more plainly that different elements are produced by successive mutations from wind, the first material element:

From It, from this Self, space came to be, from space the wind, from wind fire, from fire water, from water earth, from earth the plants, from the plants food, from food (transformed into semen) man.

(*Taittirīya Upanishad* 2. 1, trans. Zaehner, *Hindu Scriptures*, pp. 137 f.)

There is unfortunately no evidence for the currency of these physical doctrines (as distinct from the eschatology) in ancient Iran. In the ninth century A.D., the high priest Mānuščihr writes:

> He is the designer of what is intended, as it is said about his creatures and capability that fire is producing wind, fire is producing water, and fire is producing earth; wind is producing fire, wind is producing water, and wind is producing earth; water is producing fire, water is producing wind, and water is producing earth; earth is producing fire, earth is producing wind, and earth is producing water.
>
> (*Dātastān-i-Dēnīk* 37. 129, trans. West, *SBE* xviii)

But it cannot be asserted that this necessarily derives from early Zoroastrian tradition. Greek and Indian scientific and philosophical writings had been collected and translated during the Sassanid period, particularly under Šāpūr I (240–*c.* 272) and Xusraw I (531–79). In the opinion of Professor Zaehner, 'The Pahlavi books, in so far as they are philosophical, show an unmistakable Aristotelian influence, and one case at least of direct borrowing from an Indian source seems certain.'[1] The mutual interchange of earth, air, fire, and water appeared in Plato and Aristotle, and was commonplace with the Stoics.[2]

Equally, it cannot be asserted that the lack of ancient evidence from Iran rules out a historical connection between the Indian and Heraclitean theories.

The sun

Heraclitus regarded the sun and other heavenly bodies as bowls (σκάφαι) filled with fire. The breadth of the sun's bowl was equal to (the length of) a human foot.[3] No one else held the bowl theory,[4] and we are told that Heraclitus gave no details of the

[1] *DTZ*, p. 185.

[2] Pl. *Tim.* 49 b–c, Arist. *gen. corr.* 337ᵃ1 ff.; passages and references in Marcovich, ed. pp. 279–81.

[3] Cf. p. 98, n. 2.

[4] In Aet. 2. 29. 3 (Stob.) *Ἀλκμαίων Ἡράκλειτος Ἀντιφῶν κατὰ τὴν τοῦ σκαφοειδοῦς στροφὴν καὶ τὰς περικλίσεις* (*ἐκλείπειν τὴν σελήνην*), the word *σκαφοειδές* is appropriate only to Heraclitus. Alcmeon held the sun—doubtless the moon too—to be flat (Aet. 2. 22. 4); Antiphon considered the moon a solid body shining by its own light (id. 2. 28. 4).

origin and substance of the bowls. Where did the idea come from?

Scholars have thought of the sun's cup in which Heracles crossed Oceanus, and of the Egyptian idea of the sun crossing the sky in a barque. I would suggest that we might also think about the Zoroastrian fire altar, still used by Parsee communities and portrayed in reliefs of the sixth and fifth centuries B.C. and on Sassanian coins. A specimen from the Arsacid period has been excavated (Plate VIII). The fire burns in a circular basin, about a foot or at most two feet across. It is the *Vahrhān* fire, derived from the *Bərəzisavah* fire (see pp. 171 f.), and it has a certain connection with the sun. To quote Duchesne-Guillemin (art. cit., p. 39): 'it is forbidden to let the rays of the sun fall on the sacred fire: for the fire of the altar itself symbolizes the sun; or rather, it *is* in a certain way the sun, before which the other sun must disappear.' There is a suggestion of such an equivalence in the curious schematic representation of the fire on a Median relief of the first half of the sixth century B.C. (Plate VIII).

But even if this is so, does it help? Heraclitus must have seen Magi at their fire altars, but how could he confuse such an altar with the sun? Certainly, if he was told 'This is a likeness of the sun', he was not the man to believe it just because he was told it. All the same it might set him thinking. Suppose the sun—and the moon and stars—*were* contained in this sort of bowl: that would explain their definite outline, fixed size, firmly controlled motion, and the concentration of their fire. Once considered, the idea could commend itself.[1]

Dike

The regularity of the sun's movements is supervised by Dike, who must be imagined as exercising a general control over the measures of the world-fire. She will also in some way overtake

[1] There is another place where a football-sized sun appears in a Persian context. According to Dinon, a fourth-century B.C. writer of *Persica* (690 F 10 *ap.* Cic. *div.* 1. 46), Cyrus dreamed he found the sun at his feet, and tried three times to seize it, but it eluded him. The interpreters correctly forecast that he would reign for three decades.

artificers and witnesses of falsehood. We saw that Anaximander had the concept of cosmic justice, but not the cosmic deity Dike, while Parmenides presented a fairly close parallel to Heraclitus (cf. p. 137).

The government of the natural world (especially the sun) by a divine principle representing Truth or Rightness is a concept with ancient roots in Iran, India, and Egypt. In Iran and India the principle has the same name, Sanskrit Ṛta = Old Persian Arta = Avestan Aša; in Egypt it is a goddess called Maʿāt.

In Zoroastrianism, from the time of the *Gāthās* of Zoroaster himself, Aša and Druj, Truth-righteousness and Lie-unrighteousness, or Right and Wrong understood with reference to speech as well as action, are made to stand for the whole antithesis between the Good Religion, with its adherents and all that belongs to it, and the forces of evil and impiety. Thus the faithful are *ašavan* (lit. one who has acquired Aša) and the unfaithful are *drəgvant*; an evil demon is a *druj*; and the terms are liable to occur constantly in any religious context. Above this banal usage, however, we see Aša in certain special associations. To it belongs the material world that is constantly threatened with disruption by the attacks of the *daēvas* (*Yasna* 57. 17, *Srōš vāč* 3). If the sun failed to rise, they would destroy everything on earth, for the sun's light strengthens the body of Aša (*Nyāyišn* 1. 11–13 = *Yašt* 6. 1–3). It is as father of Aša that Ahura Mazdāh controls the regularity of nature:

> This I ask thee, O Lord, answer me truly:
> Who was the first father of Righteousness at the birth?
> Who appointed their path to sun and stars?
> Who but thou is it through whom the moon waxes and wanes?
> (*Yasna* 44. 3, trans. Duchesne-Guillemin, *The Hymns of Zarathustra*)

In two other *Gāthās*, the sacred fire that will bring blessings to the worshipper, and visible harm to the infidel, receives its strength from Aša (*Yasna* 34. 4 = *Nyāyišn* 5. 18; *Yasna* 43. 4).[1] By a natural projection the meting out of justice through the

[1] As an element Aša *is* fire. Cf. p. 38 with n. 4.

fire is transferred to the future day of reckoning. Ahura Mazdāh sees all that men do with the eye of Right:

> The deeds, open or stealthy, into which search is made, O Wise One,
> —Or if (?) for a trifling wrong a man should exact the greatest atonement (?)—
> Perceiving all this with thine eye, thou seest it through shining Righteousness.
>
> (*Yasna* 31. 13)

And at the end he will judge them in the name of Aša:

> The reward which thou shalt give by the spirit and the fire
> And which thou shalt divide, as Righteousness, among the two parties . . .
> Do thou tell us, that we may know.
>
> (Ibid. 31. 3)

> O Wise Lord, as this Holy Spirit,
> Through the fire thou shalt accomplish, supported by Devotion and Right,
> The apportioning of the good between the two parties.
>
> (Ibid. 47. 6)

> Then shall Evil cease to flourish,
> While those who have acquired good fame
> Shall reap the promised reward
> In the blessed dwelling of the Good Mind, of the Wise One, and of Righteousness.
>
> (Ibid. 30. 10)

Heraclitus, too, extends the idea of truth/falsehood to cover actions as well as words. Fr. 23(*f*) = B 112 *σωφρονεῖν ἀρετὴ μεγίστη, καὶ σοφίη ἀληθέα λέγειν καὶ ποιεῖν κατὰ φύσιν ἐπαΐοντας*. (Cf. fr. 1, they fail to show comprehension of these *ἔπεα καὶ ἔργα* covered by my discourse, although they hear me explain everything *κατὰ φύσιν*.) So in fr. 19 = B 28, the people threatened by Dike are the *ψευδέων τέκτονες καὶ μάρτυρες*, where *τέκτων* can mean either 'inventor' or 'worker'.[1] They correspond exactly to Zoroaster's *drəgvants*.

[1] Cf. [Hes.] fr. 343. 14 (*Μῆτις*) τέκταινα δικαίων, Aesch. *Ag.* 1405–6 νεκρὸς δὲ τῆσδε δεξιᾶς χερὸς / ἔργον, δικαίας τέκτονος, Eur. *Med.* 409 κακῶν δὲ πάντων τέκτονες σοφώτατοι.

The Old Persian equivalent of *aša̋van* is *artāvan*, and it is something that Xerxes hopes to be after death.[1] In the Vedas, *ṛtāvan* is applied to gods, to death, and to the ancestral dead.[2] It is not necessary for my purpose to discuss the Indian *ṛta* at length, for the parallels with *aša* only serve to show that the concept is much older than Zoroaster. (In fact *ṛta* falls into disuse as a cosmic principle after the *Ṛgveda.*) I shall simply note its connection with fire and the sun. Agni, the fire-god, is 'guardian of *ṛta*', *Ṛgv.* 1. 1. 8; so is the sun (1. 83. 5, cf. 105. 12). 'The meaning of the word as applied to the natural world connects itself with the alternation of day and night, the regular passage of the sun through the heavens, or the unswerving motion of the rain in its fall from heaven and of the streams along their courses.'[3] By the will of Mitra-Varuna, it is established at the place where the sun's horses go forth (*Ṛgv.* 5. 62. 1; cf. Parm. B 1. 9–14).

The Egyptian Maʿāt is daughter of Reʿ. 'The fundamental idea of the word is "straight", and from the Egyptian texts it is clear that *maʿāt* meant right, true, truth, real, genuine, upright, righteous, just, steadfast, unalterable, etc.'[4] In a hymn to Reʿ in the *Book of the Dead* it is said: 'Thoth and the goddess Maʿāt mark out thy course for thee day by day and every day.'[5] She herself is stationed at the sunrise and sunset: 'The goddess Maʿāt embraceth thee at the two seasons of the day (i.e., at morn and eve).'[6]

It is she who leads the souls of the dead to judgement. The deceased's heart is weighed against her, or against the ostrich feather that is her symbol, and if it fails to balance is eaten by the monster Āmām.[7] Maʿāt's spheres of action thus agree with those of Aša-Ṛta. You may say that they are natural spheres in which to find a personification of Rightness acting. Yet we do not find an analogue in Greek before Heraclitus and Parmenides.

[1] Inscription XPh 48, 55. Cf. Gershevitch, *JNES* 23, 1964, 19.

[2] F. B. J. Kuiper, *Indo-Iranian Journal* 3, 1959, 215.

[3] H. W. Wallis, *Cosmology of the Ṛigveda*, 1887, p. 93.

[4] Budge, *Book of the Dead*, p. 185; cf. J. A. Wilson in Frankfort and others, *Before Philosophy*, 119 f.; S. G. F. Brandon, *The Judgment of the Dead*, 10 f.

[5] Budge, *Book of the Dead*, p. 343.

[6] Ibid., p. 340.

[7] Ibid., pp. 199, 236, 340 n. 3.

The Wise

The fragments of Heraclitus do not specify Dike's relationship with *τὸ σοφόν*, and the complete book may not have done so either. But *τὸ σοφόν* is 'Zeus', and from Hesiod onwards, Zeus is the father of Dike.

Aša's father, as was mentioned, is Ahura Mazdāh. He was identified by the Greeks with Zeus (Hdt. 1. 131. 2, etc.), but his name means simply the Wise God.[1]

τὸ σοφόν is 'one'; the existence of other gods is admitted, but, as 'Zeus', he/it is the greatest. God (or a god) is wiser than a man as a man is wiser than a child. With Heraclitus' supreme god we must take Xenophanes' *εἷς θεός, ἔν τε θεοῖσι καὶ ἀνθρώποισι μέγιστος, οὔ τι δέμας θνητοῖσιν ὁμοίιος οὐδὲ νόημα* (B 23).

The Persians admitted other gods besides the Wise God, but Zoroaster says 'I know none other but you; then save us, through Righteousness.'[2] The *Yasna* liturgies begin:

I offer, I fulfil for the creator Ahura Mazdāh, the mighty and exalted, the greatest and best and finest and firmest and wisest and comeliest and highest in Righteousness.

(1. 1, after Wolff; cf. 26. 2, *Vidēvdāt* 19. 14)

Heraclitus' god watches men the whole time, not only by day: *τὸ μὴ δῦνόν ποτε πῶς ἄν τις λάθοι;* Earlier poets had said that Zeus sees all men's wrongdoing, or has subordinates who report it to him.[3] But they had said similar things of the sun; the sun sleeps at night, even Zeus sleeps sometimes according to Homer. The emphasis on the sleepless, unrelenting watchfulness of the divine power is something new in Greece.

[1] Sometimes he is Ahura alone, or Mazdāh alone. In the *Gāthās* the two words stand independently, usually separated from one another, Mazdāh often coming first. In the younger Avesta too they are treated as two words, in the Achaemenid inscriptions usually as one. Ohrmazd is the Pahlavi form.

[2] *Yasna* 34. 7. There is a grammatical difficulty in the plural 'you'. Hymns to Amen-Reʿ (Budge, *Book of the Dead*, pp. 108 ff., 195 f.) praise him as 'ruler of all the gods' and as 'One Only', 'thou One, thou Only One who hast no second', 'One One'. (Cf. the interpretation of the Syrian Adad as *unus unus*, Macr. *Sat.* 1. 23. 17.) 'The Lord he is God; there is none else beside him' (Deut. 4: 35, cf. 6: 4, Isa. 45: 5).

[3] Hes. *Op.* 248–69, *Od.* 13. 213–14, Solon 1. 17 ff. Diehl.

Ahura Mazdāh sees all that men do (*Yasna* 31. 13, quoted on p. 178; cf. *Yašt* 1. 8), and is not to be deceived (*Yasna* 45. 4). He is never asleep, and never dulled by narcotics (*Vidēvdāt* 19. 20).[1] He is not contrasted with the sun that sets; on the contrary, in *Yasna* 1. 11, 3. 13, 7. 13, the sun is said to be his eye, and he can be represented pictorially by the solar symbol, as on the Behistun relief. In India, however, τὸ μὴ δῦνόν ποτε has a striking parallel. I have pointed to a similarity between Heraclitus' fire—which, if not identical with 'that which never sets', was close enough to be identified with it by Plato's time—and the Indian *prāṇa* (pp. 173 f.). In the hymn referred to on p. 105, it is said of Prāṇa:

Erect, he stays awake when others sleep,
He never falls down prone:
That he should sleep while others sleep,
None has ever heard.

In the *Bṛhadāraṇyaka Upanishad* this is put as follows:

Just as breath holds the midmost position among the human faculties, so does the wind among natural phenomena; for the other natural phenomena fade away; not so the wind. The natural phenomenon known as wind never sets (as does the sun).

(1. 5. 22, trans. Zaehner)

This wind is the breath of life that stirs the whole world. According to the *Kaṭha Upanishad* (6. 2; perhaps contemporary with early Buddhism) it derives from the Brahman, which is the same as man's inmost Self. This is 'the upraised thunderbolt', for fear of which the fire burns, the sun blazes, the gods of storm and wind fly, and death itself. If this reminds us unexpectedly of our κεραυνός, it is only one of a series of reminders of Heraclitus in the context. How was the Self discovered?

The self-existent (Lord) bored holes facing the outside world;
Therefore a man looks outward, not into (him)self.
A certain sage, in search of immortality,
Turned his eyes inward and saw the self within. (4. 1)

[1] Mithra is described in similar terms. He is 'a chief in assemblies, with a thousand ears, well-shapen, with ten thousand eyes, high, with full knowledge, strong, sleepless, and ever awake' (*Yašt* 10. 7, cf. 24).

Heraclitus, accounting for his knowledge, said *ἐδιζησάμην ἐμεωυτόν*.[1] The Self resembles a smokeless flame (4. 13). It dwells in *ṛta* and is born of it and is it (5. 2). It remains awake when all things sleep (5. 8). The next verses—

> As the one fire esconced within the house
> Takes on the forms of all that's in it,
> So the One Inmost Self of every being
> Takes on their several forms, (remaining) without (the while).
>
> As the one wind, once entered into a house,
> Takes on the forms of all that's in it,
> So the One Inmost Self of every being
> Takes on their several forms, (remaining) without (the while)—

recall the god who changes like fire (?) mixing with incense.[2]

Those changes were specified as day and night, winter and summer, war and peace, satiety and starvation. The proposition that God is these things is without parallel in Greek. In the *Praśna Upanishad*, matter and the breath of life issue from Prajāpati (cf. p. 33). The breath of life is the sun, and matter is the moon. The sun envelops everything in its rays by day:

> So arises this universal life breath which has every (possible) form,—(I mean) fire. (1. 7)

In other words there is a universal fire-soul, emanating from the sun and thus from Prajāpati, which takes on the form of every thing.

> The year too is Prajāpati: it has a southern and a northern path. (1. 9; cf. p. 34)

God is summer and winter, in other words.

> The month too is Prajāpati. Its dark half is matter, the light one the breath of life. (1. 12)

[1] Fr. 15 = B 101. Cf. Somigliana, *Monismo*, pp. 16–19, 202–6.

[2] Compared by Somigliana, p. 152. Cf. also the Pahlavi *Mēnōk-i-Xrat* 60. 6–10: 'Because it is said, that whoever joins with the good brings good with him, and whoever joins with the bad brings evil—just like the wind which, when it impinges on stench, is stench, and when it impinges on perfume, is perfume.'

Day and night too are Prajāpati. Of these day is the breath of life, night matter. People who cohabit voluptuously by day waste their life-breath. True chastity consists in cohabiting voluptuously by night. (1. 13)

Food too is Prajāpati. Semen proceeds from it, and from semen (all) these creatures are born, they say. (1. 14; cf. p. 158)

Sleep (cf. pp. 147 ff.)

ἄνθρωπος ἐν εὐφρόνῃ φάος ἅπτεται ἑωυτῷ, ἀποσβεσθεὶς ὄψιας.

'When both sun and moon have set, Yājñavalkya, when the fire has gone out and (all) voices are stilled, what is the light of man then?'

'The self becomes his light then. Lighted by the self alone he sits down, moves away, does his work and comes back.'

(*Bṛhadāraṇyaka Upanishad* 4. 3. 6)[1]

θάνατός ἐστιν ὁκόσα ἐγερθέντες ὁρέομεν, ὁκόσα δὲ εὕδοντες ὕπνος.

'Which one is the self?'

'(Abiding) among the senses there is a "person" who consists of understanding, a light within the heart: this is he. Remaining ever the same, he skirts both worlds, seemingly thinking, seemingly moving. For, having fallen asleep, he transcends this world,—the forms of death.' (Ibid. 4. 3. 7)[2]

ζῶν ἅπτεται τεθνεῶτος εὕδων, ἐγρηγορὼς ἅπτεται εὕδοντος.

This 'person' has two states (of consciousness), that of this world and that of the other world. There is a third twilight state (of consciousness),—that of sleep. Standing in this twilight state, he sees the (other) two, that of this world and that of the other world. Now, however, when he approaches the state (of consciousness) of the other world, he fares forth (towards it) and descries both evil and joyful things. (Ibid. 4. 3. 9)

Cf. Pindar, *ἀτὰρ εὑδόντεσσιν ἐν πολλοῖς ὀνείροις δείκνυσι τερπνῶν ἐφέρποισαν χαλεπῶν τε κρίσιν.*

Death

The bodies of the dead are for Heraclitus an abomination, more to be cast out than dung (pp. 151 f.). This treatment would involve

[1] Somigliana, p. 83. [2] Somigliana, p. 75.

maltreatment by dogs and birds, and would be repulsive to ordinary Greek sentiment. It is, however, the Zoroastrian practice, still kept up by some Parsee communities; in antiquity it was the practice of the Magi, and well known as such to the Greeks.[1] A large part of the *Vidēvdāt* is concerned with the pollution attending a recent corpse and means of minimizing it (especially chapters 5–12). Burial and cremation are both sins, invented by Angra Mainyu, since they transmit the pollution to earth and fire respectively (1. 13, 17, 3. 8, 8. 73 ff.). If a man or a dog has been buried, it is a sin not to dig him up again (3. 36–42). The proper thing to do with a corpse is to expose it on a hilltop (6. 44–8). For once the soul has departed the body is invaded by Nasu the Druj, who stays upon it until it has been eaten by dogs and birds, or at least seen by a dog of a certain sort.

Heraclitus' conception of the soul's history is, from a Greek point of view, novel. It has a deep 'account' that increases itself. What happens to it after death is not yet clear to us, but it smells things. It can die by liquefaction, yet mortals are immortals, exchanging lives with them. The cycle proceeds water–earth–water–soul. We hear that there are ψυχαὶ καὶ δαίμονες everywhere.

Zoroaster increased his soul by a good deed.

> On the way, Zaratušt gave their two horses water, on account of their thirst, and he thought thus: 'Unprofitable was my going to the residence of the Karaps, except in this manner, when, through giving water to the horses, my soul was then expanded.'
>
> (Zātspram 18. 7, trans. West, *SBE* xlvii)

Elsewhere in the Pahlavi books, the good works themselves are said to increase annually during life for the soul's benefit, like savings bonds.[2] At death, the soul's good and bad deeds are counted up, and determine its fate.[3]

[1] Hdt. 1. 140, Strabo 15. 3. 20 p. 735, Cic. *Tusc.* 1. 108. Cf. p. 68.

[2] *Dātastān-i-Dēnīk* 10. 2, *Saddar* 41. 21–3, 45. 4–5, 58. 2–3, *Dēnkart* 9. 52. 11.

[3] *Dātastān-i-Dēnīk* 12–14, *Mēnōk-i-Xrat* 12. 12, 18. 3, 37. 28, 41. 13, 42. 16, *Saddar* 18. 16, 36. 5, 58. 5, 87. 9, 100. 2, *Dēnkart* 8. 14. 8, *Škand-Gumānīk Vičār* 4. 91–6. Cf. *Chāndogya Upan.* 5. 10. 5.

The rewards and torments that await the good man and the sinner are detailed in *Yašt* 22 and *Vidēvdāt* 19. 27 ff. Curious emphasis is laid on the smells that the soul will experience.

At the end of the third night (after death), when the dawn appears, it seems to the soul of the faithful one as if it were brought amidst plants and scents: it seems as if a wind were blowing from the region of the south, from the regions of the south, a sweet-scented wind, sweeter-scented than any other wind in the world. And it seems to the soul of the faithful one as if he were inhaling that wind with the nostrils.

(*Yašt* 22. 7–8)

The soul of the sinner is assailed by a terrible stink (ibid. 25–33; cf. *Dātastān-i-Dēnīk* 26–7, *Mēnōk-i-Xrat* 2. 140–4, 7. 15, 30).

The man that is laden with sins is a *daēva* and becomes a spiritual *daēva* at death (*Vidēvdāt* 8. 31–2). *Daēvas* fear the soul of the good man, which they apparently recognize by its smell.

As to the godly man that has been cleansed, the wicked evil-doing Daēvas tremble at the perfume of his soul after death, as a sheep does on which a wolf is falling.

(*Vidēvdāt* 19. 33; cf. *Yašt* 24. 27)

The smell that *daēvas* particularly hate is that of fire:

The perfume of fire, pleasant to the Maker, Ahura Mazdāh, takes them away from afar.

(*Yašt* 24. 51)

So that is perhaps what the pure man's soul smells of. A burning fire kills *daēvas* by the thousand (*Vidēvdāt* 8. 79–80, cf. *Šāyast Lā-Šāyast* 10. 4), so it is natural that the smell of it makes them feel like sheep before a wolf.

The world is thus full of unseen spirits and demons. Distinct from these, and from the 'souls' that experience an odorous after-life, are the Fravašis or 'external souls'. The Fravaši is the immortal spirit that exists before a man's life as well as after it, from the beginning of time to the end. The Fravašis are loyal supporters of Ahura Mazdāh, resembling mounted warriors in the sky with spears in hand. They are venerated by men; a whole *Yašt*

(13) is devoted to them, and it tells how they fight the *daēvas* (33), and how they contribute to the maintenance of the cosmos.

Ahura Mazdāh spake unto Spitama Zarathuštra, saying: 'Do thou proclaim, O pure Zarathuštra! the vigour and strength, the glory, the help and the joy that are in the Fravašis of the faithful, the awful and overpowering Fravašis; do thou tell how they come to help me, how they bring assistance unto me, the awful Fravašis of the faithful. Through their brightness and glory, O Zarathuštra! I maintain that sky, there above, shining and seen afar, and encompassing this earth all around' (and also the waters of the world, the earth, natural life, etc.). (1 ff.)

Through their brightness and glory the sun goes his way; through their brightness and glory the moon goes her way; through their brightness and glory the stars go their way. (16)

We worship the good, strong, beneficent Fravašis of the faithful, who showed their paths to the stars, the moon, the sun, and the endless lights, that had stood before for a long time in the same place, without moving forwards, through the oppression of the Daēvas and the assaults of the Daēvas. And now they move around in their far-revolving circle for ever, till they come to the time of the good restoration of the world. (57–8)

Here, then, we have a parallel to Heraclitus' hero-spirits and to his immortals that live the death of mortals.

Even the cycle of transformations, soul–water–earth–water–soul, has a counterpart in the east, one which offers a more attractive solution to the riddle than the one proposed on p. 154, and seems to fit Heraclitus well in other ways. It is the Indian doctrine that was adduced in Chapter 2 (pp. 63 f.) to throw light on Pherecydes and Pythagorean ideas. It is set out in those two oldest *Upanishads*, *Bṛhadāraṇyaka* and *Chāndogya*, that have already provided a number of striking parallels to Heraclitus in the present chapter. Inferior souls become rain, and then plants: rice or barley, sesame or beans, herbs or trees. With luck they are eaten by someone, metabolized into semen, and poured into a womb for rebirth. Soul, water, earth, water, soul.[1]

[1] I owe this important comparison to Somigliana, p. 101.

And at each stage its home is fire: the heaven is a fire, the storm is a fire, the earth is a fire, man is a fire, woman is a fire.[1]

In the last chapter I asked in vain how souls might turn to water after death. In the chapter before I asked in vain what were the 'dark exhalations' that rose from the earth but fell back as rain, besides being responsible for winds and for the diminution of the celestial fire at night and in winter. It now appears that the one problem is the solution of the other. The 'exhalations' were souls—as Aristotle told us all the time (p. 150).

Consider the account of the *Chāndogya Upanishad*. The superior souls pass from the flame of the funeral pyre into the day, the bright half of the month, the summer months of the year, and eventually to the sun and the Brahman world. The others pass from the smoke of the pyre into the night, the dark half of the month, the winter months of the year, to the moon, into wind, mist, cloud, rain—everything for which in Heraclitus the 'dark exhalations' are responsible.

Theophrastus also tells us that Heraclitus placed the moon lower than the sun and in a less pure region (D.L. 9. 10). What is the significance of that likely to have been: astrophysical, or eschatological? Alcmeon of Croton held that the soul is immortal because it maintains constant motion like the sun; and that the region of eternal nature begins at the level of the moon (24 A 1, cf. 12). 'Empedocles', we read in Hippolytus (*Ref.* 1. 4. 3 = *Doxogr.* 559 = DK 31 A 62), 'said that the region we live in is full of ills, and that they reach up from the region round the earth as far as the moon, but do not go further, because the whole region above the moon is more pure; and this was also Heraclitus' view.' Ills stretching up to the moon can only be of concern to the ascending soul. If it is in this region that souls are converted into water, to become successively earth, water, and soul again, the assumption of a theory closely corresponding to the Indian becomes virtually inescapable. If this is the Hades where souls go a-smelling, we can perhaps connect

[1] Above, p. 172 n. 2.

it with the myth that the inhabitants of the moon nourish themselves on smells.[1] We are bound to welcome an explanation at which so many puzzling details tumble into place; and we shall take solemn note of how the Peripatos in search of physical theory sternly converts the souls of the wicked into an exhalation.

The evidence suggests, then, that Heraclitus' doctrine was as follows. Superior souls, being drier, rise to the pure region of sun and stars and survive there indefinitely, perhaps as part of the body of the unique Wise that is separate from everything else. The damper souls do not rise so high (rather as in Plato, *Phaedo* 108 a–b the more sensual soul is reluctant to abandon the body, and lingers in the impure lower air). They cluster round the moon, making its fire seem dimmer than the sun's, and from there they become wind and rain and so die. Their gathering is confined by Dike to the night and the winter. It is in this way that the world is full of ψυχαί and δαίμονες.

And now we have a niche for the guardians that rise up and watch over living and dead: at the highest level, as that which never sets and therefore cannot be hidden from. These are the immortal hero-spirits whom I compared with the Fravašis of Zoroastrian theology. It remains to add that the Fravašis too have the function of watchers.

> Spənta Mainyu maintained the sky (when it was set up), and they sustained it from below, they, the strong Fravašis, who sit in silence, gazing with sharp looks; whose eyes and ears are powerful.
>
> (*Yašt* 13. 29)[2]

Hades

When Heraclitus refers to the conversion of man's soul to water, its death, in theological terms, he sees in it the agency of Hades:

[1] Perhaps Pythagorean, see Burkert, *WW*, p. 324 n. 53.

[2] In the Pahlavi books (*Mēnōk-i-Xrat* 49. 22–3, cf. *Dātastān-i-Dēnīk* 37. 24–31) they are identified with stars. The idea that the dead become stars is of wide popular currency (p. 66; Frazer, *GB* iv. 64 ff., xiii. 310 ff.); it is found in Egypt and India, and in Greece from the fifth century (Ar. *Pax* 832–3). In Pl. *Epin.* 984 d–5 b and Plaut. *Rud.* 6–16 (from Diphilus) the stars act as watchers of mankind, reporting their behaviour to Zeus. (Cf. E. Fraenkel, *CQ* 36, 1942, 10–14 = *Kl. Beitr.* ii. 37–44.) For Heraclitus only the circumpolar stars could come into question: the rest are extinguished daily.

the traditional 'god of death', but not a god usually thought of as present in the world of men. I have pointed out (p. 158) that he is the antagonist of Zeus, at least in this psychic sphere, and possibly on the cosmic scale too. If the dry souls of the dead make up the body of 'Zeus', perhaps the damp ones make up the body of Hades.

The Wise Lord of the Persians, he who never sleeps, he who is never deceived, the father of fire, is opposed throughout the world by a spirit of contrary nature who is hostile to all life and growth, the 'Destructive Spirit', Angra Mainyu. It was he who first introduced death into the world. He is the author of all evil, attended and represented by the *daēvas* who do his work. Associated with them is Aēšma, the spirit of furious violence, whom one might render as Ὕβρις. In a verse in praise of the haoma, the drink of immortality, we read:

> And honour to Haoma, for all other liquors are attended by Aēšma that swings the bloody club, but it, the Haoma liquor, is attended by Aša itself.
>
> (*Yašt* 17. 5, cf. *Yasna* 10. 8)

The Greeks, besides identifying Ahura Mazdāh with Zeus, identified Angra Mainyu with Hades.[1]

Strife

I am not suggesting that Heraclitus presented the antithesis between Zeus and Hades as a grand cosmic war. Yet his novel emphasis on the function of Eris or Polemos in determining the apportionment of the natural world, his conviction that opposition is the essence of the universe as we know it, has long seemed to comparativists a counterpart of the Zoroastrian doctrine of agelong war between Ahura Mazdāh and Angra Mainyu, in which the two powers are ranged against each other together with their respective subordinate spirits and creations. This is not only a moral antagonism. It is seen in physical phenomena such as the increase or failure of a fire, and the alternation of

[1] Theopompus 115 F 65, Arist. fr. 6 *ap.* D.L. 1. 8, Plut. *Is. Os.* 369 e, Hesych. s.v. Ἀρειμανής.

summer and winter. Āzay ('greed, hunger'), made by the *daēvas*, strives against fire, to put out its light if pure fuel is not brought (*Vidēvdāt* 18. 18–22). Fire is strengthened by Aša, and itself kills *daēvas* (pp. 177, 185). Winter is a creation of Angra Mainyu (*Vidēvdāt* 1. 2–3). According to the *Bundahišn*, it comes from the north to do battle with the summer:

The appearance of winter is in the direction of the north, where the regions Vōrūbaršt and Vōrūjaršt are; the original dwelling of summer, too, is in the south, where the regions Fradatafš and Vīdatafš are; on the day Ohrmazd of the auspicious month Āvān the winter acquires strength and enters into the world, and the spirit of Rapītvīn goes from above-ground to below-ground, where the spring of waters is . . . until the end, in the auspicious month Spendarmat, winter advances through the whole world . . . As the day Ohrmazd of the month Fravardīn advances it diminishes the strength which winter possesses, and summer comes in from its own original dwelling, and receives strength and dominion. (25. 10–13)

It is a manifestation of Angra Mainyu's aggression against Ahura Mazdāh and his world.

On the evil-doing of Ahriman and the demons it says in revelation that the evil which the evil spirit has produced for the creation of Ohrmazd it is possible to tell by this winter. (Ibid. 28. 1)

By serving Ahura Mazdāh and living in righteousness men enhance the strength of the sun, but wickedness increases the strength of winter.[1] Already in the Avesta, Angra Mainyu and the *daēvas* belong in the north.[2] We remember that the southern sky for Heraclitus is the boundary of Zeus, and that in his imitator (*de victu* 1. 5) Zeus and Hades stand for light and dark, in the same context as the changing lengths of day and night, the advances of fire and water, and the north–south movement of the sun.

The great year

Considered from the Greek point of view, Heraclitus' great year will seem to be a development of Hesiod's myth of ages, the

1 *Vidēvdāt* 7. 25–7, *Dēnkart* 7. 8. 19, 9. 52. 11–13.
2 *Yašt*. 3. 17 = *Srōš vāč* 3; *Vidēvdāt* 7. 2, 19. 1.

'year' itself being an original construction based on the analogy discovered between day and generative cycle. Is this a sufficient account? Would that analogy of itself put into a man's head the notion of a vastly greater cycle than any earlier Greek had contemplated?

I have described on pp. 30 ff. the Zoroastrian theory of 'Time for long autonomous'. It is a single, non-recurrent period.[1] But it is on a similar scale to the Heraclitean period, Zātspram likens it to a year (p. 67 n. 2), and it is given its shape by division into quarters, and by the supremacy of Angra Mainyu giving way to the supremacy of Ahura Mazdāh.

The Avesta refers to another Iranian myth which may be relevant. It concerns Yima, the first man. Yima ruled over mankind for a thousand years, a golden age of prosperity and abundance unspoiled by excessive heat or cold, old age or death. One might say it was a great springtime. When the millennium came to its end, Ahura Mazdāh warned Yima that worse times were ahead, and instructed him to retire to a cavern below the earth, taking with him perfect specimens of every living creature. Yima did as he was told, and is now king of a subterranean realm where men live a perfect life. He will stay there until a terrible winter, the worst the world has ever known, with rain and snow falling for three years on end, heralds the end of the present condition. Then he will return to the upper world and repopulate it with his ideal race.[2] In Heraclitus' system, if winter represents a predominance of damp souls, then the moral depression of the great year ought logically to produce an actual physical great winter.

His year is arrived at by multiplying a given figure by 360. We have seen this principle applied in the *Vishṇu Purāṇa* (p. 94),

[1] Van der Waerden, *Hermes* 80, 1952, 147, argues that originally it was cyclic. Cf. p. 67 n. 2.

[2] *Yašt* 9. 10, 17. 30, 19. 32, etc.; Zaehner, *DTZ*, pp. 134 f. The first part of the story resembles the Greek myth that Kronos once ruled over a blessed generation of men on earth, and now rules over them in a paradise below, or in the far west: Hes. *Op.* 109–26, cf. 166–73c (divided between two generations, but united in [Hes.] fr. 204. 94 ff., cf. 1. 6 ff.); Pind. *Ol.* 2. 56 ff., fr. 129 Snell. The great winter that will end this world and be followed by the creation of a perfect new one has a parallel in Norse mythology, where the cataclysm of Ragnarøk begins with a series of seven 'Monster Winters' (*fimbulvetr*).

where the (hundred) years of Vishṇu's Brahman-life are equivalent to 360 × (1,000 × 12,000 years). It is said of this Time-Vishṇu:

Vishṇu being thus manifest and unmanifest substance, spirit, and time, sports like a playful boy, as you shall learn by listening to his frolics. (i. 2)

Αἰὼν παῖς ἐστι, παίζων, πεσσεύων.[1]

Resurrection

Heraclitus' guardian-spirits behave in an un-Greek way when they 'stand up' from the dead. Resurrection of the dead is a typically Zoroastrian doctrine.[2] It was believed that at the end of time, when all existence is renewed, the bodies of the dead will rise up and be reunited with their souls, and enter upon immortal life. The Greeks knew of the Magian teaching at any rate by the fourth century.[3] I have remarked (pp. 153 f.) that Heraclitus' resurrection is of a different variety, involving continuous selection, and more recently (p. 188) come to a conclusion on its nature. Possibly, however, his terminology is influenced by the Zoroastrian conception.

The prophet

Heraclitus ridicules men who pray to statues as foolish and ignorant. He is not alone among the Greeks of his time in his rejection of anthropomorphism; Xenophanes makes fun of it at any rate. But this is just another of the ideas current in Ionia at that period which magically agree with those of the Persians. Hdt. 1. 131. 1 *Πέρσας δ' οἶδα νόμοισι τοιοισίδε χρεωμένους, ἀγάλματα μὲν καὶ νηοὺς καὶ βωμοὺς οὐκ ἐν νόμῳ ποιεομένους ἱδρύεσθαι· ἀλλὰ καὶ τοῖσι ποιέουσι μωρίην ἐπιφέρουσι, ὡς μὲν ἐμοὶ δοκεῖν, ὅτι οὐκ ἀνθρωποφυέας ἐνόμισαν τοὺς θεοὺς κατάπερ οἱ Ἕλληνες εἶναι.* This was the feature of Persian religion that the Greeks and Romans found most noteworthy; it is mentioned again by Strabo (15. 3. 13 p. 732, from Herodotus) and Cicero (*Rep.* 3. 14, *Leg.* 2. 26).

[1] Compared by Eisler, *Weltenmantel*, p. 507.

[2] It was probably from the Persians that the Jews took the idea; cf. Zaehner, *DTZ*, pp. 57 f.

[3] Theopompus 115 F 64, Eudemus fr. 89 Wehrli *ap.* D.L. 1. 9.

Diogenes Laertius, whose account of the teachings of the Magi is based on various sources including several fourth-century writers, reports that their contempt for idols was particularly directed at the idea that gods are male and female (1. 6). Xenophanes' God remains male, but Heraclitus' is *τὸ σοφόν, τὸ μὴ δῦνόν ποτε*. It is in Aeschylus (*Oresteia*) and Herodotus that we first meet *τὸ θεῖον*.

With his intolerant attacks on established religious usages, his threats of future punishment for all contrivers of falsehood, his warnings against drunkenness and *ὕβρις*, Heraclitus strikes a prophetic note that has reminded more than one reader of Zoroaster.

For these deeds shall ruin overtake
The race of the sacrificers and the magician priests
Through those whom they prevent from living as they should;
These shall be borne far away from them to the dwelling of the
  Good Mind.

(*Yasna* 32. 15)

Let Fury be suppressed! Put down violence,
You who would ensure yourselves, through Righteousness,
The reward of the Good Mind, whose companion is the holy man.
He shall have his abode in thy house, O Lord!

(Ibid. 48. 7)

When wilt thou smite this piss of drink
Through which the sacrificers wickedly
And the evil masters of the countries of their own will
Commit their deeds of malice?

(Ibid. 48. 10)

But the wicked who have evil power,
Evil deeds, words, conscience, and thought,
The souls shall go to meet them with evil nourishment.

(Ibid. 49. 11)

Without the extensive parallels of doctrine this would remain a generality. With them it becomes a significant point.

Miscellaneous details of thought and expression provoke additional comparisons. There are the proverb-like illustrations from animal life. *πᾶν ἑρπετὸν πληγῇ νέμεται* (fr. 80 = B 11): even to do what they do naturally, willingly, and well, they need prodding. 'Even the swiftest horse requires the whip—and the wisest man requires counsel': that is a saying found in the Pahlavi books,[1] and shown to be ancient in origin by *Proverbs* 26: 3, 'A whip for the horse, a bridle for the ass, and a rod for the fool's back'. ὕες βορβόρῳ ἥδονται μᾶλλον ἢ καθαρῷ ὕδατι (fr. 36 = B 13, 37) echoes an oriental proverb that meets us in the story of Aḥiqar: 'My son, thou hast been to me like the swine that had been to the baths, and when it saw a muddy ditch, went down and washed in it, and cried to its companions, "Come and wash".'[2] Perhaps such an illustration as that of the poisonous sea-water that is vital to fish (fr. 35 = B 61) derives from a similar popular tradition.[3] And fr. 10 = B 22 χρυσὸν διζήμενοι γῆν πολλὴν ὀρύσσουσι καὶ εὑρίσκουσιν ὀλίγον, resembles a comparison in the *Chāndogya Upanishad* 8. 3. 2,

For, just as (a group of people) who do not know the country might wander about and pass over a hidden hoard of gold time and again without finding it, so too do all these creatures go on day after day without finding the Brahman-world within them, for they are led astray by unreality.

In the seventh century, when a Greek wanted to say that a certain kind of man was worth many others, he said just that:

Callinus 1. 21 ἔρδει γὰρ πολλῶν ἄξια μοῦνος ἐών.

Il. 9. 116 f. ἀντί νυ πολλῶν
λαῶν ἐστιν ἀνὴρ ὅν τε Ζεὺς κῆρι φιλήσῃ.

Il. 11. 514 ἰητρὸς γὰρ ἀνὴρ πολλῶν ἀντάξιος ἄλλων.

When Heraclitus says it, he uses a much stronger expression: εἷς ἐμοὶ μυρίοι, ἐὰν ἄριστος ᾖ (fr. 98 = B 49). That is how they talked in the east.

It is said in revelation that one truthful man is better than a whole world speaking falsehood. (*Saddar* 62. 5)

[1] *Saddar* 85. 3, *Čitradāt Nask ap. Šāyast Lā-Šāyast* 10. 28.

[2] 8. 18 (Syriac), trans. J. Rendel Harris in Charles's *Apocrypha and Pseudepigrapha of the O.T.* ii. 772. Cf. 2 Pet. 2: 22.

[3] Zātspram (34. 35, Zaehner, *Zurvan*, p. 351) uses the simile of 'a frog that liveth in the water—so long as it defileth the water, it liveth by it, but when the water is withdrawn from it, it dieth, parched'.

What is the one recital of the praise of Holiness that is worth ten thousand others in greatness, goodness, and fairness?

(*Yašt* 21. 12)

Though a million of men, unacquainted with the *Ṛgas*, were to dine at a (funeral sacrifice), yet a single man, learned in the Veda . . . is worth them all as far as spiritual merit is concerned.

(*Laws of Manu* 3. 131)

Better one day in thy courts than a thousand days at home.

(Psalm 84: 10)

Heraclitus' recommendation about corpses, too, is noteworthy for its form. He does not just say that they should be cast out, but that they are more to be cast out than another thing that no one would hesitate to cast out. Similarly fr. 102 = B 43 ὕβριν χρὴ σβεννύναι μᾶλλον ἢ πυρκαϊήν. I do not know an earlier Greek example of a prescriptive sentence in this form. But Ahura Mazdāh said to Zoroaster, about whores,

Verily I say unto thee, O Spitama Zarathuštra! such creatures ought to be killed even more than gliding snakes.

(*Vidēvdāt* 18. 65)

And the Pahlavi *Dēnkart* says of certain wicked men:

Concerning them, too, I tell thee that they are more to be destroyed than the leaping serpent which is like a wolf or a lion.

(7. 8. 45, in *SBE* xlvii)

Heraclitus complains that his hearers will not hear. They are ἀκοῦσαι οὐκ ἐπιστάμενοι (fr. 1(*g*) = B 19); κωφοῖσιν ἐοίκασιν (fr. 2 = B 34). They have eyes and ears, but those are no use without understanding (fr. 13 = B 107). Zoroaster says, 'Now will I speak to those who will hear' (*Yasna* 30. 1); and

Remembering your commands, we proclaim words
Unheard by those who by the precepts of Evil[1]
Deprave the creatures of Righteousness,
But beneficial to those who are faithful to the Wise One.

(Ibid. 31. 1)

[1] H. Humbach (*Die Gathas des Zarathustra*, 1959) translates 'die von denjenigen nicht gehört werden sollen'; but this seems worse sense.

According to the *Mēnōk-i-Xrat* (26. 6),

he who is sound-eyed, when he has no knowledge and understanding, and even that which they teach him he does not accept, then that is worse than even a blind eye.

'All this'

Early Greek has no term for 'the world'. It has to say 'earth, sea, sky, and Tartarus' (Hes. *Th.* 736) or the like. Anaximenes uses 'what was, is, and shall be', perhaps under oriental influence (p. 105). Heraclitus speaks of 'this set-up', ὁ κόσμος ὅδε (fr. 51 = B 30), and probably of 'all this', τάδε πάντα (fr. 79 = B 64). The first of these expressions is only a variant of the second, and it is the second that interests me here. Xenophanes B 27 says

ἐκ γῆς γὰρ τάδε πάντα καὶ ἐς γῆν πάντα τελευτᾷ.

(So Theodoretus; τὰ for τάδε Stob., om. [Plut.].) Parmenides B 19. 1 speaks simply of τάδε. Empedocles has τοῦτο τὸ πᾶν (17. 32), τάδε πάντα (35. 5), τὰ νῦν ἐσορῶμεν ἅπαντα (38. 2). Plato has τὸ ὅλον τοῦτο (*Gorg.* 508 a), or τὸ πᾶν τόδε (*Tim.* 29 d, 37 d, 41 a, c, 48 a, 69 c). In later verse we again encounter τάδε πάντα ('Linus' *ap.* Stob. 1. 10. 5, verse 4; Orph. fr. 168. 7 = 169. 1; *Orac. Chald.* p. 35 Kroll). See Addenda.

Here, then, we have an accepted idiom for 'the universe', using the deictic 'this', which first appears in Heraclitus and Xenophanes. Kahn, who noticed only one of the above passages, acutely observed (p. 228 n. 2): 'Precisely the same expression is used in early Sanskrit for "the universe": *sárvam idám*, "all this", Rigveda x. 129. 3.' Often it is just 'this'. Examples occur in passages from the Upanishads that I have quoted in this book. The deictic idiom is not only Indian: Darius and his successors proclaim 'a great god is Ahuramazda, who created this earth, who created yonder sky' (*imām būmīm, avam asmānam*; references on p. 31 n. 8).

The death of Heraclitus

Of all the singular modes of death recorded by the ancients as having carried off their most famous writers, there is none to compare with that of Heraclitus. Different accounts vary a little, but the essentials of the story are as follows. Disgusted by Ephesian life, Heraclitus retired into the mountains and lived on grasses and herbs, as a result of which diet he developed dropsy. He returned to the city, went to the doctors, and asked them if they knew how to change wet weather into drought. They were not intelligent enough to grasp his meaning, and he was constitutionally incapable of plain speech, so he left them and attempted to cure himself. His method was to plaster himself from head to foot in cow-dung, and lie in the sun for the moisture to evaporate. Some authorities say simply that the treatment failed, and he died; others that dogs came and ate him as he lay helpless in his horrid integument.[1]

The basic datum here is the dropsy; and the dropsy is pure legend. As with other fabled deaths of great men, the circumstances were intended to be ironically appropriate to the person. Heraclitus had urged men to keep their souls dry, because the liquefaction of the soul means death. It would be a nice turn of fate that made him die of the dropsy;[2] the tale might have ended with that, and originally, no doubt, it did.

The rest is secondary elaboration by some Hellenistic biographer, based on deductions of a type often represented as the irresponsible fictions of men who merely wanted to tell piquant stories regardless of truth. Perhaps we should regard them rather as imaginative attempts, by men avid for knowledge of the past, to reconstruct what might well have happened, in default of records of what did happen. Their reasoning might be fanciful, but it was a kind of reasoning, not just scurrilous invention.[3]

[1] The fullest account in D.L. 9. 3–4. Three versions are there distinguished, one being attributed to Hermippus and another to Neanthes of Cyzicus (84 F 25). Neanthes' version is the one with the dogs in it. This appears also in the *Suda*. Marc. Ant. 3. 3 mentions the dropsy and the dung but not the dogs. In the two Epistles addressed to Amphidamas (5–6), Heraclitus speaks of his dropsy and the doctors' bafflement, and declares that he is going to cure himself on cosmic principles. Ancient evidence and modern opinions are reviewed by J. Haussleiter, *Altertum* 10, 1964, 9–13; Marcovich, *RE* Supp. x. 252–4.

[2] See Marc. Ant. 3. 3.

[3] Apollodorus' chronological studies are to be judged in the same light. To date a man's birth by the *floruit* of his teacher is obviously unsound by our standards, but the ancients accepted it as being better than having no date at all.

The thought of a dropsical philosopher at once suggested the stock type of the water-drinking, vegetarian tramp so dear to Comedy.[1] The encounter with doctors may have been suggested by fr. 46 = B 58, which could be interpreted as a bitter criticism of the profession. But Heraclitus could not be supposed to have swallowed his characteristic pride and asked them for help. He must hold the upper hand. Hence the riddle about wet weather and drought.[2]

The final events are the most puzzling. R. Muth, an expert on excrement, has pointed out that there is evidence for the external application of dung as a treatment for dropsy.[3]

> Plin. *NH* 28. 232 *hydropicis auxiliatur*...*fimum uituli masculi* ⟨*uentri*⟩ *inlitum*.[4]

> Diosc. *de simplicibus* 2. 66 καταπλασσόμενα δὲ ὑδρωπικοὺς ὠφελεῖ... βόλβιτα ξηρὰ θερμανθέντα σὺν ὀξυκράτῳ καὶ μέλιτι· προσέμπασσε δὲ θείου ἀπύρου τέταρτον μέρος.

It is to be noted firstly that according to Pliny the dung is applied to the stomach, not all over, and secondly that in both authors this is only one among many cures for dropsy, and one not specially emphasized in any way. On both counts, Muth's description of Heraclitus' procedure as 'eine bekannte Therapie der Volksmedizin' is exaggerated. It is by no means explained why our biographer picked on this particular method of cure and developed it to a dramatic conclusion involving hungry dogs. According to Kirk, 'He is said to have buried himself in dung because he had said in fr. ⟨76 = B⟩ 96 that corpses are more worthless than dung'[5] (I confess I cannot see the logic). 'The expectation that the dropsy would be evaporated is based upon the theory that the sun feeds on evaporation from the sea.'[6]

[1] DK 58 E; cf. *Maia*, N.S. 20, 1968, 196.

[2] For this ἐπομβρία and αὐχμός cf. Emp. 111. 6–8; K. Deichgräber, *Philol.* 93, 1939, 17 n. 9. Lassalle thought that some Heraclitean passage lay behind it.

[3] *Anzeiger f. d. Altertumswiss.* 7, 1954, 253; 8, 1955, 252.

[4] I have restored *uentri* from the epitome, 'Pliny *de medicina*' 3. 22 p. 96. 8 Rose.

[5] Kirk–Raven, p. 183; less positively in *HCF*, p. 5.

[6] *HCF*, p. 5, cf. Kirk–Raven, loc. cit.; Marcovich, *RE* Supp. x. 253.

Heraclitus' personal teaching is hardly relevant here, since the knowledge that things are dried out by the sun is common to mankind; they are not dried out more effectively if first covered with dung, and it is not said by the medical authorities that the dung-treatment had any such rationale. According to Fränkel,[1] the point is that constant evaporation is the basis of life, and Heraclitus hopes that the inward exhalation from the warm dung will fortify his failing soul. Ingenious, but hardly likely to have been thought up by a biographer. Fränkel has a further argument, that Heraclitus had spoken of unenlightened mankind as being 'buried in the slime', *βορβόρῳ κατορωρυγμένοι* or some such phrase,[2] and that it pleased the biographer's malicious humour to show the haughty sage forced by his disease to subject himself to the same indignity.[3] He explains the dogs who do not recognize Heraclitus, and eat him, by reference to fr. 22 = B 97 *κύνες καταβαΰζουσιν ὧν ἂν μὴ γινώσκωσιν*.[4]

This is all very well on the view that the biographers who tell the story were mere pantaloons who set out to make a long-dead philosopher look ridiculous by inventing crude and absurd misadventures for him, and all because they 'resented his superior tone'.[5] But they were not. They were researchers into the past, however silly their methods may have been. In the absence of historical evidence their guiding principle was the consistency of Heraclitus' character as they saw it. If he condemned men for burying themselves in filth, it is all the more strange that he should be represented as doing the same himself.

1 *AJP* 59, 1938, 310 = *W. u. F.*, pp. 254 f.

2 The argument is brilliant. It is criticized by Marcovich, *RE* Supp. x. 260; ed. p. 183.

3 '*βόρβορος* ist nicht dasselbe wie *τὰ βόλιτα*', Marcovich, *RE* Supp. x. 254. It generally means 'stinking mud'. It is also said to be the *κύριον ὄνομα* for 'Attic' *ὀχετός* (Helladius *ap.* Phot. *bibl.* 535 b, cf. 'Trypho' *de tropis* 18 (in *CQ* 1965), Hesych.), and in that sense presumably means 'sewage'.

4 Marcovich, *RE* Supp. x. 253 (after Gigon, p. 133) compares Diogenes the Cynic, who according to one account died of being bitten by a dog while feeding it with octopus (D.L. 6. 77)—'ein kynischer Zug beim H.-Bild'. But the dog is so peculiarly appropriate to Diogenes that it is hard to believe in its being transferred to Heraclitus just because he was another ascetic.

5 Kirk–Raven, p. 183.

The Avesta prescribes a curious method of purification for the man who has touched a corpse while Nasu the Druj is still on it, and so tainted himself with the miasma of death. He must rub himself all over with bull's urine. Until it dries, a dog is set in front of him to look at him. When it is thoroughly dry, he washes in water, and then he is pure again.[1] Bull's urine was regarded as a peculiarly cathartic fluid, and used also for purifying contaminated clothing and other articles. A Pahlavi text emphasizes that things cleansed with it must be properly dried with dust and laid out three months in a place to be viewed by the sun.[2]

The procedure laid down in the Avesta corresponds with that attributed to the sick Heraclitus in the following respects.

1. The man is covered all over in bovine excreta.[3]
2. He exposes himself to the sun to dry.
3. As he is drying in the sun, he becomes the object of a dog's attention.
4. The object of the operation is to purify him from deadly pollution.

These correspondences are too striking, surely, to be fortuitous. But how are they to be explained? Gladisch, who first noticed them, thought that as Heraclitus' views on fire and corpses were the same as Zoroaster's, it was necessary for him to harden his feelings against Greek funeral custom, and we should not be surprised if he arranged a Zoroastrian funeral for himself.[4] This assumes a historical kernel in the story, and a conflation of purification-ritual with exposure of the dead. But we cannot really suppose that Heraclitus indulged in or commended any such exercise. He ridiculed those who tried to cleanse blood-pollution with blood, comparing them to men who had trodden in mud and tried to wash it off with more mud (fr. 86 = B 5).

[1] *Vidēvdāt* 8. 38.

[2] *Šāyast Lā-Šāyast* 2. 98, cf. 112 f.

[3] Urine in the Persian ritual, dung in the Heraclitus-legend. In one version he rolls in a byre, in another he makes children plaster him. The *Dēnkart*, p. 182. 6 ff. Madan, describes worshippers of Ahriman who prowl around in secrecy, keeping home, clothes, and body in a state of filth, smearing themselves with dead matter and excrement and calling on the demons by name. Cf. Zaehner, *Zurvan*, p. 16.

[4] *Herakleitos und Zoroaster*, pp. 65–7.

Now suppose that that passage continued on these lines:

καθαίρονται δ' ἄλλως αἵματι μιαινόμενοι, οἷον εἴ τις ἐς πηλὸν ἐμβὰς πηλῷ ἀπονίζοιτο· μαίνεσθαι δ' ἂν δοκοίη, εἴ τις αὐτὸν ἀνθρώπων ἐπιφράσαιτο οὕτω ποιέοντα. ἄκεα δὲ κρέσσω τὰ βαρβάρων, ὁκόσοι βοὸς τῷ μιαρωτάτῳ ἄνθρωποι ἐόντες καθαίρονται· οὗτοι γάρ, ἐπείτε ἂν τέρσωνται σώματα πρὸς ἥλιον, κυσὶ προβάλλουσιν ἑωυτούς, κάρτ' ἄξια ποιέοντες.

Our biographer, if he knew that application of dung was a treatment for dropsy, would be delighted to find in such a passage Heraclitus' own preference, or perhaps even a hint of his ailment.[1] It is a tenuous hypothesis; it has the one merit of bridging the gap between Persian ritual and Hellenistic biography, and I prefer hypotheses with at least two merits.

Conclusion

'Some of Fränkel's conclusions and deductions are indeed too adventurous: he is misled by his concept of Heraclitus as a metaphysician, and it is surprising, after his diversion on the *Upanishads* (pp. 241 ff.)—always a danger signal in Heraclitus-studies—that he returns to as sound a summary of the general force of fr. 67 as appears on pp. 243–4.'[2]

See how the Greek scholar fears Upanishads. He does not merely think they are dangerous, he is really surprised to find that interest in them can coexist with sound interpretation. In a tidy world, I daresay, a Greek thinker would be fully explicable from Greek material. The facts are otherwise. The fact is that the *Bṛhadāraṇyaka Upanishad* alone throws more light on what Heraclitus was talking about than all the remains of the other Presocratics together.

[1] It would help if Heraclitus had used the word ἄκεα. He did use it somewhere of religious rites, apparently of those involving indecent sights or sounds (fr. 88 = B 68; one thinks of fr. 50 = B 15). Plato uses ἀκεῖσθαι of what ἀγύρται and μάντεις promise to do, *Rep.* 364 c. Cf. *Od.* 22. 481, Aesch. *Cho.* 71, Pl. *Lg.* 910 a, etc. Zoroaster calls himself 'an initiate, a healer of existence' (*Yasna* 31. 19), and Fire is prayed to as 'a full source of healing' (*Nyāyišn* 5. 6).

[2] Kirk, *HCF*, pp. 196 f.

It is a long walk from Ephesus to India. But the distribution of the human race proves that people, and what they carry with them, have travelled a good deal further in the course of years. In Heraclitus' time, Ephesus and India were linked by the Persian empire. Indians came to mainland Greece with Xerxes' army. The connections between Heraclitus' thought and Persian religion (as we know it from the literature of Zoroastrian orthodoxy) are proportionately strong.

'Heraclitus must have been somewhat aware of the nature of the wide-spread mazda-worship with which his successors were so familiar. For the Persian forces which looked to Auramazda for victory and hated Angra Mainyu as the author of defeat, surged for years up to the very gates of Ephesus when Heraclitus was in his prime.'[1] One may wonder, however, how much cosmology and theology the inhabitants of a city are likely to absorb from forces surging at their gates. What we have found in Heraclitus seems to presuppose a deeper intercourse with a more learned class of person.

[1] L. Mills, *Journal of the Royal Asiatic Soc.*, 1902, 903.

7

THE GIFT OF THE MAGI

THE reader who has had the patience to follow the necessarily detailed and sometimes complicated argumentation of the foregoing chapters will have seen how the assumption of non-Greek influences, and particularly Iranian influences, again and again forces itself upon us as we examine the theological and cosmological systems of the later sixth and early fifth centuries. It is now time to look at them in a wider context, to turn from the trees to the wood. Surveying the development of Greek thinking on cosmological matters from the beginnings of the age of literacy down to the second half of the fifth century, I shall try to show that the period of active Iranian influence stands out sharply in the middle, lasting from about 550 to about 480 B.C., and that it succeeded a period in which, while eastern influences are clearly operative, they are more Babylonian in appearance.

Hesiod and Homer

In the period before about 650 B.C. only Hesiod can give us an idea of the condition of Greek cosmological thinking. Perhaps he was not representative, how can we tell? At least we can say that his theogony had no serious rivals, and established itself as an acceptable statement of how the world and the gods came into being. The orientalizing conceptions that we find coming in later do not seem to have to compete against a native tradition that differs substantially from the Hesiodic view.

The first thing to note is that although Hesiod's chosen subject, the *θεῶν γένος* (*Th.* 33, 105), entails some account of the origins of the physical world, he displays little interest in the question, and has nothing to offer but a perfunctory genealogical scheme. (Overleaf.) It does not stand out by itself, but has to be abstracted from the ampler genealogies in which it is embedded. It does not come out cleanly, for non-cosmic figures like Theia and Kreios have to come out with it; and when we have got it out by this artificial operation, it does not strike us as the product of any profound reflection. Genealogy as a cosmogonic form clearly had a long history before Hesiod, and we may say that

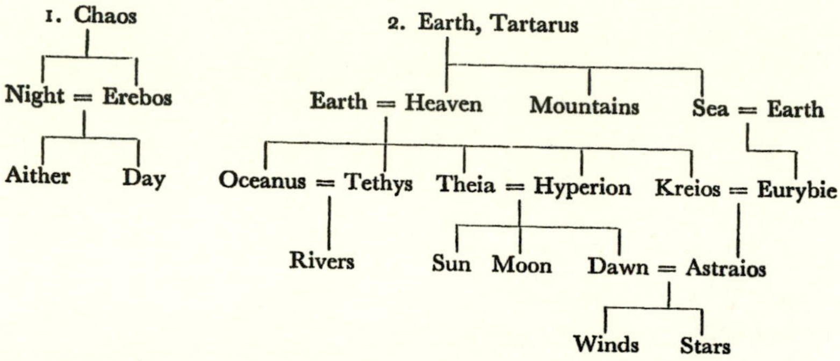

he is bound to it by the poetic tradition in which he has chosen to write. But even in the form of a genealogy it is possible to say much or little. Anaximenes' cosmogony could have been, and to some extent may have been, expressed in genealogical language (p. 101). Is Hesiod saying anything by means of his genealogy? Translate it into mechanistic terms, and the result is sometimes sense but just as often nonsense. The proposition that heaven was born from earth, or Oceanus from the marriage of the two, is evidently not the answer to the question 'How was the firmament or the fabled Oceanus created?', but to the question 'What is the best way to combine these divine names in a genealogy?' It is a story, not an explanation, not even a silly explanation.

I have noted elsewhere (p. 97) that physical speculation existed in Hesiod's time. It seems, however, to have been limited to the interpretation of man's immediate environment. Man is earth and water. Thunder and lightning are somehow caused by wind. Rain is moisture drawn up from the rivers by ἀήρ and conveyed across land by the wind. Ask what the stars are, and the only answer is that they are children of Eos and Astraios. Ask about night and day: Night is the daughter of Chaos, the sister and wife of Erebos, the mother of Aither and Day, death and sleep, and various others. Night and Day go in and out of a certain house, in turn, crossing a great bronze threshold, at appointed times. What is the sun made of, or what makes it rise and set? No answer. How was the earth formed? It simply *ἐγένετο*, after Chaos *ἐγένετο*.

We get the impression that Hesiod and his audience did not bother their heads about such questions, probably because it had not occurred to them that there was any way open to mortals by which an improved understanding could be reached. (Certainly there were many in the sixth and fifth centuries who did not bother their heads about such questions either; but they knew that others did, and they did not repeat the old myths in the same matter-of-fact way.) Hesiod was writing in central Greece, at the end of the eighth century, at the end of a long period in which Greece was culturally isolated. Some of his myths are of eastern origin, but it seems more probable that they came to Greece in the Mycenaean period, and reached Hesiod by way of Greek tradition, than that they were brought in by the renewal of oriental contacts in or shortly before his time.[1] I would be more ready to recognize a neo-oriental element in the cosmic myths alluded to in the *Iliad*, a poem composed east of the Aegean and a couple of generations later than Hesiod.[2] Oceanus and Tethys as the primeval parents, long estranged from one another (14. 200–7), recall the Babylonian cosmology in which Apsû and Tiâmat were originally united, the chthonic water

[1] See *Hes. Th.*, pp. 28 f., and for a different view, P. Walcot, *Hesiod and the Near East*, 1966, pp. 47 ff., 104 ff.

[2] The descriptions of hoplite warfare bring it down to *c.* 650 (*Hes. Th.*, p. 46 n. 2; other possibly seventh-century elements are the seated statue of Athena in 6. 303 (but this may really be an interpolated passage), the outbidding of Hesiod (?) in 8. 13–16, the gorgon blazon in 11. 36, and latter-day rulers in Troy in 20. 307 f.). On the other hand it existed as a whole by *c.* 630, as the reader of K. Friis Johansen's *The Iliad and Early Greek Art* will be persuaded. East Greek provenance is indicated by certain similes (2. 144, 460; 4. 275, 422; 9. 5; 14. 395) and by knowledge of local antiquities in Lycia (the tomb of Sarpedon) and especially the Troad. Knowledge of Phoenician trade is admitted in 6. 290 f., 23. 743 f.

and the brine, and their children were created inside them.[1] That cosmology also played a part in the prehistory of Hesiod's Succession Myth, but there Heaven and Earth are the parents.[2] If Hesiod's account represents an old, long-Hellenized version, as I have supposed, the *Iliad* story may reflect either an independent line of tradition from Mycenaean times, or a renewal of exposure to oriental accounts. There is a similar problem—not necessarily with the same answer—in the sea-dwelling Atlas of the *Odyssey*.[3]

Alcman

I have mentioned the Homeric poems as possibly showing signs of a revival of oriental influence in cosmic mythology in the latter part of the seventh century. One would not expect epic poems to reveal whether there was any interest in cosmological speculation, as distinct from story-telling, at the time they were composed. Nor would one expect this of songs composed for a Spartan girls' chorus. Yet it is in fact from this surprising source that we get our first glimpse of 'philosophical' cosmogony: from a poem of Alcman, composed in the latter part of the seventh century, or possibly early in the sixth.[4] No doubt his system is not his own creation *ex nihilo*, but follows some contemporary line of thought. As far as we can make out, it seems to have begun as follows:

In the beginning there was a waste of waters, conceived as trackless and featureless (ἄπορον, ἀτέκμαρτον). In it Thetis was or came to be, and upon her appearance, or perhaps as a result of

[1] *Enûma Eliš* i. 1–20; Hölscher, *Hermes* 81, 1953, 386 f. = *Begriffswelt*, pp. 128 f.; Kirk–Raven, pp. 18 f.

[2] In the Vedas Father Sky (*Dyāush pitā*) is paired with Mother Earth; Ohrmazd's marriage to Spandarmat (p. 52) may be a trace of the same Indo-European myth. So in Greece, Zeus the father of gods and men must originally have been the consort of Earth the mother of all. When the oriental Succession Myth was adopted, the marriage of Sky and Earth kept its place, but Zeus now had to take the role of the young conqueror; as primeval father and husband of Gaia he was replaced by Uranos, who has otherwise no importance in myth or cult.

[3] 1. 52 ff.; see p. 49.

[4] On the dating of Alcman see *CQ* 59, 1965, 188 ff.; on the reconstruction and antecedents of his cosmogony, ibid. 57, 1963, 154–6, and 61, 1967, 1–7, where some of what I say below is explained more fully.

something she did, the boring uniformity of the primeval ocean was disturbed by the emergence of Track and Feature (*Πόρος*, *Τέκμωρ*). There was darkness then at first, but it was followed by day, and the moon and stars.

The derivation of our world from water is a primitive enough conception (cf. Schwabl, col. 1510), but it is something to find a Greek conceiving the cosmogony in physical terms, even if no causal principle was invoked but the divine agent Thetis. What is more remarkable is that it is the formal and not the material aspect of the original chaos that is put in focus and treated as needing modification: not 'out of the waters came earth', but 'out of the *ἄπορον καὶ ἀτέκμαρτον* came *πόρος καὶ τέκμωρ*'. This is truly abstract thinking. Alcman makes Poros and Tekmor gods,[1] to suit the traditional theogony-form, but he cannot have conceived them as active powers. We do not know whether he went on to mention the appearance of earth as a concrete consequence of the appearance of Poros and Tekmor. At any rate his assumption would seem to have been that it came from the sea, and perhaps that it still rests on water.

Several features point to influence from the Near East, with which, as archaeology shows, Sparta had had direct or indirect contacts throughout the seventh century. The original dark watery chaos characterized in negative terms is paralleled on the one hand by Egyptian,[2] on the other by Semitic accounts.[3] Thetis, the goddess who lives and has power in the waters, and is associated by Alcman with the cosmogonic process, can perhaps be compared with Tiâmat. In Genesis, too, it is a divine presence that takes steps towards creation, albeit an external one with different affinities (p. 29). Finally, the opening-up and marking-out

[1] In the cosmogony-poem he apparently called Poros *πρέσγυς*; in the Louvre Partheneion 13–14 he coupled him with Aisa as 'oldest of the gods' (though there he must mean something different).

[2] See Wilson in Frankfort and others, *Before Philosophy*, p. 61.

[3] *Enûma Eliš* i. 1–9; Gen. 1 : 2; the world was 'without form, and void', *tōhû* and *bōhû*, cf. p. 29. (The translation of the Authorized Version is acceptable here, cf. Skinner's commentary.) 'Darkness was upon the deep', i.e. darkness (instead of earth) covered *t*^e^*hôm* (~ Tiâmat). The idea is also Indian; see especially *Ṛgv.* 10. 129.

(Poros, Tekmor) that are at first linked with Darkness, but soon followed by daylight and the luminaries, may be put beside Gen. 1: 3–4, 6–7, 14–18, and the more mythical account of *Enûma Eliš* iv. 137–v. 13.

Thales

Aristotle and the entire doxographical tradition ignore Alcman's contribution to cosmological theory, and we had no inkling of its existence until the publication in 1957 of a papyrus commentary on some of his partheneia. To Aristotle it might have seemed to fall into the same intermediate category of philosophy as the work of Pherecydes (p. 14). It would not have conflicted with his view that a new kind of physical philosophy began with Thales.[1] To us, however, it may now appear that the question of Thales' originality calls for some reconsideration.

That he had a comprehensive cosmology is not to be doubted; but he may never have put it down in a book. Aristotle has to rely on report for opinions of Thales, and does not commit himself on their authenticity.[2] What he has heard includes, apparently devoid of context, the *πάντα πλήρη θεῶν* elsewhere ascribed to Pythagoras or Heraclitus,[3] so that one might be afraid that the tradition consisted of nothing more than apophthegms of the sort attributed to the Seven Sages—of whom, after all, Thales was commonly reckoned to be one.[4] Yet we find specific physical theories attributed to him such as that kind of tradition can never have trafficked in. One of the theories about the Nile inundation recorded by Herodotus (2. 20) is ascribed to Thales by Aetius (4. 1. 1); it seems likely that the ascription goes back to Theophrastus (it does not look like a Stoic construction), and that he found it in an earlier written source. Might Theophrastus and Herodotus both be dependent on Hecataeus? That

[1] p. 99 n. 2.

[2] *Metaph.* 984^{a}2 *Θαλῆς μέντοι λέγεται οὕτως ἀποφήνασθαι περὶ τῆς πρώτης αἰτίας* *de cael.* 294^{a}29 *τὸν λόγον ὅν φασιν εἰπεῖν Θαλῆν τὸν Μιλήσιον.* *de an*, 405^{a}19 *ἔοικε δὲ καὶ Θαλῆς, ἐξ ὧν ἀπομνημονεύουσι, κινητικόν τι τὴν ψυχὴν ὑπολαβεῖν, εἴπερ τὸν λίθον ἔφη κτλ.*

[3] p. 145 n. 2.

[4] Pl. *Prot.* 343 a, Dicaearchus, fr. 32 Wehrli, etc.

would not be the earliest mention of Thales, but it would be much the earliest report of his teachings. In favour of the hypothesis, it may be recalled that Hecataeus was himself a Milesian, and that his map of the world links him with Anaximander (Hellanicus 4 T 13). He was consulted by Herodotus on Egyptian matters,[1] and in fact the next of the theories about the inundation that he quotes seems to be that of Hecataeus.[2] Still in the fifth century, Hippias mentioned Thales' idea that the magnet possesses a 'soul', i.e. is 'alive'; perhaps also his view that everything comes from water (and perishes into it?), and that the earth rests on water.[3]

Theophrastus felt able to construct a fuller account, the outlines of which are preserved by Hippolytus.[4]

Hippolytus	Parallels and notes
(1) λέγεται Θαλῆν τὸν Μιλήσιον ἕνα τῶν ἑπτὰ σοφῶν πρῶτον ἐπικεχειρηκέναι φιλοσοφίαν φυσικήν.	Simpl. *in Phys.* 23. 29 Θαλῆς δὲ πρῶτος παραδέδοται τὴν περὶ φύσεως ἱστορίαν τοῖς Ἕλλησιν ἐκφῆναι, πολλῶν μὲν καὶ ἄλλων προγεγονότων, ὡς καὶ Θεοφράστῳ δοκεῖ, αὐτὸς δὲ πολὺ διενεγκὼν ἐκείνων ὡς ἀποκρύψαι τοὺς πρὸ αὐτοῦ.
οὗτος ἔφη ἀρχὴν τοῦ παντὸς εἶναι καὶ τέλος τὸ ὕδωρ. (2) ἐκ γὰρ αὐτοῦ τὰ πάντα συνίστασθαι πηγνυμένου καὶ πάλιν διανιεμένου.	~Aet. 1. 3. 1. (After Aristotle.) Assimilation to Anaximenes (Diels, *Doxogr.* 145): characteristic of Theophrastus (cf. p. 129), after Arist. *de cael.* $303^{b}13$.

[1] 2. 143; 70–3, cf. Porph. *ap.* Eus. *PE* 10. 3. 16 = 1 F 324; Diels, *Hermes* 22, 1887, 411–44 = *Kl. Schr.*, pp. 93 ff.

[2] Cf. Diod. 1. 37, sch. A.R. 4. 259: 1 F 302.

[3] The magnet: Hippias DK 86 B 7, Arist. *de an.* $405^{a}19$. Water: Arist. *Metaph.* $983^{b}6$–$4^{a}3$, *de cael.* $294^{a}28$. Hippias as the source: Snell, *Philol.* 96, 1944, 170–82 = *Gesammelte Schr.*, pp. 119–28; cf. C. J. Classen, *Philol.* 109, 1965, 175–8.

[4] *Ref.* 1. 1. 1–3 = Diels, *Doxogr.*, p. 555. The passage is omitted from DK and from Maddalena's *Ionici*, probably in consequence of Diels's decision that it came from the 'Vitarum epitome, Laertio Diogene multo et brevior et futtilior sed haud absimili forma' (*Doxogr.*, p. 145) which supplies the more anecdotal of Hippolytus' material. So D. R. Dicks, *CQ* 53, 1959, 301.

Theophrastus next gave reasons for Thales' choice of water (*Phys. Op.* fr. 1, cf. Aet. 1. 3. 1), which derive from Aristotle's conjectures in *Metaph.*

ἐπιφέρεσθαί τε αὐτῷ τὰ πάντα· ἀφ' οὗ καὶ σεισμοὺς καὶ πνευμάτων στροφὰς καὶ ἀέρων κινήσεις γίνεσθαι. (*συστροφὰς καὶ ἄστρων* Cedrenus.) (3) *καὶ τὰ πάντα φύεσθαί τε καὶ ῥεῖν τῇ τοῦ πρώτου ἀρχηγοῦ τῆς γενέσεως αὐτῶν φύσει συμφερόμενα.*

After Aristotle.
~ Aet. 3. 15. 1, 9; Sen. *QN* 3. 14.

There follows a sentence which defines divinity as that which has neither beginning nor end. This appears in Diogenes Laertius and Clement as an apophthegm (cf. Diels ad loc.), but seems to derive from Arist. *Phys.* 203^b4–15, applied by some doxographer generally to *οἱ ἀπὸ Θάλεω.*

Most of the information is clearly derived from Aristotle, but the last two sentences quoted offer new details. What do they say, and where did Theophrastus get his knowledge? The sense of the earthquake theory is plain enough;[1] only it was unknown to Aristotle, who says that three people are on record as offering explanations of earthquakes, Anaximenes, Anaxagoras, and Democritus.[2] Perhaps Theophrastus found the reference to it in the course of a more thorough reading of the literature.

For what follows we may hazard a more specific guess. The best reading is *πνευμάτων συστροφὰς καὶ ἄστρων κινήσεις*, as Cedrenus has it.[3] But, while we know that Thales thought about

[1] Thales might have been struck by the way the timbers of a raft or pontoon bridge grind together even in calm water. Note Aet. 3. 15. 9 *καθάπερ τὰ πλαταμώδη καὶ σανιδώδη ἐπὶ τῶν ὑδάτων*, and Seneca's *more nauigii*. For late references for the idea of the world as a ship, cf. Eisler, *Weltenmantel*, p. 576 n. 4.

[2] *Meteor.* 365^a15 ff.

[3] Diels quoted Apuleius' *uentorum flatus, stellarum meatus* (*Flor.* 18), but it may be asked whether the words do not allude rather to the *Ναυτικὴ ἀστρολογία*. However, *ἀέρων κινήσεις* would come oddly after *πνευμάτων συστροφάς*, and the corruption could be explained from *ἄστ^{ερ}ρων* (cf. Hipp. 1. 2. 2 *ἄστρων* (. . . *τὴν κίνησιν*) BT, *ἀστέρων* C).

the interaction of wind and water (Etesians and Nile), and we can see that he might have held that winds were produced by the movements of the sea,[1] why should he be specially concerned with *whirl*winds; and how could he make the water supporting the earth account for the revolution[2] of the stars? The two questions answer each other. The link between the sea and the stars is the winds.[3] As in Anaximenes the stars ride on aer, so already for Thales, it would seem, they are carried round by winds, which are caused by the movements of the waters round the earth. The wind movement is circular precisely because it has got to explain the visible motions of the stars. That would naturally lead Thales to think of a circular flow of water round the earth, and to conclude that that was what Homer meant by his 'river' Oceanus. But really it was not a river, but the exposed part of a great pool, so that the rotatory motion was of the nature of a δίνη—something that can obviously develop spontaneously in a body of water.[4] Rotating clockwise, it generated winds which lifted the sun, moon, and stars into the sky in the east,[5] but abated towards the west, so that they sank into the water and were carried round by the current under water till they reached the east again: Homer's 'baths of Ocean'.[6]

[1] Cf. Xenoph. B 30 πηγὴ δ' ἐστὶ θάλασσ' ὕδατος, πηγὴ δ' ἀνέμοιο κτλ.

[2] Cf. Hipp. 1. 7. 6 on Anaximenes οὐ κινεῖσθαι δὲ ὑπὸ γῆν τὰ ἄστρα κτλ.

[3] The three winds and the stars are born together from Astraios and Dawn in Hes. *Th.* 378–82.

[4] In *CQ* 57, 1963, 172–6, I suggested that Thales' cosmology, being based on water, was the likeliest source of the δίνη-metaphor which appears in later systems. But I assumed too confidently that the idea appeared in Anaximander and Anaximenes, I overlooked the Theophrastean evidence, and I constructed a picture of Thales' cosmos that differs considerably from what I am now arriving at.

[5] 'Oceanus' starts in the east: Hdt. 4. 8. The winds are the children of Dawn, and in fact tend to rise at dawn in Greece (*Hes. Th.*, pp. 270 f.).

[6] Cf. p. 98. The sun goes below earth, *Od.* 10. 191. According to Aet. 2. 13. 1, 20. 9, Thales held the sun and stars to be solid bodies, γεώδη. This might come from Theophrastus, but Aetius makes several other statements about Thales which derive from Stoic interpretation and are often anachronistic (2. 12. 1, 24. 1, 27. 5, 3. 10. 1). The post-Theophrastean tradition has in general nothing of value in it concerning Thales. Sen. *QN* 3. 13 *adiciam, ut Thales ait, 'ualentissimum' elementum est* (sc. *aqua*) might correspond to something like πάντων κρατεῖν (Diog. Ap. 64 B 5, Anaxag. 59 B 12, [Hp.] *vict.* 1. 10); or it might be related to the exegesis which connected Pindar's ἄριστον μὲν ὕδωρ with Thales (sch. *Ol.* 1. 1).

There is an author who might very well have recorded some of this, and who was certainly read by Theophrastus: Anaximenes. In arguing that the earth floats (not on water but) on aer, in propounding his own theory of earthquakes (13 A 21), and in denying that the heavenly bodies pass under the earth ('as others have supposed', adds Hipp. 1. 7. 6), he might have referred to the mistaken views of his predecessor. It is true that the fifth-century philosophers and scientific writers rarely attack a predecessor by name, but speak of 'many' or 'certain' people.[1] Anaximenes may have done just this; Theophrastus would have been able to identify the person who thought the earth floated on water.[2]

The remaining sentence quoted from Hippolytus would seem to refer to plants and rivers, if the transmitted text is right.[3] The language is strange, however, and Roeper's *φέρεσθαί τε καὶ ῥεῖν* attractive. This would assimilate Thales to the Heraclitizers (cf. Pl. *Crat.* 411 c–d, 440 b), a liaison that might have been suggested by Hippias' discussion.[4]

A conjectural reconstruction of Thales' cosmogony, then, would run on the following lines. Before our earth existed, there was a great ocean. A circular eddy developed, in the middle of which the earth grew. Round about it the air is driven along by the whirling current, and the luminaries alternately soar up with the wind and plunge down through the water. So this whole cosmos is borne on the sea like a vessel, controlled and steered (*κυβερνᾶν*) by the water itself, which, immortal and ageless, mover of things outside it, shaker of earth, owns the attributes of divinity.[5]

[1] Walter Burkert made this objection when I suggested that Anaximander was the primary source for knowledge of Thales' views (*CQ* loc. cit., after P. Tannery, *Pour l'histoire de la science hellène*, ²1930, p. 92 n. 1; cf. Classen, *RE* Supp. x. 937).

[2] There remains the difficulty that if Aristotle knew Anaximenes' earthquake theory from his book, he should have known of Thales' too.

[3] Cf. perhaps Sen. *QN* 3. 14 *ait enim terrarum orbem aqua sustineri et uehi . . . non est ergo mirum si abundat umor ad flumina profundenda cum in umore sit totus*. But that looks like Seneca's own comment (see context).

[4] Cf. Pl. *Crat.* 402 b+Arist. *Metaph.* 983^{b}27 ff., with Snell, art. cit.

[5] If the magnet *ψυχὴν ἔχει* because it moves other things, the same should be true of the water. But Aet. 1. 7. 11, 8. 2 (> Athenag. 23)+Cic. *ND* 1. 25 represents a Stoicizing construction deriving from Arist. *de an.* 411^{a}7. On Hipp. 1. 1. 3 see above, p. 210.

In time, presumably, the δίνη will run down and vanish; but perhaps there are and will be others elsewhere.

Here, as in Alcman and as in the Babylonian account, we have the primeval water with the divine force inside it. The difference is that the divine force is the water itself, and its powers are the observed powers of water. Apsû and Tiâmat are the waters in a sense, but they are also more: mythical persons whose speech and actions are subject to no natural limitations. Much the same must be said of Thetis. What raises Thales' system to the rank of 'philosophy' is that he eliminates the possibility of arbitrary intervention that is presupposed in the personalization of divinity.[1] If it was he who said 'gods are everywhere', he meant that nature is no inert mass but full of living forces. He has not changed the shape of the cosmos; sun and stars take their daily dip in Oceanus as they did in Homer; but he has made it automatic.

The period of Iranian influence. Pythagoras

There is no evidence here for increased influence from the east, whatever may be thought of Thales' supposed achievements in astronomy and geometry.[2] But soon afterwards there is a marked change. Anaximander, who was Thales' fellow citizen and must at least have heard him, shows himself dependent on a Greek tradition of materialistic speculation, particularly in the meteorological field, but at the same time he introduces a throng of non-Greek, non-materialistic conceptions, partly Babylonian in character (from our viewpoint), partly distinctively Iranian (pp. 87–97). At the same period, Pherecydes of Syros comes up with a rich mixture of lore which, though seldom overlapping what we find in Anaximander, has similar provenances, with the Iranian element prominent in the foreground. Like Anaximander, he is at pains to assimilate it to native Greek traditions. The probability that his father was an immigrant from southern Anatolia, and that that is the source of some of his exotic material,

[1] Cf. Frankfort, *Before Philosophy*, p. 253.

[2] Cf. Kirk–Raven, pp. 80–4; Burkert, *WW*, pp. 393 f.; van der Waerden, *AA*, pp. 121–3.

may make Pherecydes an exceptional case. But migration may be a significant fact in itself. This *was* a time when barbarians became Greeks. Thales was of Phoenician ancestry (Hdt. 1. 170); his father's name, Examyes, is certainly Anatolian, perhaps Carian. Another of the Seven Sages, Bias of Priene, was the son of Teutames: this is another Asiatic name, probably Phrygian.

Anaximenes, much more than Anaximander, follows in the footsteps of Thales. But he too betrays the influence of eastern and specifically Iranian cosmology, in things that he cannot have taken from Thales (northern mountain; luminaries not passing under earth) or from Anaximander (eclipses caused by dark bodies) (pp. 104–9). Meanwhile, twenty miles away, an intellectual priest-prophet was propagating a new sort of wisdom. His name was Pythagoras. He claimed to be Hyperborean Apollo, he is said to have dressed in a gold crown, white robe, and trousers,[1] and while some judged him an impostor,[2] he evidently made a considerable impression. He may have become politically dangerous; at any rate, Samos was too small to contain both him and Polycrates, and he departed.[3]

He appealed to the authority of poems by Orpheus, in which, however, he was believed to have made alterations.[4] Of his

[1] Ael. *VH* 12. 32; the white robe also in D.L. 8. 19, Iambl. *VP* 149. (Max. Tyr. 1. 10 puts him in purple.) The same garb is worn by the highest god in *P. Mag.* 4. 698 (Dieterich, *Eine Mithrasliturgie*, p. 14; *Abraxas*, p. 105): ἐν χιτῶνι λευκῷ καὶ χρυσῷ στεφάνῳ καὶ ἀναξυρίσι, κατέχοντα τῇ δεξιᾷ χειρὶ μόσχου ὦμον χρύσεον. On the wearing of imposing costume by Anaximander and Empedocles see p. 77. Of the latter, who gives his own testimony in B 112. 6, Alcidamas (*ap.* D.L. 8. 56) said that he followed Pythagoras in his σεμνότης τοῦ βίου and σχῆμα. Bright-coloured clothing was worn to attract attention; so by sophists (Gorgias, Hippias: Ael. loc. cit.) and rhapsodes (Pl. *Ion* 530 b, 535 d).

[2] For Heraclitus he is a deluded polymath, master of κακοτεχνίη, prince of charlatans (fr. 16–18 = B 40, 129, 81).

[3] Aristox. fr. 16 Wehrli.

[4] Ion of Chios *ap.* D.L. 8. 8 and Clem. *Strom.* 1. 131; cf. Hdt. 2. 81, and perhaps Heraclitus 17 = B 129 (p. 2 n. 3). Other 'Orphic' poems (*Diktyon, Peplos, Physica, Krater, Katabasis, Hieros Logos*) are said to have been composed by early Pythagoreans—Brontinus, Zopyrus, Cercops—and show connections with Pythagorean thought. Some, perhaps all, of the ascriptions go back to Epigenes (Orph. t 229 Kern), who must be dated in the fourth century B.C. I shall discuss all this more fully in a book on the Orphic theogonies. It is interesting that the first mention of Orpheus in extant literature comes from Ibycus, a south Italian poet who moved to Samos and was a member of Polycrates' circle.

personal doctrines, we can say confidently that he believed in metempsychosis through animal bodies, at least for certain people.[1] His teaching was passed on to his later followers in the form of *ἀκούσματα*, also called *σύμβολα*, laconic maxims and riddles, many of which expressed religious tabus and superstitions.[2] Among those that have come down to us, a group that have cosmological or eschatological reference deserve our attention.

βροντᾷ ἀπειλῆς ἕνεκα τοῖς ἐν τῷ Ταρτάρῳ ὅπως φοβῶνται. (Arist. *Anal. post.* 94^{b}33.)
ὁ σεισμὸς σύνοδος τῶν τεθνεώτων. (Ael. *VH* 4. 17.)
ἡ ἶρις αὐγὴ τοῦ ἡλίου. (Ibid.)
ὁ πολλάκις ἐμπίπτων τοῖς ὠσὶν ἦχος φωνὴ τῶν κρειττόνων. (Ibid.)
τί ἐστιν αἱ μακάρων νῆσοι; ἥλιος καὶ σελήνη. (Iambl. *VP* 82.)
ἐπὶ κολάσει ἐλθόντας δεῖ κολασθῆναι. (Ibid. 85.)
ἡ θάλασσα Κρόνου δάκρυον. (Porph. *VP* 41 = Arist. fr. 196.)
αἱ ἄρκτοι Ῥέας χεῖρες. (Ibid.)
ἡ Πλειὰς Μουσῶν λύρα. (Ibid.)
οἱ πλανῆται κύνες τῆς Περσεφόνης. (Ibid.)

Some of these can be treated as self-contained and self-explanatory propositions, but others are only intelligible as allusions to a larger system—fragments, though not in the sense that the tradition once contained a continuous exposition. Kronos and Rhea appear as cosmic figures. The sun and moon are the Isles of the Blessed, i.e. where the souls of the dead most desire to arrive; but there are also the planets, Persephone's dogs, which we must suppose to have the office of Cerberus, guarding the passage and devouring souls or turning them away. (The planets are therefore below the sun and moon.) Some of the dead, then, loiter in the lower air; their voices are to be heard in the ringing of the ears.

[1] Burkert, *WW*, pp. 98 ff., cf. 110 f. on the imprecision of the term metempsychosis without qualification.

[2] Burkert, *WW*, pp. 150 ff. There is no telling how many of the recorded *ἀκούσματα* go back to Pythagoras himself, but their general character cannot have changed. (Burkert, *WW*, pp. 172 f.)

Others are in Tartarus, below the earth. Earthquakes occur when they hold their conventions, and thunder is a warning to them.[1]

This is all beguilingly coherent. Is it Pythagoras' scheme? It is tempting to think so, for no period suits it so well as the second half of the sixth century. Pherecydes had combined his metempsychosis-doctrine with a cosmic mythology that had an important place for Chronos (and his secretions), and some sort of a place for Rhea; he had made the moon a source of ambrosia, and he had a Tartarus for unruly gods. Planets collectively below the sun and moon recall the arrangement of Anaximander's cosmos, except that he spoke generally of 'the stars'. The next stage after the primitive division sun, moon, stars (p. 86 n. 2) is to separate the planets as a group from the fixed stars (Burkert, *WW*, p. 298). We see this in Alcmeon (Aet. 2. 16. 3 = A 4), and perhaps in Anaximenes (p. 102); Parmenides is already going further (A 40 a). The explanation of the rainbow as a reflection of sunlight appeared in Anaximenes (A 7 § 8; 18). When early fifth-century Pythagoreans such as Brontinus and Zopyrus worked out ideas of the same character—'the earth is the robe of Persephone', for instance—they did not inject them into the *ἀκούσματα* but embodied them in new 'Orphic' poems.[2]

It is probable that Pythagoras also attached a cosmic significance to number, not in the sense that he applied himself to mathematics as we understand it, but in the sense that he was fascinated by some of the simpler properties of numbers and recognized therein a basic secret of nature.[3] One of the *ἀκούσματα* answers the question *τί σοφώτατον;* ('cleverest') with *ἀριθμός· δεύτερος δὲ ὁ τοῖς πράγμασι τὰ ὀνόματα θέμενος*.[4] It is less clear that he knew that the basic musical intervals involve numerical

[1] Thunder can frighten those in a subterranean Tartarus, see Hes. *Th.* 839/851, *Il.* 20. 56–65. Cf. Iambl. *VP* 156 *ὅταν δὲ βροντήσῃ, τῆς γῆς ἅψασθαι παρήγγελλε μνημονεύοντας τῆς γενέσεως τῶν ὄντων.*

[2] p. 214 n. 4; p. 230. One of these poems contained a reference to 'tears of Zeus', which according to Epigenes meant rain (Orph. fr. 33).

[3] Cf. Burkert, *WW*, ch. VI.

[4] Iambl. *VP* 82, Ael. *VH* 4. 17. The second part implies a fascination with etymologies; its assumption of a clever name-giver is also that of Plato's *Cratylus*.

relationships;[1] but there are other connections between number and music which can perhaps be traced before his time,[2] and which may have engaged his interest. The Pleiades as the Muses' lyre hint at a belief in a celestial music. Burkert (*WW*, pp. 333–5) has suggested, on the basis of several ancient references[3] and parallels among other peoples, that the later theory of a harmony of the planetary spheres developed from a simpler conception of a correspondence between the four seasons and four notes or intervals. This would make sense of the saying about the Pleiades, for it is the Pleiades, more than any other sign, that mark the onset of summer and winter by their rising and setting.[4]

The 'ethos' (if I may use the word) of these cosmological fancies reminds us of Pythagoras' supposed teacher Pherecydes more than of anyone else. And we find in Pythagoras a similar blend of Greek and barbarian wisdom: Greek religious custom, barbarian cosmology and eschatology. Many of the *ἀκούσματα* are obviously traditional precepts, some of which indeed appear in the *Works and Days*.[5] The *ἄκουσμα* about the rainbow gives an

[1] The more plausible tradition associates it with Hippasus, see Burkert, *WW*, pp. 355–7. It is apparently presupposed by the *ἄκουσμα* 'What is the oracle at Delphi?—Tetraktys, which is to say Attunement, in which the Sirens are.' See *CQ* 61, 1967, 12.

[2] Ibid. 11–14, on Alcman's eleven Sirens.

[3] First collected by Lobeck, pp. 944–6. Add Aristox. (?) *ap*. Hipp. *Ref*. 1. 2. 13, who seems to make this part of what Pythagoras learned from Zaratas.

[4] Cf. Hes. *Op*. 383 f. with Sinclair; Arat. 266 f. They would be a seven-, not a four-stringed lyre, but it would be pedantic to make that an objection; and cf. [Hp.] *hebd*. 4 *ὧραι δὲ ἐνιαύσιοι ἑπτά, εἰσὶ δὲ αὗται· σπορητός, χειμών, φυταλιά, ἔαρ, θέρος, ὀπώρα, μετόπωρον*. (The work is a fourth-century construction from mainly fifth-century material with marked Pythagorean affinities; cf. Burkert, *WW*, p. 269 n. 76, and Addenda to p. 231 below.)

Another possible factor is suggested by the *ἄκουσμα* concerning 'the ringing that often comes into the ears', and the tradition that Pythagoras was the only person who could actually hear the heavenly music (Porph. *VP* 30 + Iambl. *VP* 65, from Nicomachus; cf. sch. *Od*. 1. 371 (Thesleff, *Pythagorean Texts*, p. 172)). Did he perhaps suffer from a defect of hearing? Smetana, before he went deaf, was troubled by the sound of a persistent high note, finding it musical enough to put into his quartet *Aus meinem Leben*.

[5] *πρὸς ἥλιον τετραμμένος μὴ οὔρει* Iambl. *Protr*. 21 (+ D.L. 8. 17) ~ *Op*. 727; *παρὰ θυσίᾳ μὴ ὀνυχίζου* ibid. (+ *VP* 154) ~ *Op*. 742–3; perhaps *ἐν ὁδῷ μὴ σχίζε* (*χέζε*?) ibid., cf. *Op*. 729. On the other hand the avoidance of woollen clothes seemed to Herodotus (2. 81) to be Egyptian, and the ban on sacrificing a white cock because it is sacred to the god Men points to Persia and Babylon (Burkert, *WW*, p. 156 n. 47).

explanation that springs from Greek speculation. On the other hand, the doctrine of metempsychosis, with sun and moon as Isles of the Blessed, points to the east (Ch. 2). The lower position of the planets resembles the Anaximandrean–Iranian position for the stars; if they challenge and repulse the soul that aspires to paradise, we might compare the later attested Iranian view of them as evil powers that try to intercept the benefits destined for mankind by the sun, moon, and constellations.[1] The tears of Kronos, the hands of Rhea, recall the oriental idea of the world as the body of a mythical person or god, particularly one whose activity belongs in the past.[2] Further than this we shall not go.[3]

Parmenides

'Presocratic philosophy is divided into two halves by the name of Parmenides. His exceptional powers of reasoning brought speculation about the origin and constitution of the universe to a halt, and caused it to make a fresh start on different lines.'

These sentences, which open the second volume of Guthrie's *History of Greek Philosophy*, exemplify what I find most objection-

[1] *Mēnōk-i-Xrat* 12. 4–5, 24. 5 (Zaehner, *Zurvan*, pp. 400, 404). (The Zoroastrian names for the planets mark them as good powers, *yazatas*, not *daēvas*.) Cf. also the Platonist and Mithraic idea of the soul's ascent to the stellar firmament by way of the planetary spheres: Cumont, *TM* i. 38, 309; *Symbolisme*, pp. 139 f.

[2] Cf. pp. 38 (Purusha, Ohrmazd), 42 (Tiâmat), 94 (Vishṇu). The cardinal directions are the arms of Prajāpati, *Ṛgv.* 10. 121. 4. See also the hymns to Skambha, *Atharvav.* 10. 7–8 (Zaehner, *Hindu Scriptures*, pp. 18 ff.); *Mundaka Upan.* 2. 1; *Mahābh.* (Poona ed.) iii. 187. 7; T. Jacobsen in Frankfort and others, *Before Philosophy*, pp. 145 f.; A. Götze, *Zeitschr. f. Indologie u. Iranistik* 2, 1923, 60 ff., 167 ff.; R. Reitzenstein and H. H. Schaeder, *Studien zum antiken Synkretismus* (Stud. Bibl. Warburg, 7), 1926, 69–103; *Vorträge d. Bibl. Warburg* 4, 1924/5, 10 ff. (= E. Heitsch (ed.), *Hesiod*, 1966, 534 ff.); W. Kranz, *GGN*, 1938, 121–61 (= *Studien zur antiken Literatur u. ihrem Nachwirken*, 1967, 165–97); A. Olerud, *L'Idée de Macrocosmos et de Microcosmos dans le Timée de Platon*, Diss. Uppsala, 1951, 128 ff.; Duchesne-Guillemin, *Harv. Theol. Rev.* 49, 1956, 115 ff.

[3] Pythagoras (D.L. 8. 20) agreed with the Persians (Hdt. 1. 133. 3) in not urinating in view of others. His rumoured trousers suggested to Burkert a Persian or Scythian connection (*WW*, pp. 136, 178 n. 18), but there may be more significance in the circumstance that they are worn by the Thracian Orpheus. (Vase paintings; cf. Philostr. *VA* 1. 25.) Nor shall we exaggerate his foreign aspect by using labels like witch-doctor, mage, or shaman, whose proper application lies in other cultures.

able in the conventional approach to the study of the Presocratics: the exaggeration of the achievement and influence of individuals, the failure to see beyond surface differences to underlying relationships, and the implicit assumption that nobody contributed to the development of thought except the few whose writings survived them.[1] To talk of speculation being 'brought to a halt' is sheer fancy. A good half-century after Parmenides, Diogenes of Apollonia propounds a cosmogony that stands very much in the tradition of Anaximenes. For Guthrie he is an 'ostrich-like' figure who 'fell back on a reaction to earlier Ionian ideas which ignored the genuine advances in thought initiated by Parmenides' (ii. 120 f.). Can we be sure that an Ionian living by the Black Sea necessarily knew about Parmenides? What reason is there to suppose that those who did know Parmenides' poem necessarily thought that he had raised a real problem which they must try to deal with? Empedocles, perhaps also Anaxagoras, knew the poem, but they pursue a very different kind of philosophy from Zeno and Melissus: why, then, must we suppose that they are seeking an alternative answer to 'the problem posed by Parmenides', and that their ultimate material elements are to be seen as modifications of the Eleatic ἓν ἐόν?[2]

But first things first. What was this new view of things that Parmenides' 'exceptional powers of reasoning' attained? He presented it, in fact, not as his own construction but as a divine revelation. 'The team that conveys me as far as my spirit goes'[3] were taking him on 'the way of divine utterance, which of itself carries the wise man over all',[4] and maidens showed the way (B 1. 1–5). The burning axle sang as the Maidens of the Sun

1 Cf. my remarks in *CQ* 61, 1967, 1, and above, p. 99.

2 Cf., e.g., Kirk–Raven, pp. 368 f.: the opening of Anaxagoras' book, being totally unlike Parmenides, shows 'how extreme was the reaction of Anaxagoras against the Eleatic monism'. When he denies that matter can come into being or perish, 'it cannot be doubted that Anaxagoras is explicitly accepting one of the Parmenidean demands'. But 'there can be little doubt either that the rejection of the other demands, in 495 (= B 1), is equally deliberate'.

3 Read ἱκάνῃ, or cf. Emp. 100. 23 for the optative.

4 Reading δαίμονος and (with Hermann) αὐτῇ φέρει.

hurried him on; they came out of the house of Night into the light, throwing the veils back from their faces, and they persuaded Dike, who holds the keys of exchange, to open the gate where day and night go forth (6–20).[1] Straight through went maidens, horses, and chariot along the carriage-way; and the goddess[2] welcomed Parmenides, shook hands, and said: ' "Welcome, lad[3] whose team-that-conveys-you has brought you to my house. It is far removed from the beaten path of men, but it was Themis and Dike that guided you here, not any evil luck. It falls to you to hear all: the firm heart of reality, and the unreliable views of men" ' (20–30). As regards the latter, he will learn 'how (*or* that) the appearances ought to stand apparent and universal', i.e. a really acceptable explanation of them such as has not been found before (31–2); it will not be ultimate reality (ἀπατηλός, 8. 52), but it will be ἐοικώς, and no mortal man will be able to improve on it (8. 60 f.).

The firm heart of reality consists of Being, uninterrupted and changeless; the 'unreliable views of men' correspond to the phenomenal world with its colour, movement, and impermanence. Parmenides is thus making a division between objective and subjective; but he differs from most of the later philosophers who operated with this distinction in the radicalism with which he excludes from the first category every quality except existence itself. Being, however, is not for him something noumenal, beyond perception, but intimately connected with human cognition. Non-being is excluded by the impossibility of thinking

[1] Cf. Hes. *Th.* 744–57; above, pp. 137 with n. 3, 179.

[2] Or, just possibly, Theia, the mother of the Sun, whom Parmenides might have interpreted etymologically as Beholding (cf. Pind. *Isth.* 5. 1 ff., 478 B.C.?), and who would suit the solar setting. She is normally Θεία, though Θέα is perhaps to be recognized in *H. Dem.* 64. Cf. *Hes. Th.*, p. 203.

[3] Despite Burkert, *Phronesis* 14, 1969, 14 n. 32, I do not see why this should not be taken at face value, with (most recently) Hölscher, *Anfängliches Fragen*, p. 161. According to Pl. *Parm.* 127 a–c (cf. *Soph.* 217 c, *Theaet.* 183 e), Parmenides was about 65 in a Panathenaic year when Socrates was σφόδρα νέος (πάνυ νέος, νέος), presumably 454, 450, or 446. If the details are not invented, Parmenides should have composed his poem in the 490s. Hölscher thinks that Plato may have lowered his dates in order to make a meeting with Socrates possible. But if there had been a chronological difficulty, Plato could reasonably have made Parmenides somewhat older than 65.

or speaking of it.[1] Thinking and being are the same.[2] Parmenides obviously does not mean to say that everything anyone thinks must be true; on the contrary, he seems to mean that all perceptions of size, shape, motion, colour, heat, and so on, never have more than a local and temporary validity, and only the fact of being is not subject to revision.

As the goddess presents it, this conclusion is arrived at by the following process of reasoning.[3] You start with three possible 'roads of inquiry', (*a*) that *it is*, and necessarily is, (*b*) that it is not, and necessarily is not, (*c*) that it both is and is not.[4] You reject (*b*) as inconceivable, and (*c*) as confused and self-contradictory. This enables you to dismiss the concepts of coming-to-be and passing-away, because they imply non-being. Then it strikes you that there can be no separation of being from being, either by non-being or by something more than being; being is therefore one and continuous, without moving parts. This leaves no room for anything else but Being itself, an argument which is allowed to exclude not only becoming, perishing, and motion, but even changes of colour. Being is finite in extent, for without a completion it would be deficient—a characteristic of non-being.[5] Finally, it must be spherical, because no non-being can interrupt its equal extension in every direction, nor can being differ from being (in different directions) by being greater or less.

Of course these were not the actual stages of Parmenides' thinking. A man does not start by weighing Being against Non-being, and then find himself forced by pure logic to the position that Being is a great, still, homogeneous sphere, while the visible world is a sham. So far from testifying to exceptional powers of

[1] B 2. 6–8; 6. 1; 8. 8, 17, 35–6. Note the constant association of 'thinking' and 'saying', which also appears in 8. 50, 53.

[2] B 3, cf. 8. 34. Distant things are present to the mind: it follows that all being is connected (B 4). Men's 'naming' of light and night determines how the apparent world 'is' (B 9, cf. 19).

[3] B 1–3 and 6–8 (10 . . . 11) can be combined in one almost unbroken text; 4 logically belongs after 8. 25, while 5 is unplaced. Diels estimated the total length of the poem at 500 lines; I would put it at more like 300.

[4] Reinhardt, *Parmenides*, pp. 36 ff.

[5] This is the best sense I can extract from 8. 33, reading ἔστι γὰρ οὐκ ἐπιδεές, μὴ ἐὸν δ' ἂν παντὸς ἐδεῖτο.

reasoning, the arguments are in several instances contrived and artificial, lending a show of logic to opinions that must have been reached in other ways. The denial of reality to the whole range of perceptible qualities might plausibly be interpreted as a hasty and extreme generalization of the recent discovery that certain qualities formerly considered to be absolutes were really relative, and might simultaneously be present and not present in a thing according to one's point of view.[1] The denial of becoming and perishing may already have been a commonplace of materialist cosmology,[2] owing nothing to thoughts about the inconceivability of non-being. The spherical shape of Being would suit a cosmos, and may have been influenced by one.[3] As Parmenides treats Being openly as a correlate of mental apprehension, we may suspect that his account of its characteristics—one indivisible continuum, immobile, timeless—is not derived from cold deduction but from a direct perception, a mystical experience.[4]

Acute awareness of the unity of all things with each other and with the self is a characteristic feature of such experiences. Space and time remain present to the consciousness, but seem to lose all significance. A nature mystic of the last century, describing his experiences, writes:

> 'It is eternity now. I am in the midst of it. . . . Nothing has to come: it is now. Now is eternity; now is the immortal life.'[5]

Similarly Huxley in *The Doors of Perception* tells of his mescalin-induced experience 'of an indefinite duration or alternatively of

[1] Examples were given by Xenophanes (B 38) and Heraclitus (cf. p. 139).

[2] As later, Anaxag. B 17, Emp. B 8, 9. Anaximander and Anaximenes at least made their Boundless eternal; others had assumed gods without beginning (Pherec. B 1, Xenoph. A 12, B 14; Orph. *ap.* Arist. *Metaph.* 1071^{b}27, 1072^{a}8; apophthegm ascribed to Thales, D.L. 1. 35; cf. Epicharm. 170 a = B 1). The maxim *nihil ex nihilo* appears as early as Alcaeus (fr. 320). Heraclitus' world-fire is everlasting, and he is able to see one's death as another's life.

[3] Cf. pp. 84 f. on Anaximander. The encompassing bond in which Ananke/Moira holds Being fast (8. 30–31, cf. 37, 42) resembles the *οὐρανός* described in 10. 5–7.

[4] Cf. C. M. Bowra, *Problems in Greek Poetry*, pp. 39, 53; Jaeger, *Theology*, p. 107; W. J. Verdenius, *Mnem.* (4th ser.) 2, 1949, 120 ff.; especially H. Fränkel, *D. u. Ph.*, pp. 417–19.

[5] Richard Jefferies, *The Story of my Heart*, 1912, p. 30, quoted (with comparison of Parmenides) by Zaehner, *Mysticism Sacred and Profane*, 1957, p. 47.

a perpetual present made up of one continually changing apocalypse'. These statements well illustrate Parmenides'

οὐδέ ποτ' ἦν, οὐδ' ἔσται, ἐπεὶ νῦν ἔστιν ὁμοῦ πᾶν (8. 5).

If it was in this way that he first came to his inner conviction of the unbroken unity of Being, however, it took nourishment from current reflections on cosmic unity (p. 129), the fallibility of the senses, and the relativity of some qualities. In attempting to provide it with a logical foundation, Parmenides shows himself a rationalist by training. He betrays the influence of recent speculation not only in the interpretation he puts upon his visionary insight, but in his analysis of the phenomenal world.[1]

At the same time, features of the picture point to the east. The light–darkness dualism of the *doxa*-world corresponds to an Iranian belief that we know was established before Aristoxenus (p. 32). The idea that the opposites are actually bundles of qualities, light–fire–gentle–rare and night–thick–heavy (B 8. 56–9), recalls the Indian Sāṁkhya philosophy, according to which the material world is woven together from three 'strands', each comprising under its one name a complex of qualities. As for Parmenides the mixture of light and dark in our bodies determines our thought and perception at any moment (A 46, B 16), so in the Sāṁkhya 'all mental operations, such as perception, thinking, willing, are not performed by the soul, but are merely mechanical processes of the internal organs, that is to say, of matter'.[2] The Sāṁkhya developed over a long period, but its concepts can almost all be traced back to the Upanishads.[3] The *Chāndogya Upanishad*, for example, teaches that everything can be reduced to the three constituents light/heat (*tejas*), water, and nourishment, each with its own powers and visible colour (red, white, and black respectively). These are the only reality, the

[1] Interaction of opposites (8. 53 ff., 9): presupposed by Heraclitus (p. 139), less clear in Anaximander and Anaximenes (p. 84). Rings of fire and night (A 37/B 12): detailed interpretation obscure, but reminiscent of Anaximander. Moon reflects sun's light (B 14–15): discoverer uncertain, but not likely to have been Parmenides in person.

[2] Macdonell, *History of Sanskrit Literature*, p. 333.

[3] A. B. Keith, *The Sāṁkhya System*, 1918, pp. 46, 51.

rest is mere names—a most important antithesis, which was to appear in Greek with Parmenides.[1]

Even more reminiscent of Parmenides is the account of the origin of the three constituents (6. 2):

> In the beginning, my dear, this (universe) was Being only,—one only,—without a second. True, some say (*Ṛgv.* 10. 72. 2, *al.*) that in the beginning this (universe) was Not-Being only,—one only,—without a second, and that from that Not-Being Being was born.
>
> But, my dear, whence could this be? said he. How could Being be born from Not-Being? No, it was Being alone that was this (universe) in the beginning,—one only, without a second.
>
> It had this thought: 'Would that I were many; fain would I procreate!' It emitted light-and-heat. This light-and-heat (too) had the thought: 'Would that I were many; fain would I procreate!' And it emitted water. So whenever a man is very hot or sweats from the heat, water is produced.
>
> This water (too) had the thought: 'Would that I were many; fain would I procreate!' It emitted food. So whenever it rains, there is food in abundance; for it is from water that edible food is produced.

The procreation of three physical elements from an unbegotten, metaphysical entity momentarily recalls Pherecydes rather than Parmenides, for whom Being and the two-element cosmology are irreconcilable alternatives, one true, the other false. But this antagonism is no less at home in Indian thought. In opposition to the Sāṁkhya philosophy stands the Vedānta, the 'doctrine of non-duality' (*advaita-vāda*), an idealistic monism which holds that the multiplicity of apparent phenomena is an illusion (*māyā*). The illusion is the result of ignorance (*avidyā*; cf. Parmenides' εἰδότα φῶτα 1. 3, βροτοὶ εἰδότες οὐδέν 6. 4). In this developed form, Vedāntic philosophy emerges somewhat later than Parmenides. It is seen in some of the younger Upanishads (*Śvetāśvatara*, *Muṇḍaka*, *Praśna*, *Māṇḍūkya*), in the *Brahma-sūtras* of Bādarāyaṇa, and above all the work of Śaṁkara (born

[1] *Chāndogya Upan.* 6. 3–4; Parm. B 8. 38, 19. 3. Cf. also *Bṛhadāraṇyaka Upan.* 1. 4. 7: 'Now, at that time this (world) was undifferentiated. What introduces differentiation is name and form (individuality), so that we can say: "A man has this name; he has this form." '

A.D. 788).[1] But it was a natural development from the characteristic doctrine of all the Upanishads: that the life-breath of man, *ātman*, is identical with the force that sustains the whole world, *brahman*, so that the apparently many and separate beings merge into a single continuous one. 'This indescribable reality, the "Real of the real" (*Bṛhadāraṇyaka Upanishad* 2. 1. 20, 2. 3. 6) reveals itself in a flash; the astonished mortal realizes himself as immortal, unconditioned, beyond space and time and causation.'[2] This might as aptly have been said of Parmenides.[3]

There is a more specific point of similarity. The goddess's revelation is set forth in the form of a logical demonstration; it is nevertheless a divine revelation. Parmenides portrays himself speeding out in a chariot from the direction of the house of Night, through the gate where day and night alternately go forth, with the daughters of the Sun as his companions. He is apparently on the path of the sun itself. But once he is through the gate, out above the world, he is at his destination: it is there that he is shown the unity of Being, the falseness of all apparent contrasts. He seems to intend the horses as a metaphor for his powers of thought.[4] The general idea of a meeting with a god, who then imparts wisdom, may be put down to literary convention.[5] But where does the cosmic setting come from? Diels and others have rightly drawn attention in this connection to the heavenly journeys undertaken by Asiatic shamans.[6] Now it

[1] The stanzas quoted by Reinhardt, *Parmenides*, pp. 65 and 221, are from Śaṁkara's predecessor Gauḍapāda.

[2] Zaehner, *Hindu Scriptures*, p. ix.

[3] Somigliana has observed that the use of the terms 'being' for ultimate reality and 'not being' for the illusory sensory world is Indian (*Monismo*, p. 76).

[4] 1. 1, 25. Cf. the poet's chariot of song in Bacch. 5. 176 (476 B.C.), Pind. *Ol.* 6. 22 ff. (468 B.C.; detailed comparison by Fränkel, *W. u. F.*, p. 158), Emp. B 3, 5, etc. (Bowra, *Problems*, pp. 41 f.). (Paths of song already in *Od.* 8. 74, etc., cf. ib. 492, 499, Hes. *Op.* 659, Ibyc. 1. 24. Bergk conjectured ἐλῶν for ἑλών in *Od.* 8. 500.) Cf. also p. 143 n. 1. In the *Kaṭha Upan.* 3. 3 ff., the body is represented as a chariot, driven by the soul, with the senses as steeds. The man whose charioteer is wisdom reaches the journey's end, the 'Person' who is the goal, the All-highest Way; 'abiding, endless, beginningless, soundless, intangible, It knows not form or taste or smell, eternal, changeless,—. (such It is,) discern It!'

[5] Hesiod, etc., see *Hes. Th.*, pp. 159 f. 'Epimenides' is the closest parallel to Parmenides, but perhaps later.

[6] Cf. Burkert, *WW*, p. 263; Guthrie, *HGP* ii. 11.

has been noted (p. 48 n. 2) that these Asiatic cultures show affinities with that of ancient India. In the *Atharvaveda* (19. 53. 1), Time (Kāla) is said to drive as a horse with seven reins, and 'him the inspired poets mount; his wheels are all beings'.

Closer to Parmenides' experience, however, is what is described in the continuation of the passage quoted on pp. 63 f. from the *Kaushītakī Upanishad.* After passing the moon and following the 'way of the gods' (cf. ὁδὸν δαίμονος) to the sun and the world of Brahman, the soul of the deceased is received by five hundred celestial nymphs (cf. the Heliades) bearing fruit, unguents, garlands, etc. By using his mind, he successfully crosses the lake Āra (which drowns those who know the present only), the moments Yeshtiha, and the river Vijarā ('ageless'). And now:

> As a man riding in a chariot looks down on the two chariot-wheels on either side, so does he on either side look down on day and night, deeds good and evil, and all dualities (*dvandva*). Delivered from both good and evil works, and knowing Brahman, to Brahman he draws near.

This comes from the same eschatological account that I have used to throw light on Pherecydes, Pythagoras, and Heraclitus. We need not suppose that Pythagoras was the sole carrier of eastern wisdom to the western Greeks, or that there is any importance in the tradition of Parmenides' association with a Pythagorean called Ameinias.[1] His father and teachers may have been among the original Phocaean founders of Elea, bringing minds fresh from Ionia.

The closing of the sluice

From the time of Anaximander and Pherecydes perhaps half a century had elapsed. The potency which oriental influences maintained at the end of this period may be gauged from Heraclitus (Ch. 6). They do not continue through the fifth century. Greek thought turns in on itself and digests what it has taken in.

[1] Sotion *ap.* D.L. 9. 21; cf. Burkert, *WW*, pp. 259 n. 17, 260 ff. There is nothing identifiably Pythagorean in his system.

One obvious cause is the Persian War and its aftermath. The expulsion of pro-Persian rulers from the Ionian towns would not in itself make much difference. But orientals, of all stations, may have suddenly found themselves *personae non gratae*; Xerxes' discomfiture certainly produced a new national awareness and pride; and it may have become difficult or impossible for Greeks to travel into the Asiatic interior.[1] At the same time the growth of the Athenian empire facilitated communication between different parts of Greece.[2] There was another factor, however, which may have been the most important of all: the growing self-sufficiency of Greek rationalism. Observation of the natural world increasingly prompted the (sometimes premature) formulation of general principles which offered more appealing solutions to the problems of cosmology than the non-empirical postulates that foreign thought had to offer. This soon produced results in the field of medicine. As early as the time of Polycrates, a doctor from Croton, Democedes, was called in by the king of Persia and found to be more effective than any practitioner of his own realm.[3]

As an instance of a cosmologist who practised a thoroughgoing empiricism, and consequently reveals no barbarian influence to speak of, Xenophanes presents himself. It is a pity that, although we know when he lived to within a few years, we have little idea when he formed his philosophical opinions. Some of them were evidently known to Heraclitus (fr. 16 = B 40), but that does not help much. Certain scientific data used by him point to his having already reached the west when he wrote about them;[4] we may also say that the quantity of his preserved works—there were five books of *Silloi*, at least—implies a collection accumulated by himself rather than one scraped together at a later period, and thus that it is not likely to have contained anything that he violently regretted in the last years of his life. On the other hand,

[1] Burkert, *WW*, p. 295.

[2] It is interesting to observe that the visit of Parmenides and Zeno to Athens to attend the Panathenaea fell at a time when Athens was making treaties with several cities of the west (Egesta, 458/7; Rhegium, Leontini, after 450; envoys from Rome, 451/0).

[3] Hdt. 3. 125–37; DK 19.

[4] Kirk–Raven, p. 178.

it is not likely that he only began to think about these matters, or fundamentally changed his approach to them, in his eighties and nineties. His basic attitudes will have been formed well before 500.

No other Presocratic shows himself so emancipated from conventional theories. Seeing no evidence that the earth is surrounded or supported by anything other than itself, he declares that it is infinite in extension and in depth. Seeing no evidence for a solid heaven, he substitutes infinite air from the earth upward. His picture has been called naïve, but it is really bold, novel, and imaginative. By exploiting a recent discovery about perspective, and assuming that the approach of the luminaries to the western horizon is a false appearance,[1] he achieves a ruthless simplification of the traditional cosmos. He then realizes that the sun and moon seen by us will fail to illuminate most of this boundless earth to the north and south of us, and that if ours is not to appear a peculiarly favoured latitude, their number must be multiplied. He does not shrink from drawing this bizarre conclusion. As he regards the luminaries as formed by clouds that are produced and nourished by water vapour from below, it is in fact reasonable that they should occur all over the earth.

His theology is equally radical, though here one must suspect assistance from current trends.[2] Again he argues from empirical evidence (the Thracians and Negroes have conflicting conceptions of the gods, based on their own physiques), and generalizes it (animals no doubt do the same) (cf. Epicharmus 173 = B 5). He was quite a collector of recherché information. He mentioned in various connections frogs, the bird-cherry, and the dripping of water in certain caves (B 37, 39, 40). He knew about fossil

[1] So Anaximenes, p. 103. The principle is being abused, of course. If the world were as Xenophanes supposed, the sun would keep getting closer to the horizon but never actually set.

[2] He rejects the notion of the gods' human shape, birth, and immoral behaviour, and divination. He says there is one great god whose every part is percipient; he does not breathe or move about, but moves everything else by power of thought (A 1 § 19; 52; B 11, 12, 14–16, 23–6). Cf. pp. 141 f., 222 n. 2. Another westerner who probably objected to the 'immorality' of the Homeric gods was Theagenes of Rhegium, the allegorist said to have lived in the time of Cambyses.

impressions to be seen in Paros, Malta, and the quarries at Syracuse, and inferred from them that sea gives way to earth and back again over immense periods of time (A 33). Regularity and periodicity were what he expected to find everywhere. He referred to Thales' prediction of an eclipse (B 19), and offered an ingenious explanation of eclipses which went with their being periodic.[1] He recorded the fact that Stromboli once erupted after sixteen years of inactivity (A 48): here too, perhaps, he was attempting to discover a periodicity.[2] Surely this was the kind of *πολυμαθίη* that Heraclitus had in mind when he bracketed Xenophanes with Hecataeus. Heraclitus thought little of it, but it was to lead to great things.

'*Pythagoreans*'

The trend towards the scientific approach can be seen among the Pythagoreans of the first half of the fifth century. By Pythagoreans I mean generally all those who recognized Pythagoras as their great inspiration and regarded themselves as humbly carrying on traditions that he established. Assuming that this was also the

[1] A 41a (*κατά τινα καιρόν*); p. 98.

[2] His mention of a solar eclipse that lasted a month (distinguished from one that produced darkness as of night) (A 41) has caused puzzlement. A conspicuous dimming of the sun could in fact have been caused by a layer of dust in the upper atmosphere following an eruption of a major volcano such as Etna. (We know from Thuc. 3. 116 that Etna erupted sometime between the late eighth century and 474.) Similar cases are described in *The Eruption of Krakatoa and subsequent phenomena*, Report of the Krakatoa Committee of the Royal Society, 1888, 264 ff., 384 ff. After the eruption of Kötlugia (Iceland) in 1721, the sun was seen red and hazy for two months. In 1783, after the eruption of another Icelandic volcano, Skaptar Jökull, a thick dry mist spread as far as north Africa, and lasted more than a month. 'In Languedoc, its density was such that the sun was not visible in the morning up to 17° altitude above the horizon; the rest of the day the sun was red, and could be observed with the unprotected eye.' Even in Syria it was much obscured, and blood-red when seen. In 1831, a year of three major eruptions, a fog was observed in various parts of the world; on the African coast the sun became visible only after passing an altitude of 15° or 20°. The eruption of Krakatoa in 1883 produced many atmospheric effects all over the world. At Aux Cayes, Haiti, a perpetual haze or dense veil round the sun lasted from the end of August to 1 March 1884. After the eruption of Etna on 21 May 1886, vapours spread over the eastern and presently the whole horizon of Palermo; on 3 June fog blotted out the sun, after several days of mist all over Italy. After that the sun on rising was purple-red or reddish-yellow, and at about 30° of altitude was a neutral grey.

basis for the use of the term by fourth-century writers,[1] we find that at that time different classes of Pythagorean were distinguished. In particular, the ἀκουσματικοί, the pious custodians of the old ἀκούσματα, were contrasted with the μαθηματικοί, who busied themselves with μαθήματα, music, geometry, etc. Both parties regarded themselves as the genuine heirs of Pythagoras, but the former seem to have had more of the truth on their side.[2] The division clearly goes back to the early fifth century, though it will have been less marked then. Hippasus of Metapontum is associated with mathematical and musical discoveries which others attributed to Pythagoras, as well as having a physical theory in which, as in Heraclitus, fire played an important part.[3] Brontinus and others followed Pythagoras' example in making 'Orpheus' their mouthpiece, and took their inspiration from the kind of cosmic imagery seen in Pherecydes and the ἀκούσματα, but they made it into something more rational. Brontinus' *Peplos* may have developed the idea of the robe woven for Chthonie (cf. Epigenes in Orph. fr. 33 Kern). The *Diktyon* ascribed to Brontinus or Zopyrus probably likened the formation of a living being to the knitting of a net (fr. 26). This weaving and knitting is something more than a metaphor, it is an insight into the process involved in the growth of vegetation and of the soul.[4] Zopyrus' *Krater*, similarly, must have made use of the concept of mixing which is so fundamental in Empedocles. These men had no inclination to discard the picturesque and the mythical as Xenophanes had done, but they were equally keen, in their own fashion, to explain the unseen from the seen.[5] Only the

[1] Subsequently it seems to have become usual so to label every native of Magna Graecia known to have been intellectually active in the first half of the fifth century, or at least to say that he heard Pythagoras or associated with disciples.

[2] For all details see Burkert, *WW*, pp. 187 ff.

[3] Arist. *Metaph.* 984^{a}7 and others, DK 18; Burkert, *WW*, pp. 188–90, 199–202, 355–7, 433–6. Perhaps the number-cosmogony of Philolaus (58 B 26+30; Burkert, *WW*, pp. 219–21) had an antecedent in this period; we saw the requisite power of abstraction already in Alcman (p. 207; cf. *CQ* 61, 1967, 7).

[4] Brontinus is also credited with the *Φυσικά*. For the analogy between plant and animal life cf. Anaxagoras A 116 and Empedocles (pp. 233 f.).

[5] Xenophanes treats existing knowledge as a partial revelation of the whole by the gods, B 18, 36. Likewise Alcmeon of Croton, an earnest investigator of

Diktyon shows an oriental idea that we have not clearly seen before; and Anaximenes, who gave me occasion to describe it (p. 105), may have hinted at it. There is no sufficient reason to think that the Pythagorean poets were getting fresh inspiration from the east.

This tradition of science coloured by poetry and myth continued down to Philolaus and Plato. By then it had given rise to a developed discipline of pure mathematics allied to astronomy and harmonic theory. The *μαθηματικοί* prevailed; the *ἀκουσματικοί* degenerated into the feeble tramps of the Middle Comedy, pale famished water-poters with vegetarian convictions and dirty clothes.

Anaxagoras

Mathematics was never a Pythagorean monopoly. Good and early tradition regards Thales as the father of geometry,[1] and the influence of mathematical thinking can be seen in Anaxagoras, whose cosmology is obviously cast in the Milesian mould. He starts with an infinity of undifferentiated matter in which aer and aither hold controlling shares; world systems form within it, as small vortices[2] develop and expand; the earth is flat and supported on aer. Naturally some new ideas have emerged in the sixty years or so since Anaximenes. Anaxagoras thinks in terms of opposites, like Heraclitus (p. 139) and Alcmeon; it is not clear that the Milesians did (p. 84). The idea that one thing, e.g. air or fire, can turn into other things, is rejected: *πῶς γὰρ ἂν ἐκ μὴ τριχὸς γένοιτο θρὶξ καὶ σὰρξ ἐκ μὴ σαρκός;* (B 10, perhaps not verbatim), an argument which can be compared with Parm. 8. 12 f. (reading *τοῦ ἐόντος* with Reinhardt). His alternative, that

natural history, aims *περὶ τῶν ἀφανέων τεκμαίρεσθαι*, as far as men can; only the gods know the truth (cf. Parmenides; Emp. B 2, 3). He belongs to the same circle as Brontinus. (*τάδε ἔλεξε Βροντίνῳ καὶ Λέοντι καὶ Βαθύλλῳ* (B 1) should be taken literally, of a private discussion group.) He may seem a very different type: but the knitting-image would throw an unexpected light on his dictum that men die *ὅτι οὐ δύνανται τὴν ἀρχὴν τῷ τέλει προσάψαι* (B 2), and his theory of the *mixture* of opposing qualities (B 4) makes a link with the *Krater*.

[1] Emphasized by Burkert, *WW*, pp. 390 ff.

[2] In the verbatim fragments we find *περιχώρησις*, not *δίνη* or any cognate.

there is a portion of every substance in every thing, presupposes two more new concepts: infinite divisibility, which we also find Zeno playing about with,[1] and mixture.[2] The latter goes together with the realization that opposites are not exclusive absolutes: οὐ κεχώρισται ἀλλήλων τὰ ἐν τῷ ἑνὶ κόσμῳ οὐδὲ ἀποκέκοπται πελέκει, οὔτε τὸ θερμὸν ἀπὸ τοῦ ψυχροῦ οὔτε τὸ ψυχρὸν ἀπὸ τοῦ θερμοῦ (B 8). A white thing has some black in it, and vice versa (B 10). This is not the same as Heraclitus' way of dealing with the problem of opposites, but it is akin. The ability to see that what is a small quantity in one regard can always be large in another, while again most easily derived from the divided line, is a particular application of the relativist principle which we see in both Heraclitus and Xenophanes. Anaxagoras recognizes only one thing that is not mixed with the rest: νοῦς, which has no opposite and can only vary in the quantity in which it is present. Again we think of Heraclitus, with his σοφὸν πάντων κεχωρισμένον.

Several details add to the evidence for progress made since the time of Anaximenes. Thales and Hecataeus had given mistaken explanations of the Nile flood; the correct one appeared in Anaxagoras, and (perhaps in consequence of his teaching at Athens) in Aeschylus and Sophocles.[3] He knows that the moon is earthlike and has its light from the sun (Parmenides, cf. p. 223 n. 1); he knows the true causes of eclipses, solar and lunar, though he still retains Anaximenes' 'earthy bodies' as an additional cause of lunar ones.[4] The doctrine that the sun and

[1] Anaxagoras wrote after 467 (Aegospotami meteorite); Zeno, born *c.* 490, wrote (one of his works) as a young man, Pl. *Parm.* 128 d. Anaxagoras' words in B 1 show that the idea of the infinitesimal was less familiar than the idea of the infinite multitude. It would most easily be arrived at by the mathematician dividing a line. In B 3 he explains carefully that every quantity is both small and large; this is exactly what Zeno (29 B 1) rejects as an absurd contradiction. Guthrie states that the conception of the infinitely small 'had been put into his head by a reading of Zeno' (*HGP* ii. 294). I can see no ground for such an assertion.

[2] Parm. B 12, Alcmeon, Zopyrus; cf. Heraclitus' κυκεών, fr. 31 = B 125.

[3] Aesch. *Memnon*, fr. 193 Mette (has been thought a late play, cf. L. D. Caskey and J. D. Beazley, *Attic Vase Paintings in the Museum of Fine Arts, Boston*, iii. 44), *Suppl.* 559 (between 468 and 456); Soph. fr. 882 Pearson (inc. fab.); Anaxag. A 42, 91; cf. Hdt. 2. 22.

[4] Above, p. 101. The reason may have been that lunar eclipses are more frequent. Cf. 'some Pythagoreans' (= Philolaus) *ap.* Aet. 2. 29. 4, with Arist. *de cael.* 293^{b}23;

stars are stones may have been suggested by the meteorite that fell at Aegospotami in 467.[1] Anaximenes' northern mountain is ignored: the heavenly bodies pass under the earth as before. There is no void, for air has substance (A 68). Men are cleverer than animals because of their hands (A 102: cf. Xenoph. B 15). Plants are ζῷα (A 116; cf. Alcmeon, Brontinus, p. 230 n. 4). The sex of a baby is determined by whether conception occurs in the right or left side of the womb (A 1 § 9, 42 § 12, 107; so Parm. B 17). The head is the seat of consciousness (A 108; Alcmeon A 5, 8). *ὄψις τῶν ἀδήλων τὰ φαινόμενα* (B 21a; Alcmeon B 1, Xenophanes).

Empedocles

Empedocles' doctrine of metempsychosis, and his fulminations against the eating of meat or beans, would seem sufficient to make a Pythagorean of him, were his personal pretentions not clearly incompatible with deference to a master. He builds on a theory of transmigration like the one seen in the (Pythagorean) Orphic fragments (p. 161), and his cosmic force *Νεῖκος* might be derived from the same source.[2] His treatment of the cosmic Sphere as a god with 'limbs' makes a link with the *ἀκούσματα* (p. 218); he makes the sea 'the sweat of the earth' instead of 'the tear of Kronos' (B 51; cf. p. 230), while he makes springs the tears of Nestis (B 6. 3). The painter-simile of B 23 can be related to the notion of divine artistry which we found in Pherecydes and the *Peplos*. His constant assumption of parallelism between plant

Leuc. 67 A 1 § 33; O'Brien, *JHS* 88, 1968, 127 n. 72. Differently Guthrie, *HGP* ii. 307; P.J. Bicknell, *Acta Classica* 12, 1968, 56 ff.

[1] On the notice that Thales regarded them as earthy cf. p. 211 n. 6. Contrast Anaximenes, Xenophanes, Heraclitus. The account of comets (A 1 § 9; 81) may also be post-467, see *Journ. Brit. Astron. Ass.* 70, 1960, pp. 368 f. Another statement that may be based on inference from a specific astronomical event is the one that the sun is many times larger than the Peloponnese (A 42, 72). In 557 B.C. the track of a total eclipse crossed the Peloponnese from west to east. Discovering memories of this, Anaxagoras might have argued (falsely) 'the moon's shadow must be the same size as the moon' (so Emp. B 42), 'therefore the moon is as big as the Peloponnese, therefore the sun, which looks the same size but is much further away, must be that much bigger than the Peloponnese.'

[2] Cf. A.R. 1. 498, with p. 22 above; also Heraclitus' Eris/Polemos.

and animal life (e.g. B 29. 1, 82, 99) confirms the promise of the *Peplos* and *Diktyon*, while his reliance on mixing as a cosmic process, and particularly the use of *ζωρός* and *ἄκρητος* in B 35. 15, makes a link with the *Krater*. In some cases a Pythagorean connection is wanting, but we can find echoes of Pherecydes. The doctrine of four elements is often classed with Anaxagoras' theory of matter, as a pluralism designed to escape the consequences of Parmenides' logic. But it has a pre-Parmenidean antecedent in Pherecydes' fire, water, and wind (cf. p. 40), which were disposed in different parts of the world and gave birth to different gods. Empedocles' elements have the same connections: they are world-masses and deities as well as materials.[1] He calls them *πάντων ῥιζώματα*, B 6, which could be connected with Pherecydes' world tree (p. 59). (A Pythagorean line of tradition might be suggested by Philolaus B 13 *πάντα γὰρ καὶ θάλλουσι καὶ βλαστάνουσι*.) Finally, the cave of B 120 recalls Pherec. B 6.

Admittedly one can find some of these things elsewhere. Empedocles certainly has other sources of inspiration. One is Parmenides, whose influence is evident in his language. His spherical, unique cosmos, and his judgement that becoming and perishing, because they involve non-being, cannot be real, though they do have a nominal existence (B 8–9, 11–12, 15, 17. 30–3, etc.), look Parmenidean. His *Φιλότης* ('Aphrodite' in 22. 5, cf. 17. 24) takes over the role of Parmenides' Aphrodite (B 13; 12. 3?).

For other features we find parallels in the Ionians, though we do not get the impression that we are looking at Empedocles' sources. The principle of eternal alternation between extreme states of the world recalls Heraclitus (great year, not ecpyrosis) and Xenophanes (A 33). So does the divine mind that darts throughout (p. 143). The attack on the idea that aither and earth are infinitely deep (B 39) seems aimed directly at Xenophanes, though it is described as the teaching of many. The *δίνη* (B 35. 4)

[1] Zeus, Hera, Aidoneus, Nestis, B 6; *ἠέρος ἄπλετον ὕψος* 17. 18, *ἴδος καὶ ἀργῆς αὐγή* 21. 4, cf. 62. 5, *οὐρανός* 22. 2, *αἰθήρ* 71. 2, 98. 2, *al.*; *πῦρ* 17. 18, 73. 2, *al.*, *ἠέλιος* 21. 3, 71. 2, *al.*, *ἠλέκτωρ* 22. 2, *Ἥφαιστος* 96. 3, 98. 2; *ὕδωρ* 17. 18, 71. 2, *al.*, *ὄμβρος* 21. 5, 73. 1, 98. 2, *θάλασσα* 22. 2; *γαῖα* 17. 18, 71. 2, *αἶα* 21. 6, *χθών* 22. 2, 73. 1, 96. 1, 98. 1.

had its counterparts in Anaxagoras and perhaps Anaximenes and Thales; the ideas that the inclination of the poles is secondary (A 58) and that the revolution was set off by an imbalance between heat and cold (A 30) correspond to views attributed to Anaxagoras and Archelaus (59 A 1 § 9, 60 A 4 §§ 2, 4); the denial of void, not on the ground that non-being cannot exist but on the ground that even air is substantial (B 13, 14, 100), is Anaxagorean; the abuse of reflection in accounting for celestial phenomena (A 30, 56, B 44) has dubious parallels in Anaxagoras[1] and the *de hebdomadibus*,[2] certain ones in Ionians who wrote a decade or two later than Anaxagoras.[3]

Only one oriental comparison must be made. According to Empedocles (B 62, 63) the sexes were produced by division of 'whole-natured' creatures, who were themselves evolved from earlier forms of life. According to the *Bṛhadāraṇyaka Upanishad*, 1. 4. 1–3, the universe began as the Self in human form. He was lonely and bored.

> Now he was the size of a man and a woman in close embrace. He split this Self in two, and from this arose husband and wife.

The same idea, certainly. But it must be admitted that there is no need to think of interdependence. The neatness with which the male and female bodies fit together makes the idea of an original unity a natural one, and it might be thought to be implicit in the widespread myth of the separation of a personified Heaven and Earth.

Eleatics, atomists, and others

The general picture remains the same in the rest of the century: evolution from what was there, without new contributions from outside. Zeno and Melissus develop Parmenides' logic of Being

[1] A 1 § 9+42 § 10 = Theophrastus; Aristotle in A 80 ascribes a different theory to *οἱ περὶ Ἀναξαγόραν καὶ Δημόκριτον*, and associates the reflection-theory with people who have a similar explanation of the comet, i.e. Hippocrates of Chios and his pupil Aeschylus (42 A 5, 6).

[2] 1. 2 *τὴν τῶν ἄστρων ἀνταύγειαν καὶ μάνωσιν*. Meaning obscure.

[3] Hippocrates and Metrodorus of Chios (42 A 5–6, 70 A 9), Diogenes of Apollonia (64 A 13); also Philolaus (44 A 16, cf. 45 A 37).

without sharing his poetic vision or troubling with the world of appearances.[1] Zeno's approach is mathematical;[2] Melissus' aim seems to have been to prove that true being is incorporeal, and probably that it is identical with God (30 A 13, B 9).[3] If Leucippus came from Miletus, as the most plausible account says, he was close to Melissus in space and time, and he certainly seems to take account of Eleatic reasoning. The general shape of his cosmology is in the Ionian tradition, and his analysis of matter as made up of minute particles shows a similar approach to that of Anaxagoras. But he calls a halt to infinite divisibility, which had worried Zeno, and defines his particles as 'indivisibles'; he finds it necessary to provide for movement by explicitly positing void, calling it *μὴ ὄν* in the Eleatic fashion (67 A 7, 8); where Anaxagoras had spoken of his *σπέρματα* as containing every colour and savour (59 B 4), Leucippus denies all such qualities to his atoms, as if to do justice to the arguments of Melissus—who had indeed devoted a paragraph to the thesis *εἰ ἦν πολλά, τοιαῦτα χρὴ αὐτὰ εἶναι οἷόνπερ ἐγώ φημι τὸ ἓν εἶναι* (30 B 8). Leucippus accepts, in fact, the Eleatic idea that the variegation of the phenomenal world is based on illusion or convention (A 32). These are important modifications of the old Ionian pattern; but the central axiom of Eleaticism is completely contradicted, as it had to be.

It is difficult to discern any difference from Leucippus in the physical system of Democritus. But he may have repeated his predecessor's cosmology merely as the background to an account of the origin and development of human life and civilization.[4] Archelaus stands in a similar relationship to Anaxagoras. He follows him so closely in his physical theory that he is often

[1] Cf. R. Otto, *Mysticism East and West*, 1932, p. 31 n. 2.

[2] Two Chinese paradoxes attested *c.* 320 B.C. provide striking parallels to Zeno (Guthrie, *HGP* ii. 100); I would not rule out the possibility that they came to Greece along with the oriental ideas seen in Parmenides.

[3] Xenophanes had given God attributes like those Parmenides gave his Being, though for different reasons; it is not surprising that the two merged, and that Xenophanes came to be regarded as a proto-Eleatic (Pl. *Soph.* 242 d, etc.). Cf. McDiarmid, *Harv. Stud.* 61, 1953, 118 f.

[4] Cf. Guthrie, *HGP* ii. 385.

dismissed as a second-rate thinker who had hardly anything of his own to say. But he went on to give an account of the growth of civilization, in which he showed that law and justice are conventions (60 A 4 § 6, cf. A 1, 2). This is where his originality lies. The Theophrastean tradition of course concentrates on his physics, and this distorts the picture. The same must be said on behalf of Diogenes of Apollonia. The main topic of his book was human physiology, a subject of which he had considerable detailed knowledge, but he set it against a background of general cosmology, an approach not without parallel in the Hippocratic corpus.[1]

Astronomy in the late fifth century

Burkert (*WW*, pp. 289–96) finds evidence for renewed contacts with the east in certain features of Greek astronomy in the period following *c.* 440. I do not find it convincing evidence, but a brief discussion is in place.

1. Detailed knowledge about the planets: their exact number, and the treatment of them as individual objects that need not all be at the same distance from us.

(*a*) According to Tzetzes, *Chil.* 10. 527 ff., 12. 212 ff., Meton taught that the world is destroyed when the seven planets come together in Aquarius, the house of Saturn, after many thousands of years. This is of course the Stoic theory (p. 155), and the attribution of it to Meton, with the astrological system it implies, is a gross anachronism. Tzetzes has allowed himself to be confused by some account like that in Censorinus, *De die nat.* 18, where discussion of intercalary cycles like those of Meton leads on to cosmic *magni anni*.

(*b*) Democritus is said to have written a work on the planets (68 B 5 b), and to have separated Venus from the others by putting

[1] In referring back to his account of the *ἀρχή*, he said something like *ὡς λέλεκταί μοι πρότερον ἐν τοῖς περὶ μετεώρων*, and elsewhere he gave as a reference *ἐν τοῖς περὶ ἀνθρώπου φύσιος* (64 A 4). Simplicius mistook these for references to lost works (Diels). Cf. Kirk–Raven, pp. 428 f. (The passage of Galen there cited by no means proves that Diogenes wrote more than one book.)

it below the sun.[1] Burkert (*WW*, pp. 292, 296) says that this points to influence from Babylon, where Venus traditionally stood in a triad with the sun and moon (sc. on boundary-stones; cf. p. 41). But the Babylonians, like Hesiod (*Th.* 381), picked out Venus because of its brilliance; Democritus, like Parmenides (28 A 40a), put it in a special position in the cosmos because of the peculiarity of its movements, always close to the sun. (The identity of the morning and evening stars was a discovery of Parmenides' time or shortly before.) If Venus was the only planet that Democritus so treated, he cannot have known as much about Mercury. He knew that the direction in which the planets commonly move with the respect to the stars is eastwards (59 A 78); but this was already known to Anaxagoras (ibid.), and it is not clear that Democritus' knowledge of the planets was in any respect more advanced than that of his predecessors.

(*c*) Philolaus knew that there were five planets (44 A 16); this is the earliest evidence for knowledge of the number in Greece ([Hp.] *hebd.* 2 is irrelevant). It is not in itself an indication of Babylonian knowledge, and scarcely presupposes more systematic observation than do the discoveries mentioned by Parmenides and Anaxagoras.

2. Meton's intercalary cycle of 19 years 'was in practical use only at Babylon' (*WW*, p. 294)—but (as Burkert acknowledges in a footnote) it was only introduced there in 381/0 B.C.[2] Since it is a natural cycle based on the close equivalence of 235 lunations to 19 solar years, it could have been discovered from observation by Greeks and Babylonians independently, given a general parity in their level of scientific achievement.

[1] Aet. 2. 15. 3 (*Placita* only = A 86). Hipp. *Ref.* 1. 13. 4 (A 40) τοὺς δὲ πλανήτας οὐδ' αὐτοὺς ἔχειν ἴσον ὕψος need not mean anything more. Burkert misinterprets Sen. *QN* 7. 3. 2 (A 92). It does not say 'Democritus suspected that there were more planets', sc. than the five; Seneca is talking about comets, and saying 'Democritus suspected that they were conjunctions of planets' (Anaxagoras' theory repeated; also attested for Democritus by Alexander), 'but he did not lay down how many, or which ones' (which would throw light on Seneca's problem, whether they are periodic): 'the courses of the five planets (= their sidereal periodicity?) had not yet been understood, for this knowledge was introduced by Eudoxus.'

[2] A. Sachs, *Journal of Cuneiform Studies* 6, 1952, 113 f.

3. Meton drew up an astronomical calendar which related weather changes to the risings of different stars through the year. A similar work was ascribed to Democritus (68 B 14). There are Babylonian parallels; but there was also a long-standing Greek tradition, as we see from the *Works and Days*, of determining the seasons by the stars. When Hesiod comes to rules for sailing, the relationship with the weather becomes particularly important and is made explicit (619–21). We may guess that it played its part in the *Ναυτικὴ ἀστρολογία* ascribed to Phocus or Thales (cf. p. 210 n. 3), and in the *Ἀστρολογίαι* of 'Hesiod' and Cleostratus (DK 4–6; Hes. fr. 288–93 M.–W.). By Meton's time prose had become the natural medium.

4. A late doxographic source says that Meton measured distances between stars, again something that was done at Babylon. The text runs: *περὶ δὲ ἀποστάσεως ἄστρων* (from each other) *ἄλλοι τε πολλοὶ καὶ οἱ περὶ Εὔδοξον καὶ Ἵππαρχον καὶ Διόδωρον τὸν Ἀλεξανδρέα ἐπραγματεύσαντο καὶ Λᾶσος (οὐχ ὁ Ἑρμιονεὺς ἀλλ' ἕτερος), καὶ Ἐρατοσθένης ὁ γραμματικὸς καὶ Μέτων ὁ γεωμέτρης* (sch. in Basilium p. 196.24 Pasquali (*GGN* 1910)). It is suspicious that the list starts with Eudoxus, Meton being tagged on at the end. In any case the information is too general to be of much use. It may be based simply on Meton's determination of the solstice points.

Conclusion

It has not been my aim in this chapter to write a history, but only to survey the ground sufficiently to justify the thesis stated in the first paragraph: that a period of active Iranian influence stands out sharply in the development of Greek thought, from *c.* 550 to *c.* 480 B.C. For a century or so beforehand, milder oriental influences can be seen; afterwards, it is as if they had been shut off with a tap.

How did it happen? What set in motion this wave that washed into Miletus between Thales and Anaximander, and into other Ionian towns at a similar period? I have noted that this is close to the time when the Persians reached the Aegean. But it was not just a matter of conquest, for Miletus retained its independence from Cyrus as from Croesus, and a garrison is in any case not a likely source of enlightenment to an Anaximander. The occupation of neighbouring towns after 547 may have brought a variety of civilian metics in its wake, priests, tradespeople, and so on;[1] but any influence upon Miletus from this source would come too late to explain the facts. To put a different question: what sort of people would we expect, in Iranian lands, to possess the knowledge in which we are interested? The answer that immediately proposes itself is 'the Magi', that formidable caste which held a controlling influence in all matters of religion.[2] The Iranian cosmological doctrines recorded by Aristotle, Eudemus, and Theopompus, which I have used in chapters 2, 3, and 6, are attributed by those authors specifically to the Magi. They were the people one talked to about such things.

It is not to be supposed that all Magi upheld the same doctrines. There will have been considerable regional and personal variations.[3] Ideas known to us only from Indian or Babylonian texts may, for all we know, have been familiar to many of them. Xerxes' famous *daēva*-inscription shows that he set himself to impose a single form of religion on an empire which supported some signal heterodoxies. Zaehner has put forward the theory that Xerxes' act drove a number of Magi to emigrate, and that after absorbing some Babylonian ideas they transported their beliefs to Asia Minor and eventually contributed to the creation of Roman Mithraism.[4] But Xerxes is much too late to help with our problem. It is not at all likely that there was any attempt to impose an orthodoxy as early as the mid sixth century. However, there was another historical event of that time which might have produced a similar effect as far as the Magi are concerned: the defeat and annexation of Media by Cyrus in 549 or slightly

[1] The amount of ethnic intermixture before the fall of the Lydian kingdom may be gauged not only from personal names, such as those of Thales' and Bias' fathers, but from the language of Hipponax with its plethora of foreign words. Hipponax is deliberately 'putting it on', but he must have had reason.

[2] See Zaehner, *DTZ*, pp. 161 ff.

[3] Zaehner, *DTZ*, pp. 163–8.

[4] *Zurvan*, p. 20.

earlier. The Magi were Medes, and remembered it (Hdt. 1. 101). Upon the fall of their country, many of them may have sought refuge abroad, in India[1] and in the west. Anaximander wrote his book in 547/6, if we accept and so interpret Apollodorus' dating (p. 1). Then there is Pherecydes. If we are right in thinking that he owed much of his learning to a Cilician father, he may perhaps be another case of a priest–theologian who emigrated to the west under the threat of Cyrus, presumably at the time of Croesus' defeat (547/6) or soon after. Apollodorus, we remember, put Pherecydes' *floruit* in 544/3. If we wonder why a holy man should choose Syros to settle in, there may be significance in its proximity to Delos, the great Ionian centre of Apolline worship. The Median Magi, no seafarers, probably felt they had gone far enough when they reached the coast. There were Miletus and Samos, the strongest and proudest of the Greek cities; or Phocaea, whose inhabitants were to abandon it sooner than accept Persian dominion, and found Elea.

If the diaspora was a direct result of the campaigns of Cyrus, and was not reinforced by emigrations on the same scale in subsequent decades, it is natural that its impact on the Greeks should have lost its power after a time. And there were other reasons, as I have said, why its influence should dwindle and disappear in the early fifth century. In general, foreign contributions were no longer wanted; not because they were foreign to Greece, but because they were foreign to inquiry based on empirical data. The maturing of this scientific approach coincided with a change in international relations which made Greece perforce more introspective. It was not until Eudoxus, after the political situation had changed again, and scientific speculation about cosmology had played itself out, that barbarian seed once more fell upon hospitable soil.

But what invaded Greek speculation in the mid sixth century was no mere convolvulus that withered away when its season was past, leaving the sturdy stems of Hellenic rationalism to grow unimpeded as they had always meant to. It was an ambrosia

[1] Cf. J. Przyluski, *Rev. Hist. Rel.* 122, 1940, 85 ff.

plant, that produced a permanent enlargement where it touched. In some ways one might say that it was the very extravagance of oriental fancy that freed the Greeks from the limitations of what they could see with their own eyes: led them to think of ten-thousand-year cycles instead of human generations, of an infinity beyond the visible sky and below the foundations of the earth, of a life not bounded by womb and tomb but renewed in different bodies aeon after aeon. It was now that they learned to think that good men and bad have different destinations after death; that the fortunate soul ascends to the luminaries of heaven; that God is intelligence; that the cosmos is one living creature; that the material world can be analysed in terms of a few basic constituents such as fire, water, earth, metal; that there is a world of Being beyond perception, beyond time. These were conceptions of enduring importance for ancient philosophy. This was the gift of the Magi.

ADDENDA

p. 31. The Elamite tablet is no. 2084 in R. T. Hallock, *Persepolis Fortification Tablets*, Chicago, 1969, p. 658; the name is Izrudukma, 'born of Zurvān's seed' (I. Gershevitch in *Studia Class. et Orient. A. Pagliaro oblata*, ii, 1969, 197). The god himself appears in the form Turma (Hallock, pp. 560, 563, nos. 1956–7; Gershevitch, *Trans. Philol. Soc.*, 1969). The tablets belong to the period 509–494 B.C.

p. 85 n. 2. J. J. Hall, *JHS* 89, 1969, 57–9, interprets πρηστῆρος αὐλός as the funnel of a tornado or waterspout. But a person in the uncomfortable situation of looking up such a funnel would not see fire.

p. 98. For the geographical localization of the sun cf. also 'Hp.' *aer.* 12–13 and 19.

p. 122 n. 2. Another consideration relevant to the dating of *De victu* is its assumption in 2. 38. 3 of a spherical earth divided into polar, temperate, and tropical zones, a conception not reliably attested before Eudoxus, frs. 288–9 Lasserre, and Aristotle, *Meteor.* 362ᵇ.

pp. 154, 156. [Hp.] *vict.* 1. 25. 1 (cf. 6. 3) speaks of the soul 'growing' in the body, and of its being used up in the juvenile increase and senile decrease of the body.

p. 157. The winter and summer rising- and setting-points of the sun are similarly used to delimit north, south, east, and west by 'Hp.' *aer.* 3–7.

pp. 160 f. 'Hp.' *aer.* 23 says that semen coagulates (to form the foetus) differently in summer and in winter, and in wet weather and in drought. The author of *De victu* (1. 35. 4, 3. 68. 5) holds that winter and wet weather are better for intercourse, especially for older men or those in whose constitution water slightly predominates over fire.

p. 188. Besides the *Phaedo*, compare the Pythagorean eschatology described by Alexander Polyhistor *ap.* D.L. 8. 31–2 (273 F 93), from a perhaps third-century source (Burkert, *Philol.* 105, 1961, 26 f.): Hermes leads pure souls to the highest region, but unpurified ones are kept in bondage by the Erinyes. The whole air is full of souls, known to men as heroes and daimones and sending them dreams, portents, and diseases. Cf. pp. 215 f.

p. 196. τάδε πάντα also in Eratosthenes' *Hermes*, fr. 15. 1 Powell. Cf. Aeschylus' Ζεύς τοι τὰ πάντα χὤτι τῶνδ' ὑπέρτερον (fr. 105 Mette). The Hellenistic Pythagorica edited by Thesleff contain additional examples of τὸ ὅλον τόδε ('Eurytus', p. 88. 11) and ὅδε ὁ κόσμος ('Aristaeus', p. 53 1; 'Philolaus', p. 150. 8; 'Timaeus', pp. 206. 18, 207. 14, 213. 22, 217. 13); the latter also in Cleanthes, *Hymn to Zeus* 7.

p. 198 n. 2. See also 'Hp.' *morb. sacr.* 4 and 21.

pp. 215 f. Cf. above, addendum to p. 188.

p. 231. The cosmology of the Hippocratic *de hebdomadibus* shows many points of contact with Philolaus. Its principle that everything in nature is arranged by sevens represents number-speculation in a form best paralleled in the *Taittirīya Upanishad* (1. 7; Zaehner, *Hindu Scriptures*, p. 135; cf. also Ion of Chios B 1 with *Bṛhadāraṇyaka Upan.* 1. 6. 1), and its assumption that man is constructed on the same pattern as the universe may be seen as a development of something that came to Greece from the east (p. 218 with n. 2). In both cases the oriental line of thought had been adopted by Pythagoreans, and I take it as further evidence for the Pythagorean character of the text, not as evidence for renewed foreign influence. The relation of different parts of the earth, and their inhabitants, to parts of the body (*hebd.* 11) may have had an Egyptian antecedent. On all this I must refer to an article forthcoming in *CQ*.

INDEX OF PASSAGES DISCUSSED

** signifies that the author also appears in the General Index.*

GENERAL INDEX

* *signifies that an author also appears in the Index of Passages Discussed.*